GW01079900

First published 2016 by Warc
85 Newman Street, London W1T 3EU
Telephone: 0207 467 8100
Fax: 0207 467 8101
Email: enquiries@warc.com
www.warc.com

A CIP catalogue record for this book is available from the British Library

ISBN: 978-1-84116-228-7

Typeset by HWA Text and Data Management, London
Printed and bound by CPI Group (UK) Ltd, Croydon, CR0 4YY

Contents

SECTION 2 GOLD WINNERS

SECTION 3 SILVER WINNERS

SECTION 4 BRONZE WINNERS

Partners

Ipsos Connect

Sponsor

The success of the 2016 IPA Effectiveness Awards is in no small part down to its partners and sponsors, and the IPA would like to thank the companies listed here for their continuing support.

Acknowledgements

Many people worked hard to make the Awards a success, especially the following: Chris Hirst, Chairman of the IPA Effectiveness Leadership Group; Bridget Angear, Convenor of Judges and Neil Godber, Deputy Convenor of Judges.

At the IPA, the team were: Tottie Faragher, Georgia Fox, Helen Goddard, Tessa Gooding, Carlos Grande, Conor Harte, Roger Ingham, Jonathan Kemeys, Fergal Kilroy, Alice Meekins, Kathryn Patten, Sylvia Wood and Kate Woodford.

We also owe a debt of gratitude to:

The IPA Awards Board

1980/82 Convenor of Judges, Simon Broadbent (d)	
1984/86 Convenor of Judges, Charles Channon (d)	
1988/90 Convenor of Judges, Paul Feldwick	
1992/94 Convenor of Judges, Chris Baker	Bacon
1996 Convenor of Judges, Gary Duckworth	
1998 Convenor of Judges, Nick Kendall	Bro-Ken
2000 Convenor of Judges, Tim Broadbent (d)	
2002 Convenor of Judges, Marco Rimini	Mindshare
2004 Convenor of Judges, Alison Hoad	RKCR/Y&R
2005 Convenor of Judges, Les Binet	adam&eveDDB
2006 Convenor of Judges, Laurence Green	101
2007 Convenor of Judges, Richard Storey	M&C Saatchi
2008 Convenor of Judges, Neil Dawson	SapientNitro
2009 Convenor of Judges, Andy Nairn	Lucky Generals
2010 Convenor of Judges, David Golding	adam&eveDDB
2011 Convenor of Judges, Charlie Snow	MullenLowe
2012 Convenor of Judges, Marie Oldham	VCCP Media
2014 Convenor of Judges, Lorna Hawtin	TBWA/Manchester
2016 Convenor of Judges, Bridget Angear	AMV BBDO
IPA Effectiveness Leadership Group Chairman, Chris Hirst	Havas
IPA Director General, Paul Bainsfair	
IPA Director of Communications, Tessa Gooding	
IPA Head of Awards and Events, Kathryn Patten	

IPA Effectiveness Leadership Group

Chris Hirst (Chairman)	Havas
Bridget Angear	AMV BBDO
Jo Arden	23red
Tom George	MEC London
Lorna Hawtin	TBWA\Manchester
Matthew Hook	Carat
Janet Hull	IPA
Joyce Kelso	IPA
Jem Lloyd-Williams	Vizeum
Stephen Maher	MBA
Sera Miller	Material
Kathryn Patten	IPA
Frances Ralston-Good	Hearts & Science
Ed Shorthose	Woolley Pau Gyro

The Judges

Bridget Angear
Convenor of Judges
Joint Chief Strategy Officer, AMV BBDO

Neil Godber
Deputy Convenor of Judges
Head of Planning, J. Walter Thompson

INDUSTRY JUDGING PANEL

Fiona Blades
President & Chief Experience Officer
MESH

Morag Blazey
Chief Executive Officer
Ebiquity

Fran Cassidy
Founder
Cassidy Media Partnership

Neil Dawson
Chief Strategy Officer, Europe
SapientNitro

Laurence Green
Founding Partner
101

Steve Hatch
Regional Director
Facebook UK & Ireland

Matt Hill
Research & Planning Director
Thinkbox

Alison Hoad
Vice Chairman
RKCR/Y&R

Vanella Jackson
Chief Executive Officer
Hall & Partners

Nick Kendall
Founding Partner
Bro-Ken

Dr Paul Marsden
Research Psychologist
London College of Fashion and Syzygy Group

Ian Maude
Group Development Director
Be Heard

Andy Nairn
Founding Partner
Lucky Generals

Marie Oldham
Chief Strategy Officer
VCCP Media

Marco Rimini
Chief Executive Officer
Mindshare Worldwide Central

Charlie Snow
Chief Strategy Officer
MullenLowe London

Richard Storey
Global Chief Strategy Officer
M&C Saatchi

Denise Turner
Insight Director
Newsworks

Nick Turner
Partner
Deloitte

Caroline Walker
Managing Director
Ipsos Connect

David Wilding
Director of Planning
Twitter UK

CLIENT JUDGES

Dame Dianne Thompson DBE
Chairman of Judges
Former CEO, Camelot

Malik Akhtar
Category Lead – Agency Services
Bayer

Jonathan Allan
Sales Director
Channel 4

Ed Aspel
Executive Director of Fundraising and Marketing
Cancer Research UK

Alexandra Dimiziani
Head of Marketing EMEA
Airbnb

Andrew Geoghegan
Global Head of Consumer Planning
Diageo

Jan Gooding
Group Brand Director
Aviva

Sue MacMillan
COO
Mumsnet

Wendy Proctor
Head of Marketing
Ministry of Defence

Sarah Warby
Marketing Director
Sainsbury's

Georgina Williams
Head of Marketing
Volvo Cars UK

TECHNICAL JUDGES

Louise Cook
Managing Director
Holmes & Cook

Masood Akhtar
Managing Partner
Bottom Line Analytics EMEA

Alan Bloodworth
Managing Partner
Gain Theory

Peter Cain
Managing Director
Marketscience Consulting

Andrew Deykin
Senior Analytics Manager
RBS

Introduction

By Bridget Angear
Joint Chief Strategy Officer, AMV BBDO

As I write this introduction Andy Murray has just won Wimbledon for the second time, cementing his status as one of the great players of the game. He is one of only ten players to have won the title more than once, and is the first Briton to have achieved this since Fred Perry in 1936. The commentators of the Wimbledon Men's Final made mention of how Murray spends long hours watching recordings of other tennis players in action, in order to continue to improve his own game. While Andy Murray may indeed be a master of tennis, he is also one of its greatest students. And perhaps his mastery of the game is indeed a consequence of how he views himself as a constant student; ever curious, believing there is always more to learn.

This desire to learn is a trait that can be seen in many successful people. The humility to think they don't know it all, and the curiosity to understand more.

In the words of one of the greatest thinkers of all time,

I have no particular talent. I am merely inquisitive.
Albert Einstein

So I would like to salute the authors of the thirty-nine cases, and seven chapters contained within this book. Their curiosity to understand more has added to the overall body of effectiveness learning that continues to help build the professional regard for our industry, and provide a valuable wealth of knowledge for anyone seeking answers to their specific challenges. They have contributed towards making the IPA Databank a treasure house of learning that all of us can benefit from.

With over 1,300 cases spanning 35 years, with another 72 added this year, it is a rich source of knowledge and inspiration. Seeing how others have overcome challenges provides valuable insight for those facing similar ones. The comprehensive evidence base can be useful when seeking to persuade a client to follow a recommended course of action.

I am sure every author will have gone on their own personal voyage of discovery and taken something valuable away from the experience, beyond a resolution to start earlier next time. They will have emerged with a deeper understanding of how and why their communications worked and what they might do more or less of in the future as a result. They will have grown as strategists through this endeavour.

The judges also reported having benefited from the process, and that what they learnt more than repaid the time and effort it took to read and debate the cases. They left the experience full of new ideas for tackling the challenges they face.

There is a danger that the day job gets in the way of learning. That we are too tired or too busy to invest the time required to write, read or evaluate an IPA paper.

But in the words of another great scholar,

> *Learning never exhausts the mind.*
>
> Leonardo da Vinci

Perhaps we need to rethink the Effectiveness Awards from being an onerous chore to being an enriching learning experience. Perhaps it's time we also stopped thinking of effectiveness as the preserve of the 'geeks in glasses' and make it our collective responsibility. Given that effectiveness is the objective of everything we do, creativity the means; it makes no sense to view it as a separate discipline.

In case you need one further piece of evidence as to why learning is so important, think of it as vital to your career.

In *The Wind Rises*, Hayao Miyazaki's 'last' animated feature, the protagonist Jiro, who designed the Mitsubishi Zero that gave the Japanese air superiority early in WWII, constantly dreams of the Italian planemaker Caproni. In one dream, Caproni, standing on a biplane wing with Jiro says:

> *Artists are only creative for 10 years ... we engineers are no different. Live your 10 years to the full.*

It has been proven that most of the great thinkers from the worlds of art, science, literature and music have, on average, a ten-year period when they produce most of their great work. The only way to extend this period is to put yourself in situations that expose you to new learning experiences. It might sound obvious, but learning new things helps you stay creative for longer. But how many of us truly make the time to learn?

The fact that you are reading this book suggests you are one of those people who values learning, and that you have curiosity to know more and understand more.

So as I suspect some of you might be testing your knowledge, the ten tennis players who have won Wimbledon Men's Final more than once are:

Pete Sampras, Roger Federer, Bjorn Borg, Boris Becker, Novak Djokovic, John McEnroe, Jimmy Connors, Stefan Edberg, Rafael Nadal and Andy Murray.

And in the spirit of never stop learning, enjoy the rest of this book.

SPECIAL PRIZES

Grand Prix
John Lewis

Best New Learning (The Channon Prize)
The Economist

Best International (The Tim Broadbent Prize)
Speeding (New Zealand Transport Agency)

Best Multi-Market
Snickers

Best Small Budget
Narellan Pools

Best Commercial Effectiveness for Good (President's Prize)
Dove

Best Dedication to Effectiveness (The Simon Broadbent Prize)
Unilever

Effectiveness Company of the Year
adam&eveDDB

Effectiveness Network of the Year
BBDO

SECTION 1

New learning

The commercial value of purpose in advertising

By Tom Knox
IPA President & Chairman, MullenLowe London

The concept of 'brand purpose' has become ubiquitous in marketing discussions. As a result, there is a risk of the idea falling into disrepute through misunderstanding and misapplication.

So it's probably best to start with a definition of what I mean by 'purpose'.

To my mind, one of the best articulations of what 'purpose' in the world of commerce means is Simon Sinek's rightly admired TED talk, 'How great leaders inspire action', in which he distinguishes between the 'what you do' (product features) from the 'how you do it' (positioning and benefits) and the '*why* you do it' (values, belief, *purpose*).

The reason that the concept of purpose has become so important to marketers is that there have now been a number of high-profile attempts to prove that articulating and delivering a purpose can add to the commercial value of brand or company.

From the 50 high-performing organisations listed in Jim Stengel's book, *Grow*, which have harnessed brand ideas to surpass their competitors to academic analysis by Joshua Margolis (Harvard), Hillary Elfenbein (Washington) and Jim Walsh (Michigan), there is now a wealth of quantitative data to show that purpose-driven businesses outperform. (Notwithstanding Byron Sharp's acerbic criticism of Stengel's research methodology.)

Numerous books, like John Mackey's *Conscious Capitalism*, have been devoted to proving that having a broader social purpose and making money are not mutually exclusive.

This is because the economist Milton Friedman was wrong. Friedman's famous diktat that '*the social responsibility of business is to increase its profit*' tells only a very small part of the story of why businesses exist and thrive. Profit is necessary but not sufficient to creating and maintaining a successful business.

Going back to the nineteenth century, the strongest enterprises (such as Cadbury) have known that shareholders are only one group of stakeholders that need to be served, alongside customers, suppliers, employees, the community at large, and the environment.

But whilst the commercial value of purpose in business is now widely recognised, it has to be conceded that the study of the specific role that advertising plays in this field is still very much a work in progress, with relatively little available research. In particular, the development of sophisticated measurement tools for quantifying the relationship between purpose-based advertising and ROI is, arguably, in its infancy.

One challenge, alluded to by Gruber, Kaliauer and Schlegelmilch in 'Improving the effectiveness and credibility of corporate social-responsibility messaging' (*Journal of Advertising Research*, December 2015), is that paid-for advertising has less credibility compared to other channels when it comes to the communication of brand purpose.

This scepticism is important because we cannot ignore the extent to which consumer trust has eroded, not just trust in advertising, but in brands, media, and even governments. In an uncertain world where we know that consumers are increasingly values-driven, but also cynical about the claims brands make, purposeful brands can and will win.

But brands better mean it and they better realise that advertising can only add value in an era of radical transparency, fuelled by the web and social media, if all aspects of a company and brand are aligned around the brand purpose.

It's certainly worth bringing a healthy dose of scepticism to the debate. I remember witnessing a feisty exchange between two members of the planners' pantheon – Paul Feldwick and Nick Kendall – who were talking about the celebrated BBH 'Keep walking' campaign for Johnnie Walker whisky.

To Paul, the campaign's strength lay entirely in its strong brand identity and not at all in the brand purpose of progression and self-actualisation (which in any case was at odds with the essential intoxicating attributes of the product!).

My thinking in creating the IPA President's Prize was that I wanted to find a way to reward commercial campaigns that could demonstrate having delivered both great economic and societal value. I specifically wanted to exclude charities, NGOs and government campaigns from the prize to concentrate on celebrating advertising's contribution to showing that brands doing good for society are also doing good for business.

I know that the judging of this award provoked a lot of vigorous debate among the 2016 jurors. One particular subject of scrutiny was how connected the societal 'good' highlighted by prize entries was to the featured brand's core purpose and actual behaviour.

This is something that comes up time and again in any discussion of purpose in advertising. Unilever is rightly cited as a leader in the field of purpose-driven brands. Its 'Sustainable living plan' is truly embedded in the entire operating model of the company. This is reflected in the decision by its Chief Marketing Officer, Keith Weed, to abolish the company's corporate social responsibility (CSR) function and absorb it into marketing.

What's clear from this example and explains why the worthy winner of the first President's Prize is a Unilever brand (Dove) is that in order to be effective, advertising has to be the peak of a triangle, the base of which is everything else which the brand does and is.

The inverse of this, where the advertising is based on a CSR type initiative (big or small) but in no way based on the strong, long-term foundations of what the brand actually does in the real world, is destined for failure.

Other key lessons from the winning Dove paper include:

1. For FMCG brands, your purpose must have a clear link to your functional attributes. Dove has earned the right to have a purpose focused on female confidence and self-esteem through beauty by virtue of the products it markets.
2. Almost by definition, advertising campaigns that relate to a brand's core purpose will be long-term, with a consistent message repeated over many years (even if the creative expression may vary).
3. Because purposeful brands have to deliver on their vision in the real world, the best campaigns are likely to involve experiential elements which can then be amplified online and in PR.
4. A strong purpose-based brand platform allows you to take advantage of tactical opportunities and to respond to events and the *zeitgeist*.
5. Finally, purpose-based 'masterbrand' advertising can have a multiplier effect on traditional 'product' advertising's effectiveness.

I think that one of the reasons that the whole idea of purpose in advertising has become so popular (to the point of risking being labelled as a temporary fad) is that it holds out the promise of engendering outstanding, emotionally engaging creative work.

What creative team is not going to feel inspired by Persil's purpose-driven belief that 'Dirt is good', compared to the category generic product claim that 'Persil washes whiter?' It is obviously highly motivating for clients and agencies alike to be associated with the creation of campaigns of which they can be proud.

And this in itself has commercial value because, thanks to the work of Les Binet and Peter Field in *The Long and Short of It*, we know that emotionally-involving campaigns and, in particular, fame-based approaches '*outperform across the range of standard business mid-term metrics*'. Being able to connect brands to big, emotional, human values and issues creates the possibility of producing highly effective work.

There are also other indirect commercial benefits of purpose-driven advertising. Put simply, the best millennial talent wants to work for and on brands that are contributing to a better, more sustainable future for the planet. Brands with overt purpose at their heart can attract and retain not just committed customers but also employees and partners.

So, I think we can state with some certainty that companies and brands that have a clearly articulated purpose, *a reason why* they do what they do, are at an advantage.

Provided that this purpose is fully integrated into every aspect of the business (as opposed to being stuck on top as a marketing campaign). It must also be understood and appreciated by all stakeholders.

This represents both an opportunity and a challenge for advertising agencies, as Mike Barry, Director of Sustainable Business for Marks and Spencer, said at the IPA's 'Conscious capitalism' event in early 2016.

The opportunity lies in the chance to influence the boardroom. Agency executives often lament being pushed down the corporate food chain, but the articulation of brand purpose offers the promise of extending the influence of marketing all the way through an organisation.

The challenge is the need for humility and wisdom in understanding the role of advertising itself and I think we are going to have to develop new skills and techniques in measuring non-sales advertising effects and relating them to marketing activity.

Attitudinal shifts (e.g. female self-esteem) and behaviour change are difficult to measure, isolate and attribute to specific marketing activities.

Above all, it's important to bear in mind that purpose-based advertising is not a one-size-fits-all panacea for all marketing problems.

As Paul Feldwick eloquently points out in his book, *The Anatomy of Humbug*, there are many ways to use advertising and I am certainly not arguing that only campaigns that explicitly leverage brand purpose can work. There are many categories where the simple *what* and *how* of a brand is all that it is required to communicate.

But I'm sure that the concept of purposeful brands and advertising is not a passing fashion. Human beings will continue to believe that the world can be made a better place and brands will continue to play their part (small or large) in making it so.

People power

How brands are changing their fortunes by changing the world

By Alex Lewis
Director of Strategy, BBDO EMEA

I remember when I first experienced Save the Children's 2012 Christmas appeal. It was 14 December. I was sitting on the tube. Looking at the most ghastly piece of knitwear I'd seen for a long, long time.

Throughout that Friday I would go on to see dozens of God-awful jumpers all over London. Then there it was in the *Evening Standard* (just some of the £1.4 million earned media value that day). I may not have known it, but I was witnessing the birth of Christmas Jumper Day.

The following year I would join them (a tasteful Rudolf number, in case you wondered). So did over 1.5 million others. Collectively we donated £1.3m to Save the Children. And the campaign enjoyed an ROI of £3.16 for every £1 spent.

Except of course, Christmas Jumper Day wasn't really a campaign at all. It was a movement. And by 2014 donations were over £4m thanks to an amazing four million of those knitwear crimes.

Whether it's men being challenged to #sharetheload or women reconsidering what it means to be #likeagirl, those brands that encourage their audience to join them in changing something are being rewarded in terms of fame, admiration and (as we see in these cases) sales.

Each of them has enjoyed their success because they had people on their side. Rather than launching another campaign, they chose to kick-start a crusade.

Sure, each of these was probably born out of a brand purpose, a mission, a North Star or whichever other synonym might have sat proudly atop of their brand template.

But it wasn't the purpose that got people to tag a bragger with #holidayspam. It was the way Three Mobile found an enemy and launched a movement to tackle it. Inviting people in like this provided a 19% increase in conversation volume on the way to a profit ROI of £1.46.

Both 'Christmas Jumper Day' and 'Sorry for the holiday spam' represent a new type of creative platform. One that provides a way for people to be involved and impact the world they live in.

These brands recognised that the most powerful media channel they could invest in was people. And the good news is that any brand can do this.

The seven ingredients common to the most successful of these revolutions are not only clear, they are replicable.

1. You need a spark that defines what you want to change

Gandhi told us to be the change you want to see in the world. But when you *brand* that change, it can pull in an army of support that will multiply your impact.

First, you need a definitive goal. If people are to be part of change, they need to know when you've succeeded. For Paddy Power's 'Rainbow laces', this will be when sport is free from homophobia. It's a change which is as unequivocal as it is simple.

Next, you also need something that's right for the brand. For some years, John Lewis had created great ads, but in 2015 they did things a little differently. They found an issue they were going to change.

It made sense to act during Christmas given the affinity they have built up around the season. By encouraging people to 'Show someone they're loved this Christmas' the retailer struck a chord. Involving people in this way provided their greatest press coverage, their highest social media response and their most number of video shares to date. Indeed, the cost per view of £0.03 was under a third of previous Christmas campaigns.

Finally, you need a new angle. Even if the issue is familiar, the best revolutions spark something fresh, new and distinct. Ending holiday spam photos certainly did the trick for Three. Holiday bragging was bang on the cultural *zeitgeist* but hadn't gone mainstream.

Einstein once said that if he had an hour to save the world, he would spend 59 minutes working out what the problem was and one minute on the solution. Even if you already have a good sense of the issue you're tackling, it's worth taking the time to define the precise change in the most inspiring way.

Go for broke only once you've found something that's really broken.

2. You need an action that inspires others to make the difference

People are the power in any revolution. But first you need to be clear about how they can fuel change.

Often it can only happen thanks to top-down changes in policy. When this is the case, you need to use your audience as a means to an end and ask them to raise pressure. Much of Jamie Oliver's quest to improve kid's cooking skills has relied upon his followers lobbying for compulsory practical food education in schools.

Once you have a clear sense of what needs to happen then you can start creating the actions themselves.

Raising funds was the *aim* for Save the Children. But getting the country to sport a Christmas jumper is the *action*.

Changing shopper's behaviours might be the goal, but creating 'Small business Saturday' provides them with an action that makes it happen.

By creating something unique, the Christmas jumper itself became a vital part of the movement's identity. And featured prominently on every piece of publicity Save the Children ran.

So start with your aim, scout around for inspiration and then give the world a new action that is going to inspire your army of followers to create real change.

3. You need a rally cry that acts as statement of intent

The rally cry is a revolution's call to arms. And very often its most public face. It's the thing you want people to chant, to write on walls and to create #s for.

Your rally cry might explain who you are and why you're on this crusade. You need the shortest possible way of communicating what you want to change.

Or it might point followers towards your action. It's telling that the most consistent ingredient in memorable rallying cries is often the use of a powerful verb.

But most importantly, you need to get inside people's heads. 'Ban the bomb'. 'This girl can'. 'Dirt is good'. Perhaps start with the rule of three. The best seem disarmingly simple. Though of course, the shorter the line, the harder the write.

4. You need a symbol that lets others show their allegiance

Whether it's on the web or on the streets, your followers need to revolt around something tangible, and nothing does this better than iconography, images and symbols. It's why so many become shorthand for the revolution itself.

But beyond simply acting as a badge, a great symbol can be an invitation to participate. The Christmas jumpers themselves were built for sharing, and it helped the revolution to spread. When people use symbols in this way it turns followers into both the media and the message.

5. You need mind bombs to catapult your cause into culture

No matter how meaningful the cause, unless you can get your revolution in front of lots of people, its success will always be limited.

This is where the *mind bomb* comes in. It's the image that's going to open the world's eyes, shock people out of their indolence and lead them to act. It's the image that will capture what's wrong in an instant. It's the image that can't be ignored.

Elle magazine's #morewomen revolution sought to boost the number of women sitting at the top table. So they simply showed what these tables would look like with the men photoshopped out – from comedy panel shows to the G20, the series of images made their point much more starkly than words ever could.

Not that it has to be a static image of course. For Dove, this has typically been a powerful film. For REI it was the act of closing their stores on Black Friday. The only requisite is that it galvanises enough people for your revolution to break out of the niches and into the mainstream.

And like all great communications, the alchemy behind all great mind bombs is feeling. Publicity is paid for with a currency called emotion. Ask Always. Ask Chipotle. Ask Lifebuoy. Each found out just how many people can care enough to share when you spoon-feed the facts and force-feed the goose bumps.

6. You need propaganda that gets others talking and writing about it

No matter how loudly you've launched your revolution, people quickly move on. If the mind bomb attracts a following with the fireworks, think of your social strategy as the roaring fire that keeps them there.

The good news is that there have never been more opportunities. An explosion in new networks, from YouTube to Snapchat to Medium, actively rely on compelling content for their success. You need to think about how your news can sit at the top of these.

The answer tends to lie in how you can add to people's experience of the revolution with your generosity. By providing tools for over 600,000 teachers and 1.5 million parents, Dove has helped deliver self-esteem workshops to young people in 112 countries.

The lesson? Inspire, don't interrupt.

7. You need allies that spread fame and create change

It can be tempting to not let anyone into your revolution for fear it may dilute the vision. Yet revolutions have always been ideas that spread with passion through a community. And in the end it's these partners who will ultimately make it a success.

Take the celebrities that helped weave the Christmas jumpers into popular culture themselves. Or the way Asda, Costa and Primark came on board to increase their exposure even further.

These allies can also be there in your time of need. An essential part of your planning should be thinking about how you might counter any criticism. This is especially useful for brands as that can be most open to attack if they're seen as seeking commercial gains out of social causes.

When John Lewis highlighted the issue many elderly people face at Christmas, it made sense to bring in Age UK as a charity partner. And actually making a second ad specifically for them to raise awareness of the issue helped show just how serious they were about making a difference.

The world needs more revolting brands

Great brands have always added to the culture that surrounds them in order to make themselves famous. Tide created the first soap operas. Guinness wrote the *Book of Records*. Mr. Kipling invented a mythical baker that most people still assume to be a real person.

Today's most successful brands still add to culture. But if the likes of Always and John Lewis and Ariel are anything to go by, the most effective way to do that in 2016 is by taking a social stance.

For some time, society has been trending towards greater empathy, diversity and citizen engagement. Initially brands were able to benefit from this shift through corporate social responsibility or the odd act of charitable giving. But doing the right thing has become a hygiene factor. It no longer gets you much attention.

Today it's the socially conscious brands that take a strong stance that are benefiting. Instead of focusing on what they've done internally, they look at what they could do in the wider world. They find their spark and seek change.

This can take different forms for different brands. For some, it will be about a shot of fame in the arm of their communications. For others, it will represent a way to effectively channel their trade spend. The boldest will make the change central to their brand idea itself.

All will begin as storms brewing in the minds of people who want change. They will start with a no and end with a yes.

But their weapon of choice won't be the commercial, or the campaign. It will be the revolution.

Making small successful

Small budgets; big effects

By Laurence Green
Founding Partner, 101

The IPA Effectiveness Awards have long provided succour and inspiration for any advertiser with a small budget.

There are case histories in every competition that demonstrate the disproportionate returns 'the little guy' can achieve if (s)he marshals resources wisely and executes with imagination.

Although industry Goliaths tend to snatch the bigger prizes, the roll call of Effectiveness Award-winning Davids is a long one.

Indeed, my formative years as a strategist were informed as much by the small budget winners as the large ones. Campaigns and case studies as varied as Clark's desert boots; the impassioned defence of the Greater London Council; and even Charlton Football Club supporters' efforts to save their precious home ground, The Valley, all climbed into my head as best practice.

But above and beyond each year's specific small budget winners, their papers and their learnings, the awards have long been a more *general* source of encouragement to those who compete with the size of their ideas rather than the size of their budgets. This is not least because they invariably demonstrate the multiplier effect of creative communication: that how you spend matters, not just how much you spend, and may even matter more than how much you spend. (Though we must now add a caveat to this, to which I will return.)

There's a romance attached to the competitor with a small budget, of course, both in the marketing microcosm of the awards and in the wider world. Like some effectiveness version of the FA Cup, one of the delights for the awards judges is that the small club can be drawn alongside the big club and prevail by dint of superior demonstration of results (even if their cash return is lower at an absolute level). An Australian swimming pool manufacturer is given the same chance to claim a place in the advertising effectiveness hall of fame as the big guns of financial services, retail and FMCG.

Indeed, there's often more to learn from those brand owners and not-for-profits that have demonstrably punched above their weight than there is from the heavyweights, if only because their resource constraints have forced them to think harder, to be more strategic in their choices and/or more creatively precocious.

These are of course the very behaviours outlined by some of our most thrillingly contrary marketing minds, not least Adam Morgan's challenger brand thinking, crystallised most recently in his book, *A Beautiful Constraint*. The IPA's small budget winners all evidence his basic premise: that constraint – viewed *'as an opportunity, not a punitive restriction'* – can be good for you, as *'stimulus to find a new or better way of achieving our ambition'*. In both the spirit of their campaigning and the content of their papers, they are all true to Morgan's mantra: *'embrace constraint, leverage it, love it'*, just as they remind us also of the broader but equally counter-intuitive principles floated in Malcolm Gladwell's *David and Goliath*.

Gladwell's book, subtitled *The Art of Battling Giants*, offers a robust challenge to the way we conventionally think about obstacles and disadvantages. Drawing on a typically varied 'data set' he encourages readers to look beyond the superficial balance of power in competitive situations and, by extension, markets.

At a time when some form of constraint is the new norm for advertisers, and when so many markets have been disrupted by apparent underdogs, Morgan and Gladwell's thinking seems especially pertinent. There are echoes of both books in this year's winning papers and in the small budget effectiveness lessons outlined below.

It's worth pointing out first, though, that in an era when 'owned' and 'earned' rival 'paid for' on the modern media plan – and when ideas can take root and spread with a will of their own – we might have expected to see rather more entries with the most beautiful constraint of all: a media budget of zero. After all, the returns on successful campaigns without a 'paid-for' component (something genuinely viral, for example) should look very healthy indeed.

In fact, this year's shortlist still boasts a healthy representation of big, 'paid-for' budgets, even if they are increasingly embellished by amplification into owned and earned channels (the John Lewis Christmas campaigns are still a masterclass in this respect).

Perhaps more tellingly, and with only the odd exception, even this year's *small budget* winners typically have some kind of paid-for media on their plan, or indeed *only* paid-for media, bought brilliantly. I'll touch on these different models as I ask the obvious question: what patterns can we see across this new data set and what lessons can we draw? My conclusions are not intended to be definitive, by the way. Keen readers will, and should, reach their own.

Think creatively about your budget(s)

For some of our winners, success springs first from the re-imagination of their budgets, often in advance of any contemplation of creative and media execution. The Department for Education understood that disparate, local campaigns to encourage adoption were a sub-optimal use of funds and rolled these efforts together to demonstrably better effect. Wrestling with a long tail of advertising-worthy but individually un-fundable ice-cream brands, Wall's took the bold step of scooping each one into a single, multi-product 'master' campaign, transforming the economics of support as well as opening up rich new creative turf.

Both profited from a sideways look at how they were spending their money *overall*, rather than staring at the line item in front of them. (A similar story, albeit on a bigger budget, plays out in this year's McVitie's paper also.)

Make sacrifices

Other winners simply used their limited media monies with astonishing precision and/or just a good deal of focus: one of Gladwell's 'advantages of disadvantages', you might say.

For some, this was a question of *where* they chose to compete. The Conservative Party overcommitted dramatically against the small number of marginal constituencies where the 2015 general election would be won or lost. Its wonderfully written paper draws a sharp distinction between the party's success in those constituencies and the 'control' of the broader, national picture. The difference was advertising – not much, but spent wisely.

In a similar vein, the arts charity, Art Fund, (full disclosure: my agency authored this awards paper) and car hire brand, Sixt, also eschewed national coverage in order to make a bigger splash in their core geography of London, the latter drilling down to a media laydown dominated by the takeover of a single tube station, Canary Wharf.

For others, it was a question of *when* they could most effectively or efficiently compete. Save the Children crystallised its campaigning around a one-off fundraising event, Christmas Jumper Day, to create cut-through. The aforementioned Aussie pool brand, Narellan Pools, faced with a collapsing market, dug deep enough into its sales data to conclude that its limited media monies would work hardest if they were exclusively spent in the limited window created by two consecutive days of above average temperatures, since this was what triggered genuine sales intent.

All of the above are classic examples of strategy as the art of sacrifice, of advertisers knowingly trading aspirations for 'year round' or 'nationwide' presence for spikes of attention and impact. After these spikes it is, incidentally, often easier to see a clear 'before' and 'after' sales picture, in turn helping to make the case for more heavyweight advertising spend.

Sharpen your creative content

As previously noted, and as evidenced by these awards down the years, creativity is the effective advertiser's friend, as the source of emotional engagement and potential fame. The Ehrenberg-Bass Institute has concluded that the most effective copy actually works 10 to 20 times harder than the least effective, and the IPA estimates that creatively awarded campaigns are six times more efficient than non-creatively awarded ones. It's no surprise therefore to see that our winning small budget advertisers not only make astute strategic calls but also boast likeable or punchy creative work: from Wall's 'Goodbye serious' and Sixt's 'Drive smug' to The Conservative Party's depiction of former Labour leader Ed Miliband in Alex Salmond's pocket.

The most noteworthy paper in this respect, however, might also be the most unusual. *The Economist* has been a determinedly creative advertiser for 30 years or so. For its most recent campaign, however, it embraced data not just to find the right (younger) audience online, but also to serve them genuinely bespoke advertising. It's a wonderful demonstration of 'narrowcast' effectiveness, not least because it comes from a brand once famous for its beautifully written and strikingly art-directed posters.

Finally, our small budget winners also remind us that – beyond the smart strategic choices and creative calls we make at 'advertising level' – there's also a deeper contribution that we can all make to effective marketing investment.

Think of product as advertising

Agencies are increasingly being asked to include product ideas in their response to briefs, and rightly so. The initiatives that flow can often be at the marketing margins (my agency has created everything from T-shirts to tea-towels) but occasionally take centre stage as comms, or the new hero of comms, themselves.

101's answer to Art Fund's dwindling charity coffers, for example, was not to shake the advertising tin harder but to repackage the incidental benefits of 'arts giving' as a product in its own right: the National Art Pass. Rather than enjoying free or reduced price access to museums and art galleries as a byproduct of donation, this access was now available to buy directly (your charitable contribution now a 'happy consequence' of purchase). And so the role of advertising duly became to sell these terrific value passes, rather than to champion a cause. *En passant*, the idea reinvented the charity as a retailer, and transformed its advertising effectiveness.

Grey London's LifePaint idea for Volvo serves to prove much the same point, but even more vividly. It arrived at the Effectiveness Awards trailing a blaze of creative awards glory for its brilliantly inventive contribution to the mother brand's safety credentials but – to the great credit of the IPA and successive generations of judges – all that matters not a jot if the profit needle has not been moved and/or payback credibly proven. It's a story not just about laterally cementing Volvo's mission – to prevent any *death by*, rather than just in, one of the auto-maker's vehicles – but also of creative entrepreneurialism at its best.

Which brings me onto my caveat. It's easy to fall in love with these tales of 'advertising' derring-do on a small budget (is LifePaint even advertising?). And it's equally easy to believe that the rules of the advertising game have changed so profoundly that all you need to succeed these days is a good idea and a lucky bounce. (I speak as someone whose agency launched a wonky 'Christmas shopper simulator' on the gaming website Twitch last year and watched it rack up a million downloads in only three weeks.) Now while this may be *more* true than it used to be, there's another, less convenient truth: quite simply, that there is exponentially more content than ever fighting for our attention, and 'branded content' (including advertising) is often the least desirable of all.

So, while we honour the small budget expertly spent, it's important to remember that established rules of effectiveness thumb still largely prevail: most notably, that sales growth still correlates to excess share of voice (IPA, Field and Binet) and that – like it or not – paid-for media is still our best guarantor of that share of voice.

Peter Field's latest contribution to the advertising effectiveness narrative, *Selling Creativity Short*, is especially worthy of note and the source of the caveat mentioned earlier. The author notes that the excess share of voice typically enjoyed by creatively awarded campaigns has fallen away over the last few years and is, in fact, now running below the level needed to maintain market share. '*Misled by a completely false logic, marketers are using creativity as a substitute for budget rather than as a multiplier of it*', he warns.

It's an important coda to the excitable commentary, this essay included, around our industry and awards' small-budget winners. A reminder that, for now at least, media spend still matters. While there are myriad new ways to outsmart others, outspending your competitors – or even just your own market share – is still business-critical as a reliable engine of growth. The real win for advertisers is allying small budget thinking to 'big budget' funding.

Adopting a test and learn mindset

Marginal gains theory in marketing

By Jonathan Allan
Sales Director, Channel 4

The most impactful and effective advertising has always been the product of blending art and science. Advertising adds most value when it's at its most creative and innovative, and is applied to a business context with clear objectives and an expectation that it will drive sales, change perceptions or influence behaviour.

If the creative teams focus more on the art, then the science is brought into the mix by the account/media planners. The alchemy they create together has probably resulted in most of the IPA Effectiveness award-winning campaigns over the years.

However, as the world has become more complex, noisy and saturated through the proliferation of channels and the march of technology, it is now potentially more difficult to gain cut-through for the art in advertising, and more intellectually challenging to deal with the science.

As this piece is focused on the application of a more scientific approach to marketing, it is helpful to look at how science itself is defined:

> *The intellectual and practical activity encompassing the systematic study of the structure and behaviour of the physical and natural world through observation and experiment.*

So a scientific approach to marketing should involve more 'systematic study' and 'observation ***and*** experiment' in how we develop our strategy and execution and how we design in-built experiments into everything we do.

Historically, this type of approach has been more visible and evidenced in below-the-line, more direct forms of communication, where creating test environments and subsequent observation have been a great deal easier due to adopting shorter-term, more easily measurable objectives. However, through the development and improved reach of above-the-line digital channels and more sophisticated forms of measurement, it is now easier to apply more science to more of your marketing investment and to test and learn in real time.

By analogy, there is also much focus in sports coaching on marginal gains theory, most famously led by Clive Woodward in rugby and Dave Brailsford in cycling, where the aggregation of tiny improvements across the breadth of activity can add up to a significant competitive advantage.

> *England winning the Rugby World Cup was not about doing one thing 100% better, but about doing 100 things 1% better.*
>
> Clive Woodward

> *We are always striving for improvement, for those 1% gains, in absolutely everything we do.*
>
> Dave Brailsford

The marginal gains theory translates directly into marketing and advertising activity and is an underlying maxim of optimisation strategies. Past Effectiveness Award-winning cases by Everest (2014 – Silver), The National Lottery (2012 – Silver) and others show how the theory can be successfully applied in practice.

Nevertheless, within a more experimental approach to marketing communications, it is important to remember that when you design your marketing experiments, you are testing and measuring the correct things. Too much 'optimisation' is focused on intermediate or even meaningless metrics and/or only looks at a few channels in the mix or short-term sales results. This is misleading because your display ROI might look great this month, but the halo of your longer-term brand equity and awareness may be suffering as a result of off-brand creative, or diversion of budgets.

Additionally, it is possible to optimise strongly in the latter stages of the purchase funnel to deliver a very strong ROI through, for example, using re-targeting. However, the total volume of sales or revenue may dip significantly, or you may start to compromise the 'top of the funnel' that the business relies on for future success.

The 2016 Effectiveness Award winning cases have managed to create a consistently strong blend of long- and short-term objectives, and ensured that their approach is consistent with long-term brand and business health, whilst also delivering short-term sales impact.

They demonstrate how a more scientific approach can help us all take advantage of incremental marginal gains in marketing and communications without undermining the transformative potential of great insight or creativity.

Experimenting, testing and learning is a marketing philosophy, not a campaign approach

As Clive and Dave would no doubt attest, you can't play at marginal gains theory for a couple of months and then move on to the next flavour of the month. It only works if the leadership and the team commits and truly believes in the theory's benefits and incorporates the approach into the DNA of their culture. Indeed, many of the ideas for the 1% gains will come from the teams themselves (being at the coalface of training, competing and living) as opposed to their coach. Additionally, these 1% gains need time to accumulate and yield their true benefit.

This is also true in developing a marketing approach. There is no point in just having one of your campaigns or a single channel that adopts this approach. It needs to be a holistic, long-term endeavour to gain learnings and optimise your approach across all of your marketing activity.

In its case study, *The Economist* demonstrates a significant commitment to a new way of communicating to a new audience to grow subscriptions. It did so in a way that allowed continuous learning and optimisation of both media and message to maximise the impact of the investment over a two-year lifecycle, and this will no doubt continue on the basis of the success so far.

Plusnet has focused on testing and learning across five years to drive growth in an extremely dynamic and competitive market. The Yorkshire-based broadband company adopted a suite of measurement techniques to modify its tonality, messaging and media approach over the period to maintain its upward momentum.

You still need great insights to form usable hypotheses to test

When brands are using multivariate testing and learning on the fly, there is clearly a danger that not enough thought will be put into the initial strategy, proposition or creative because people may think 'hey, we can always change it as we go'. However, the 2016 winners highlight how much a strong insight drives success.

For example, through deep data-mining, Narellan Pools not only identified the 'dive-in' moment, when Australian consumers first aspired to buy a swimming pool, but also a clear tipping point where customers were most likely to move from consideration into purchase mode. This drove the brand's entire strategy, and the brand was able to optimise further as it went to market.

Plusnet appreciated that its marketing message of being 'from Yorkshire' might be interpreted as being 'for Yorkshire only' so it shifted its messaging to appeal to a broader national audience.

Similarly, Wall's recognised that it needed to drive mental awareness through showing ice creams as close to point of purchase as possible – and used this insight to drive the brand's creative and media approach.

Be very clear on your target audience and what it wants

All effective communications campaigns have a very acute sense of their target audience, and this is further amplified when you are planning a more scientific approach to your advertising optimisation, as you need a clear segment against which to measure your success.

The Economist realised that to attract a broader audience of subscribers, it had to enable potential new readers to experience the reality of *The Economist*'s journalism to challenge any false assumptions they might have about the title. This moment was known as *The Economist* 'epiphany'.

They also created a deep understanding of a group of the 'intellectually curious', which it coined 'the progressives' to help with its messaging and global media placement. The brand then measured the campaign's performance against this specific audience from a tracking and sales perspective.

Narellan Pools not only focused on qualified-lead pool buyers, but it also found out that if the mean monthly rolling average temperature was higher for two or more consecutive days, then conversions spiked. Based on this insight, the brand created the best modal opportunity to run its activity and maximise ROI.

In another example, Eurotunnel completely changed its marketing approach, building a customer segmentation to identify the most valuable customer groups and then communicating to them separately. Over five years, the integration of this segmentation across all Eurotunnel's marketing, messaging and media activity, effectively measured and optimised, culminated in a 20.8% increase in cars carried through the tunnel. Over the same period the 'cross-channel with car' market declined by 0.7%.

Using science doesn't mean you can forget the art

It's the testing of the combination of the targeting, placement and the message itself and its adjustment on the fly that will deliver the uplift in a test and learn approach.

However, it can be the case that when using multiple copy and optimisation techniques that the initial creativity goes out of the window and the ads become very utilitarian. It is crucially important that as much effort goes into the creative development as with any other campaign.

The Economist used excerpts of news stories as ad copy and placed them contextually to the target audience, delivering *The Economist* 'experience' in bite-size chunks and helping change potential readers' perceptions.

In the client statement that accompanied its case, *The Economist* added: '*We tested machine-generated, dynamic creative and it was consistently and significantly outperformed by crafted communications*'.

Likewise, Plusnet maintained its focus, but optimised its creative approach and tonality over time to match its growth plans and consumer perceptions.

Measure your results holistically and cross-channel, not in silos

The world is unfortunately not simple and therefore to benefit substantially from a scientific marketing approach one has to put as much effort into the measurement of the experimentation as into the creation of the marketing communications themselves.

Too much so-called 'optimisation' and ROI focuses on single channels, short-term impact and binary metrics such as click-throughs or cost per acquisition (CPA). Also, some clients and agencies working in individual silos are targeted and rewarded with improving a specific channel or KPI, with little regard for the broader picture and how things will hang together for the brand and business as a whole.

This means famous brands can follow you round the internet imploring you to buy things you have already purchased, just to chase clicks. In other cases, little account is taken of the impact of mass-brand communications when measuring the ROI of more direct channels.

The best 2016 Effectiveness Awards cases have a range of objectives around long-term brand equity, consumer awareness and perception, sales and short-term acquisition. They also use a variety of tracking, sales analysis, and econometric modelling to help understand how each channel impacts on the others in the long and short term.

Further, case studies from Wall's, *The Guardian* and the Department for Education demonstrate how measurement can have wider additional benefits such as creating benchmarks for future activity by supporting more risk-taking and innovation in an organisation, and in spreading industry learning.

Don't kick yourself for mistakes, instead see them as opportunities to improve

Marginal gains theory uncovers and pays attention to all those 1% possibilities to improve. Therefore it requires everyone involved to celebrate those areas in which they are not operating at 100%, as an opportunity to improve and create advantage.

In business, there is generally too much negativity around failure. As a result, people tend to cover up any mistakes or errors when things don't go according to plan. Instead, we should view everything we do in marketing as an experiment in which there are lots of opportunities for those 1% improvements the next time round.

Rather than apologising for suboptimal results, we should look forward to identifying areas for improvement and be much more open about how we tackle them for our next campaign. After all, that is what learning is all about ...

The benefits of tailored targeting

Challenge Byron Sharp and grow your brand

By Marie Oldham
Chief Strategy Officer, VCCP Media

The ubiquitous Byron Sharp has sold over 50,000 copies of his book, *How Brands Grow*, however, this year's entrants demonstrate that many in the advertising and marketing industry refuse to adopt his arguments as sacrosanct.

Is this because we simply think we know better? Or is it because, no matter how many times Sharp tells us that his laws are based on hard evidence and apply across different countries, time periods and market conditions, practitioners know that brands can also grow by breaking rules.

In case you do not have them pinned up above your desk, let me remind you of Sharp's laws (or rather, the laws created using the seminal research by Ehrenberg and Goodhart and brought to market by Sharp).

Sharp's seven rules for brand growth:

1. *Continuously reach all buyers of the category:* (communication and distribution – don't ever be silent).
2. *Ensure the brand is easy to buy:* (communicate how it fits with the user's life).
3. *Get noticed:* (grab attention and focus on brand salience to prime the user's mind).
4. *Refresh and rebuild memory structures:* (respect existing associations that make the brand easy to notice and easy to buy).

5. *Create and use distinctive brand assets:* (sensory cues that get noticed and stay top of mind).
6. *Be consistent:* (avoid unnecessary changes, whilst keeping the brand fresh and interesting).
7. *Stay competitive:* (keep the brand easy to buy and avoid giving excuses not to buy).

(Byron Sharp: *How Brands Grow*)

As a broadly contemporaneous set of cases rewarded for convincingly demonstrating how marketing activity has generated a financial return, the 2016 shortlisted Effectiveness Awards submissions provide a distinctive body of evidence against which to test some of these rules.

It would be possible within this year's papers to examine how well several of these rules hold up (e.g. Do brands sometimes succeed by being disruptive rather than consistent? Or a price rise may give consumers a 'reason not to buy' but can equally be financially necessary for long-term brand health).

However, arguably, rule number one is the most contentious and most discussed of the laws and there is much to challenge it in current industry best practice.

Sharp argues that blanket coverage is the most effective way to grow your brand, that targeting is a waste of time and indeed reduces brands' ability to attract more buyers. He is particularly tough on the '*esoteric quackery concerned with segmentation, differentiation and how buyers perceive brands*'.

Contrast this with the following quote from OMD's Eurotunnel Le Shuttle Effectiveness Award paper:

> *We completely changed our marketing approach, building a customer segmentation to identify the most valuable customer groups and then communicating to them separately and appropriately. Over five years, the deep integration of this segmentation across all marketing, messaging and media activity, effectively measured and optimised, has culminated in a 20.8% increase in cars carried through the Tunnel. Over the same period the cross-channel with car market declined by 0.7%.*

Not only did team Eurotunnel identify segments to target (and segments to ignore), it embedded the philosophy of segmentation in all activity.

It pursued a strategy of segmented messaging, highlighting very distinct brand benefits to different audiences, even differentiating between 'social adventurous families' and 'summer holiday families' segments who on paper could look like the same demographic but who Eurotunnel believe to have different attitudes to travel and different purchase behaviours.

In fact, the Eurotunnel team goes so far as to say that broad targeting and single messaging risk '*making messages less salient for our core audiences and best prospects, generating less response*'. In other words, it believes that broad targeting wastes money. Instead, the operator targeted priority audiences and tracked this activity rigorously.

Eurotunnel is far from alone in its reliance on targeting. A quick review of the 39 IPA papers given an award this year reveals that 19 (49%) claim to be targeting specific audiences.

Figure 1: Eurotunnel Le Shuttle customer database segment changes 2013–2015

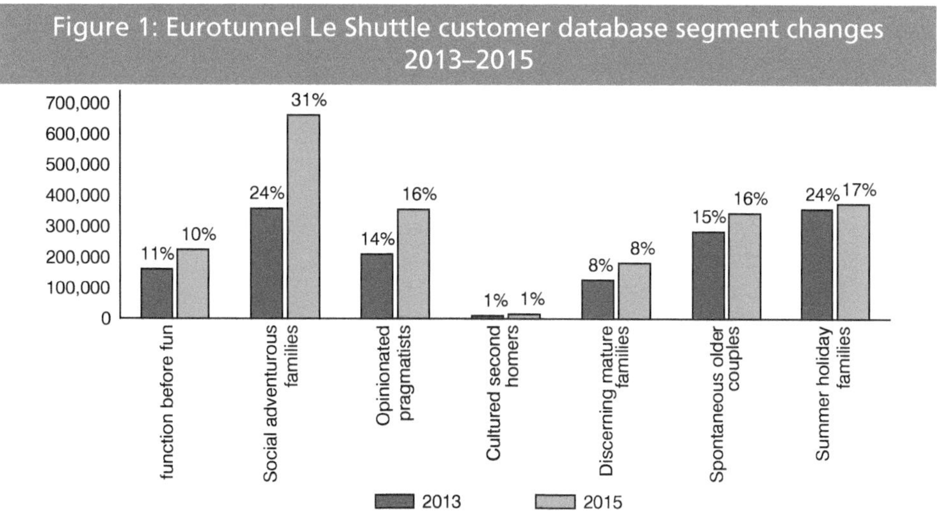

Source: OMD UK segmentation refresh. Percentages relate to the proportion of overall database accounted for by each segment, e.g. SAF contributed 24% of all customers in 2013 and 31% in 2015.

Given that the very nature of the IPA Effectiveness Awards is to reward authors for demonstrating ROMI, these teams must be doing something right and, as Eurotunnel's paper spans five years, this is not simply short-term reward.

A second brand taking targeting to extremes was Sixt, the car hire business. This struggling UK business suffered from many of the issues Sharp outlines in his book. It had competitors with higher brand penetration, a small pool of regular users, and

Figure 2: Sixt Canary Wharf takeover campaign

was trapped in a rut of 5% market share without enough budget to outshout the competition.

Sixt and its agencies decided to pursue a strategy often referred to as 'concentrate and dominate', spending all of its budget in a four-week period, with 57% of the budget spent on an OOH takeover of London's Canary Wharf Station and the majority of the remainder with *The Evening Standard*. Sixt also chose to focus on a small part of its product repertoire (premium cars) in order to maximise relevance to the Canary Wharf audience.

The 'Drive smug' campaign was created. The campaign's Effectiveness Awards submission states that *'the media strategy was to sacrifice reach for domination. This required focus'.*

Poster campaigns generally deliver high frequency of viewing, especially those targeting us on habitual journeys to work. The Canary Wharf takeover campaign would have delivered OTS beyond 20+, bombarding the audience twice each day at every possible location in the station. This was underpinned with a high-profile wrap of *The Evening Standard* and a one-day takeover of the paper's website. Perhaps unsurprisingly, campaign awareness amongst Canary Wharf users was high, the audience understood the campaign messages and people felt that they would consider the brand should they need to hire a car.

Figure 3: Sixt brand consideration uplift

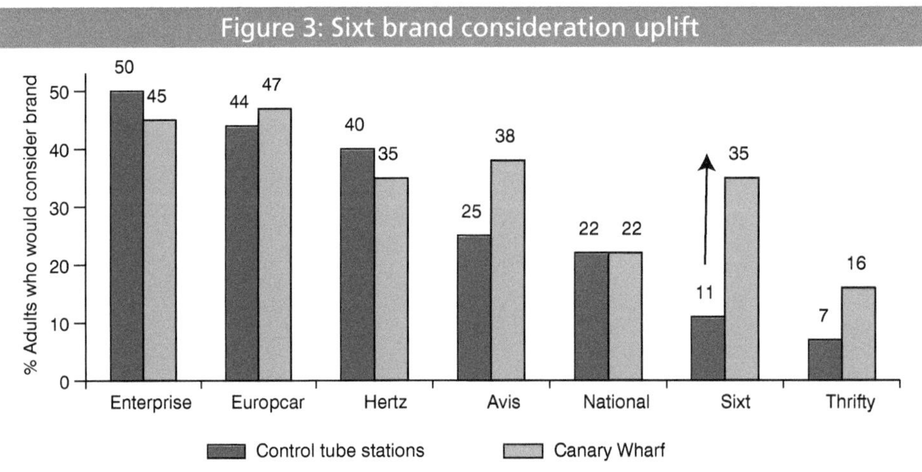

Sixt ad tracking July 2015. Base: Canary Wharf 250 adults. Control stations, 150 adults.

Sales in the east London region were also up, resulting in a positive ROMI. Some might argue that this type of campaign is short-term and un-replicable. It might have driven sales (see Figure 4) but is unlikely to have contributed to long-term penetration gain.

However, the campaign did enable the client to prove to his organisation that focused activity can drive growth and that increased marketing spend should be considered. As the client argued:

> *Small brands do not have to simply accept the big brands' category rules, or assume they knew best. There may be opportunities they have not yet spotted.*

Figure 4: Sixt London vs out-of-London growth

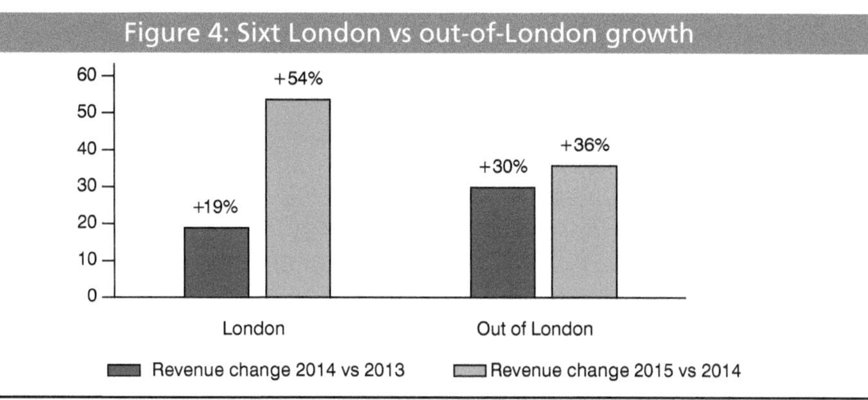

Source: Sixt sales data.

For another success driven by precision targeting, see the example of Narellan Pools, the Australian swimming pool manufacturer which successfully activated its activity only when specific climatic conditions were met and turned it off outside this restricted window of opportunity.

The Economist also put targeting of a specific segment at the heart of its successful drive to increase subscriptions.

At this point, it is worth stating that many practitioners fundamentally agree with the Sharp approach and had built brands using these principles long before Sharp and his laws appeared on TED or in the business book section of Waterstones.

Campaigns such as 'Intel Inside' and Compare the Market's 'Meerkats' are built on the principle of highly recognised, consistent communications icons, distinctive memory structures and ownable brand assets.

Offering consumers simple sensory cues to unite all brand contacts is a powerful way to maintain mental availability.

In his book, Sharp mentions Coca-Cola and Pepsi as brands which need to follow his philosophy as their customers are not loyal and maintaining both mental and physical availability is critical to retaining penetration.

However, the Effectiveness Award shortlisted paper from Pepsi Max suggests this thinking may not apply to sub-brands. Surely, sub-brands have to develop their own niche and not just cannibalise the parent's equity, particularly as a sub-brand will have a fraction of the parental budget?

Pepsi Max has focused on millennials as its hope for securing the future of the brand. After years of heavy discounting and adapting big American TV ads for the UK market, in 2012 Pepsi Max realised it had lost relevance to its primary 18–34-year-old consumer group.

Sharp argues that cola brands are heavily reliant on supermarket purchases by multi-pack buying families and that 'relevance' is not as important as we think it is. Instead, at the very least, Pepsi Max should be building a strong framework of Pepsi brand icons and assets.

Pepsi, on the other hand, re-directed marketing spend away from TV and decided to focus on the digital world, on YouTube and on content. Agency meeting rooms around the UK have all hosted the same discussion with clients, '*how can a content strategy reach out to our audience, engage them in our brand world and increase brand relevance to their lifestyle*?' Such questions are probably anathema to Sharp, since by its very nature, content is ever-changing, lightly branded, can have a relatively short shelf life, and often reflects the world of the consumer rather than the world of the brand.

However, Pepsi Max re-structured its way of working to become a creator and publisher of content – moving away from one or two big TV commercials per year to filling a whole channel with a wide variety of content.

Pepsi Max created its own YouTube channel, committing the brand to the creation of significant levels of content with the goal of becoming a brand that entertains its audience, not sells to them.

Using high-profile personalities, such as Dynamo the magician, has helped drive viewings to Pepsi content. The brand has also addressed the need to populate the channel with large quantities of content by creating a content 'hub' that has longer shelf life (although possibly less share-ability). Hub content is produced in conjunction with YouTube creators and this may help broaden coverage within follower communities.

As with all the authors of successful IPA papers, Pepsi Max and its agency team have sought to demonstrate a connection between its activities and sales. The channel itself has 110,000 subscribers, and many might argue that this is below par for a brand that needs to sell millions of cans per year. However, video views are high, content sharing is high and we have to admire the quality of commitment from the brand to exploring new ways of communicating. Only time will tell whether this is enough to sustain a brand for the long term.

So, what can we conclude from this year's papers? A topline review of papers would indicate that, as several of Sharp's laws suggest, there are still benefits to brands – particularly young ones – from investing in big, memorable brand communications across mass media channels to maximise mental availability and drive penetration.

However, mature brands such as Eurotunnel, Sixt, *The Economist* and Pepsi Max have also found new growth routes using segmentation, high levels of message relevancy, and more targeted use of budget to create impact and cut through amongst specific consumer groups.

Some brands such as first direct have used a combination of approaches. The banking group has singled out millennials in its drive to refresh its consumer base by delivering quirky communications in traditional broadcast channels such as TV alongside highly targeted digital and social activity.

All of the 2016 Effectiveness Award winners have risen to the Sharp challenge to 'grab attention' and 'be distinctive'. And many have clearly put understanding of the role of their brand in consumers' lives at the heart of their communications.

So, it is understandable why brands are attracted to the idea of following proven laws of brand growth, but any such rules always need to be tested and shaped by the real-world experience of individual brand teams and their business needs.

The 2016 shortlisted papers suggest that at the end of the day, there are different roads to ROMI for different businesses.

Great work requires more than following universal 'laws' and conventional thinking. That may be a nuisance for marketing savants. But it is the joy of our industry.

Figure 5: Pepsi Max summary of hub films

For the 'Unbelievable Uncovered' series our two vlogger presenters travelled the country to unearth great talent and inspire them to try something unbelievably good.

For the 'Unbelievable Challenges' series we collaborated with YouTube talent (performers and directors) to find out what unbelievable talents they had and help them to push them to the next level.

Taking a longer view

Learning from long- and short-term hits

By Alison Hoad
Vice Chairman, RKCR/Y&R

I'm Blue da ba dee da ba da-ee

Remember that? The biggest hit of September '99? Sold over a million copies?

It's by Eiffel 65, in case you've forgotten.

But where are they now? Just one more hit ('Move your body' reached number three in 2000). And then…? Nada.

There are one-hit-wonders a-plenty. Some, like Live Aid, were one-hit and wondrous for good reason. But most shine brightly for a few short weeks and then fade, ingloriously, from memory.

In 2002, the world went mad for 'The Ketchup Song'. It sold 6 million copies. But (perhaps thankfully) none of Las Ketchup's follow-up singles made it into the UK charts.

A couple of years earlier, Coldplay released 'Yellow'. Eighty million record sales later, with a reported net worth of $475m, they're still going strong – testament to trademark quality, an ongoing reputation for brilliant live gigs, an ability to mould what they do to changing times and a brand that's bigger than any individual song. You might consider Radiohead or U2 in the same vein.

In marketing, as in the music biz, playing the long game pays off. IPA Databank analysis has consistently found that the most potent marketing cocktail is not just creativity, but creativity invested in over the long term. It's this that builds businesses and generates disproportionate profit.

Yet as the IPA's recent *Selling Creativity Short* report shows, short-termism and declining budgets have led to a quadrupling of short-term campaigns at the expense of longer-term brand building. We've opted for more Ketchup, less Chris Martin.

In uncertain times this is, perhaps, inevitable. With good planning and creative ingenuity your short-term campaign might become a lucrative phenomenon. But examples of this instant pot of gold are few and far between. And they always fizzle out in the end. A flash in the pan will neither build nor sustain a business.

Happily, this year's crop of IPA papers includes some brilliant longer-term successes that might just persuade, support and guide marketers towards a more profitable longer-term approach.

These cases have a lot in common – and what we learn from them is reassuringly consistent with previous IPA Databank findings.

Recession-proofing

Every one of the cases this year was developed in the teeth of recession; many on the back of declining spend. It's likely that we're not yet out of the woods. So it's worth considering that long-term thinking has been fundamental in helping these brands thrive in less than perfect trading conditions.

In its home market, Guinness faced the perfect storm of an Irish economic collapse severe enough to require a bailout by the International Monetary Fund, pub closures and fewer people drinking in those pubs that survived. As if that was not enough, it faced an onslaught of cheaper and/or trendier competitors. But perseverance (more of which later) paid off. Its long-term commitment to a new idea – 'Made of more' – proved 2.3 times more effective than the advertising that preceded it.

Macmillan's 'No one should face cancer alone' campaign was born out of a need to compensate for a dramatic slowing of revenue growth when recession hit. A one-off phenomenon would not help: it was crucial for Macmillan to generate ongoing predictable revenue for investment in the services they provide. Commitment to the idea generated unprecedented 49% revenue growth – four times as much as the average for major UK charities.

Costa had become market leader in terms of distribution, but neither preference nor profits followed presence. What did follow was recession, at which point people fell back on their favourite brand – Starbucks (despite blind taste tests showing that Costa coffee was better). So Costa set out on a mission to save the world from mediocre coffee – building long-term brand values as it did so. This mission propelled Costa to brand leader – a position it has defended ever since.

Making budgets go further

Sticking with the money, it's clear that long-term campaigns aren't just more effective – they're more efficient too.

Most of this year's long-term cases show how consistent investment behind increasingly effective campaigns ensured that returns per pound spent dramatically improved over time. They benefited from a powerful combination of growing familiarity and talkability, increased PR amplification and greater interest from commercial partners – together with the ability to optimise the campaign over time. (Many of these are 'fame-effects' – which are discussed elsewhere in this book.)

Take Stoptober – an ingenious calendar event that has proven highly effective in helping the 'rump' of hardened smokers to quit. By repeating Stoptober annually, a new quitting season has emerged, generating ever more publicity year by year. In time, this has the potential to influence smokers regardless of marketing budgets. Rigorous evaluation has helped improve the effectiveness of the campaign – with significant changes made to both tone of voice and supporting tools. As a result, Stoptober has become more useful as a quitting tool and claimed quit attempts have grown dramatically year on year. This is despite the fact that the marketing budget has remained flat.

Other cases show how growing campaign reputation fuels interest from outside.

- Macmillan's mission that no one should face cancer alone is enormously helped by both Boots and Nationwide who have come on board to help ensure that people living with cancer do not have to cope with pharmacy, appearance or financial decisions alone.
- 40% of the cost John Lewis's Christmas campaign is now funded by commercial partners.
- Sainsbury's partnerships with the Royal British Legion, Save the Children and the author Judith Kerr, have brought all-important legitimacy to its Christmas campaigns – as well as creating new revenue streams either for the charity partners or from publishing and merchandising in the case of 'Mog's Christmas'.

Nothing sells quite as hard as emotion

The most powerful long-term cases this year are almost all built upon an emotional foundation.

Plusnet had, initially at least, competitive prices on its side. But its best weapon has been its brand. Building emotional connection through its good honest Yorkshire values helped Plusnet thrive when its products became less competitive. Despite having a largely dual-play offer in what is now a quad-play market, there were only *five* weeks in the period from 2011–2015 when its total customer base fell. For every sale the campaign delivered in the short term, it delivered two more over the longer term, through its aggregate brand-building effect. Doing Plusnet, as well as its customers, proud.

Both Sainsbury's and John Lewis have shied away from the Christmas norm. Both set out to win the hearts and minds of the nation over the long term rather than to simply sell this year's Christmas wares. Both have built campaigns on simple, but deeply felt emotional truths.

Sainsbury's have harnessed the old adage that Christmas is for sharing – generating £24 profit for every £1 spent. And each Christmas, John Lewis tells a new emotive tale of thoughtful Christmas giving. The feeling is the message. And it's a powerful feeling. Anticipation of what's to come has grown – as have John Lewis profits.

Of course this approach is not for the faint-hearted: each year the stakes are higher; the creative bar is raised. Roll on next Christmas ...

Emotion isn't always the answer ...

Armed with the clear evidence that in the long run, emotion sells, it's tempting to head straight to an emotionally based strategy. But for anyone with a hunch that emotion might not be the answer to their particular challenge, look no further than the Art Fund's National Art Pass campaign to support your case.

Here's a charity with a noble cause. Surely, there's a compelling emotional pull in saving art for the nation? But the charity's noble motivations turned out to be rather more noble than its audience's who were more interested in saving money than in saving art. This (together with a cut in Government funding) left the Art Fund short of income. The solution lay not in emotion but in an entirely commercial product: the National Art Pass – a membership scheme that gives members free or discounted museum entry. Relentless focus on this brilliant product has turned a worthy cause into a profitable one – generating a profit return of £4.07 for every £1 spent. What's more, the profit has been used for the charity's original cause – helping to acquire or retain an astonishing range of art which might otherwise have been lost.

Sensodyne is another exception that proves the rule. Here, education, rather than emotion has driven long-term success. For the past 10 years, its campaign has focused entirely on 'condition awareness' – waking people up to the problem of sensitive teeth. This strategy has not only helped Sensodyne grow from a minnow to a big fish, but also to fend off stiff competition from market leader, Colgate.

Long-term commitment isn't a straitjacket

Who doesn't relish the shock of the new?

Advertisers and their agencies might well be accused of getting bored of good ideas rather too quickly. We don't get famous by doing more of the same ...

But the best long-term campaigns have plenty of room for manoeuvre – usually because they're rooted in a simple, enduring idea that's big enough to accommodate fresh execution, new messages and changing conditions. Often, it's this ability to change that makes these campaigns so effective.

Guinness's 'Made of more' has stretched across 'Clocks' and 'Clouds' to 'The Society of the Elegant Persons of The Congo'. More recently, the same idea has lent credibility to Guinness's sponsorship of the Rugby World Cup.

Sainsbury's managed to capture the mischievousness of a calamitous cat and the poignancy of the Christmas Day truce under the same overarching idea.

Perseverance pays

How often do we get it 100% right first time? If you're going for a one hit wonder, then what? Start again? Get it not quite right again?

Clearly, a major advantage to playing the long game is the ability to fine-tune your campaign – feeding in learning as you go, building on what works, adjusting what doesn't, responding to changing conditions.

Guinness is refreshingly honest in this respect. It charts the ups and downs of perfecting creative against a new global platform. Grit, determination and, most crucial of all, faith in the strategy, resulted not just in highly effective, award-winning creative work – but also created a bank of learning for other markets.

In this, and all the other long-term cases, evaluation has been used as a means, not an end – and is central to their long-term success.

Wider impact

Long-term campaigns aren't just campaigns – they are intended to (or become) central fulcrums of a business, driving significant value well beyond regular advertising effects.

Take The Royal British Legion (a campaign on which my agency worked). Faced with the threat of an aging supporter base – with younger people more distant from its apparent cause – RBL took the brave step to turn its brand on its head. 'Live on' has not only driven record donations in the short term, but become a guiding light for the organisation as a whole.

Macmillan's mission that no one should face cancer alone has helped it become a more influential brand. It has successfully built its case well beyond advertising – influencing the Cancer Strategy for England and ensuring its argument was included in all three main parties' election manifestos.

It's clear from the range of examples discussed above, that this year's crop of entries is rich with long-term thinking. But there are also some brilliant examples of powerful short-term campaigns. What's interesting is that they're not simply the result of a short-termist, 'one-hit-wonder' frame of mind. They're all short term for good reason.

Short term by necessity

Sometimes you're dealing with a moment in time. You don't need to think long term. You're looking for a quick, impressive win. This calls for pinpoint accuracy: you have no time to fine-tune as you go.

The Conservative Party 2015 election campaign illustrates this brilliantly. Effectiveness on the day was the only thing that mattered. This called for forensic analysis and laser-sharp accuracy in every part of the campaign – from setting objectives to identifying exactly which behavioural change, among which audiences would push the Conservatives over the winning line. So it was no accident that the campaign targeted not Labour swing voters, but 'sway' voters who favoured other, smaller parties. It was no accident that the proposition focused not on why they should vote Conservative, but on the *risk* of not doing so. And, as we know, it was no accident that it worked.

Far-away, down-under, Narellan, Australia's leading swimming pool builder has benefited from similar forensic accuracy – built around a moment in time. You may think the window of opportunity for swimming pool brands is summer-long. But you'd be wrong. With a budget of just $10k for each of its 49 territories, Narellan needed to be sharper than that. Using big data, they identified that the tipping point to picking up the phone came if the temperature rose to above the mean monthly rolling average for more than two consecutive days and that the effect lasted for four days. So media was activated only if these specific temperature conditions were met, and turned off four days later.

How's that for precision planning?

Short-term expressions of a longer-term positioning

A well-established long-term positioning can create the conditions for brilliant short-term opportunities – one-off injections that, in turn, reignite the brand.

Volvo LifePaint is one such example: an ingenious product idea built out of Volvo's Safety Vision 2020 that 'no one will be killed or seriously injured in, *or by*, a Volvo'. By making cyclists visible at night, LifePaint does exactly that: it can keep them alive. It's an idea that has generated huge free publicity for Volvo – modernising its commitment to safety in the process. Although it was not treated as a profit centre, LifePaint is entirely self-funded, with the costs of development covered by the product's sales.

Short-term testing of a hoped-for longer-term strategy

For smaller businesses, or when budgets are under pressure, all-out commitment to a large, long-term campaign can be daunting or unaffordable or both.

This was the case for Sixt, which tested the water with a confident swagger of a campaign that ran for just one burst in Canary Wharf tube station. By sacrificing reach for domination, sales grew beyond all expectations – providing Sixt with a blueprint for future growth.

As we've suggested, these campaigns were short term for good reason. But to really build a business, longer-term thinking clearly pays off.

So if Live Aid is the right answer to your brief, then great: Go ahead. But if you're tempted by a quick win because a longer-term approach seems too hard or too costly or too, well, long term, maybe pause for a moment, let the dulcet tones of The Ketchup Song drift into your head – and think again.

Building customer experience

The need for product and service innovation

By Neil Godber
Head of Planning, J. Walter Thompson

The need to improve customer experience by innovating products and services is an increasingly common demand from clients and an increasingly pressing challenge to agencies.

It is driven by the influences of digital technology and the culture of lean start-ups in helping to develop easier, better and cheaper products and services.

By encouraging businesses to apply new tools and an entrepreneurial mindset to cut out intermediaries, disrupt channels, combine existing offerings in novel ways, and enable more personalisation, these forces are redefining all manner of expectations about products and services, and even the categories in which businesses operate.

At the same time, the internet is equipping consumers with more information and an increased ability to keep brands under surveillance.

Consumers' ability to get behind brand image and share any disappointments with what they find is forcing brands to focus more on closing the gap between a brand's promise and the reality of a consumer's experience of it. As a result, the power of communications to build unrealistic aspirations is being downgraded by many brands in favour of re-engineering and improving their products and services.

As part of this re-engineering, organisations have focused on clarifying and articulating the purposes individual brands exist to achieve. And they have put greater onus on delivering such purposes through activity programmes, experiences, partnerships and software-enabled utility rather than purely through communications.

Ultimately, for some commentators, there is no need to augment a product or service with emotional value; companies simply need to be more useful and better, or they will perish. As the mantra goes, the product is the marketing is the product is the marketing.

The same trends require agencies to ask themselves fundamental questions such as:

- What does an idea look like?
- What are brands and why do we need them?
- What is the role for agencies?
- What skills do/will agencies need?
- How should agencies be paid for their work?

The 2016 IPA Effectiveness Awards show brands and agencies grappling with these issues. They demonstrate the potential for developing products and services to meet diverse challenges, from reinvigorating interest in an established brand value as Volvo LifePaint did, to changing the relationship an organisation has with its members, as achieved by Art Fund, to Mattessons' success in building social currency to enable it to access a new audience.

Re-engineering a relationship: Art Fund

Art Fund was an organisation with a clear, authentic purpose for over 100 years, rooted in saving works of art for the nation.

But faced with stalling membership, an ageing customer base (the average was 69 years old), larger and more immediately worthy competitors, and government funding cuts, Art Fund needed a strong recruitment campaign.

Since the relationship between customers and Art Fund was traditionally characterised as being driven by donations to preserve art, the expected response to these problems would have been to devise communications to make Art Fund's purpose feel even more emotive and persuade more donors to give to the cause.

However, research revealed that the real reason most people 'donated' to the Fund was less to do with the worthy, but intangible cause of saving art for future generations, and more related to the real, quantifiable and immediate benefits of discounted entry to galleries and museums which Fund membership provided.

As a result, the Fund developed The National Art Pass as a type of art passport which codified member discounts to galleries into a concrete product, and became the centre of the Fund's advertising.

Alighting on the right motivations to recruit donors would have made a difference to a campaign's success in any scenario.

But by applying innovative thinking, the brand created an enduring product for members (not patrons) which acted as a permanent reminder of the benefits of membership.

Generating social currency amongst a new audience: Mattessons

Mattessons was a pioneer in the meat snacking category, having launched the successful Fridge Raiders brand. However, from 2012 onwards, the brand was losing ground to the category leader, Peperami, which had a higher media spend.

Mattessons faced the further disadvantage that snacking on meat was a less-established habit than eating crisps or other choices, so it was important that meat snacking became a distinctive and active preference.

Rather than compete with Peperami for established category users, Mattessons decided to focus on teen gamers, because 49 per cent of snack purchases were a response to pester power and 61 per cent of teens were gaming after school, often with snacks.

The challenge for Mattessons was to understand how to earn the right to access and make a dent in teen culture.

Using the 'hunger filler' positioning, Mattessons' first step was to change its usual approach to media channels by partnering with a famous gaming vlogger to build an authentic connection with gamers.

More importantly, the brand avoided buying its way into gamer culture via 'me too' sponsorship or giveaways. Instead, it made a genuine contribution by leveraging audience passions around gaming and technology.

Mattessons embraced the audience in a co-design competition, using the vlogger to publicise and endorse the activity, resulting in the MMM3000, a hands-free meat snacking helmet.

The second activity used F.R.H.A.N.K, an AI snacking and gaming robot, launched via the mouthpiece of Ali-A, a leading UK gaming vlogger. Unlike the first wave of Mattessons activity where the acceptance of the audience was generated by collaboration, the robot was wrapped in a longer narrative using the ET story of discovery and friendship to build wider awareness and engagement.

For both launches, by changing the brand's approach from pure communications and product messaging to understanding how it could authentically become a part of teen gaming culture, Mattessons created value through useful and fun 'products' which proved hugely successful and repeatable.

Breathing new life into a category generic: Volvo LifePaint

Volvo is the definitive car brand for safety. But over the years, other, more exciting brands have achieved equally high ratings on NCAP (the European New Car Assessment Programme on car safety). Consequently, interest in safety has gradually declined, leaving Volvo's brand as a hygiene factor, which was considered a necessary minimum rather than a significant driver of preference.

It would have been extremely difficult for Volvo to move away from safety or find a more exciting perception especially on the brand's modest budget (typically 10% of its competitors). Therefore, Volvo set itself the challenge to try and make its core attribute of safety feel relevant, aspirational, and talked about again.

Volvo took the brave decision to reverse the convention of protecting drivers within the car to protecting people outside the car, by focusing its activity on cyclists.

Car drivers and cyclists typically argue 'like cat and dog' and are a source of endless mutual frustration, so a car brand actively extending the olive branch to cyclists would generate news.

Volvo avoided approaches such as producing safety messages or car safety features which could have been interpreted as conventional advertising to help drivers avoid a nuisance on the road.

Rather, Volvo generated real interest not by talking to or about cyclists, but by providing cyclists with LifePaint, a glow-in-the-dark paint (previously applied to make reindeer more visible to drivers in Finland) that gave cyclists control.

Whilst Mattessons picked a new target audience to drive penetration, Volvo focused on the emotive subject of the tension between drivers and cyclists, giving the brand's activity immediate cultural momentum. More than that, by re-appropriating a protection product, Volvo demonstrated commitment to its safety positioning in a way communications wouldn't have been able to.

Turning the product into a service: Volkswagen Commercial Vehicles

Volkswagen Commercial Vehicles was pushing for aggressive growth at a time when its competitors were undergoing major product refreshes, cheaper brands were growing in the market, and the Volkswagen brand advertising budget was cut by 51%.

To meet this challenge, Volkswagen underwent a review of its entire marketing strategy.

Audience analysis revealed an opportunity amongst the business managers of SMEs who were having to make decisions about vehicle fleets without having the systems and support that larger firms enjoyed.

Whilst the competition focused on the different functions of vans for drivers, business managers also cared about logistics, and the wider issues of running vans.

In response, Volkswagen redefined its role from van manufacturer to business partner, shifting the focus from vans to Volkswagen services. To fulfil the brand's new 'working with you' platform, Volkswagen needed to evolve all aspects of the actual experience, to behave as a business service partner would, offering genuine understanding, advice and support, alongside new communications.

The 'working with you' platform redirected content production in a number of related directions. These included providing information on the whole life costs of vans, creating online comparison services, re-engineering the brand's website to take greater account of users' needs, developing staff initiatives in 'every moment matters' service ideas, and creating a backdrop of awareness via efficient channels and TV support.

In going beyond communications to behave as an authentic business partner to its customers, Volkswagen escaped direct competition by changing the category it worked in – from manufacturer to service partner – in order to answer the needs of the target consumer more accurately.

Brand extension by changing the category not the brand: John Lewis

John Lewis is a high street staple, famous for its iconic Christmas advertising, partner structure, service and reputation for trust.

John Lewis had strong credentials in homewares and furniture, so in a bid to transfer some of its equity of trust into new product and service categories, John Lewis rebranded its Greenbee insurance to John Lewis Insurance in 2011. The name alone automatically brought strong performance.

However, analysis showed that aggregator websites had commoditised the category and retrained the consumer to consider price as the key variable, forcing brands to cut back on the quality and service side of their offers. Consequently, in communications, brands leveraged salience markers or catastrophe threats in a bid to attract customers.

For John Lewis, obeying the category conventions would have meant abandoning the trust and service levels customers had grown used to, ostracising insurance from delivering any wider halo effect on the business and, at worst, risked damaging the brand. Rather than follow the category conventions, John Lewis remained true to its brand strengths and how it defined products and services to be worthy of bearing the John Lewis brand.

By launching to loyalists who currently felt unable to trust the quality and service of insurance brands, John Lewis realised that in order to exploit its trust positioning it needed to redesign its products with outstanding service, new tiered models of pricing and uncommonly good cover levels.

In bringing its insurance products and service up to the standard the brand's consumers expected, John Lewis was able to amplify its brand's difference in communications under the thought 'if it matters to you, it matters to us'.

Looking ahead

Each of the above cases demonstrates how a focus on behaviour and actions rather than automatically resorting to communications can help a brand meet a business challenge.

They have shown innovative thinking being applied in varied ways, from re-engineering a brand's relationship to its users, to showing commitment to an audience culture, to maintaining the integrity of a brand.

It is worth noting that these cases did not show brands spurning traditional communications activity altogether, but using it within the marketing mix and not as the first and only way of approaching a problem.

For all the seeming ease with which the brands met with success, we should not underestimate the difficulties involved. Building new products, recycling existing ones, and redesigning the services a brand offers are not quick or risk-free activities.

For clients, these kinds of product and service solutions can be harder to buy than conventional campaigns. This is because they can draw on fewer precedents within the organisation, require more people and inter-departmental co-operation, need more 'non-working' spend or resource borrowed from existing budgets, and may require organisational change, not to mention considerable staying power to see a project through.

Agencies will need their people to catch briefs earlier in the briefing process and apply their creativity and innovation in more fluid ways, to develop new partners, relationships, and ways of monetising, and redefine the notions of communications craft and what an idea is.

For all the challenges it generates, this development should be embraced with optimism, as a much-needed shift in the potential role of agencies, and the scope for their problem-solving capabilities.

In conventional thinking, wanting to change a product or service might have been seen as a bad thing, an admission of defeat that a bold repositioning or reframing couldn't be mustered to reinvigorate the fortunes of a brand.

The 2016 Effectiveness Awards examples suggest that agencies are moving back to embrace a more fluid, innovative way of thinking. Within J. Walter Thompson, the story is often told of how Mr Kipling was created by the agency as the answer to a client brief of what to do with a surplus of flour. That would feel a thoroughly modern case now.

SECTION 2

Gold winners

John Lewis

The gift that keeps on giving: John Lewis Christmas advertising, 2012–2015

By Les Binet, adam&eveDDB

Contributing authors: Kate Fanning, John Lewis; David Golding, adam&eveDDB; Ric Roberts, Manning Gottlieb OMD
Credited companies: adam&eveDDB; Manning Gottlieb OMD

Summary

This is the story of Britain's best-loved Christmas advertising. Since 2012, John Lewis has created some of the most famous and creatively awarded ads in the world. By immersing the British public in them, on TV, online and in-store, John Lewis has become Britain's most talked about retailer, and British mums' favourite brand. The ads have been watched nearly 2.5 billion times, with a further 0.5 billion exposures from PR. They have inspired mutually beneficial partnerships with suppliers, tech firms, media owners and charities – not to mention over 81,000 parodies. Sales have increased 37%, generating a profit ROMI of more than £8 for every £1 invested in the advertising.

Editor's Comment

The judges thought this was a masterclass in how to write a clear, compelling IPA case. A well-told story of how brand fame drove outstanding business results. It was a lesson for all of us on how to write a paper with a consistent, clear insight into the challenges faced over time. The campaign showed an interesting use of channels, unexpected touch-points and fantastic phasing. The judges appreciated the high-risk strategy and continuous learning that went into achieving an unprecedented level of fame.

Client Comment

Rachel Swift, Head of Brand Marketing, John Lewis

From this experience, we have learnt that in an increasingly fragmented media landscape we need to understand what consumers actually want, not what we want to tell them. That means approaching every piece of brand comms as first and foremost pieces of engaging entertainment.

We need to tell great stories, because that's what people actually care about, and immerse our consumers into the worlds we create. That means extending our campaigns beyond traditional channels but critically making sure that when we do so we respect the reasons those consumers are on those channels in the first place.

It means when we go to those places, we behave in a way that is appropriate. We will continue to remind ourselves that creativity is the key to effective advertising and a positive ROI. Our audiences have become increasingly impatient and also vocal. We can't expect them to care about our message if we haven't earned it.

Introduction

Our previous IPA paper[1] told how, from 2009 to 2011, John Lewis transformed its fortunes with a series of emotional advertising campaigns. The pinnacle was 'The long wait' (2011), a tear-jerking story of a little boy who couldn't wait to give his parents their Christmas presents (Figure 1).

Figure 1: 'The long wait', Christmas 2011

Those campaigns were outstanding in every way, delivering a ROMI[2] of 5:1.

This paper tells the story of how, from 2012 to 2015, we created a series of Christmas campaigns that were even more effective, and even more profitable.

But more than that, it's a story about the power of stories. It's a story about the power of fame, and how to harness it. It's a story about the immersive power of modern media.

It's a masterclass in how to build brands in the twenty-first century.

Objectives

Founded in 1864, John Lewis is a UK department store. With 45 shops and a thriving e-commerce business, it is now at the forefront of British retailing.

Unusually, The John Lewis Partnership (which also includes supermarket chain Waitrose) is mutually owned, making it the UK's largest employee co-operative. The stated objective of the partnership is 'the happiness of all its members, through their worthwhile and satisfying employment in a successful business'.

Every year, the board awards a bonus to all permanent employees ('partners'), depending on profits. Christmas is vital for generating those bonuses. It accounts for around 20% of annual sales and 40% of profits, and a successful Christmas sets the trajectory for good trading over the following year.

So Christmas matters a lot to the people at John Lewis. And in recent years, the pressure on the department store has been acute, as sister retailer Waitrose has suffered a profit squeeze (like all supermarkets).

But UK retail is fiercely competitive, and never more so than at Christmas. British retailers spend around £180m a year on Christmas advertising. To make things more difficult, 2014 saw the arrival of 'Black Friday' in the UK, when retailers offer deep discounts to kick-start the Christmas season. This, together with the continued rise of online shopping, has made Christmas ever more challenging for up-market stores like John Lewis.

Against this background, John Lewis set the commercial objectives shown in Figure 2.

Figure 2: Commercial objectives

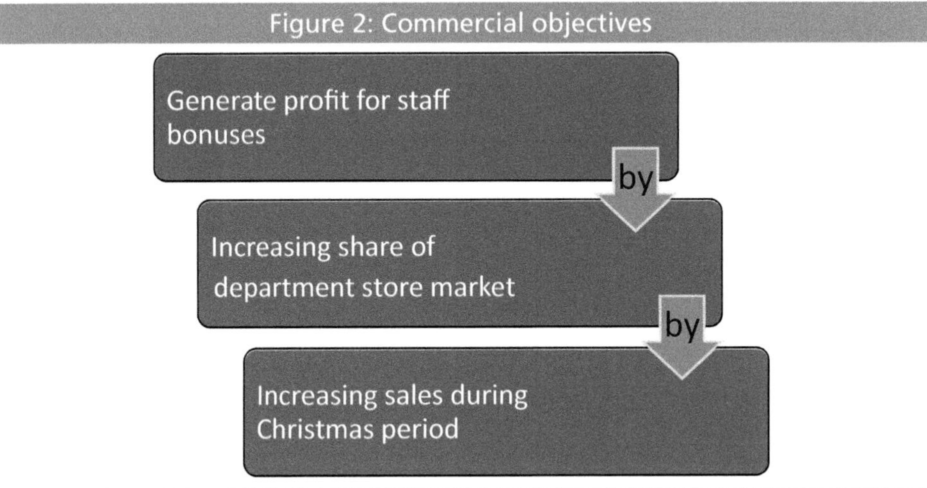

The key to high sales at Christmas is store traffic, mainly driven by gift shopping. So the marketing objectives were as shown in Figure 3.

Figure 3: Marketing objectives

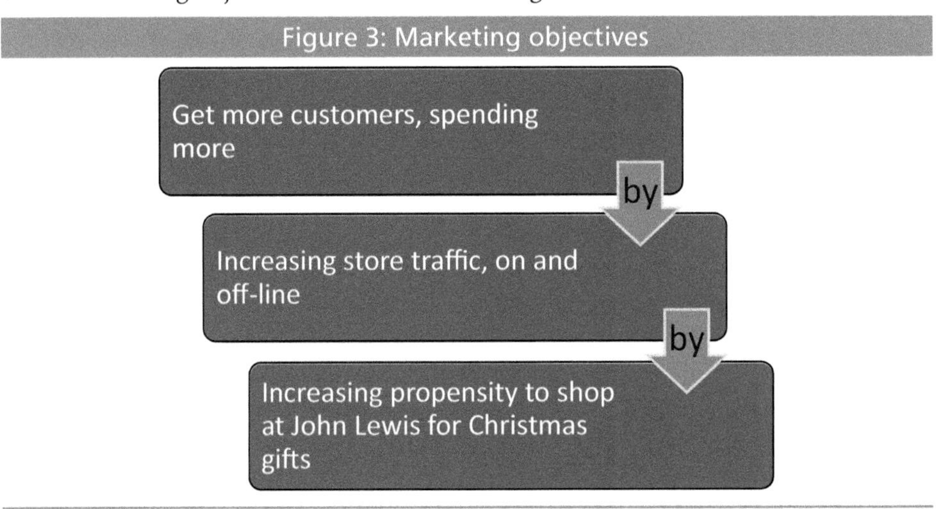

The likelihood of visiting John Lewis is in turn partly a matter of salience – in the Christmas rush, it's important that John Lewis springs to mind as first port of call. It's also a matter of emotional connection – John Lewis needs to feel 'special', a 'destination' shop.

But the impact of the John Lewis Christmas campaign goes far beyond short-term sales. This is Christmas. And this is the John Lewis Christmas campaign. This is the most high-profile marketing campaign in the UK, at the most commercially important time of the year. Each new John Lewis Christmas campaign is anticipated, analysed, debated, critiqued, rated and talked about by pretty much everyone. Failing to engage the nation would have a significant commercial, social and cultural impact on the John Lewis brand. We needed to raise the bar every year, and make each John Lewis campaign more famous than the last. With that in mind, we set the following communications objectives shown in Figure 4.

Figure 4: Communications objectives

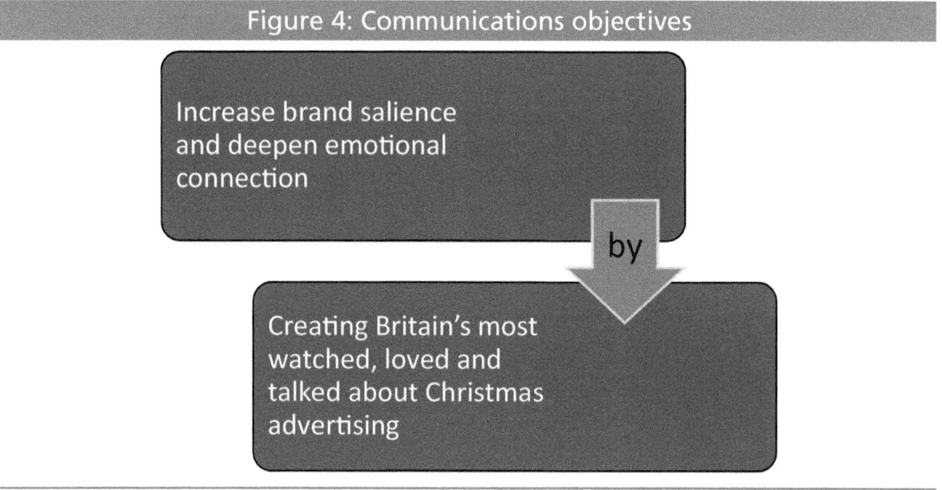

The 'thoughtful gifting' strategy

Creative strategy

John Lewis's Christmas strategy is based on three core insights:[3]

1. *Business insight:* John Lewis has more products than any other high-street retailer. So no matter who you are buying for, you will find the perfect gift there.
2. *Brand insight:* John Lewis is a calm, understated brand in all that it does. The shopping experience is quiet and unruffled. At a time of glitz, celebrities and cliché, John Lewis prefers to be considered and thoughtful.
3. *Customer insight:* John Lewis appeals to an affluent and educated customer base (typically ABC1 aged 25–55), who like to buy well, and be seen to do so. When it comes to buying presents, they like to think more carefully and

choose more thoughtfully. They want to buy the most interesting, relevant and distinctive gifts; gifts that say how important the people they love are to them.

Based on these insights, John Lewis's strategy is to be the home of 'thoughtful gifting', a place where shoppers can find gifts that demonstrate 'a little more thought' than they could elsewhere. Each year, John Lewis bring that strategy to life in a humble, charming way by telling highly emotive tales of thoughtful gifting.

Media strategy

The central role for media is to make those stories famous. To do so, we need to build anticipation; maximise awareness at launch, and embrace media and technology solutions to enhance our storytelling both online and in-store. Our media agency, Manning Gottlieb OMD aims to make the most integrated, immersive and successful retail advertising ever.

The Christmas films

The core of the campaign each year is a film designed to run on TV and online. Like 'The long wait', each is a simple, but highly emotive story of thoughtful gifting, set to music. In 2012, we told the story of a snowman's epic journey to find the perfect Christmas gifts for his snowwoman (Figure 5).

Figure 5: 'The journey', Christmas 2012

In 2013, our story was about a hare who thoughtfully gave his friend, a hibernating bear, an alarm clock, so that he wouldn't miss the Christmas fun (Figure 6).

Figure 6: 'The bear and the hare', Christmas 2013

In 2014, our tale involved a boy and his toy penguin, Monty. Seen through the eyes of the child, Monty comes to life. But Monty wants someone to love, so the boy gives him a companion called Mabel for Christmas (Figure 7).

Figure 7: 'Monty the penguin', Christmas 2014

And in 2015, we told a story of loneliness. A little girl looking through her telescope spies an old man, living on his own on the moon. Her thoughtful Christmas gift is a telescope, sent by balloon, so that he can see he's not really alone (Figure 8).

Figure 8: 'Man on the moon', Christmas 2015

Immersive story-telling

We took customers into the heart of our stories

The films were just the start. Each year, we immersed the public in the story through a myriad of touch-points. We created in-store experiences, like 'The bear cave' and 'Monty's den', using partnerships with Google and Microsoft to bring our stories to life in new ways (Figures 9 to 12).

Figure 9: 'The bear cave'

Figure 10: 'Monty's magical toy machine' allowed children to bring their toys to life[4]

Figure 11: 'Monty's winter garden' on the roof at John Lewis Oxford Street

Figure 12: In-store activity for 'Man on the moon'

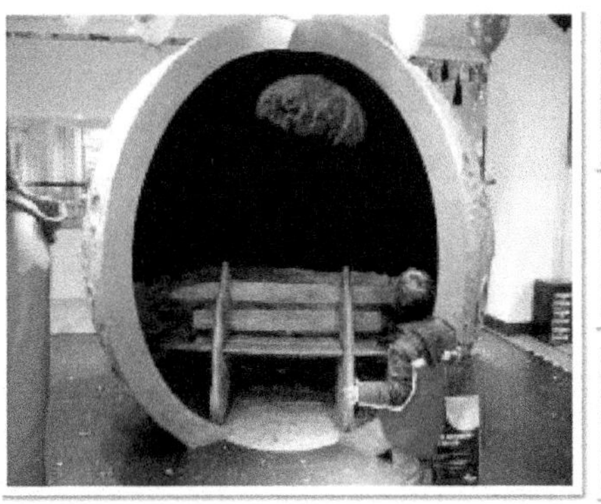

Store windows were themed around the ads, to draw people in (Figures 13 and 14).

Figure 13: 'Monty' themed window displays

Figure 14: 'Man on the moon' themed window displays

The stories continued online

We created micro-sites, where fans could explore the worlds we created, and download the songs (Figure 15).

Figure 15: Online micro-site

We created story-books for children to read, available online and in-store (Figures 16 and 17).

Figure 16: *The Bear who had never seen Christmas*

Figure 17: *Monty's Christmas*

We designed apps which told the stories interactively, and allowed users to play games and make Christmas cards (Figures 18 to 20).

Figure 18: 'The bear and the hare' Christmas card maker

Figure 19: Monty app

Figure 20: 'Man on the moon' app

These online experiences were promoted with advertising (Figures 21 and 22).

Figure 21: Online ad for 'Monty's den' in each branch, featuring 'Monty's goggles' virtual reality experience[5]

Figure 22: Press ads for the 'Man on the moon' app

Our stories came to life in social media

We encouraged the public to create their own art and music (Figures 23 and 24).

Figure 23: Examples of ad-related content uploaded to social media

Source: John Lewis social media analysis, Christmas 2012.

Figure 24: Song competition for 'The bear and the hare'

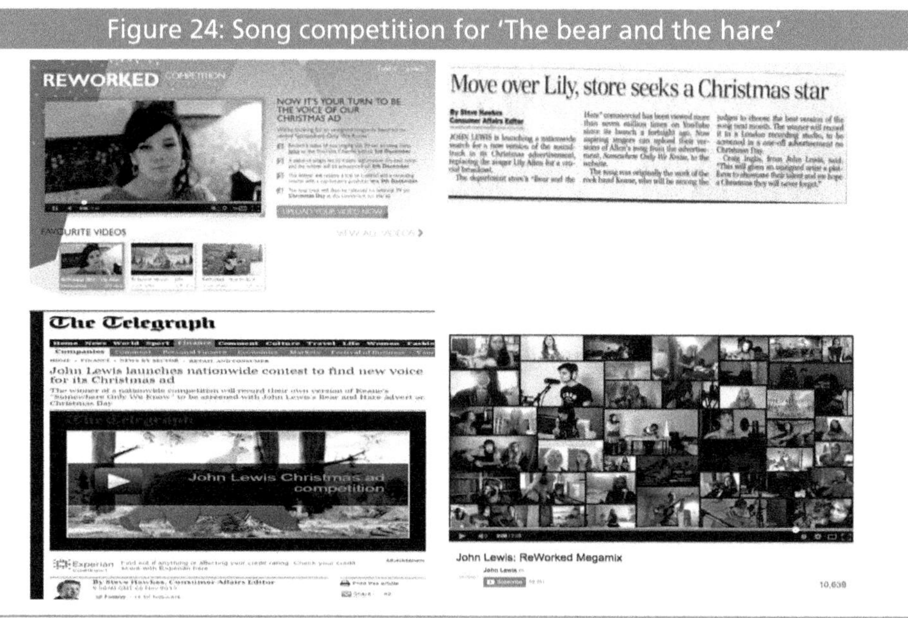

And in 2014, our two love-birds, Monty and Mabel, conducted a very public romance on Twitter, and via dating apps (Figure 25).

Figure 25: Monty and Mabel on Twitter

Customers could enjoy the story at home

In 2013, we created a range of 'The bear and the hare' themed merchandise (Figure 26).

Figure 26: 'The bear and the hare' merchandise

This proved so successful that we produced an even bigger range the following year (Figure 27).

Figure 27: 'Monty' merchandise

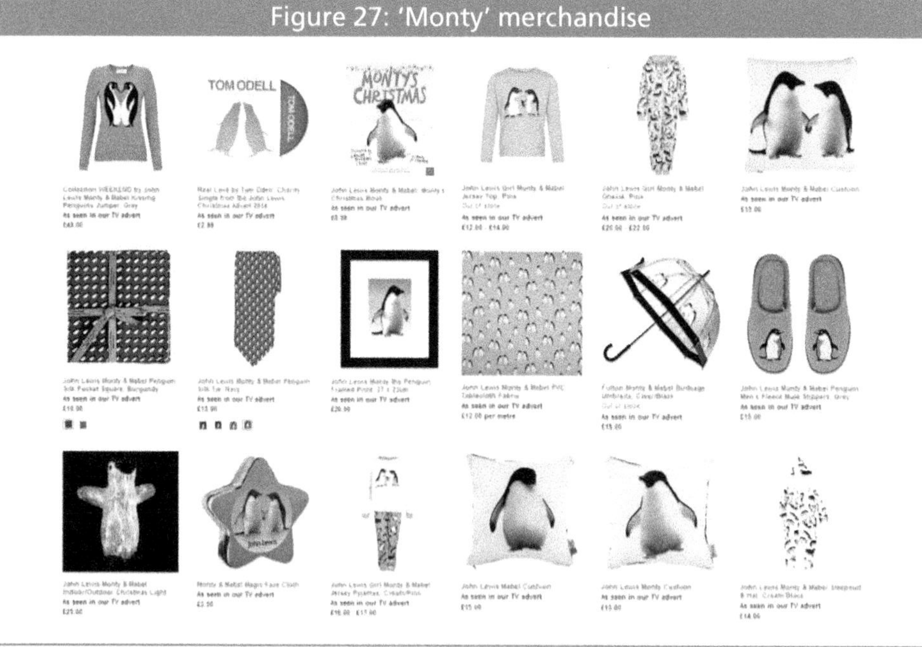

Above all there were soft toys (Figure 28).

Figure 28: 'Monty' soft toys

In 2015, we created a dedicated 'Moon Gear' shop (Figure 29).

Figure 29: 'Moon gear' shop

We rewarded special customers

Members of the John Lewis loyalty programme, My John Lewis, were given sneak peeks of the ads before everyone else, and invited to exclusive shopping evenings, competitions, and more. (Figure 30).

Figure 30: Examples of offers and other communications with My John Lewis account holders

Using the power of stories for social good

As a highly ethical business, John Lewis has always been keen to support good causes. For instance, the firm runs a free online education programme for primary schools called 'Bringing skills to life'. In 2013, we created a 'Bear and hare' section of the website, with a range of activities for teachers and children to use.

In 2014, the firm partnered with the World Wildlife Fund to encourage people to sponsor a penguin (Figure 31).

Figure 31: World Wildlife Fund partnership

But in 2015, we took things to another level. The ad featured an old man, all on his own at Christmas, and ended with the line 'Show someone they're loved this Christmas'. That suggested a natural charitable partner: Age UK.[6] For Age UK, we made a second TV ad, showing the old man on the 'Man on the moon' film set. As filming wraps up, he is left alone and forgotten, while a voice-over reminds us of the problem of loneliness amongst the aged (Figure 32).

Figure 32: The Age UK TV ad

Media and budgets

Video is the natural medium for emotional story-telling. But having great films was not enough – we needed to ensure that as many people saw them as possible. TV was the core of the media plan, because only TV can deliver audiences on the scale we needed (Figure 33).

Figure 33: UK media consumption in 2015

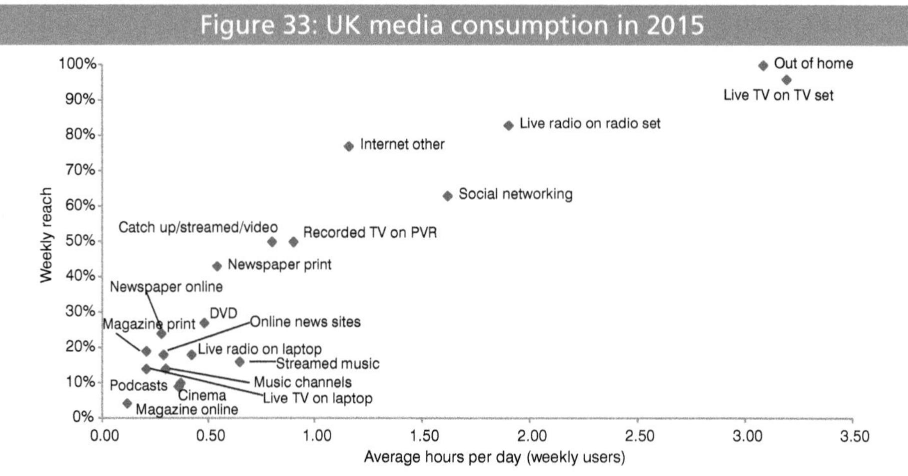

Source: UK Touchpoints 6 (February–June 2015)

But online video makes TV work harder, reaching light viewers and allowing our ads to propagate virally. So almost all of our media budget was devoted to TV and online video in various forms (Table 1).

Table 1: Christmas media expenditure

	2012	2013	2014	2015
TV	£3,722,745	£4,391,301	£4,080,862	£3,711,987
VOD	£171,994	£205,976	£141,354	£129,476
Cinema		£261,845		
Press				£159,292
Social		£48,036	£131,725	£192,107
YouTube			£64,768	£107,092
Mobile		£56,265	£30,627	£42,983
Online display			£66,000	
OOH		£96,800	£205,000	
Total	£3,894,740	£5,060,224	£4,384,337	£4,279,937

Spend by John Lewis on Christmas brand campaign. Source: Manning Gottlieb OMD

Our budgets were decent,[7] but have fallen recently, so we had to work them hard. As the campaigns evolved, we devised a three-phase approach: create anticipation, launch in spectacular fashion, then immerse the public in our story (Figure 34).

Figure 34: How the media plans evolved

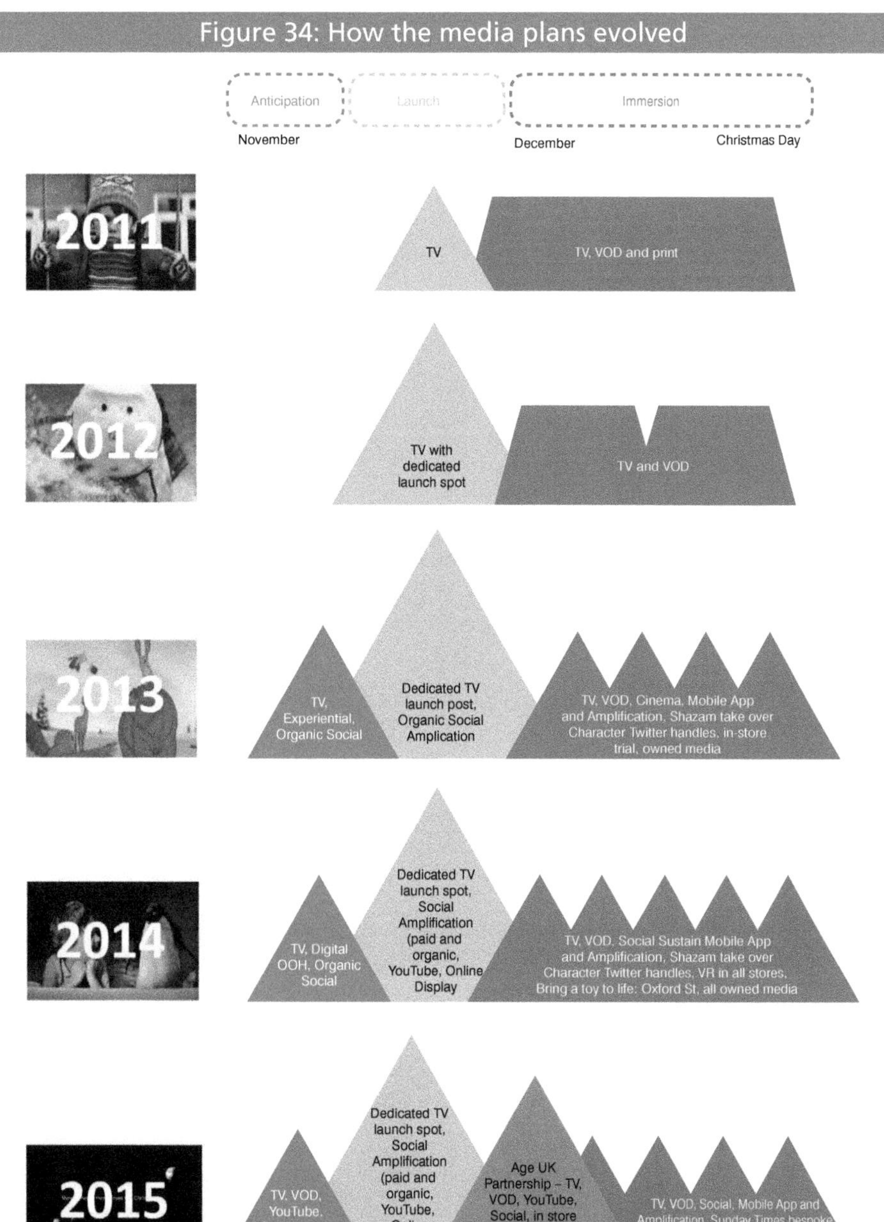

Results part one: Britain's most famous advertising

Our aim was to create the most famous advertising in Britain, on a relatively modest budget. Much has been written about the power of fame to transform brands; we're going to show you how it works (Figure 35).

Figure 35: Fame: the gift that keeps on giving

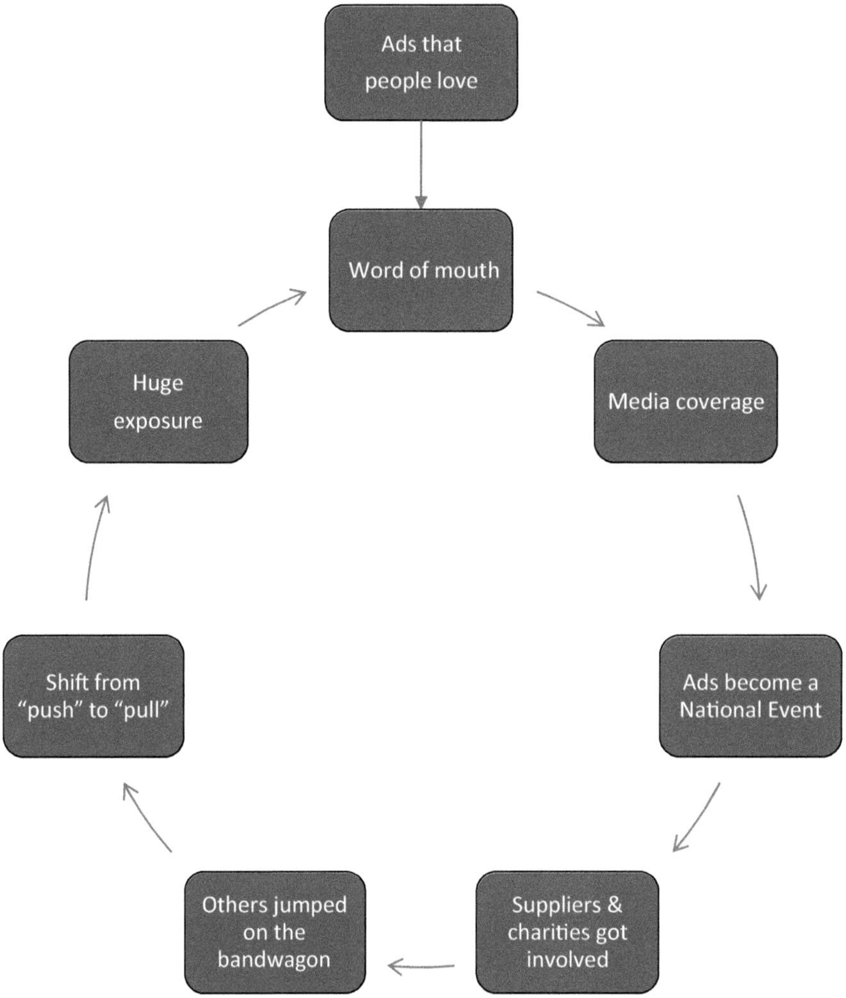

Ads that people love

Word of mouth

Media coverage

Ads become a National Event

Suppliers & charities got involved

Others jumped on the bandwagon

Shift from "push" to "pull"

Huge exposure

People loved the ads

Five years on, it is easy to forget how ground-breaking these ads were. Back then, most clients regarded advertising as a way of showcasing products and giving people reasons to buy. Persuasion was the name of the game.

We took a different approach: no overt selling messages, and few references to the store or its products. Instead, we gave the public a Christmas present each year: a lovely story about thoughtful giving.

People noticed. They rated our ads as different, impactful and memorable (Figure 36).

Figure 36: The ads were highly memorable, disctinctive and impactful

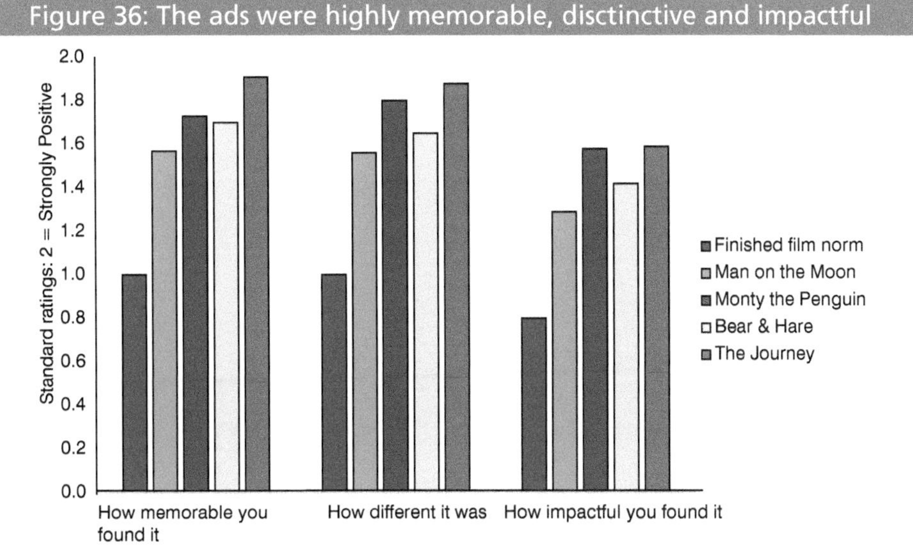

Source: Brainjuicer testing of 90″ finished ads

Emotion lay at the heart of this. We literally reduced people to tears (Figure 37).

Figure 37: Reactions to the ads

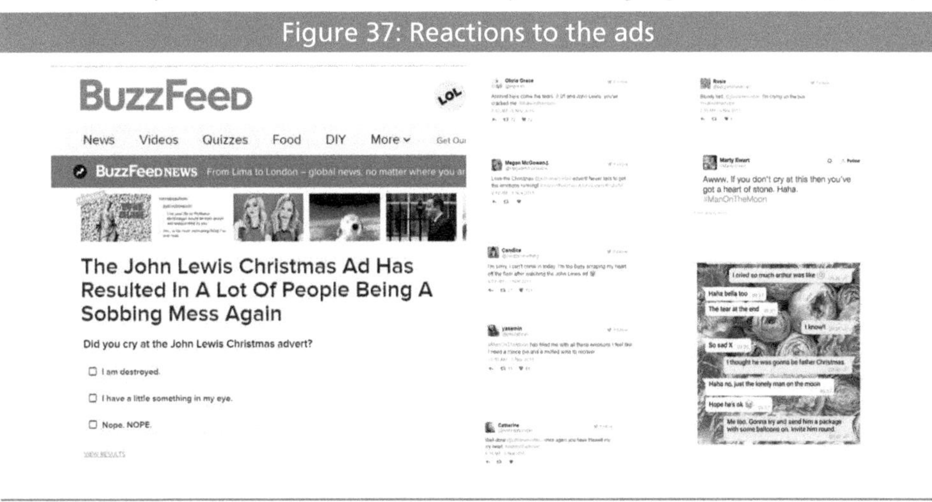

This is not how British shopkeepers usually sell stuff. Our ads were more emotional than other retail advertising (Table 2).

Table 2: Most emotive Christmas ads: UK retailers, 2013–2015

Rank	Brand	Ad	Year	Emotion into action score	Star rating
1	John Lewis	Monty the penguin	2014	83	5
2	John Lewis	Bear and hare	2013	79	4
3	M&S	Adventures in surprises	2015	78	4
4	Sainsbury's	Mog the cat	2015	77	3
5	Boots	Special because	2014	77	3
Category median	–	–	2013–2015	73	3

Source: Brainjuicer 'Feelmore 50'. Database of 402 ads tested 2013–2015

But the public loved it. They voted ours the best Christmas advertising every year (Table 3).

Table 3: Britain's favourite Christmas ads

	Christmas 2011	Christmas 2012	Christmas 2013	Christmas 2014	Christmas 2015
Netmums	John Lewis 1st	John Lewis 1st	John Lewis 1st	John Lewis 1st	John Lewis 1st
Marketing Magazine	N/A	N/A	John Lewis 1st	John Lewis 1st	John Lewis 2nd

Source: Netmums, Annual Christmas Advertising Report. sample: 2,000 mothers; *Marketing Magazine*, Adwatch Poll of Favourite Christmas ads, sample: 1,000 adults, first published 2013

People loved the music

Music played an important role. Music can evoke and intensify emotion, and so take storytelling to another level.[8] The style of music we used – acoustic cover versions, slowed down and tinged with a hint of sadness – also served as branding device, a kind of 'musical handwriting'.

The songs were incredibly popular. As soon as 'The journey' went on air, people rushed to Google to find out what the song was. And the same level of interest has been shown each year since (Figure 38).

Another popular way to find our tracks is Shazam, which identifies songs automatically. Since it was launched in 2013, we have regularly topped the 'Most Shazamed ads' chart (Table 4).

The songs have all gone on to become chart successes, including two Christmas number ones. With the songs regularly playing on the radio, in shops and at home, the public were gently reminded of our ads throughout Christmas, even when they weren't watching TV (Table 5).

Figure 38: Google searches for 'John Lewis Song'

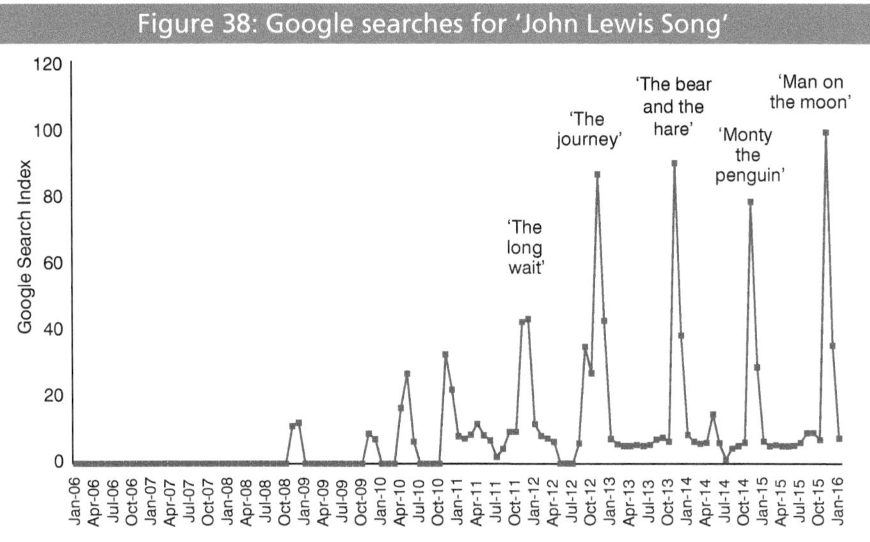

Source: Google Trends

Table 4: Most Shazamed UK ads

John Lewis advert	First aired	Featured song	Artist	Weeks in UK chart	Peak position
The bear and the hare	Christmas 2013	Somewhere only we know	Lily Allen	N/A	1
Monty the penguin	Christmas 2014	Real love	Tom Odell	7	1
Man on the moon	Christmas 2015	Half the world away	Aurora	7	1

Source: The Drum/Shazam 2013 data shows most Shazamed ads of the year. Weekly charts only available from 2014

Table 5: Each song was a chart success

John Lewis advert	First aired	Featured song	Artist	Weeks in UK chart	Peak position
The journey	Christmas 2012	The power of love	Gabrielle Aplin	14	1
The bear and the hare	Christmas 2013	Somewhere only we know	Lily Allen	15	1
Monty the penguin	Christmas 2014	Real love	Tom Odell	14	7
Man on the moon	Christmas 2015	Half the world away	Aurora	8	11

Source: Official Charts Company

The ads got everybody talking

Our emotional, story-based approach stood out and made our ads memorable. But it had another benefit: it got people talking. People love stories, and we gave them stories they could pass on. Our advertising had always generated a lot of buzz, but the new, story-based approach took things to another level (Figure 39).[9]

Figure 39: People talked about the ads with friends

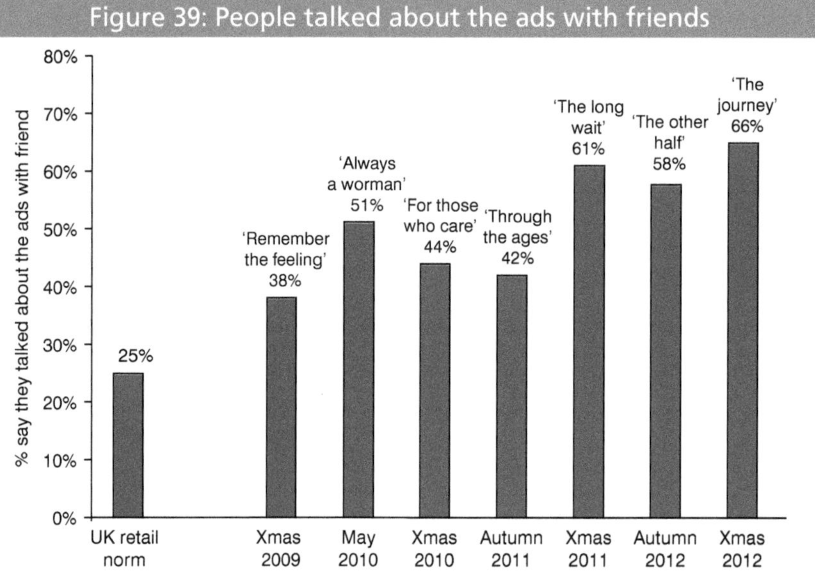

Source: Millward Brown. No data available post 2012

Social media allows us to over-hear some of that talk. Mentions of John Lewis have increased relentlessly every year, with the peak always occurring when we launch our Christmas ads (Figure 40).

Figure 40: Mentions of John Lewis in social media

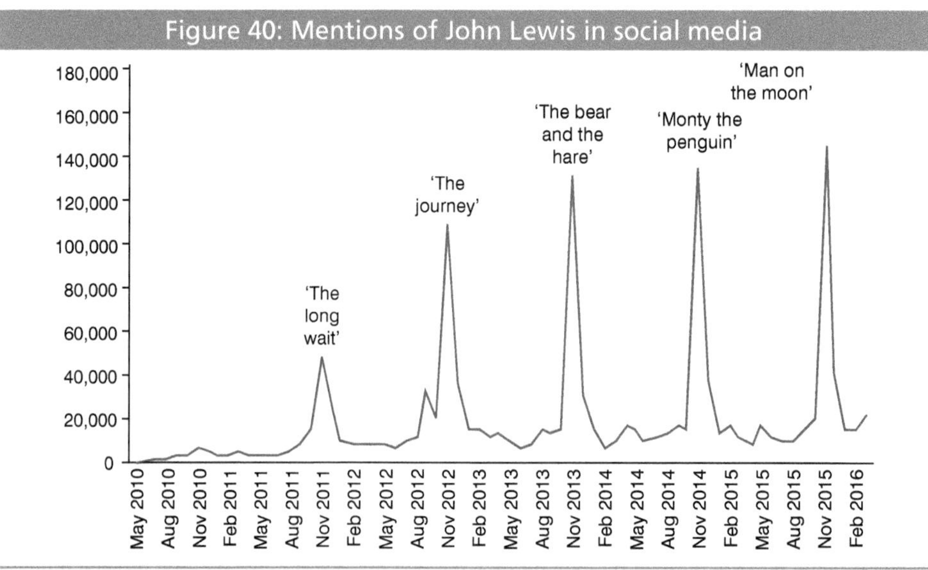

Source: Crimson Hexagon

On social media, people regularly say how much they 'love' the ads, that they are 'the best ever' and that they made them cry (Figures 41 to 44).

Figure 41: Comments about 'The journey' in social media

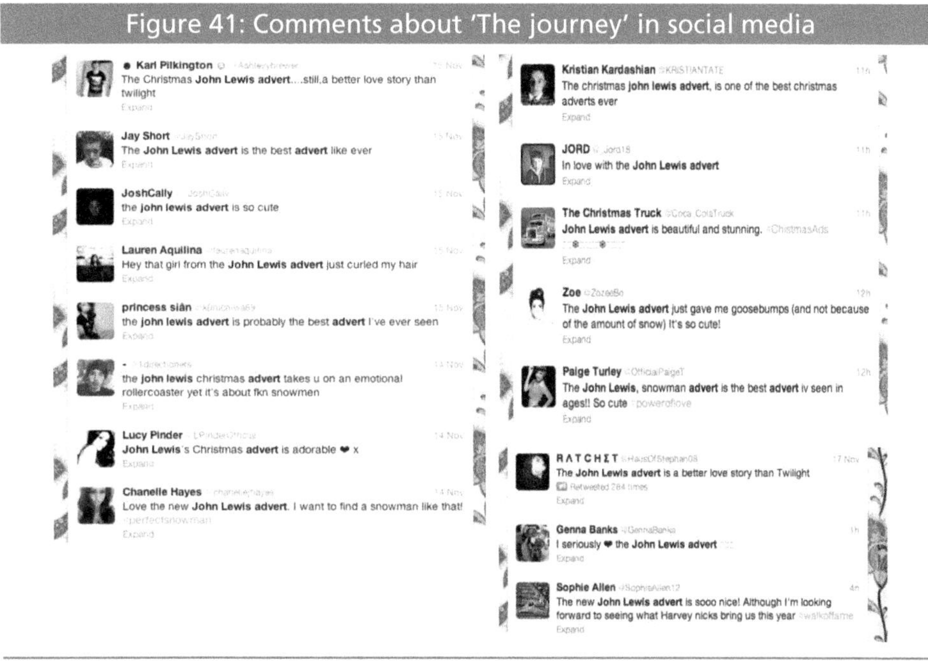

Figure 42: Comments about 'The bear and the hare' in social media

Figure 43: Comments about 'Monty the penguin' in social media

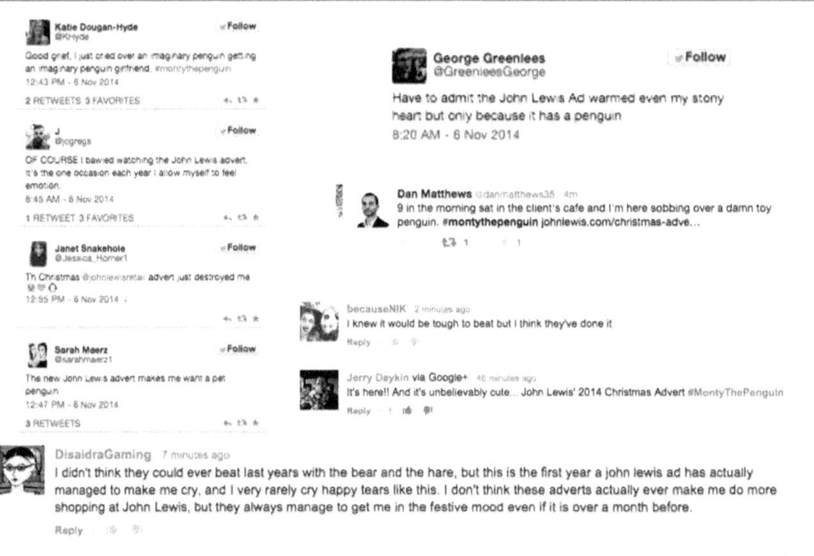

Figure 44: Comments about 'Man on the moon' in social media

As a result, John Lewis has been voted the most talked-about retailer in Britain every year, and one of the most talked-about brands in *any* category (Table 6).

Table 6: YouGov most talked-about high street retailers

Rank	2013	2014	2015
1	John Lewis	John Lewis	John Lewis
2	Marks & Spencer	Marks & Spencer	Marks & Spencer
3	Boots	Boots	B & M Bargains
4	Debenhams	Poundland	Boots
5	Lakeland	Lakeland	Home Bargains

Source: YouGov Brand Index 2013–2015

Media coverage gave us free publicity

The media picked up on this groundswell of interest. With 'The long wait', press coverage almost doubled. And it has continued to increase since. Christmas 2015 saw over 1,400 articles about our ads in the press, plus numerous references on TV and radio. Mentions in the top-selling dailies delivered *458 million impressions* over the last four Christmases (Figure 45).[10]

Figure 45: John Lewis Christmas advertising – UK press coverage

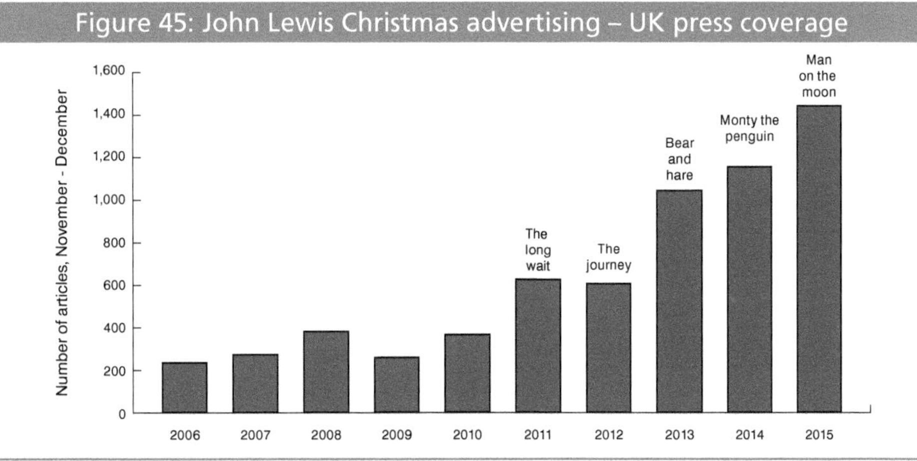

Source: Factiva

In an age of widespread cynicism about advertising, it is noticeable how overwhelmingly positive the coverage has been (Figures 46 to 49).

Figure 46: Press coverage of 'The journey'

THE INDEPENDENT
Mirror
How they made TV's most heart-melting Xmas ad
LEWIS SNOW AD WARMS HEART
hotlist
The John Lewis Xmas advert
Daily Mail
10 HOT STORIES
GRAZIA
OH SNOW! DID SHEAKE YOU TAKE THEM B/K?
SNOWMAN IS 'PHOTO-BOMBED'
I'm walking in the air
The Sun
Daily Mail
John Lewis sales soar 44% - thanks to the Snowman

Figure 47: Press coverage of 'The bear and the hare'

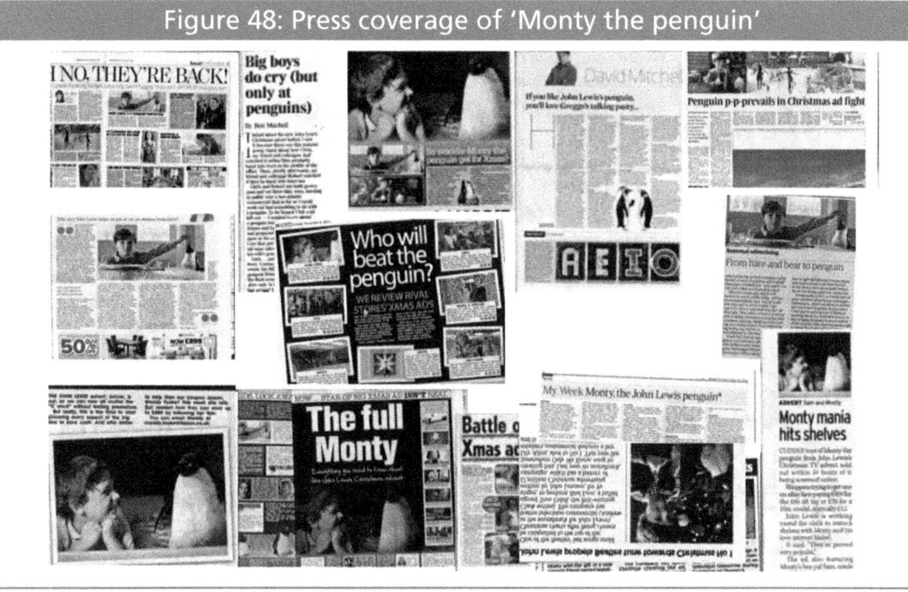
I NO, THEY'RE BACK!

Big boys do cry (but only at penguins)

Who will beat the penguin?

WE REVIEW RIVAL STORES' XMAS ADS

Penguin p-p-prevails in Christmas ad fight

From hare and bear to penguin

My Week Monty, the John Lewis penguin

The full Monty

Battle o

Xmas ad

Monty mania hits shelves

Figure 48: Press coverage of 'Monty the penguin'

Tears of the man on the moon

YULE LOVE THESE TO THE MOON & BACK!

The Christmas advert that is never knowingly undersold hits new heights

6m see John Lewis Xmas ad in one day

Man on moon stars in store's festive tearjerker

Man on Moon is beating 2014 ad

Seven weeks to go and the John Lewis Xmas ad's here already!

Hankies at the ready as stores decide it's Christmas

John Lewis puts a man on the Moon to the sound of Oasis

Figure 49: Press coverage of 'Man on the moon'

Coverage in the trade press has been equally kind (Figure 50).

Figure 50: Trade press coverage

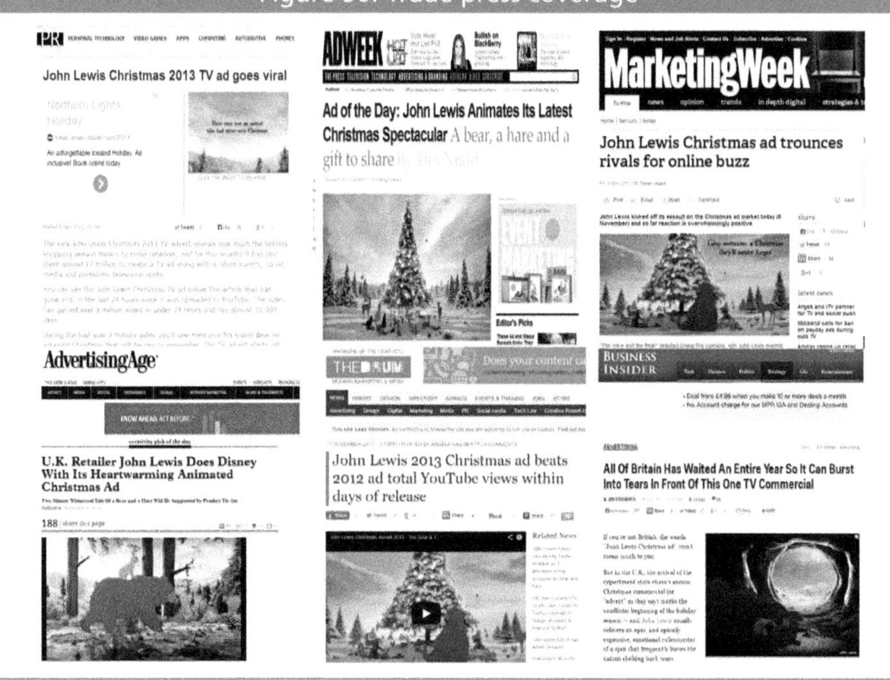

As well as writing nice things about our ads, the industry has given them a lot of awards. Since 2009, John Lewis has won 55 major creative awards.[11]

In 2015, the *Gunn Report* named 'Monty' as the most awarded film in the world (Table 7). And our hopes for 2016 are even higher.

Table 7: Most awarded film commercial in the world, 2015

Rank	Brand	Ad	Agency	Office
1	John Lewis	'Monty's Christmas'	adam&eveDDB	London
2	Leica Gallery São Paolo	'100'	F/Nazca Saatchi & Saatchi	São Paolo
3	Twix Bites	'#TBT bites'	BBDO	New York

Source: *Gunn Report*, 2015

Creating a National Event

By 2013, people were wondering what we would come up with next. So we provoked them with a series of teaser ads on ITV, leading up to a special ad break in 'X-Factor', entirely devoted to 'The bear and the hare' (Figure 51).

This brazen showmanship got us even more publicity and buzz. Within two hours of launch, the ad was trending globally on Twitter (even though this was just a UK campaign). 'The bear and the hare' became the most shared ad in the world, and press coverage leapt 73% year-on-year. C4's 'Gogglebox'[12] even devoted an entire section of the show to people watching our ad.

Figure 51: Teaser ads for 'The bear and the hare'

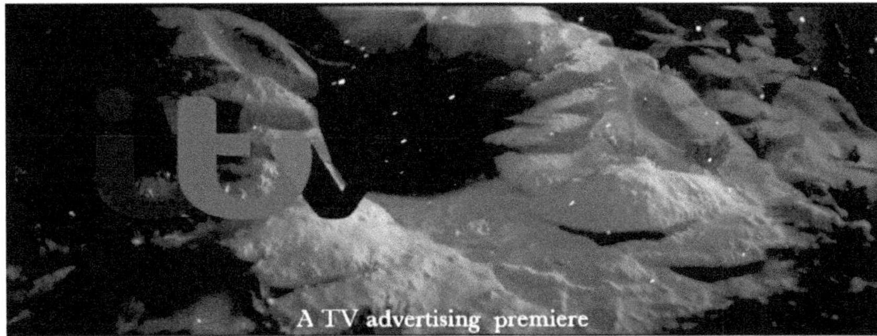

As early as September 2014, people were speculating about the next ad in social media (Figure 52).

Figure 52: Speculation about the 2014 advertising on social media

Once again, we teased them. Monty the penguin first featured unbranded on mini-trailers in C4 'idents'. At the same time he started appearing on digital outdoor sites across key cities (Figure 53).

Figure 53: Monty the penguin teasers

The teaser ads seemed to be everywhere, triggering hundreds of conversations on Twitter, with 1.5 million people overhearing them (Figure 54).

Figure 54: Social media reactions to the teaser campaign

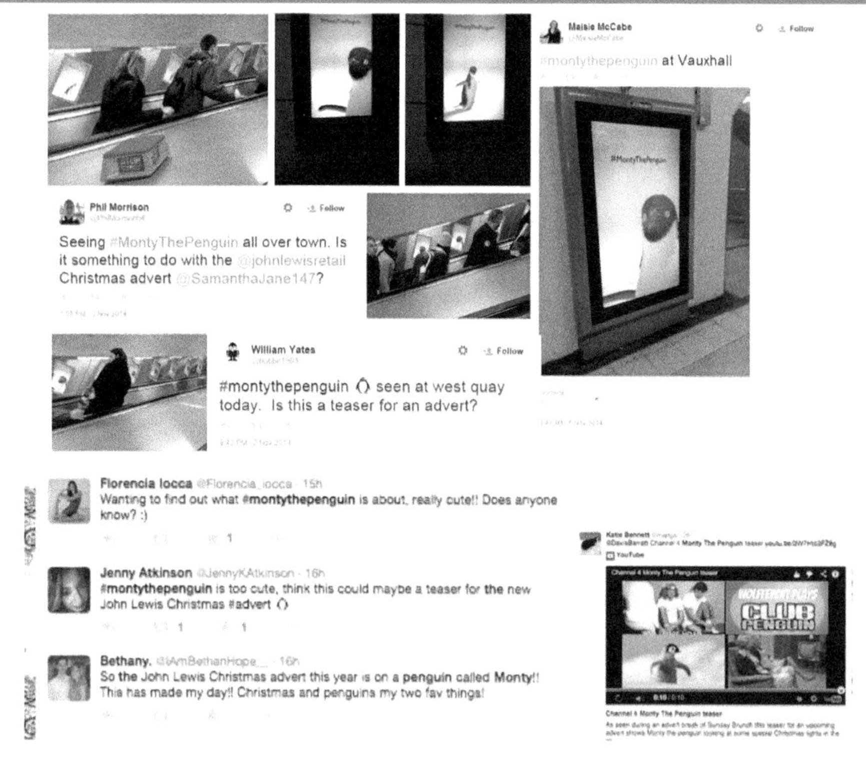

Meanwhile, we sent mysterious boxes containing penguins to journalists, bloggers and other key opinion formers (Figure 55).

Figure 55: Penguin boxes

These 'thoughtful gifts' prompted plenty of speculation on Twitter (Figure 56).

Figure 56: Reactions to the penguin boxes on Twitter

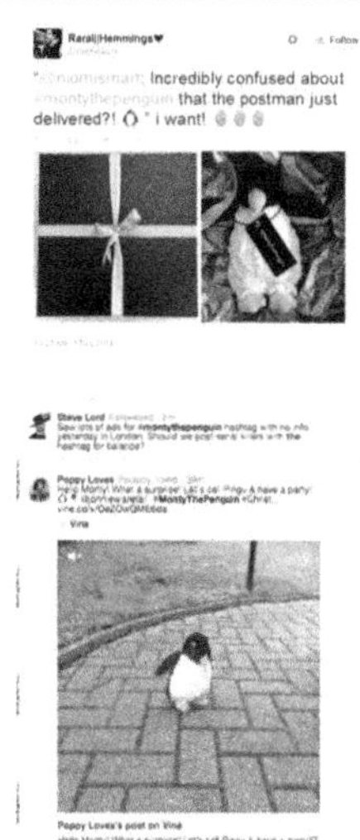

Then we took the internet by storm. The campaign launched in social media 24 hours before it aired on TV, to ensure fans got a sneak preview. We revealed who Monty really was via an online media first – scratch off digital display advertising in partnership with Google (once you scratched off the snow it would play the ad) (Figures 57 and 58).

Figure 57: Scratch-off ad online

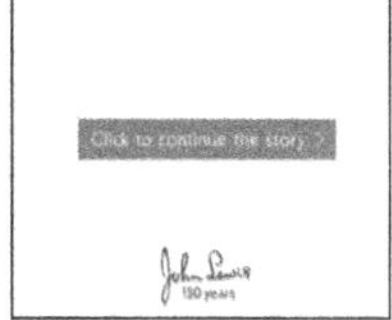

Figure 58: Online launch via social media

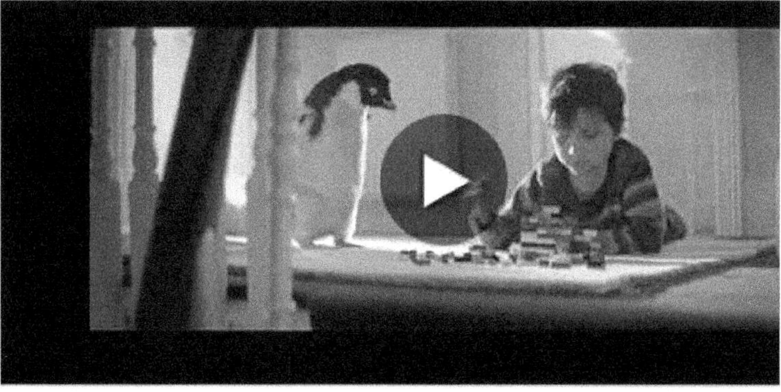

The reaction was astonishing. Within an hour, Monty was trending #1 globally on Twitter. Within 48 hours, Monty generated 124,000 Tweets, five times more than our nearest rival (Figure 59).

Figure 59: Christmas ads 2014 – Twitter mentions in the first 48 hours

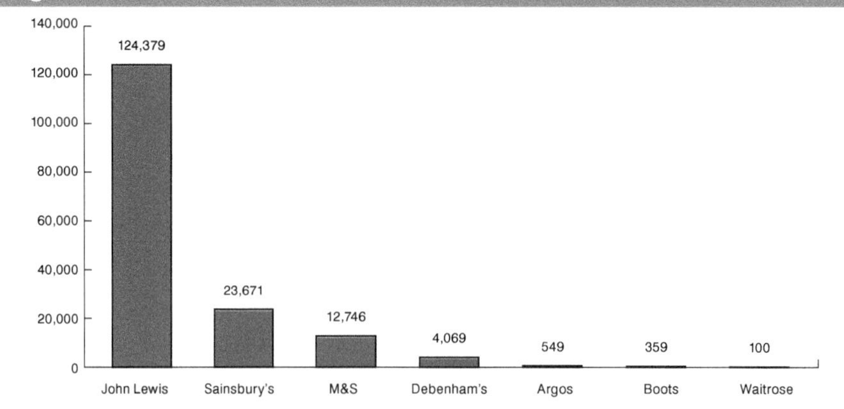

Source: Twitter

In all, there were 212,000 Tweets, plus 165,000 shares on Facebook, delivering *568 million impressions* (Figure 60).

Figure 60: Reactions to the online launch on Twitter

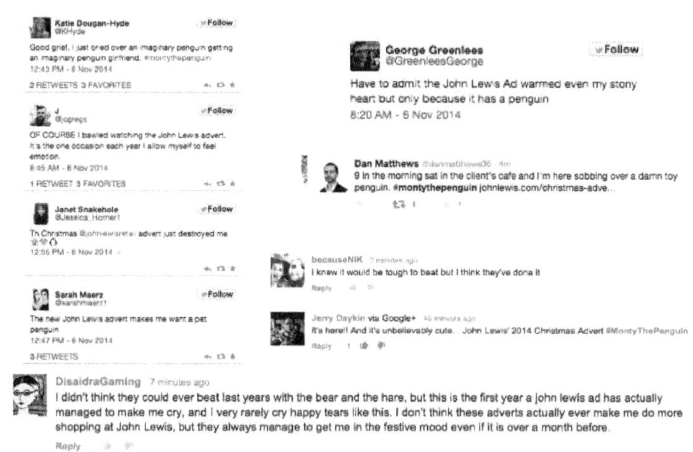

Finally, Monty aired on TV, during C4's 'Gogglebox', followed closely by a second showing in 'X-Factor', giving us huge exposure and talk value.

By 2015, the launch of the John Lewis Christmas ad had become a national event, signalling the start of Christmas for many. Teaser videos in social media, marked #OnTheMoon, were all we needed to set off a frenzy of speculation (Figures 61 and 62).

Figure 61: 'Man on the moon' teaser videos in social media

Figure 62: Press speculation about 'Man on the moon'

By now, the press were practically doing our job for us. *The Daily Telegraph* ran a countdown clock, showing precisely how long readers would have to wait for the new ad (Figure 63).

Figure 63: Countdown clock on Telegraph Online

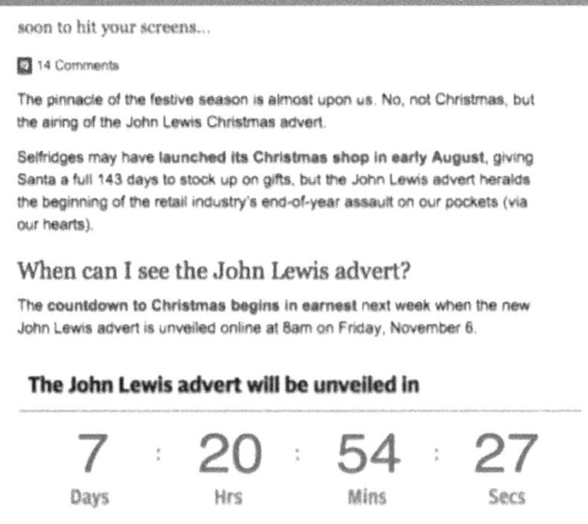
soon to hit your screens...

14 Comments

The pinnacle of the festive season is almost upon us. No, not Christmas, but the airing of the John Lewis Christmas advert.

Selfridges may have launched its Christmas shop in early August, giving Santa a full 143 days to stock up on gifts, but the John Lewis advert heralds the beginning of the retail industry's end-of-year assault on our pockets (via our hearts).

When can I see the John Lewis advert?

The countdown to Christmas begins in earnest next week when the new John Lewis advert is unveiled online at 8am on Friday, November 6.

The John Lewis advert will be unveiled in

7 Days : 20 Hrs : 54 Mins : 27 Secs

So I still have to wait another week?

This time, we trended globally on Twitter *before* the launch, and hit number one within 40 minutes of launch. We got more social mentions, more Google searches, more shares and more PR than ever before. As *FHM* reported, 'the John Lewis Christmas ad launched and the internet basically imploded'.

Suppliers got more involved

Suppliers had been funding some of John Lewis's product advertising for some time, but until 'Snowman' they had not been very involved with the Christmas campaign. Now suppliers became increasingly keen to link advertising for their products to it (Figure 64).

Figure 64: Funding of John Lewis Christmas advertising

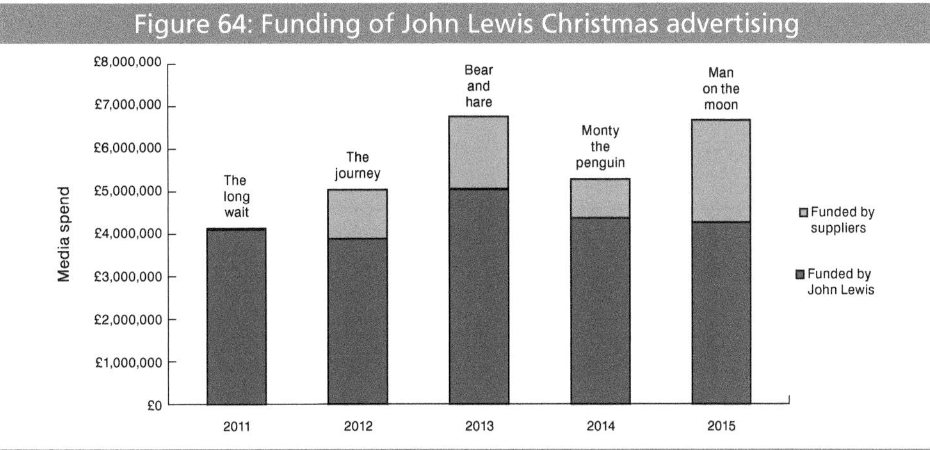

Source: Manning Gottlieb OMD

By 2015, the Christmas budget was split almost exactly 60:40 between John Lewis brand work and supplier-funded activation, in line with best practice.[13] The activation work was firmly linked to the main brand ad, with featured products floating across the lunar landscape on balloons, just like the telescope in 'Man on the moon' (Figure 65).

Charities got more involved too

Our rising fame made charities keen to partner with us too.

When we teamed up with the World Wildlife Fund in 2014, the number of Britons sponsoring penguins increased by *600%*.

But the big breakthrough came in 2015, when we joined forces with Age UK to create a second 'Man on the moon' ad. This was another 'thoughtful gift' – John Lewis were effectively giving Age UK a bit of their brand equity. The benefits to Age UK are outlined in a separate IPA paper,[14] but what about the effect on John Lewis?

In some ways, these were brave ads. It's a sad fact that old men are not as popular and appealing as animals and children.[15] And the emotions stirred were sadder and darker than anything John Lewis had tried before.

This sort of thing is commonplace in charity advertising,[16] but it's not obviously a good way to sell toasters. There was a distinct risk that it might backfire.

Figure 65: Supplier-funded video ads

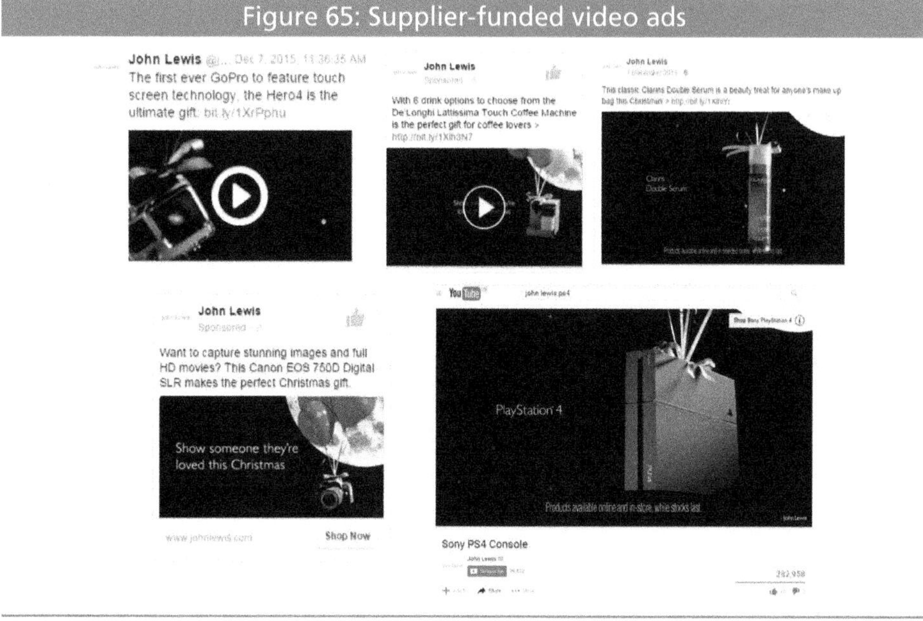

We needn't have worried. Yes, the ads were sadder than before, but all the other performance metrics went through the roof, and British mums still voted us their favourite Christmas campaign. 'Man on the moon' had an even more positive effect on brand perceptions than 'Monty', and the Age UK ad had a remarkably strong halo effect on John Lewis (Figure 66).

Figure 66: The Age UK ad had a halo effect on John Lewis

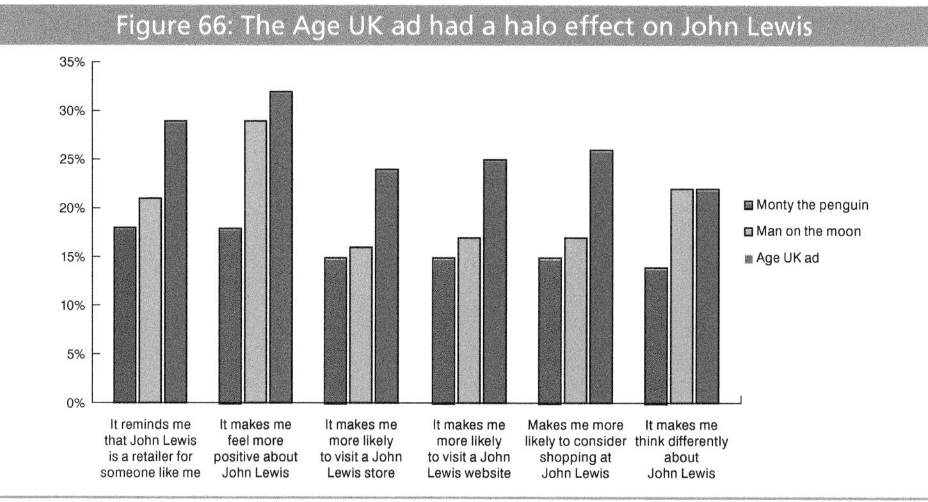

Source: Brainjuicer

Others jumped on the bandwagon

Parody is a sure sign of fame, so when people started lampooning 'The long wait', we knew we were on to a winner.[17] From then on, spoofs just kept on coming.[18] Online parodies became increasingly popular (Figure 67).

Figure 67: Google searches for 'John Lewis parody/spoof'

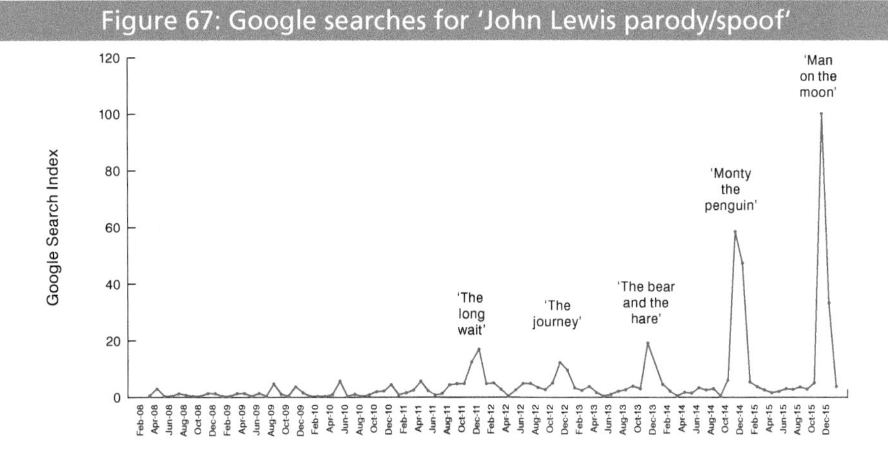

Source: Google Trends

As Figure 73 suggests, the last three campaigns were particularly popular targets (Figures 68 to 70).

Figure 68: 'The bear and the hare' parodies

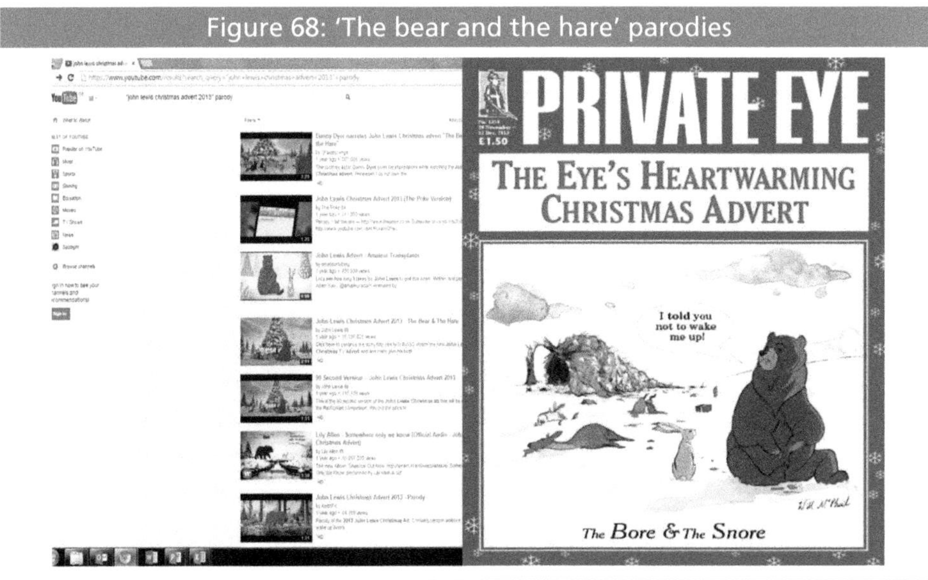

Figure 69: 'Monty the penguin' parodies

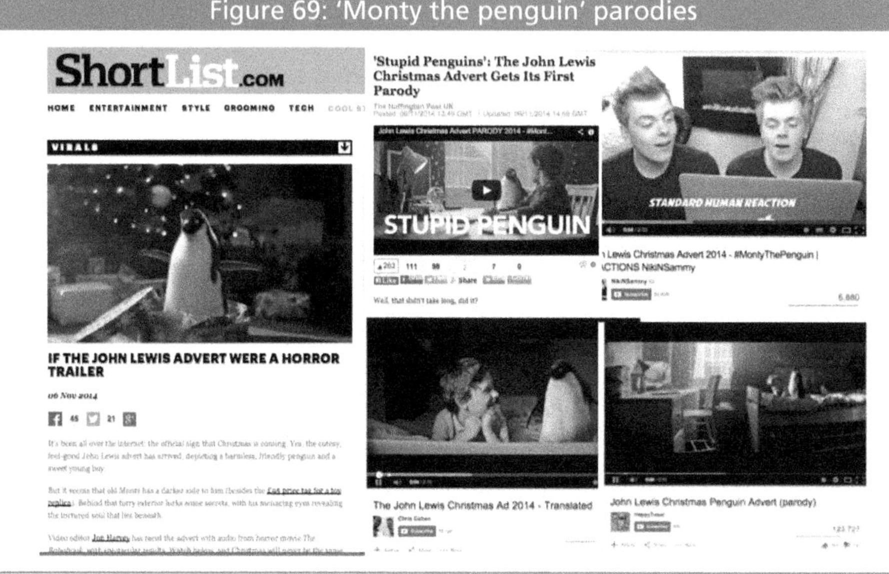

Figure 70: 'Man on the moon' parodies

YouTube currently hosts *81,200* John Lewis parodies. The top ten gathered over 7 million views, more than most retailers get for their official Christmas ads (Table 8).

Table 8: Top 10 parodies YouTube

Parody title	Source	Ad parodied	Year	Views
'Telescope Xmas ad'	Aldi	'Man on the moon'	2015	2,109,435
'Geordie the penguin'	#Geordiethepenguin	'Monty the penguin'	2014	1,253,505
'Star Wars parody'	The Poke	'Man on the moon'	2015	829,373
'X Rated'	Russell Howard	'Monty the penguin'	2014	710,574
'Rude penguin'	MRLBXv2	'Monty the penguin'	2014	571,300
'Penguin ad parody'	Happy Toast	'Monty the penguin'	2014	550,702
'JL 2015 ad parody'	Gorgeous	'Man on the moon'	2015	345,431
'JL 2014 ad parody'	Redshirt Films	'Monty the penguin'	2014	343,649
'The JL ad: recut'	John Harvey	'Monty the penguin'	2014	265,631
'Star Wars edition'	Dan Tube	'Man on the moon'	2015	240,640
Total view				7,220,060

Source: YouTube: views as of 1 April 2016

Because of this, other brands started jumping on the bandwagon (Figure 71).

Figure 71: Examples of other brands 'hi-jacking' 'Monty the penguin'

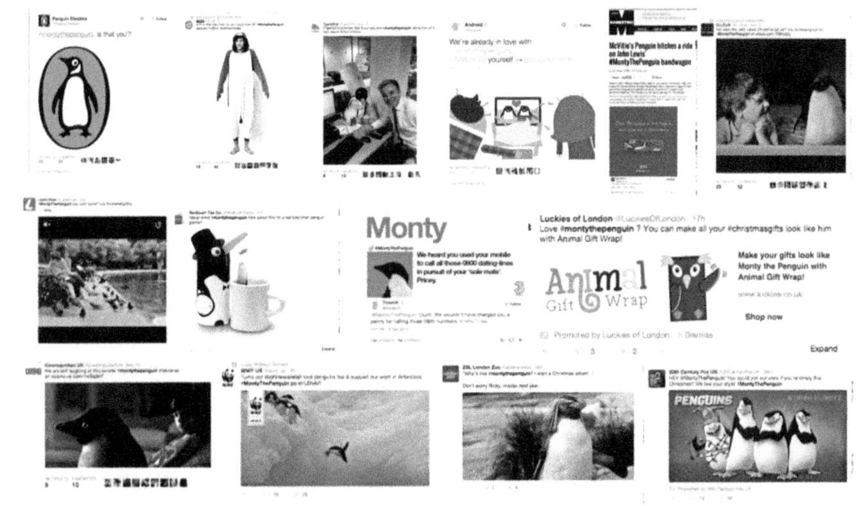

The ultimate accolade came when Aldi created their own parody of 'Man on the moon', and ran it as their Christmas ad. This gave us huge amounts of free exposure (Figure 72).[19]

Figure 72: Press coverage of the Aldi spoof

campaign

METRO

Aldi Christmas advert just spoofed the John Lewis Man on the Moon and people are crying laughing

The Telegraph

Aldi spoofs the John Lewis Man on the Moon Christmas advert

ALDI AD THE LAST LAUGH

INDEPENDENT

Aldi launches John Lewis Christmas advert parody

From 'push' to 'pull'

As the buzz around the John Lewis Christmas advertising has grown, people increasingly seek the ads out online, rather than wait for them to appear on TV. Google search volumes peak higher and earlier each year (Figure 73).

Figure 73: Google searches for 'John Lewis ad'

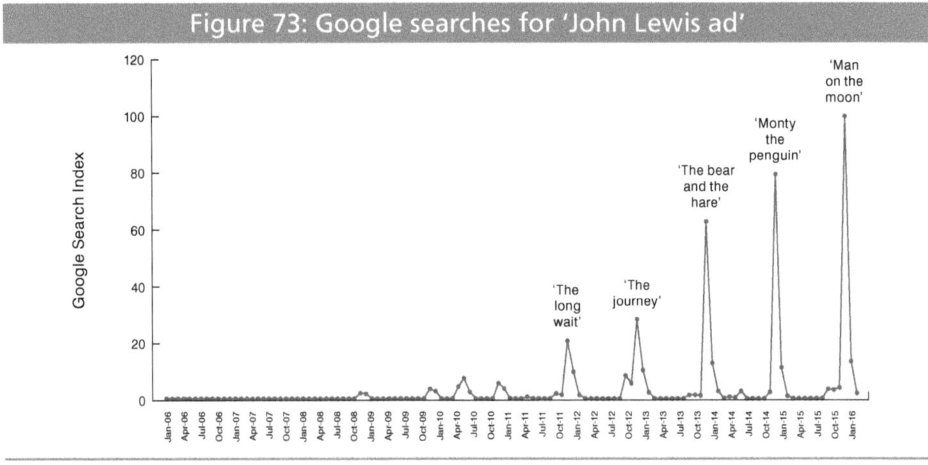

Source: Google Trends

This is must-see advertising. Everyone wants to be the first to share it with their friends. According to a 2015 poll,[20] four of the ten most shared Christmas ads in the world were ours (Table 9).

Table 9: The most shared Christmas ad in the worlds

Rank	Brand	Ad	Year	Country
1	Universal	'Minions go caroling'	2014	USA
2	**John Lewis**	**'The bear and the hare'**	**2013**	**UK**
3	**John Lewis**	**'Monty the penguin'**	**2014**	**UK**
4	Sainsbury's	'Christmas is for sharing'	2014	UK
5	**John Lewis**	**'The long wait'**	**2011**	**UK**
6	**John Lewis**	**'The journey'**	**2012**	**UK**
7	Burberry	'From London with love'	2014	UK
8	M&S	'Magic and sparkle'	2013	UK
9	Cartier	'Winter tale'	2013	France
10	Three	'Pony at Christmas'	2013	UK

Source: The Drum/Unruly 6 November 2015

And it looks like 'Man on the moon' will place even higher in the chart next year (Figure 74).

Figure 74: John Lewis Christmas ads – number of shares

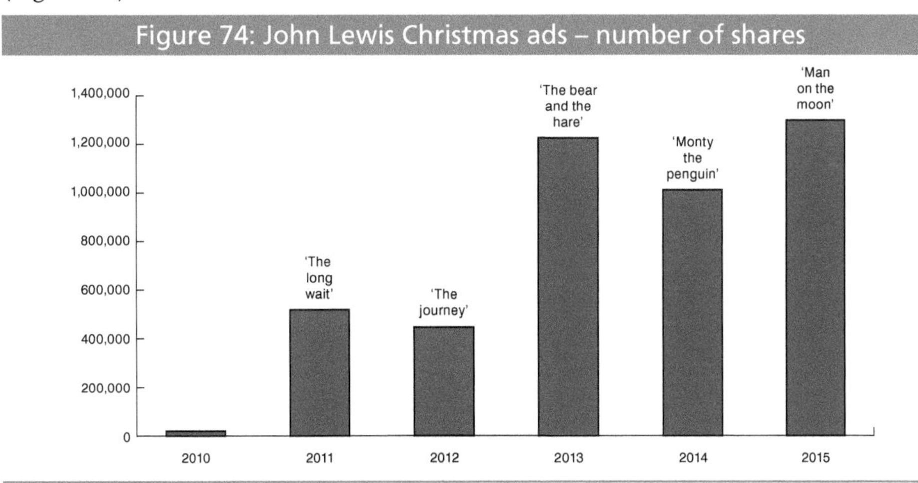

Source: Unruly

Fame made our media work harder

With people increasingly seeking our ads out online, we got massive amounts of extra exposure. Over the last four Christmases, we've had *78 million* views online (Figure 75).

Figure 75: John Lewis Christmas advertising – online views

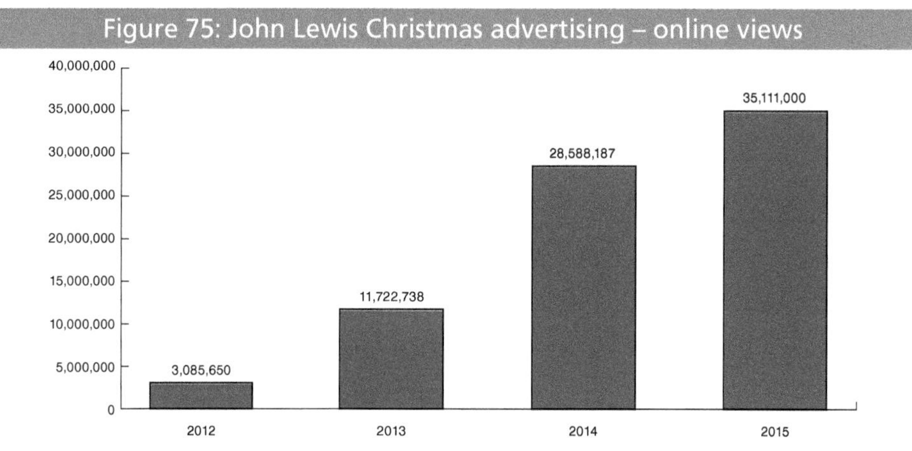

Source: YouTube, Facebook, Twitter

We don't have complete data on competitors,[21] but what we have suggests we've achieved much higher levels of views than them (Figure 76).[22]

Figure 76: Christmas ad – YouTube views

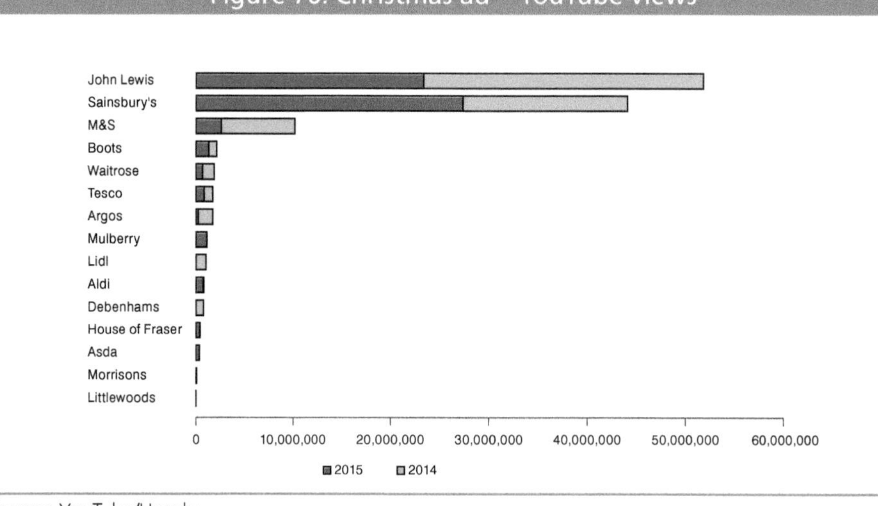

Source: YouTube/Unruly

Meanwhile, supplier-funded advertising increased our presence on TV (Figure 77).

Figure 77: John Lewis Christmas advertising – TV ratings

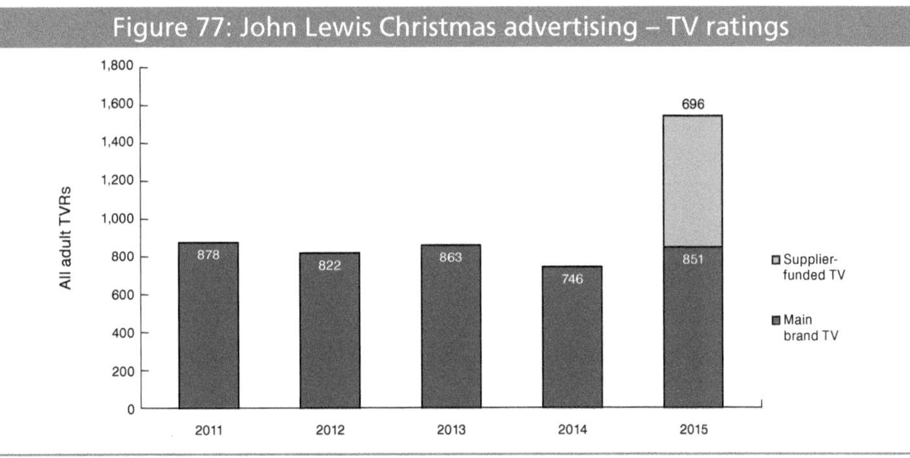

Souce: BARB

As a result we got huge exposure at low cost. Over four years, we have had an astonishing *2.5 billion views* (Table 10).[23]

Table 10: Media effectiveness and efficiency

Christmas	TV views	Online views	Total views	John Lewis spend	Cost per view
2012	403m	3m	406m	£3.9m	1.0 pence
2013	426m	12m	437m	£4.6m	1.1 pence
2014	371m	29m	400m	£3.9m	1.0 pence
2015	1,175m	35m	1,210m	£4.1m	0.3 pence
Total	2,375m	79m	2,453m	£16.5m	0.7 pence

And that doesn't take account of the free publicity we got from music, PR, parodies, charitable partnerships or word of mouth.

Results part two: The effect on John Lewis

We've seen how a steady stream of popular advertising created a virtuous circle of fame.

But that was only a means to an end. In part two, we will look at the effect on John Lewis (Figure 78).

Figure 78: The effect on John Lewis

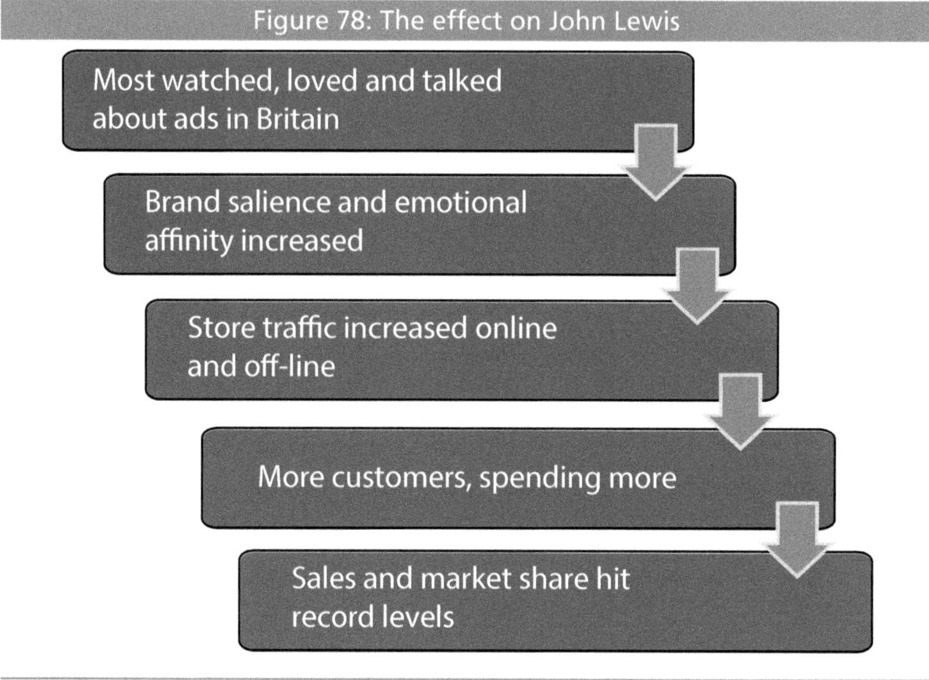

Advertising awareness increased

As we have already seen, our ads were distinctive, impactful and memorable. Combine that with increased exposure, and it's not surprising that ad awareness increased (Figure 79).

Figure 79: Ad recognition

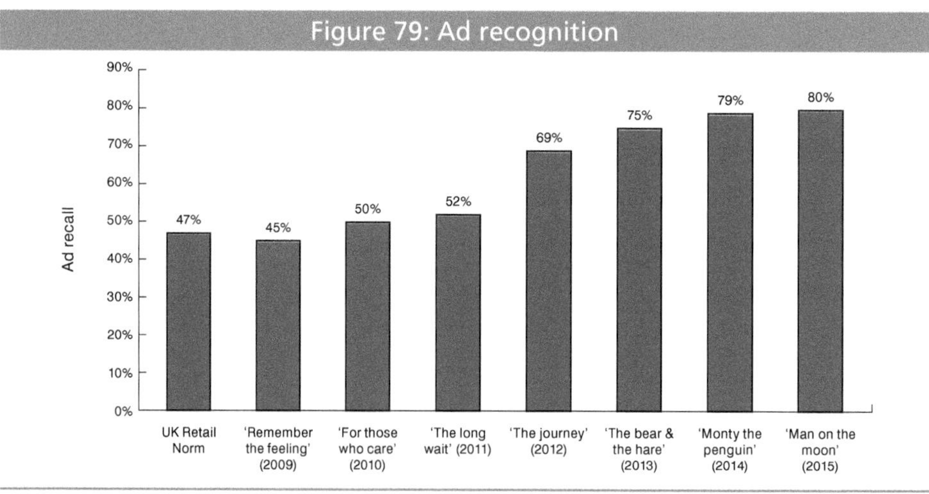

Millward Brown (2009–2012); John Lewis Image Tracker (2013–2015)

We swiftly overtook our direct competitors, and soon had higher ad awareness than any other retailer (Figure 80).[24]

Figure 80: *Marketing Magazine* – top 10 Christmas ads of 2015

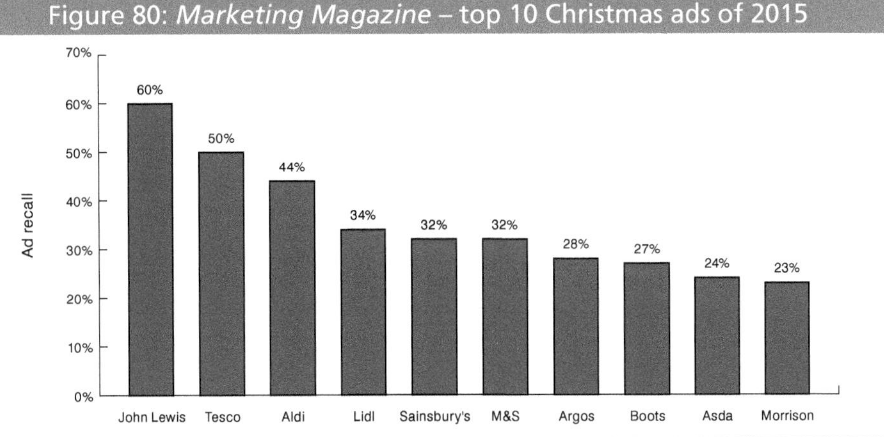

Source: *Marketing Magazine* AdWatch Survey, Ads of the Year 2015

The ads strengthened the brand

Awareness of John Lewis has always been high, and brand perceptions have always been favourable, *when prompted*. Our aim was not to *change* these perceptions, but to make them *more top-of-mind*. By making the brand famous, we would ensure John Lewis came to mind at Christmas. And by creating an emotional halo around John Lewis, we would prime people to feel better about our products and services.[25]

The best way to measure this 'emotional priming' effect is not to look at *how* people answer questions about the brand, but at how *fast* they answer.[26] Research by BrainJuicer showed that exposure to our ads produced unusually positive responses under time pressure. Respondents were quick to associate John Lewis with quality, difference and distinctiveness, in line with our 'thoughtful gifting' strategy (Table 11).

Table 11: Implicit characteristics test – key brand health metrics

Time-pressured agreement	**UK finished film norm**	**'Man on the moon' 90" (160)**	**'Monty the penguin' 90" (178)**	**'The bear and the hare' 90" (150)**	**'The journey' 90" (150)**
Famous brand	82%	93% (+13%)	90% (+9%)	85% (+4%)	83% (+2%)
High quality	76%	86% (+13%)	87% (+14%)	86% (+14%)	86% (+13%)
Trustworthy	78%	87% (+12%)	83% (+7%)	83% (+7%)	90% (+15%)
Distinctive	69%	78% (+13%)	78% (+12%)	73% (+6%)	79% (+14%)
Different	61%	75% (+13%)	73% (+20%)	72% (+18%)	64% (+5%)

Q. *In this section we're going to show you a series of words in quick succession. All you need to do is tell us whether you feel the words describe [advertised brand] by saying 'yes' or 'no' … but be quick, you only have three seconds to make your choice*

Source: BrainJuicer Implicit Characteristics Test. Figures in backets show deviation from norm

This is perhaps one reason why British mums voted us their favourite brand in 2014 (Table 12).

Table 12: Mumsnet – mums' favourite brands

Rank	Brand
1	John Lewis
2	Waitrose
3	Amazon
4	Apple
5	M&S
6	Lego
7	Sainsbury's
8	Cadbury
9	Ocado
10	Next

Source: Mumsnet survey of 1,000 mums, November 2013–January 2014

The ads increased web traffic

We have seen how people sought out our ads online. Meanwhile, a range of other activities encouraged people to interact with the brand there. There were competitions, apps, e-books, microsites and lots of activity in social media. All of this was linked to JohnLewis.com, the brand's online store, as was the supplier-funded advertising. Millions of people clicked straight through to start their Christmas shopping each year.

Over the last three years, web traffic has increased 63%.[27] People now start visiting earlier in the season, at precisely the point when we launch our ads (Figure 81).

Figure 81: Web visits vs Christmas ad campaigns

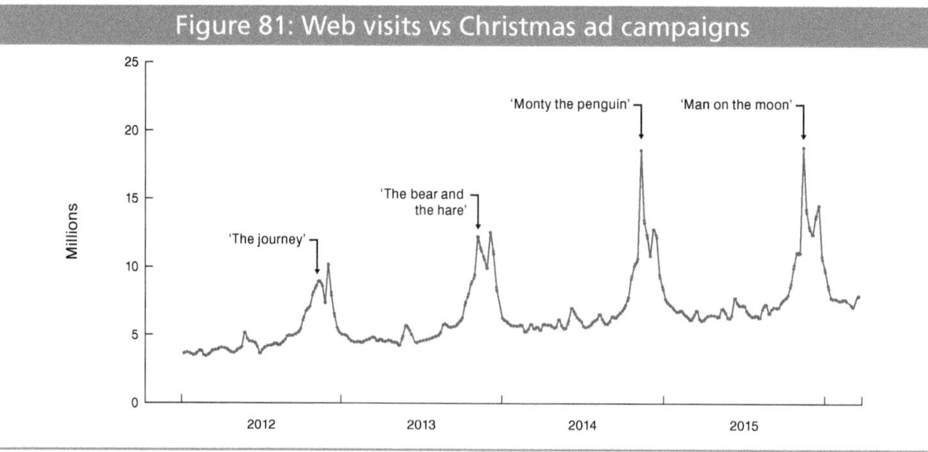

Total weekly visits to johnlewis.com. Source: John Lewis

What's more, our activity made people feel more positive about their online shopping experience (Figure 82).[28]

Figure 82: WebPulse survey of visitors to JohnLewis.com

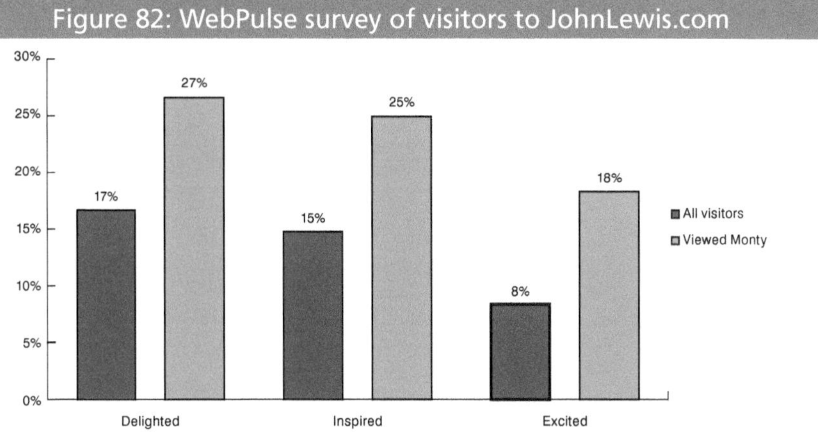

Source: WebPulse survey of visitors to JohnLewis.com all shoppers, Dec 2014. Viewed Monty Page: 240, Did not view Monty Page: 2818. All differences statistically significant at 95% confidence.

The ads increased footfall in-store

Our campaigns also got people pouring into John Lewis's shops. John Lewis have only been tracking footfall since 2013, but since then it has increased 55% (Table 13).

Table 13: Footfall increased 55%

	December 2013	December 2014	December 2015
Footfall	929,429	1,473,425	1,442,603

Source: John Lewis (all stores with cameras installed for all three years)

We got more customers, spending more

With all this extra traffic, John Lewis recruited record numbers of customers, both on and offline, who visited more often and spent more (Table 14).

Table 14: More customers, spending more

	2009	2010	2011	2012	2013	2014	2015
Number of customers	100	105	106	115	118	123	126
Average spend per customer	100	106	110	117	121	125	127
Total sales	100	112	117	134	144	154	160

Source: John Lewis GCI Detailed Customer Dashboard Indexed (2009 = 100)

The ads created new revenue streams

In 2013, we created a new revenue stream from merchandise. The products sold out quickly, and were soon selling to collectors on eBay (Figure 83).

Figure 83: Selling to collectors on eBay

sky NEWS HD

Watch Sky News LIVE — 27 November 2013

HOME | UK | WORLD | US | BUSINESS | POLITICS | TECHNOLOGY | ENTERTAINMENT | STRANGE NEWS | WEATHER

John Lewis Runs Out Of Bear and Hare Gifts

The department store sells out of merchandise linked to its £7m TV advert as people put the gifts on eBay for twice the price.

The two-minute advert cost £7m

TESCO direct

£20.00 View — £119.00 View

Top Stories

Next year, 'Monty' sold **£2.5m worth of merchandise**, including 48,000 soft toys. Some stores sold out of penguins in a day, and soon they were selling for £500 on eBay (Figure 84).

Figure 84: 'Monty the penguin' on eBay

Home | News | U.S. | Sport | TV&Showbiz | Australia | Femail | Health | Science | Money

Now you can p-p-p-pick up a penguin on eBay - the £95 toy that stars in John Lewis ad is already being sold on auction site for up to £500

- Monty the penguin starred in retailer's Christmas advert released yesterday
- The £95 cuddly toy sold out online within hours of the commercial's release
- Several versions of the gift have been listed on eBay for as much as £499
- John Lewis hopes to release more online stock today, a spokesman said

By MARTIN ROBINSON and JENNIFER SMITH FOR MAILONLINE

PUBLISHED: 09:04, 7 November 2014 | UPDATED: 13:05, 7 November 2014

Sales and market share increased to record levels

Merchandising was just the tip of the iceberg. Sales hit record levels, increasing 33% over the last four Christmases, and allowing John Lewis to beat its rivals seven years in a row (Table 15).

Table 15: Christmas sales, year-on-year

	2009	2010	2011	2012	2013	2014	2015
John Lewis	+12.7%	+7.6%	+6.2%	+13.0%	+6.9%	+4.8%	+5.1%
M&S	+1.2%	+3.8%	−1.8%	−3.8%	−2.1%	−5.8%	−5.8%
Debenhams	+0.1%	−1.3%	0.0%	+5.0%	+1.5%	+2.4%	+1.8%
Argos	+0.1%	−4.9%	−8.8%	+2.7%	+3.8%	+0.1%	−2.2%
Comet	−3.9%	−7.3%	−14.5%	Closed	Closed	Closed	Closed
Mothercare	n/a	n/a	−3.0%	−5.9%	−4.0%	+1.1%	+4.2%

Like-for-like sales, Christmas period (non-food) year-on-year. Sources: published financial information

This contributed to a spectacular run of annual sales figures. Gross sales increased 37% over four years, an amazing performance for such a venerable brand (Figure 85).

Figure 85: John Lewis full year sales

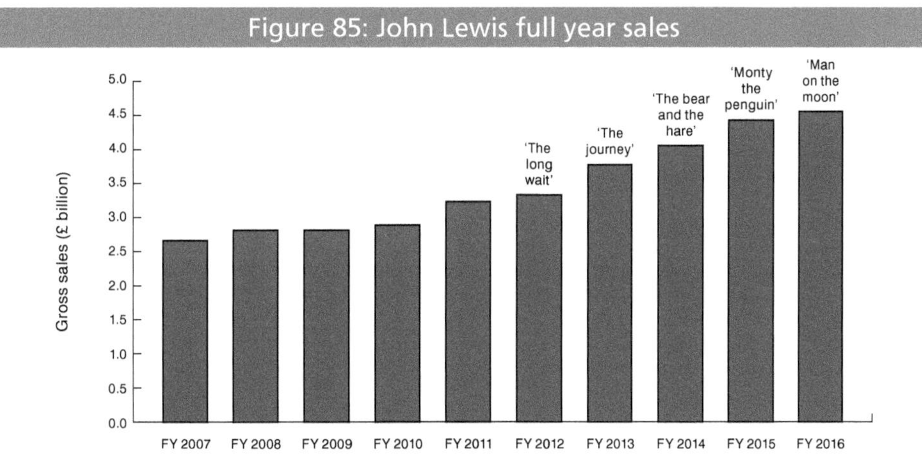

Source: John Lewis financial reports

This was not just a question of market growth. As we've seen, John Lewis beat its rivals, and more generally grew much faster than the market (Figure 86).

Figure 86: John Lewis sales versus UK retail sales

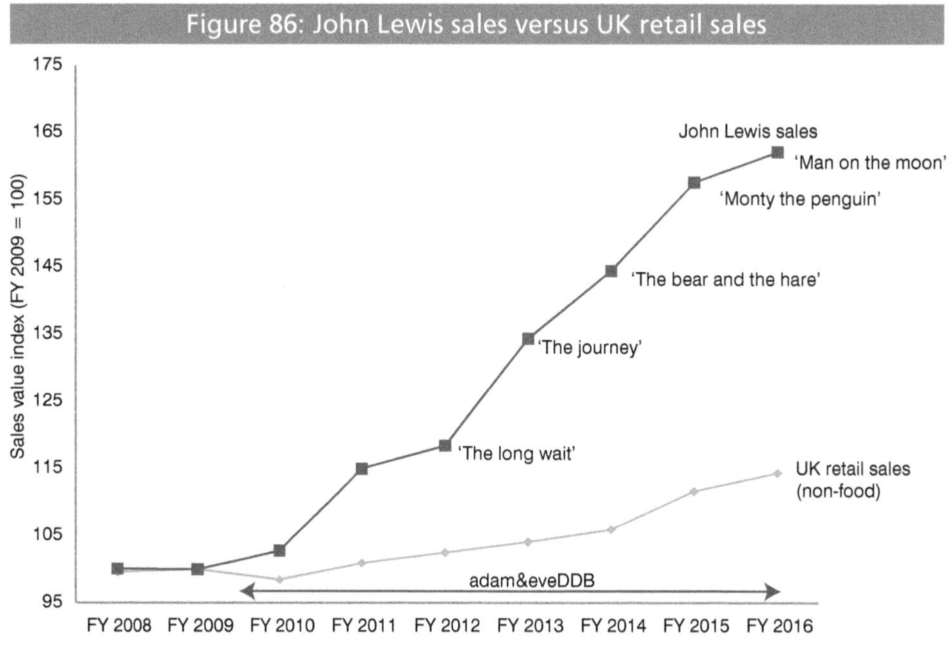

Source: John Lewis; Office for National Statistics

As a result, John Lewis's market share increased to 29.6%, its highest level ever. This dwarfs the achievements outlined in the previous IPA paper (Figure 87).

Figure 87: John Lewis market share

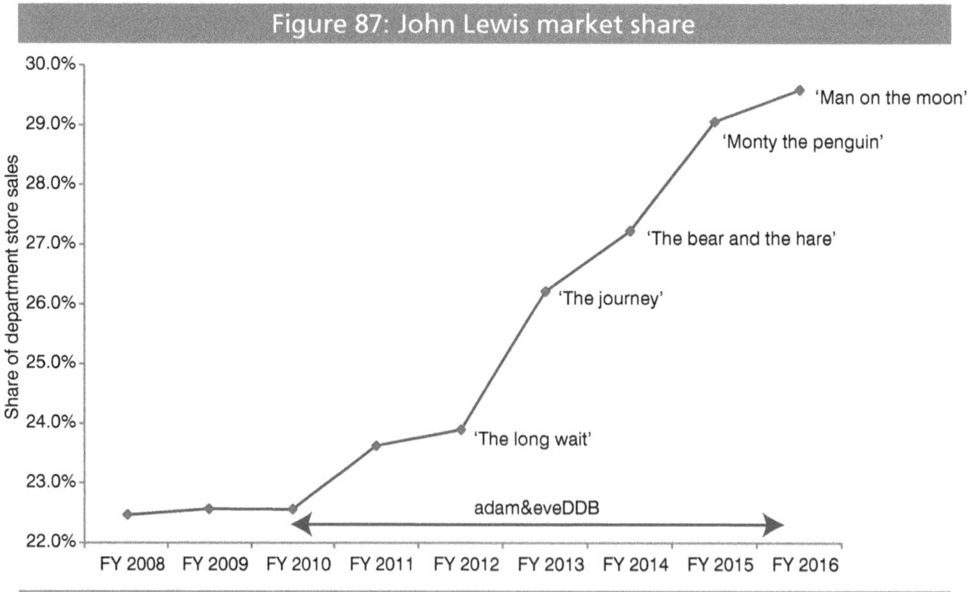

Source: John Lewis; Mintel

Isolating the contribution of advertising

The effect of advertising on sales

Since 2007, John Lewis have been using econometrics to measure the factors that influence sales.[29] Econometrics shows that advertising has played a huge role, especially Christmas advertising, which increases sales during the festive season by 16% on average (Figure 88).[30]

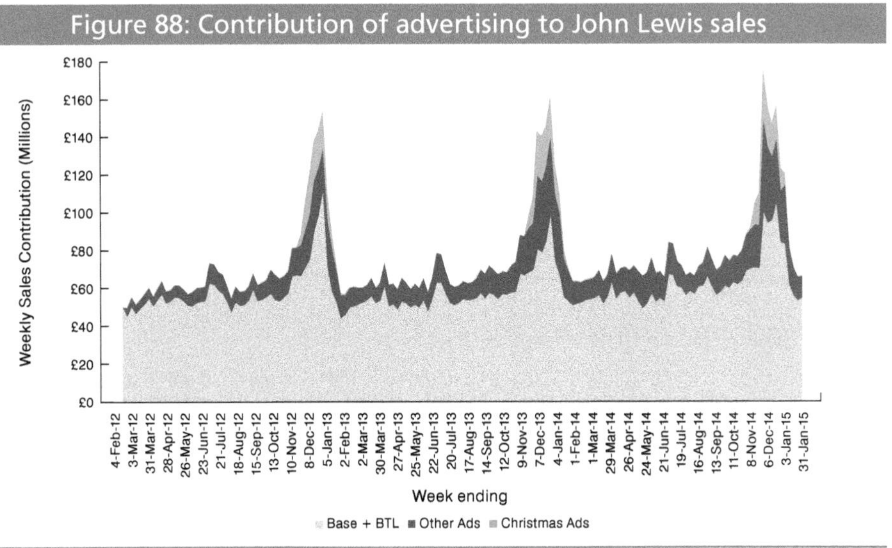

Figure 88: Contribution of advertising to John Lewis sales

Source: MarketShare Econometric Models

Market factors played a minor role

Economic growth has helped in recent years, but that's not the whole story – as we've already seen, John Lewis grew faster than the market. Econometrics shows that the overall contribution of market factors has been modest, and was actually *negative* last Christmas.[31]

New stores can't explain our success

To account for the impact of store expansion, all econometric models are based on like-for-like sales. Like-for-like sales grew strongly, so new stores were not the main driver (Figure 89).

Figure 89: John Lewis like-for-like sales

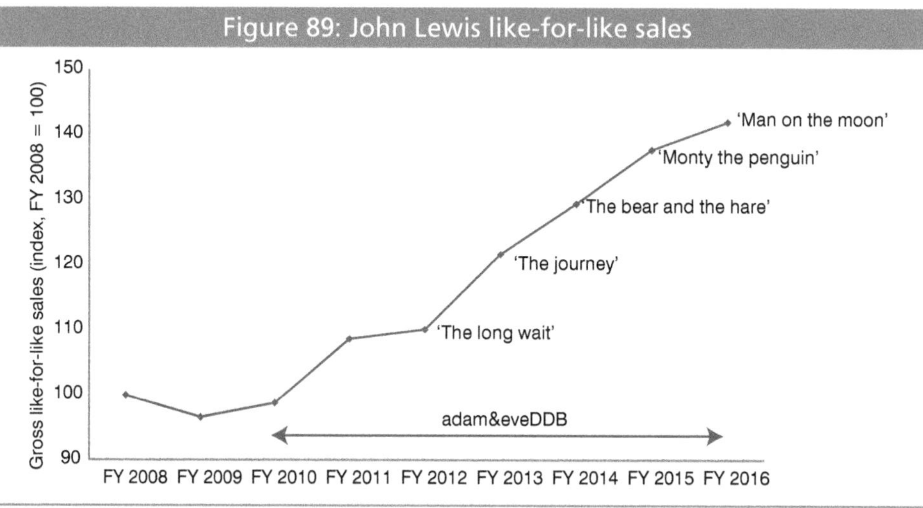

Source: John Lewis financial reports

Advertising drove online sales too

JohnLewis.com, the online store, continues to be a major engine of growth. The rise of internet shopping has helped, but JohnLewis.com grew faster than the online market (Figure 90).

Figure 90: John Lewis online sales

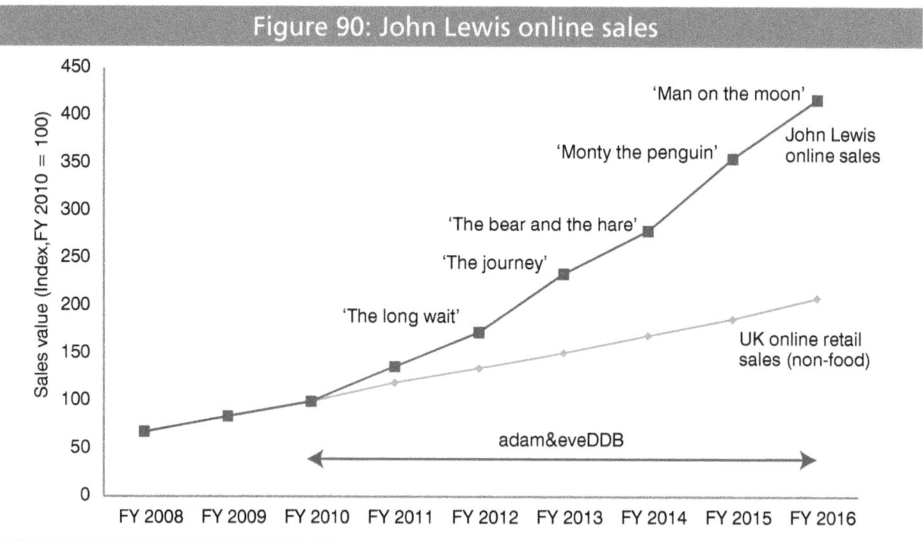

Source: John Lewis company reports; Office for National Statistics

We have already seen how our Christmas advertising increased visits to John Lewis.com. Econometrics shows that online sales are even more responsive to advertising than branch sales. Our Christmas ads boosted sales during the festive season by 19%, on average (Figure 91).

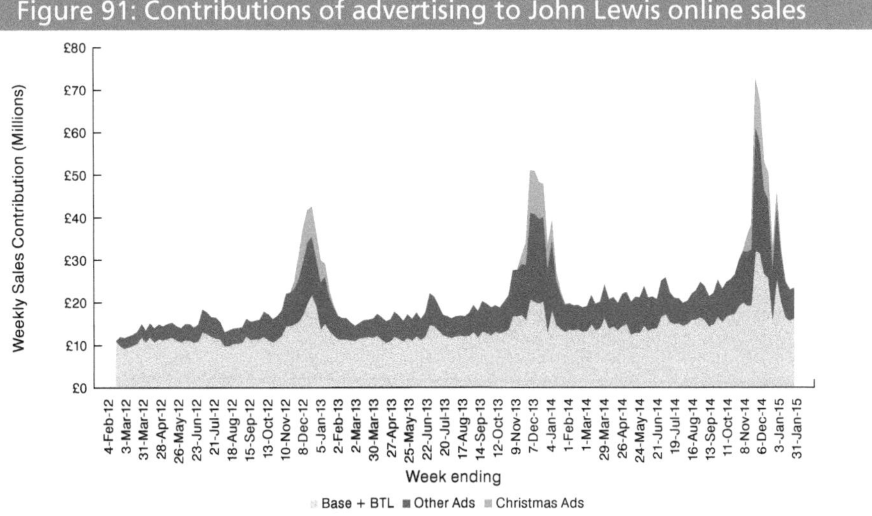

Source: MarketShare Econometric Models

Products and prices continued to be competitive

John Lewis continually strive to offer the best products and services. The effect of changes to the offer[32] varies from year to year, but the long-term effect is modest.

Loyalty scheme launch

The loyalty scheme 'My John Lewis', launched in 2013, boosted sales by 1.3% according to econometrics. This was a one-off effect, and cannot explain the long-term growth observed.

Other factors played a minor role

Econometrics has investigated the impact of many other factors that might affect sales. None was sufficient to explain the extraordinary increase in sales and market share observed.

Measuring return on investment

Our Christmas ads paid for themselves eight times over

In the previous IPA paper, we showed how advertising delivered a payback of 5:1. But this advertising was even more profitable, delivering *over £8 of profit for every £1 spent* (Table 16).[33]

Table 16: Return on investment from Christmas advertising

	2012 'The journey'	2013 'The bear and the hare'	2014 'Monty the penguin'	2015 'Man on the moon'
John Lewis Christmas ad spend	£3.9m	£5.1m	£4.4m	£4.3m
Incremental revenue generated (inc VAT)	£121.0m	£142.5m	£132.8m	£151.4m
Revenue generated per £1 spent	£31.07	£28.15	£30.29	£35.37
Incremental profit (before deducting ad spend)	£47.8m	£40.8m	£32.4m	n/a
Net profit (after deducting ad spend)	£43.9m	£40.8m	£32.4m	n/a
Net profit per £1 spent	£11.27	£8.07	£7.39	n/a
Return on marketing investment	1127%	807%	739%	n/a

Source: Econometrics by BrandScience (2012); econometrics by MarketShare (2013–2015); Figures for 2015 are preliminary estimates

That's over four times more profitable than the average IPA paper (Table 17).[34]

Table 17: These ROMIs are exceptionally high

Year	Christmas campaign	Net profit per £1 spent	ROMI
Average	John Lewis Christmas ads	£8.78	879%
Average	All IPA Effectiveness entries	£1.85	185%

Source: Econometrics by BrandScience (2012); econometrics by MarketShare (2013–2015); IPA Databank

... in a tough retailing environment

This is a remarkable achievement, given the state of British retailing. The economy has picked up in recent years, but retail profits have been meagre. Nearly 8,500 stores have gone bust in the last four years, and things seem to be getting worse, not better (Table 18).[35]

We achieved our ultimate objective

We achieved all of our campaign objectives, but our ultimate aim was to make the John Lewis partners happy. Money is only part of that, of course. Making staff feel proud to work for a famous, well-loved, charitable business is massively important.[36]

But the annual bonus is important too, and that depends on profits. According to the econometrics, our Christmas advertising generated £117m of extra profit from 2013–2014,[37] which meant more bonus income for partners and their families.

Who says advertising can't make people happy?

Table 18: UK retail failures

Year	Companies failing	Stores affected	Employees affected
2016 (to March)	12	670	8,290
2015 (12 months)	25	728	6,845
2014 (12 months)	43	1,314	12,335
2013 (12 months)	49	2,500	25,140
2012 (12 months)	54	3,951	48,142
2011 (12 months)	31	2,469	24,025
2010 (12 months)	26	944	10,930
2009 (12 months)	37	6,536	26,688
2008 (12 months)	54	5,793	74,539
2007 (12 months)	25	2,600	14,083

Source: Centre for Retail Research

10 Lessons for marketers

1. *Make stuff people want to watch, listen to and talk about:* We can no longer *command* attention – we must *earn* it. If our ads bore or irritate people, they will block, skip or avoid them. But if we make ads that people love, they will seek out, share and amplify them.
2. *Nothing sells quite as hard as emotion:* Most advertising treats emotion as a means to an end – a way of getting the 'message' across. Here, the feeling *was* the message. And the huge profits generated show just how powerful feelings can be.
3. *Tell a great story, create a world:* Nothing interests, involves and moves people more than a great story. Media and technology offer new, more immersive ways to tell stories. We drew people into the worlds we created, and then into John Lewis's stores.
4. *Create characters that have a life of their own:* Great stories have characters that live and breathe beyond their creators. Our characters came to life, in books, apps, and parodies. And when they came to life in store, they created a whole new revenue stream from merchandise.
5. *Creativity is not a luxury:* None of this would be possible without great creative. With an ROMI of 8:1, this case proves that creativity is crucial for efficiency.
6. *Scale matters too:* Creativity increases *efficiency*, but *effectiveness* is also a numbers game. With over 2.5 billion impressions, our creative got the exposure it needed to create fame.
7. *TV is still indispensable:* Only TV can deliver audiences on that scale. TV remains the core, and continues to deliver outstanding ROI.
8. *Online makes TV work harder:* Online channels extend reach, deepen involvement, and stimulate sales directly.

9. *Fame is a virtuous circle:* The more famous our ads become, the more exposure they get. The more exposure they get, the more famous they become.
10. *Dedication to effectiveness and evaluation:* To keep the wheel of fame turning, we need to deliver great campaigns every year. That means continually evaluating what we do, and trying to make each campaign work harder than the last.

Conclusion

Maybe this case teaches us something about business in the twenty-first century. In a world where jobs are being Überised, media are fragmenting, and marketing is increasingly about short-term responses, John Lewis took a very different approach.

The John Lewis story is about giving and sharing. They gave the British public heart-warming stories that they could share as a nation. They gave something back to the community, by sharing those stories with good causes. And when a grateful nation gave John Lewis their business, they shared the profits with their staff.

As a result, they became one of the best-loved and most successful firms in Britain.

It seems that giving really is its own reward.

Notes

1. 'John Lewis: Making the nation cry… and buy', Grand Prix Winner, IPA Effectiveness Awards 2012.
2. Return on marketing investment.
3. Source: adam&eveDDB qualitative research.
4. A unique technological partnership with Microsoft. As our fame grew, tech firms were increasingly keen to get involved.
5. Another tech first, partnering with Google this time.
6. For the full story of the partnership between John Lewis and Age UK, see our other IPA paper, 'No-one should have no-one at Christmas', IPA Effectiveness Awards 2016.
7. Although competitors spent more, especially those in electrical, home and beauty. For example, Boots spent an average of £8m on advertising over the last four Christmases, Argos £12m and Dixons £13m.
8. Much more could be written on this aspect of the case, but space does not permit. adam&eveDDB have worked closely with psychologists at Goldsmiths University to study the effects of music in advertising. For a summary of some of our research, see 'The Power of Music' by Binet, Müllensiefen and Edwards (*Admap,* October 2013). Of course, Hollywood producers have understood the emotional power of music since at least the 1920s.
9. Millward Brown data is not available after 2012, as John Lewis switched to another research provider.
10. Based on ABC daily circulations quoted by Newsworks for print editions of *The Sun*, *The Daily Mail*, *The Daily Mirror*, *The Daily Telegraph*, *The Daily Express*, *The Times* and *The Guardian*. Coverage in online editions will take the true total even higher. The power of news brands to deliver mass audiences is clearly alive and well.
11. As defined by *The Gunn Report*. This makes John Lewis the second most creatively awarded IPA Effectiveness Awards entrant of all time, just behind our very own Volkswagen ads. And we've been entering VW papers since 1990. [Analysis of *Gunn Report* data by Peter Field. Personal communication.]
12. Channel 4 have since worked closely with John Lewis to make 'Gogglebox' part of our Christmas plan. See our other IPA paper, 'No-one should have no-one at Christmas' for more details.
13. See *The Long and the Short of It* by Binet and Field. A cracking good read, and very reasonably priced.
14. 'No-one should have no-one at Christmas' – Age UK / John Lewis IPA Effectiveness awards paper, 2016.
15. This observation is based on bitter personal experience.

16. For this reason, based on the emotions it evoked, Brainjuicer say they would give 'Man on the moon' five stars as a charity ad, but only two as a retail ad.
17. See previous IPA paper.
18. *The Guardian*'s suggestion that the 'Man on the moon' endline be changed to 'Don't give balloons to moon Hitler, you idiot' remains a personal favourite.
19. As a food retailer, Aldi does not compete with John Lewis.
20. Conducted just before the launch of 'Man on the moon'.
21. We only have data for YouTube, and only for the last two years. Earlier ads are no longer online.
22. Only one other retailer has come close: the excellent Christmas ads for Sainsbury's. While we regard them as our biggest advertising rival, Sainsbury's is not a true competitor to John Lewis the department store.
23. To put that in context, that's almost as many views as the most watched video ever on YouTube, 'Gangnam style', has achieved globally since it was released in November 2012 (2.55 billion views). For a British department store to rival a 'global internet phenomenon' seems rather impressive.
24. Also note that no 3. in that chart is Aldi, with their parody of 'Man in the moon'.
25. This is a well-documented phenomenon, which psychologists call 'the halo effect'. If you have a positive emotional response to something, you will intuitively rate it more highly an all dimensions. So, if you like someone, you will rate them as more intelligent, for example. See Binet and Field (2013) for a more detailed discussion.
26. 'Implicit responses' rather than 'explicit responses', as psychologists put it.
27. Calendar 2014 vs calendar 2012 (earliest data available). Source: John Lewis.
28. Another example of 'the halo effect'.
29. Econometric analysis was conducted by Brand Science (2007–2012) and MarketShare (2012 onwards). Figure 87 shows the most recently available simulation.
30. Other advertising includes supplier-funded activity, 'Never knowingly undersold' (NKU) advertising (see 2012 IPA paper) and insurance advertising. In recent years, insurance ads have supplanted NKU ads as the main brand activity outside Christmas (see separate 2016 IPA for more detail).
31. Retails sales were down 1.8% year-on-year Christmas 2015, according to the latest data from the Office for National Statistics.
32. Accounted for in the econometrics.
33. The figures for 'Man on the moon' are preliminary estimates. John Lewis profit figures for 2015 had not been finalised at time of writing. But what data we do have suggests that ROI will be even higher this year.
34. It's also the second highest retail ROMI of all time, to our knowledge. The only IPA paper to record a higher figure was the 2010 entry for Waitrose, part of the John Lewis partnership.
35. The figures for Q1 2015 suggest that the rate at which retailers are closing has doubled recently, probably in response to the market contraction the previous Christmas. This makes John Lewis's recent success all the more impressive.
36. For more details of the motivating effects of the partnership with Age UK on John Lewis Partners, see our other IPA paper, 'No-one should have no-one at Christmas', IPA Effectiveness Awards 2016.
37. See ROMI calculations above. Profit figures for 2015 are not yet available.

Art Fund

The art of framing

By Joe Smith, 101
Contributing author: Laurence Green, 101
Credited companies: 101; the7stars

Summary

Art Fund is a UK charity that exists to save works of art for the nation. This paper shows how, over a five-year period, marketing has transformed the entire organisation through the art of framing; changing its category from a charity with a worthy purpose to a membership business with a compelling product. This case includes how the transformation was achieved by the creation and marketing of the Art Pass product, which provided members with discounted entry into museum and galleries, and a specific campaign to increase domestic visitors to London art galleries. At a time when the arts receive just 1% of charitable donations, the Art Fund has grown its membership and revenue significantly, delivering an incremental profit of £12.9m. This equates to a profit ROMI of £4.07 for every £1 spent.

Editor's Comment

This was a beautifully executed reframing of a product that pierced the market with its crystal-clear, unconventional thinking. The judges found the creative to be extremely well defined with a strong call to action coupled with an innovative approach to media planning.

Client Comment
Carolyn Young, Director of Marketing, Art Fund

This campaign has profoundly changed how the Art Fund approaches fundraising income. Since reframing and promoting our membership offer as a product – the National Art Pass – we now think of ourselves as an e-tailer or service provider as much as a charity.

Gifting has become a bigger part of our commercial strategy and we have been able to reach a significantly younger audience (the average age of new members has dropped by over 10 years since 2011). In addition, our online activity has become primary, seeing a major increase in traffic to our digital platforms and a significant decrease in the cost per acquisition.

Introduction

The last decade in marketing has been defined in part by the pursuit of *purpose*. Brands from every conceivable category have focused their efforts on defining their missions, organising ideas, lighthouse identities and north stars.

This is a story about a brand doing the opposite.

Since its inception in 1903, the Art Fund charity has had a very clear purpose: to save works of art for the nation, as Figure 1 shows.

Figure 1: 1920s National Art-Collections Fund advert

ONE OF THE WORKS OF ART
SAVED FOR THE NATION
WITH THE AID OF
THE NATIONAL ART-COLLECTIONS FUND
HERTFORD HOUSE, MANCHESTER SQUARE, W.1

TITIAN

ALL ART LOVERS SHOULD JOIN
THIS SOCIETY SECURES WORKS
OF ART OF ALL TIMES FOR
THE NATIONAL COLLECTIONS

MINIMUM SUBSCRIPTION . . ONE GUINEA
WITH MANY PRIVILEGES

What has been less clear and consistent over the organisation's history is the business model and marketing strategy that could turn this worthy purpose into a profitable one.

So this paper tells the story of the pursuit of profit over purpose.

Five years into a new strategy and creative approach, we show how marketing has transformed an entire organisation through the art of *framing*. By changing its category from a *charity with a worthy purpose* to a *business with a compelling product*.

At a time when the arts receive just 1% of charitable donations,[1] the Art Fund has grown its membership and revenue significantly. Our campaign has delivered an incremental profit of £12.9m, which equates to a return on marketing investment of £4.07 for every £1 spent.

Over three chapters, we show how this success has been achieved.

Background

The birth of a cause

The Art Fund charity was established in 1903 and has remained dedicated to its mission of securing works of art for the nation ever since.

It receives no government financial support and relies primarily on income from its membership subscriptions and a small number of wealthy individuals.

By 2010, the organisation had helped to acquire over 860,000 works of art for museums and galleries to display. It had become an important source of funding and support for hundreds of museums and galleries throughout the UK.

A change in fortunes

But a charity for art was losing appeal. Membership numbers had stalled at around 80,000 and the membership base was ageing. Fifty-six per cent of Art Fund members were over the age of 65 and their average age was 69.[2]

The Art Fund's most recent advertising campaign had focused on raising awareness of its cause of saving art, but had not been able to significantly increase memberships (Figure 2).[3]

A tough time for the arts

Perhaps counterintuitively, following the largest recession in living memory, charitable giving in the UK enjoyed a five-year peak in 2010 (Figure 3).

Figure 2: 'Empty frames' by Ogilvy & Mather London, 2007

Figure 3: Total charitable donations in the UK, adjusted for inflation, 2005–2010 (£billions)[4]

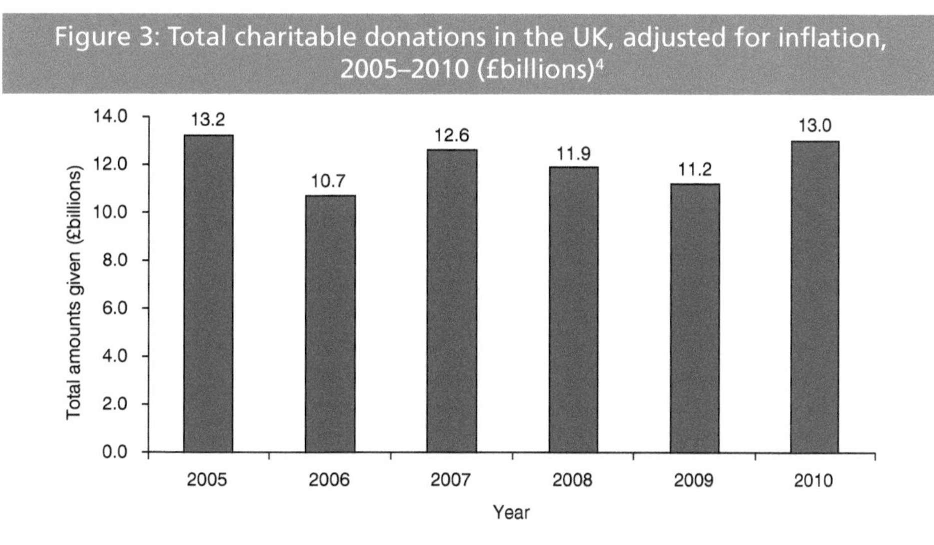

However, the picture was far less rosy for the arts sector.

First, the arts received far fewer donations than other charities, including those relating to medical research, children and animals. The 1% of all donations dedicated to the arts had to be shared amongst approximately 10,000 arts charities in the UK (Figure 4).[5]

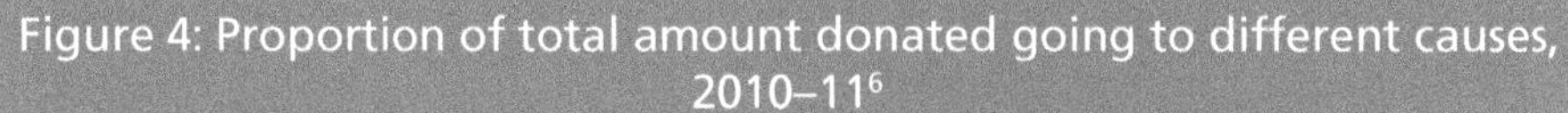
Figure 4: Proportion of total amount donated going to different causes, 2010–11[6]

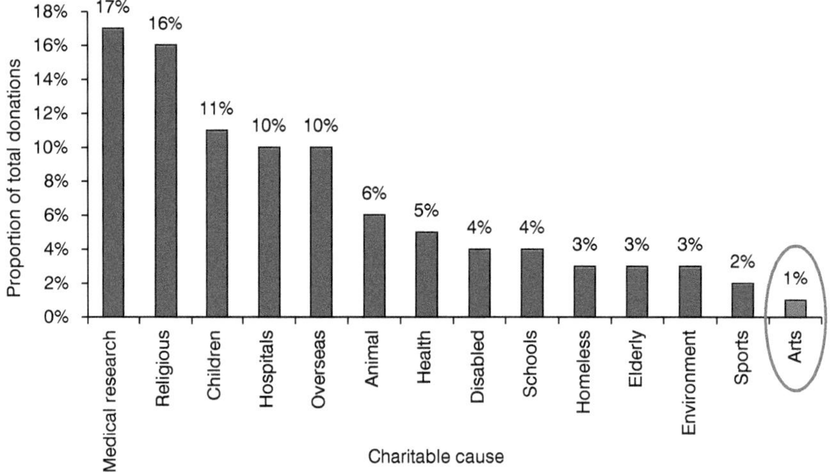

Second, the newly formed coalition government's funding cuts started to hit museums and galleries.

In 2011, the Museums Association found that 58% of museums had experienced cuts to their overall budget over the past year. As a result, 51% had reduced their number of full-time staff and 22% had reduced opening hours compared to 2010.[7]

But our targets were growing

In part to fill the void created by this funding gap, the Art Fund's Strategic Plan 2011–2014[8] sought a 50% growth in their charitable programme, driven by a dramatic increase in membership and donations.

It would not be easy. Consumer research with Art Fund members and prospects suggested that the Art Fund would struggle to grow its 'market share' versus charities with humanitarian missions such as Amnesty or Oxfam; or those with whom people had a personal connection, such as Cancer Research or the NSPCC.[9] Brands, of course, with much larger marketing budgets and greater media profiles (Figures 5 and 6).

Figure 5: Cancer Research UK 'Giving news' TV ad, 2010[10]

Figure 6: NSPCC 'Enough is enough' TV ad, 2010[11]

Solution

Rather than compete for attention with thousands of other charities, we shifted categories and reorganised the brand around a product rather than a purpose. The story of how we did this comes in three chapters (Figure 7).

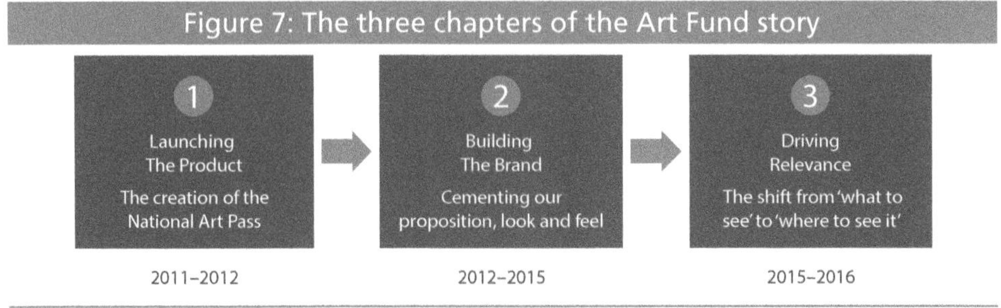

Chapter 1: Launching the product (2011–2012)[12]

Ask not what you can do for the Art Fund...

To better understand how we could grow the Art Fund's membership, we conducted research amongst members and prospects in late 2010. What we heard pointed us towards a completely new way of thinking about the Art Fund's proposition. Even amongst its current members (who you might expect to be motivated by philanthropic zeal), the primary impulse for Art Fund membership was in fact to save money on gallery and museum visits:

> *The members...hold their benefits in exceptionally high regard.*[13]
>
> *Whilst they fully support the cause, engage and believe in it, this element is an important* secondary *benefit.*[14]

So, whilst other brands were scrambling to define and then communicate their purposes, we decided to move ours to the background and focus instead on the more rational customer benefits. Prospects would be invited to join a cultural membership scheme granting them free or reduced entry to a range of galleries and museums.

A new audience

Repositioning the Art Fund as more of a cultural membership scheme drew us to two new 'psychographic' target audience segments: so called 'liberal opinions' (young, professional, urban-dwelling *Guardian* readers) and 'professional rewards' (successful folk with busy lives and expensive leisure interests).[15]

The idea of branding Art Fund membership as a kind of national 'art passport' for this new audience soon crystallised, and 101 was briefed to develop an organising idea, identity and promotional plan for this art passport. The short-term objective was to deliver 10,000 new members in 2011.

We also wanted to challenge the age distribution of our members – increasing average lifetime value by attracting a younger audience. With this aim in mind, we monitored the average age of Art Fund members and the proportion over 65.

The National Art Pass

The National Art Pass was born, designed to complement the Art Fund 'parent brand' but to reframe the organisation as a cultural membership scheme – with a visible, tangible product. 101 and the Art Fund designed the pass itself, the membership pack and the launch materials that included print and digital advertising (Figure 8).

Figure 8: National Art Pass membership cards and pack, 2011

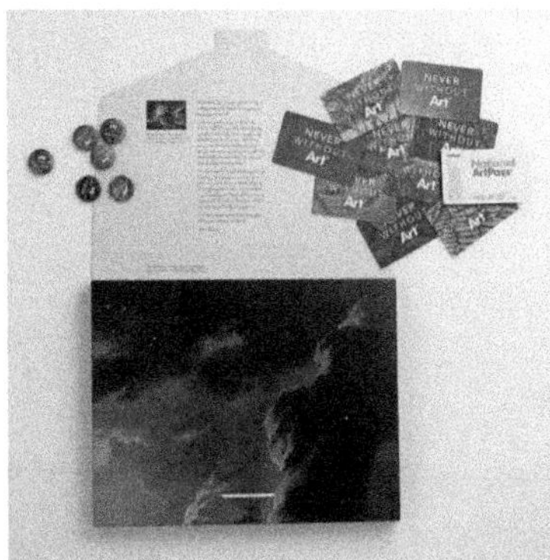

The accompanying organising idea, 'Never without art', captured both the product's ultimate benefit to members and gave the Art Fund a simple articulation of its mission.

No change was made to the Art Fund's product benefits or member privileges. The 'new' National Art Pass and the comms that followed simply re-presented the organisation's benefits in a more galvanising and desirable form.

As well as targeting direct sales, we hoped that the National Art Pass would prove to be a popular gift product and created a gift option on the Art Fund website.

Marketing the product

Launch advertising in outdoor, press and digital worked alongside PR to drive awareness of the National Art Pass under the umbrella of our organising idea, 'Never without art'. We made the pass itself the hero of the activity (Figure 9).

Figure 9: Campaign posters, 2011

We also ran the organising idea across all third-party materials, such as T-shirts, badges and bags for gallery staff (Figure 10).

Figure 10: Gallery staff materials

Finally, we devised a weekend-long promotion with the *Guardian* and the *Observer*, our prospects' newspaper brands of choice. This centred around a weekend promotion offering a free three-month 'trial version' of the pass.

Chapter 2: Building The Brand (2012–2015)

As we will cover in the results section, the 2011 campaign had an immediate impact on both awareness and, more importantly, sales.

The next challenge was to build on this success – turning this compelling product into a powerful and distinctive brand. To do this we needed a creative style and tone of voice that could help us stand out in a crowded arts sector (particularly in London) and a media approach – developed with the7stars – that could make the most of a £605k per year budget.[16]

Without the budget for TV advertising, we continued to use print formats to deliver reach and impact. Poster sites across the London Underground and key train stations also gave us a more focused way of reaching a younger London audience more effectively.

Over 70% of the marketing budget during this phase went on press and outdoor advertising.[17] Other activity included online advertising and search. We also made efforts to optimise the conversion of visitors to artfund.org into paying members, by testing different language and layout options.

Finding our voice

We noticed that advertising for museums and galleries followed a simple formula of artist/exhibition name plus work of art visual plus basic information (Figure 11).

Figure 11: Advertising for museums and galleries

Whilst this approach made sense for venues, with specific exhibitions and collections to promote, we saw an opportunity to inject more charm into the sector. As a charity, the Art Fund had traditionally adopted a fairly serious tone of voice – reflecting the seriousness of its purpose. But the National Art Pass, as a cultural membership scheme, freed us up to talk to a new audience in a new way.

We were helped in this pursuit by the scale and variety of the Art Fund's remit; we could in theory draw upon thousands of works of art from hundreds of museums, galleries and historic houses throughout the UK. This gave us the flexibility to use different styles of art, from conceptual to pop, thus broadening the Art Fund's appeal and reaching a younger audience.

Marketing the benefit

Our ambition was to raise awareness of the National Art Pass as a passport to a whole world of art. Using print as the key medium, we showcased a variety of artistic styles and developed a witty tone of voice that could stand out from the rest of the category. The ambition was to leverage art that we had saved, to highlight the indispensability of the National Art Pass.

Initially this took the form of 'single artwork' ads, each featuring one striking artwork alongside the National Art Pass visual. The ads appeared in national print titles, such as the *Guardian* and *Time Out*, as well as prominent formats on the London Underground – targeting a London commuter audience (Figure 12).

Figure 12: Campaign advertising (print and online), 2012–2013

The process of securing image rights and permissions to use the various artworks in this way was not a simple one (the ad below had to be approved by the Queen, for example), but it allowed us to visualise the breadth of art on offer throughout the UK, all accessible via the National Art Pass (Figure 13).

Figure 13: Campaign advertising (print and online), 2014–2015

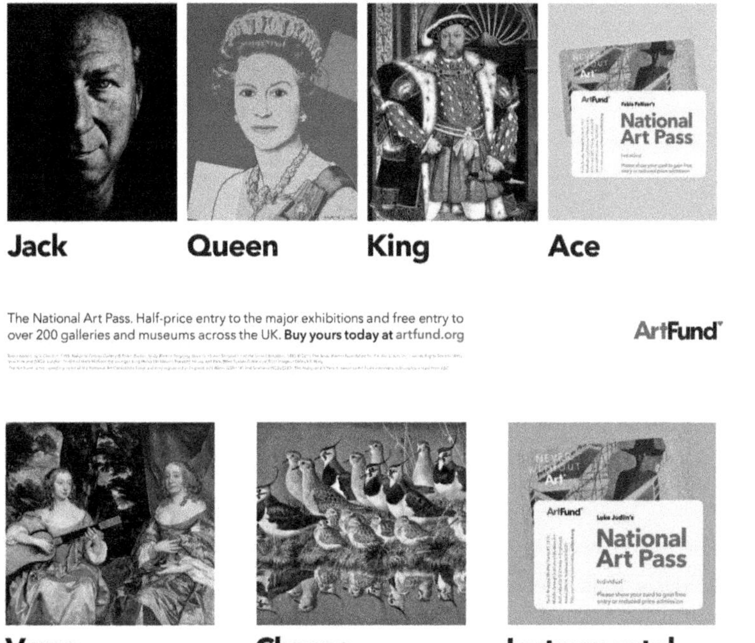

Chapter 3: Driving relevance (2015–2016)

In early 2015, the Department for Culture, Media & Sport reported a 4% increase in visits to major museums.[18] But these headline figures were hiding a worrying trend; visitor number growth was increasingly coming from tourism, rather than local residents. Whilst over 40% of holiday visits to the UK included museum or gallery trips,[19] domestic visitors to the National Gallery and the Tate Galleries had dropped 20% since 2009 (Figure 14).

Figure 14: UK art gallery visitor numbers drop

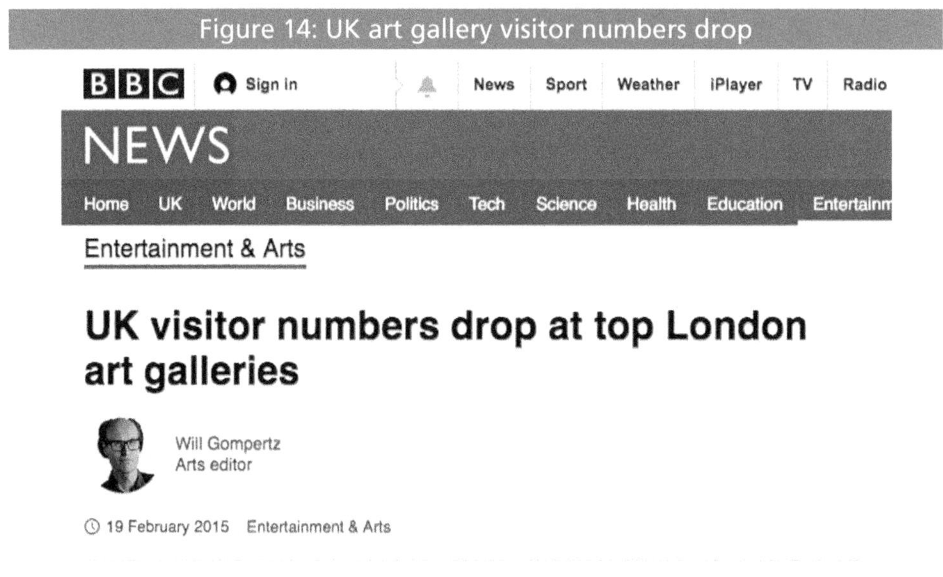

BBC Sign in News Sport Weather iPlayer TV Radio

NEWS

Home UK World Business Politics Tech Science Health Education Entertainm

Entertainment & Arts

UK visitor numbers drop at top London art galleries

Will Gompertz
Arts editor

19 February 2015 Entertainment & Arts

This presented a significant problem for the Art Fund, which relied exclusively on domestic members. So we set out to understand how we might further optimise the National Art Pass's performance.

Sleepwalking past art

Research told us that there were two main barriers to acquiring new Art Fund members:

1. *Low awareness of London's hidden gems:* People struggled to see past the internationally famous museums and galleries, such as the Tate, the Science Museum and the Natural History Museum – the majority of which offered free entry (and therefore the National Art Pass benefits were less compelling[20]). By contrast, awareness of 'hidden gems' such as the Cartoon Museum and the Courtauld Gallery was significantly lower.
2. *The category lacked urgency:* It is too easy to put off going to see art. Unlike the first weekend of a new blockbuster film or when Glastonbury tickets go on sale, exhibitions and the art world in general can lack the energy, excitement and urgency that can turn interest into action.

Marketing the location

Focusing on London, our approach to addressing these barriers was to highlight the *proximity* of art in the city, not just the variety.

Working closely with Transport for London, we developed a media approach that allowed us to tailor each ad to its location – referencing how close people were to intriguing works of art, in steps, stops or minutes.

By not showing the art, we hoped to pique people's curiosity and get them to actually visit the museums and galleries and see the art for themselves. It also gave us a more cost-effective and flexible production model (Figure 15).

Figure 15: Campaign posters on the London Underground, 2015

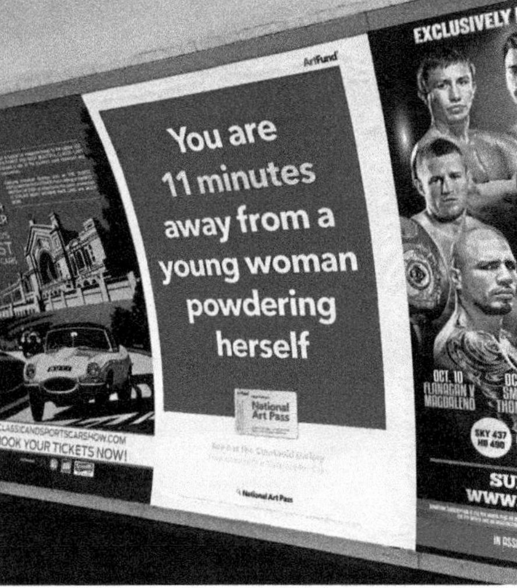

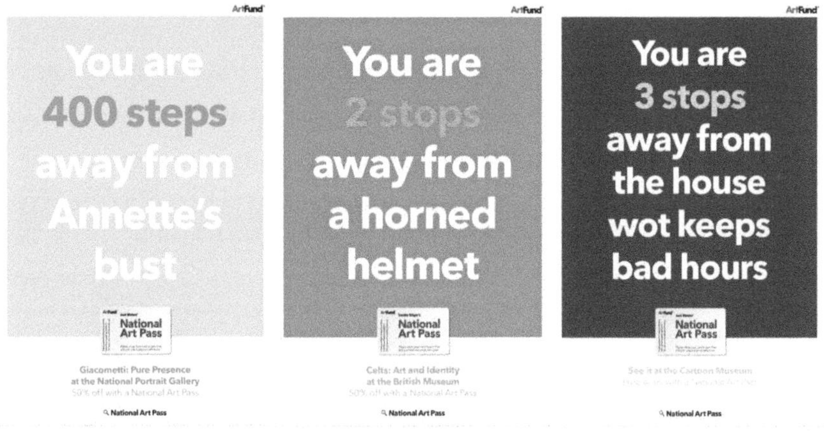

Whilst we didn't expect people to change their plans and visit these venues straight away, the work was designed to drive response and we included a prominent call to action (Search: National Art Pass) to drive people online to find out more about the National Art Pass and what was on around them.

Results

The launch of the National Art Pass has surpassed all expectations, far beyond the membership target and the ambition to lower the average member age.

The Art Fund's limited resources mean that we have not been able to produce detailed econometric analysis, but we are able to show the scale of the effect and attribute it to marketing by looking at a variety of data.

The way in which the campaign worked to increase profit can be summarised by the model shown in Figure 16.

Figure 16: Profit increase model

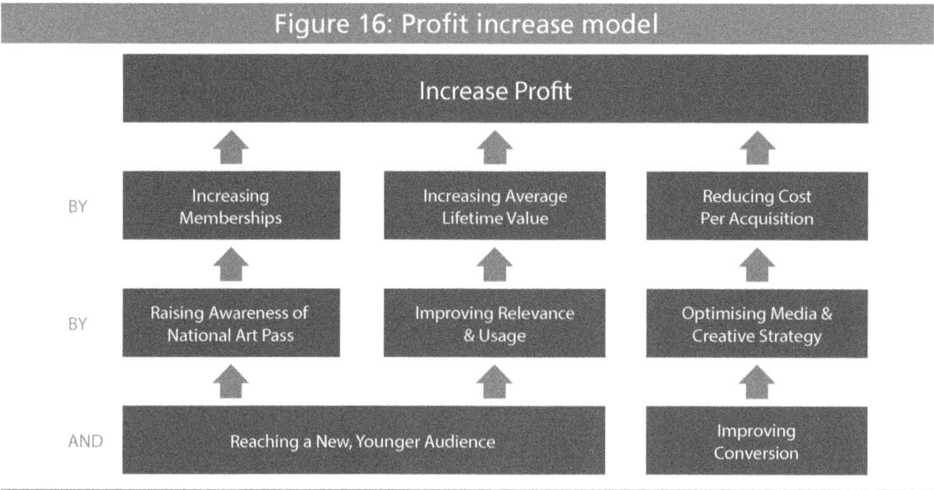

In proving the impact of marketing, we will start by looking at memberships and the National Art Pass, before moving on to consider the broader impact on the Art Fund brand and organisation.

1. The impact on memberships

New memberships more than doubled in the first year after the launch of the National Art Pass and by 2015 were 174% higher than in 2010 (Figure 17).

Figure 17: New memberships, 2008–2015

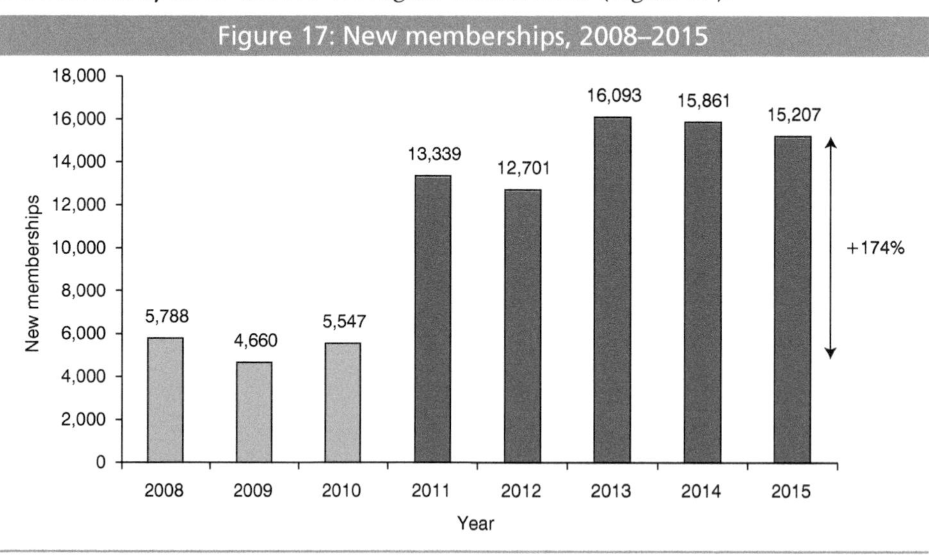

These new memberships have driven a 60% increase in total memberships between 2010 and 2015, with strong growth every year (Figure 18).

Figure 18: Total members, 2008–2015

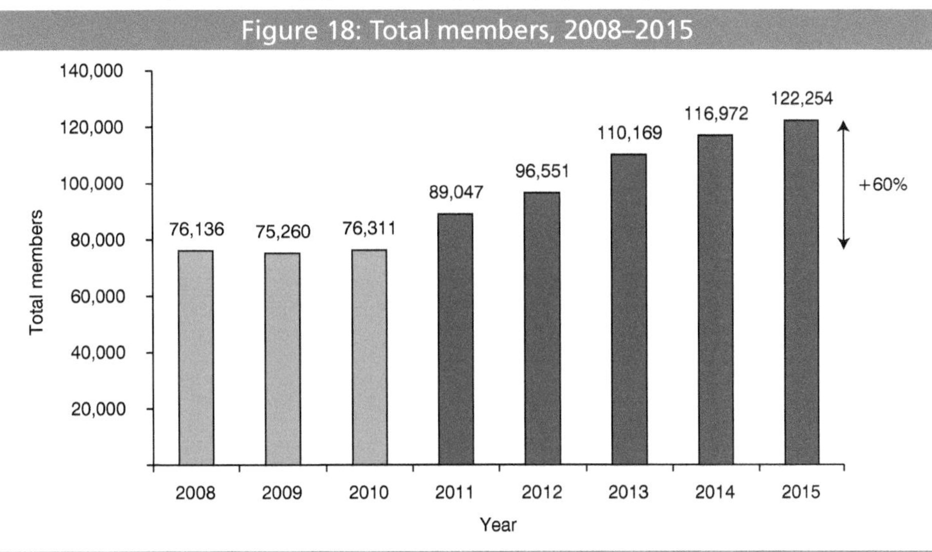

The campaign has successfully reached a new, younger audience, with the average age of new members dropping by over a decade from 2010 to 2015 (Figure 19).

Figure 19: Average age of new members, 2010–2015

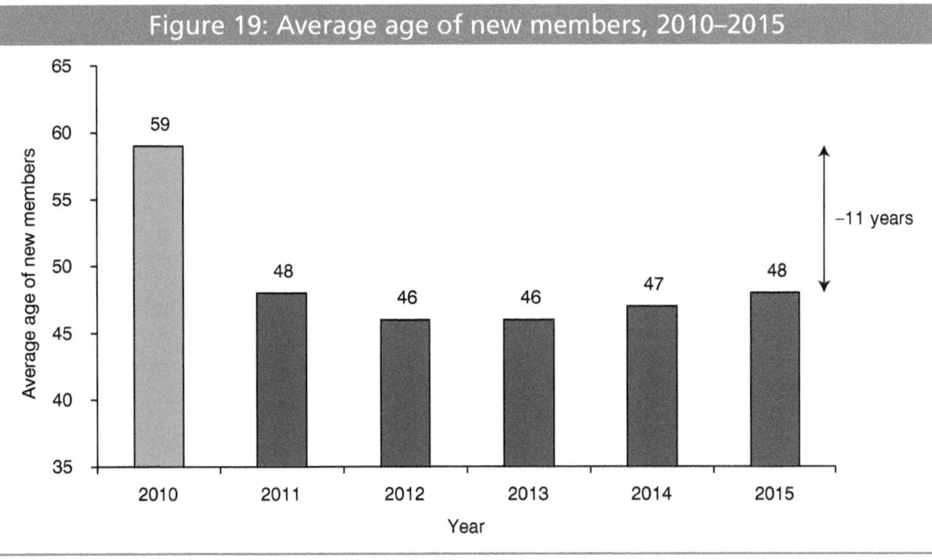

This has helped the average age of all members fall from 66 in 2010 to 58 in 2015 (Figure 20).

Figure 20: Average age of total membership base, 2010–2015

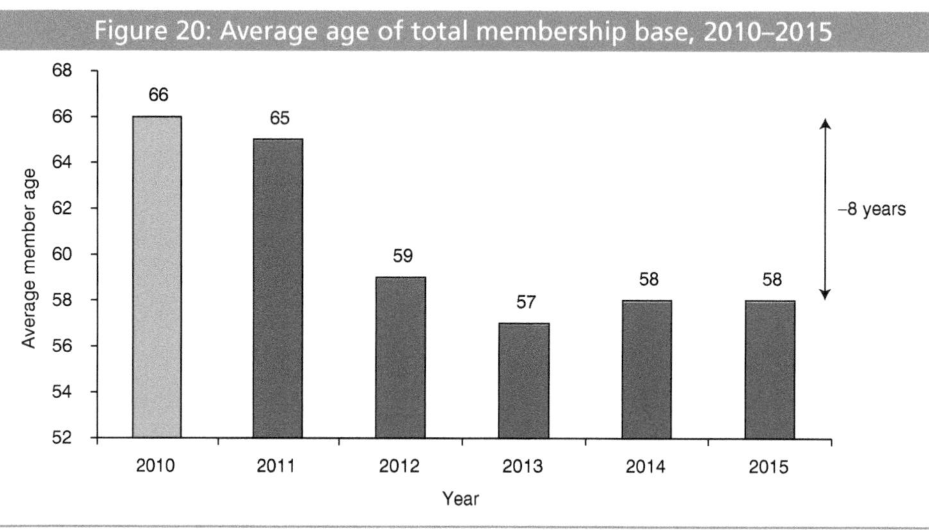

2. The impact on revenue and costs

The revenue generated from memberships (or National Art Pass sales from 2011), rather than bequests and other sources of income, has increased by 85% in five years (Figure 21).

Figure 21: Revenue from memberships / National Art Pass sales, 2010–2015

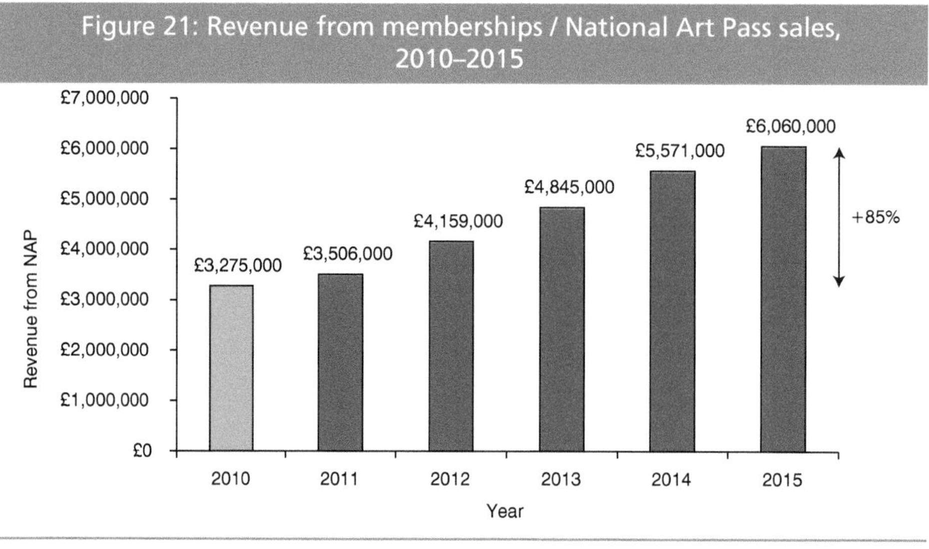

As a result, the proportion of total Art Fund revenues generated by memberships has also increased over the same period (Figure 22).

Figure 22: Memberships / National Art Pass sales as a proportion of total revenue, 2010–2015[21]

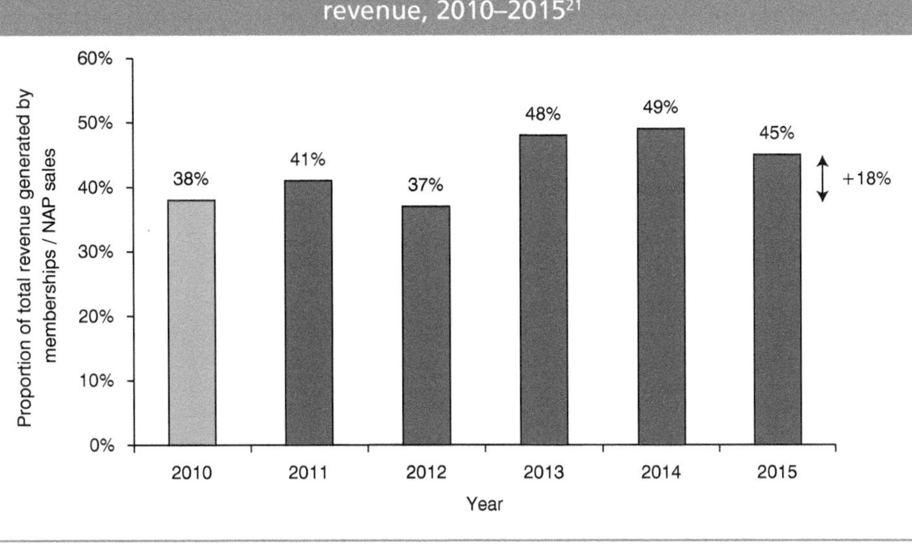

The media strategy and creative approach has also seen the cost per acquisition improve by nearly 15% since 2011, from £92 to £79 (Figure 23).

Figure 23: Average cost per acquisition, 2011–2015

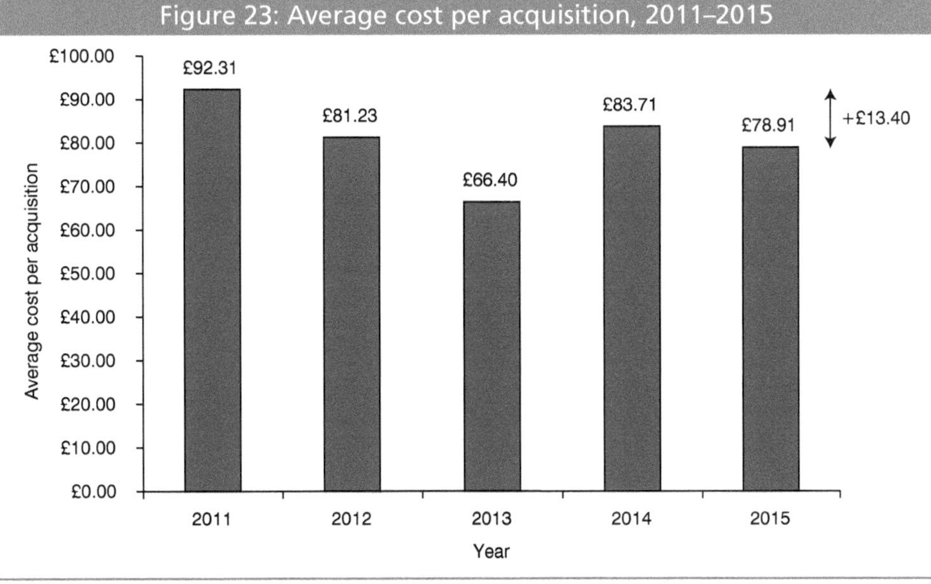

The reframing of Art Fund membership as the National Art Pass has also justified a higher membership price. The Art Fund has been able to increase the cost of an individual membership (the most popular option) by 28% in five years, at a time of disinflation.[22] The costs of double and family memberships have also increased over the same period, by 40% and 37% respectively (Figure 24).

Figure 24: Membership rates, 2006–2015

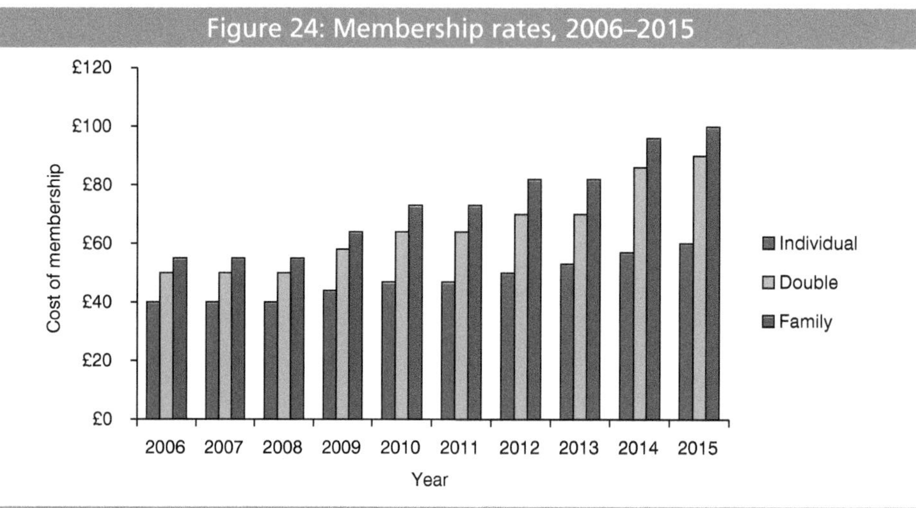

This increase has been achieved without a drop in retention rates, which have remained stable above 80% (Figure 25).

Figure 25: Average membership retention rate, 2006–2015

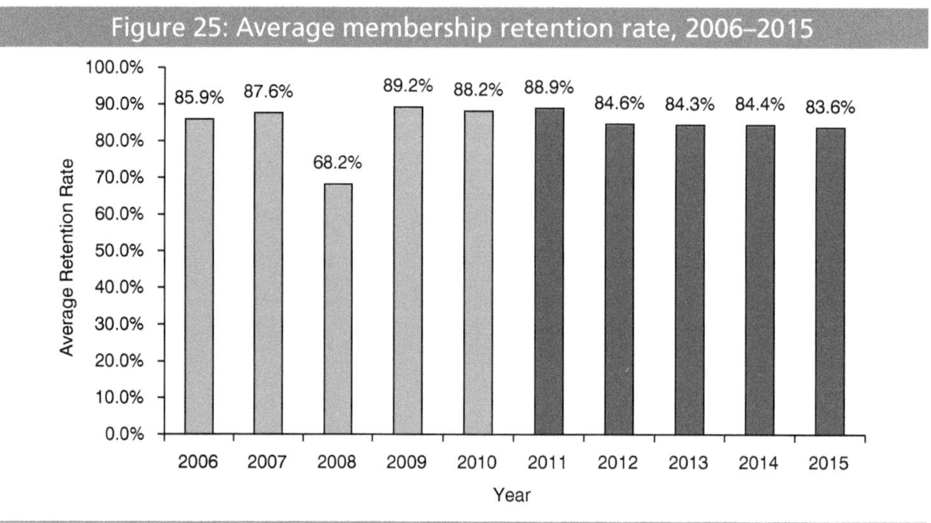

This higher membership cost and stable retention rate have seen the average lifetime value (+36%) and the average lifetime profit contribution per member (+17%) increase significantly since 2011 (Figures 26 and 27).

Figure 26: Average lifetime value, 2011–2015

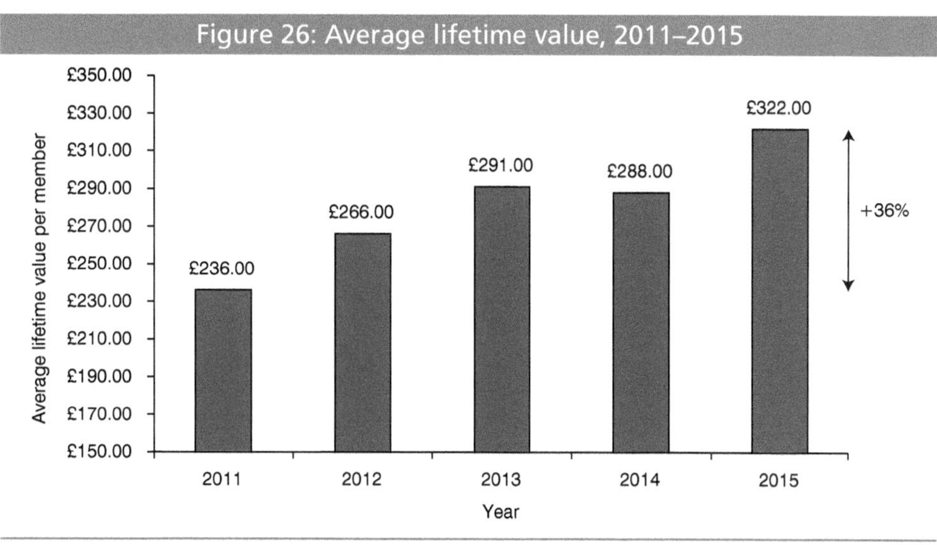

Figure 27: Average lifetime net profit contribution per member, 2011–2015

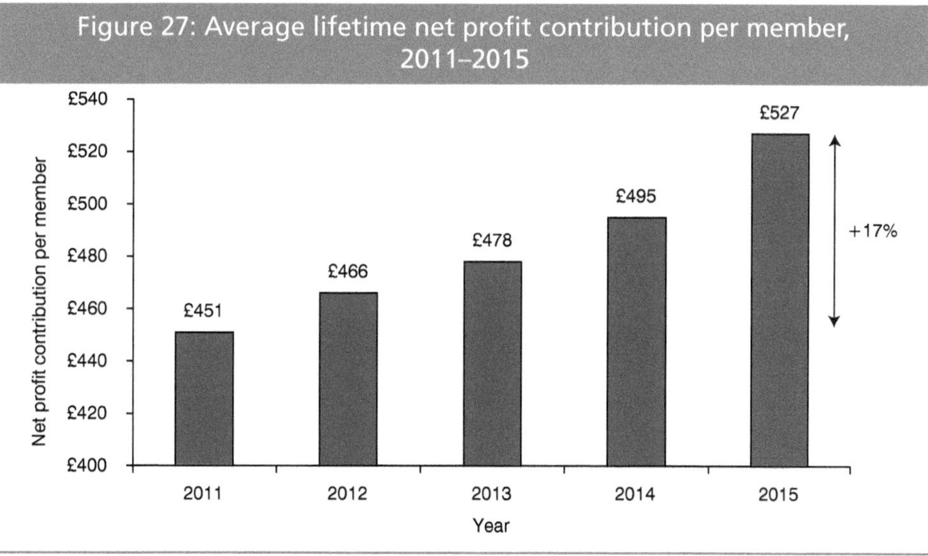

Correspondingly, payback per member has dropped from 3.9 years to 2.4 years over the same period (a 38% improvement) (Figure 28).

Figure 28: Average payback per member, 2011–2015

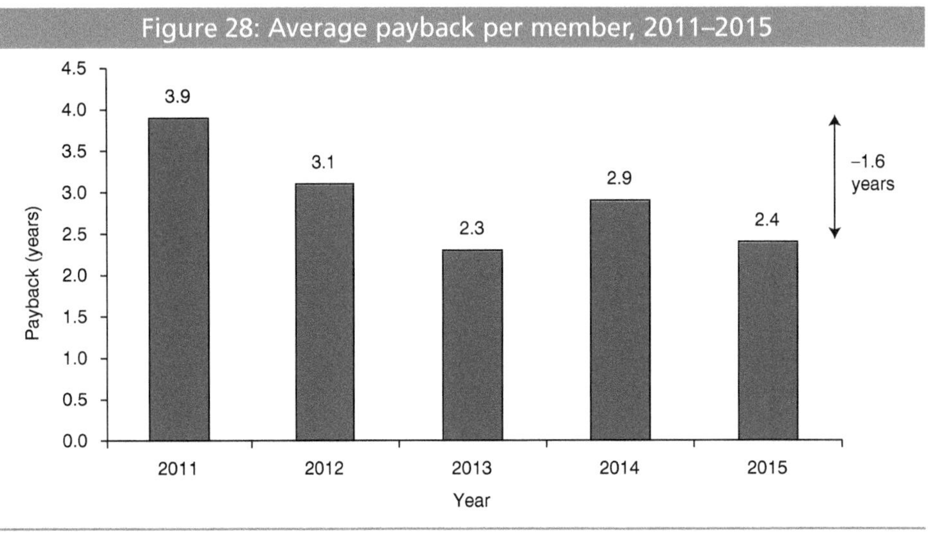

3. Proving the impact of marketing

Awareness of the National Art Pass amongst our target audience reached an impressive 22% within a few months of launch and increased by a further 150% over the next four years of the campaign (Figure 29).

Figure 29: Awareness of the National Art Pass, 2011–2015[23]

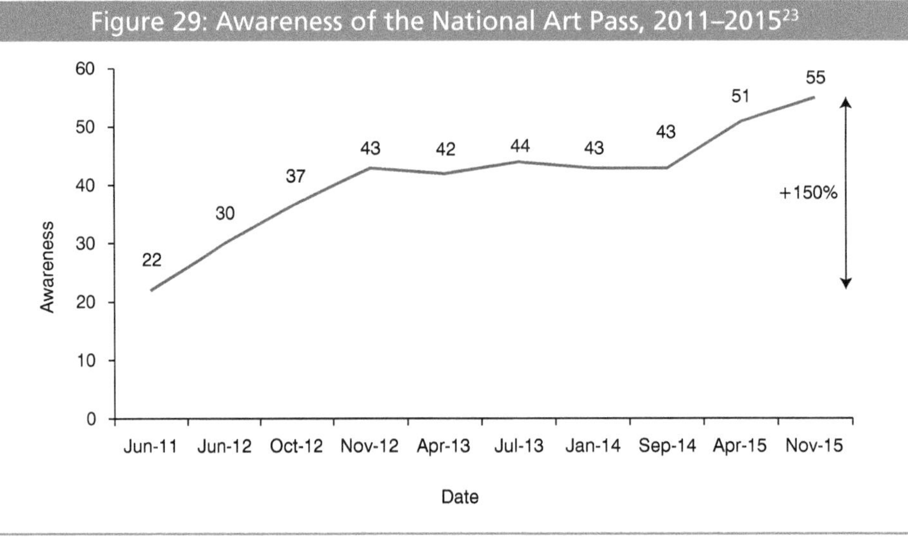

This increase in awareness has been driven by the three main channels used during the campaign (press, outdoor and online) (Figure 30).

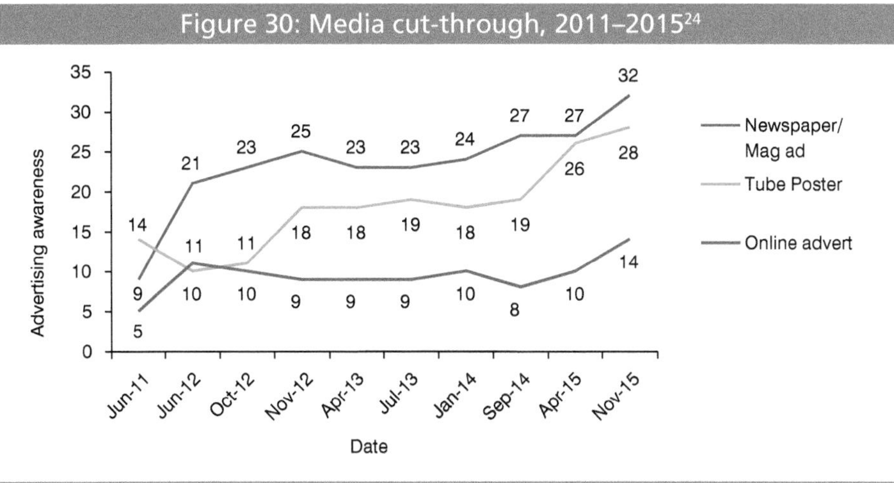

Figure 30: Media cut-through, 2011–2015[24]

There has been a strong correlation between membership sales and the dates of marketing activity. Sales in the launch year spiked precisely in line with media bursts, which gave us confidence that media could drive sales rather than just awareness (Figure 31).

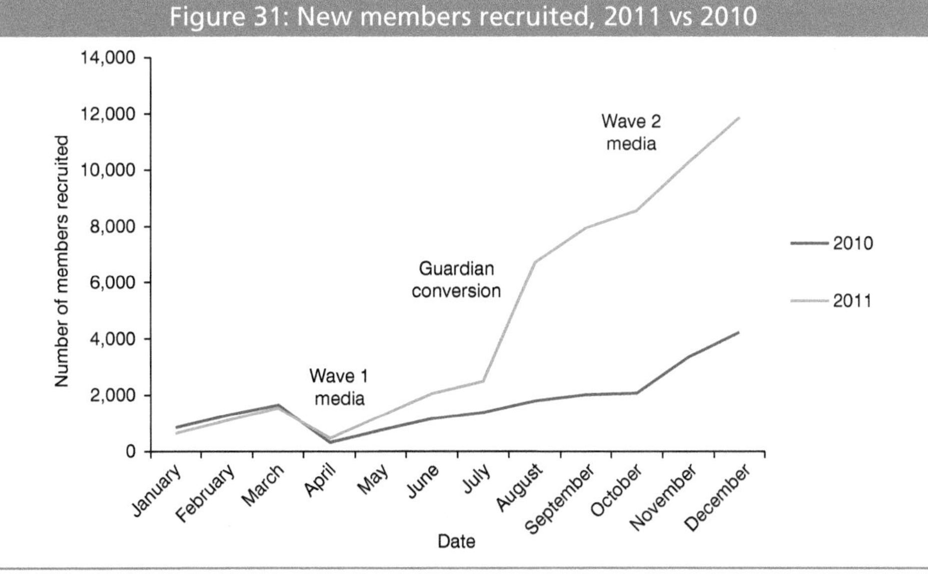

Figure 31: New members recruited, 2011 vs 2010

In subsequent years, we continued to see a clear correlation between media spend and sales, as well as a steady increase in December sales. As intended, the National Art Pass became an increasingly popular gift (Figure 32).

Figure 32: Media spend and number of members recruited, 2012–2015

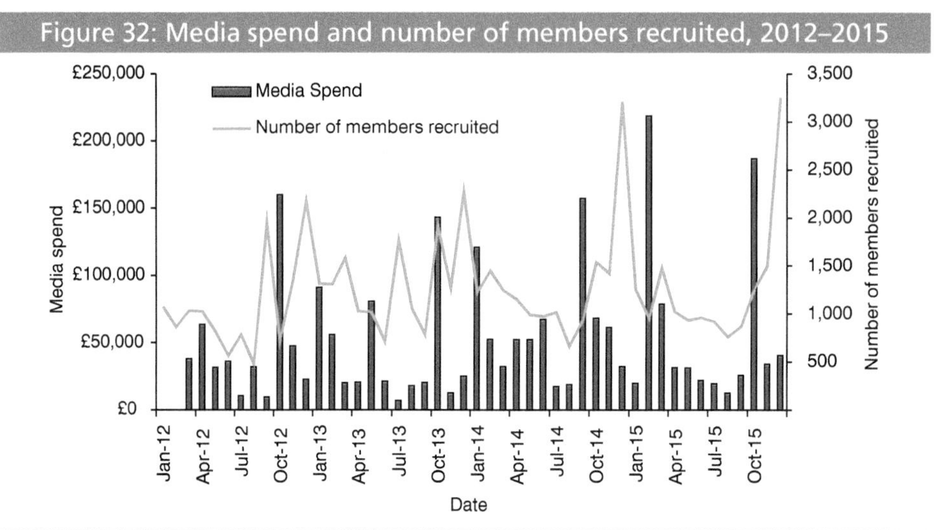

Isolating gift memberships makes this trend even clearer (Figure 33).

Figure 33: Gift membership sales, 2011–2015

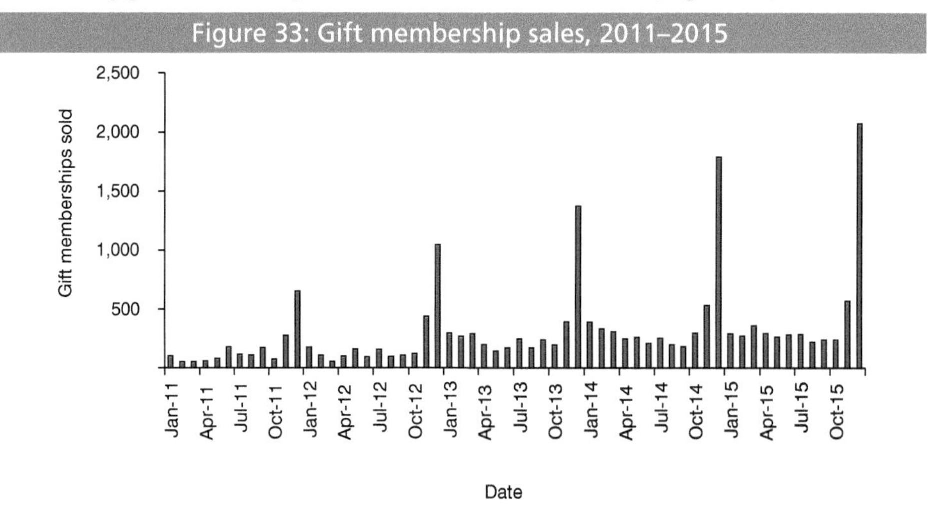

Visits to the National Art Pass page on artfund.org also show a clear correlation with campaign activity over the past five years. Taking the most recent wave of activity as an example, the outdoor ads in the autumn 2015 wave went live on 4 October (featuring a prominent search call to action), which is the same day a significant increase in unique visits can be seen (Figure 34).

Figure 34: Unique visits to the National Art Pass page on artfund.org, September–October 2015

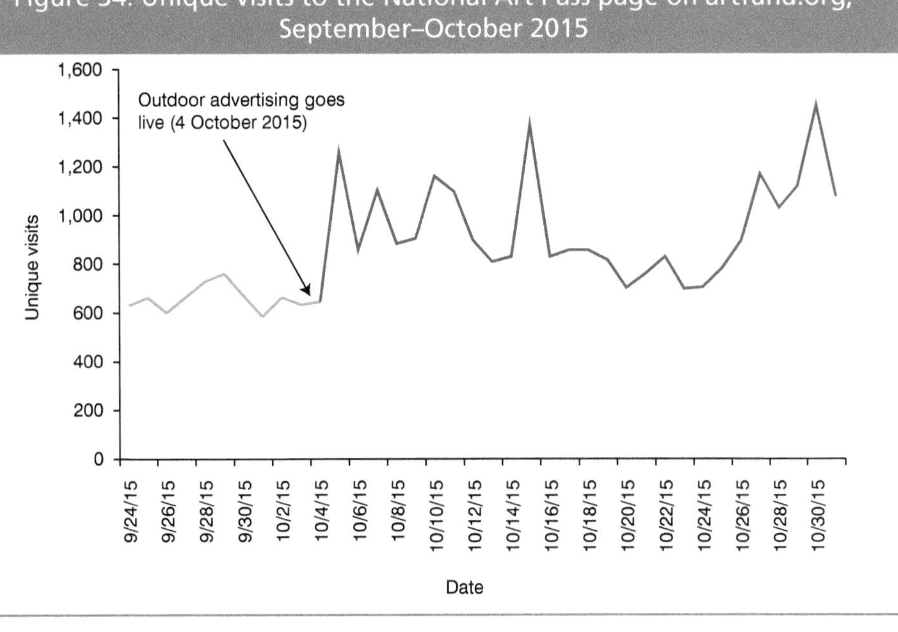

4. Changing perceptions of the Art Fund

Perceptions of the Art Fund have also shifted significantly since launching the National Art Pass in 2011. It is now perceived by most people as a cultural membership organisation, as well as a charity (Figure 35).

Figure 35: Perceptions of the Art Fund (amongst those aware), 2011–2015[25]

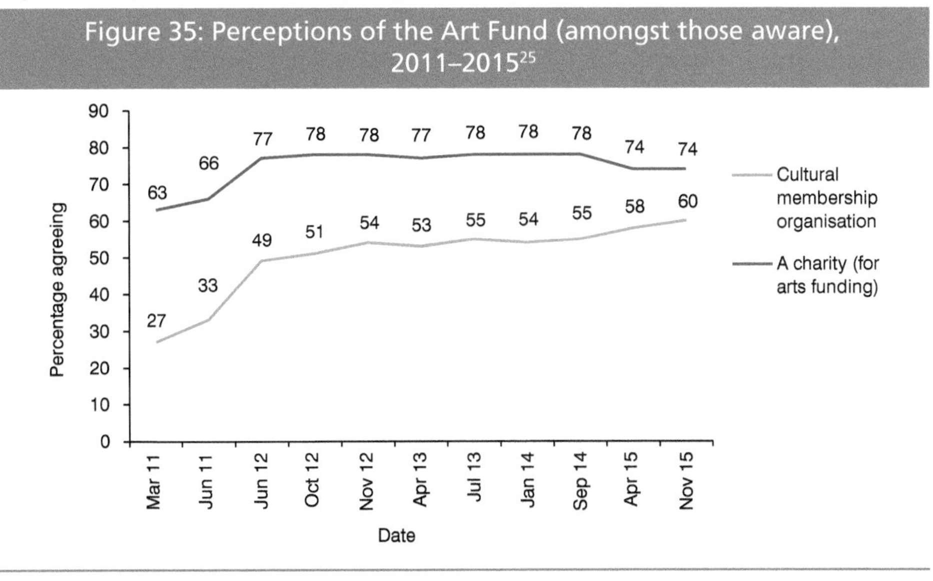

Since 2013 we have tracked perceptions of the Art Fund as a reliable and valuable source of information. Perceptions have improved by 32% in less than three years, at a time when other organisations have seen no improvements (Figure 36).

Figure 36: Perceptions of the Art Fund as a reliable and valuable source of information, 2013–2015[26]

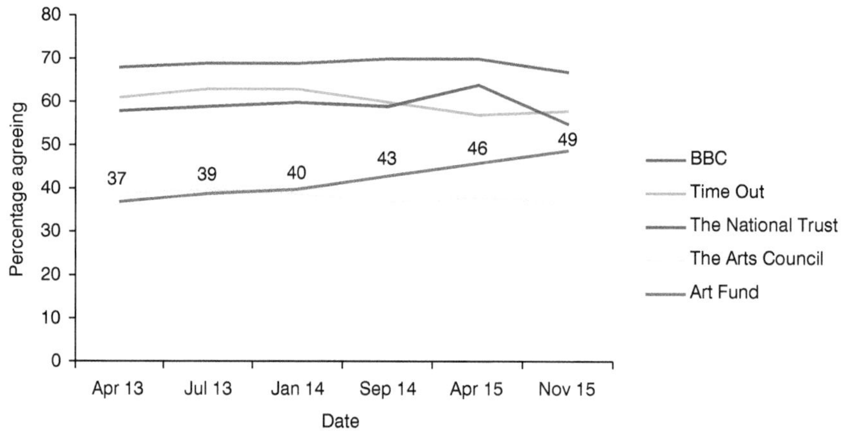

Percentage agreeing
80
70
60
50
40
30
20
10
0
37
39
40
43
46
49
Apr 13
Jul 13
Jan 14
Sep 14
Apr 15
Nov 15
Date
BBC
Time Out
The National Trust
The Arts Council
Art Fund

5. *An improved relationship with museum and gallery partners*

Since launching the National Art Pass in 2011, more venues have agreed to offer free and discounted entry to Art Fund members. We have also been able to secure shop and café discounts for Art Fund members in some locations (Figure 37).

Figure 37: The number of venues offering discounts to Art Fund members, 2011–2015

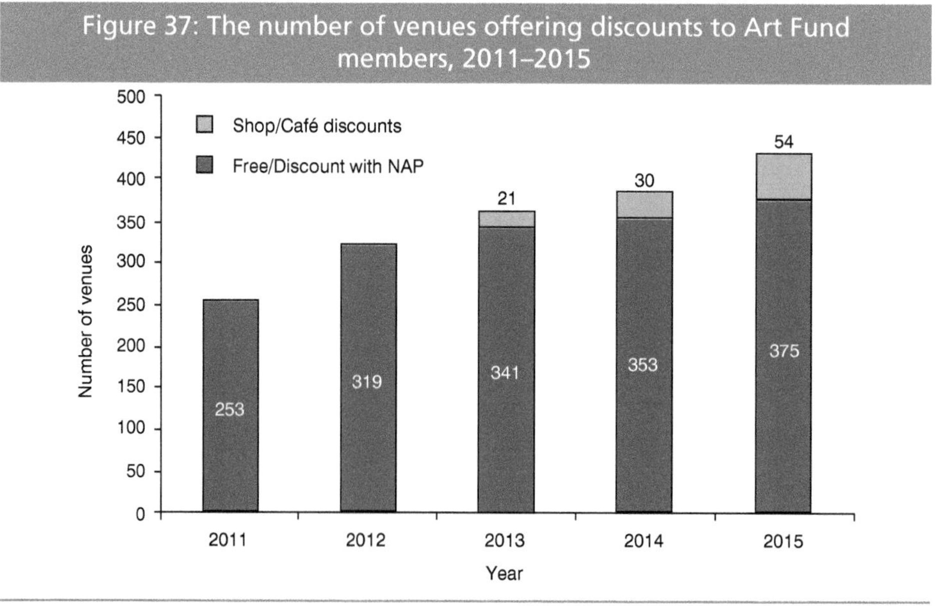

Eliminating other factors

1. The price of membership did not decrease

As we have shown, the price of membership has actually increased significantly over the period in question.

There have been sporadic trial membership offers between 2011 and 2015, but these have not been counted as memberships in the results.

2. The benefits did not significantly change

The benefits of Art Fund membership have not changed; they have just been framed and presented in a new way.

The main benefits remain free and discounted entry to museums, galleries, castles and historic houses throughout the UK. Whilst the number of venues offering free and discounted entry to National Art Pass users has grown since the campaign launched, this has not altered the way in which the benefits are communicated, either in advertising or in owned channels such as the artfund.org website. Therefore this cannot account for the growth in membership.

Indeed, we would claim increased participation of museums and galleries as evidence of effect.

3. Growth greatly outperformed the sector (Art Fund's success wasn't simply a category effect)

We don't have data for comparable membership schemes within the arts sector, but we did track awareness of them, which shows clearly that the National Art Pass was the only scheme in growth over the period in question (Figure 38).

Figure 38: Awareness of the National Art Pass and other membership schemes, 2011–2015[27]

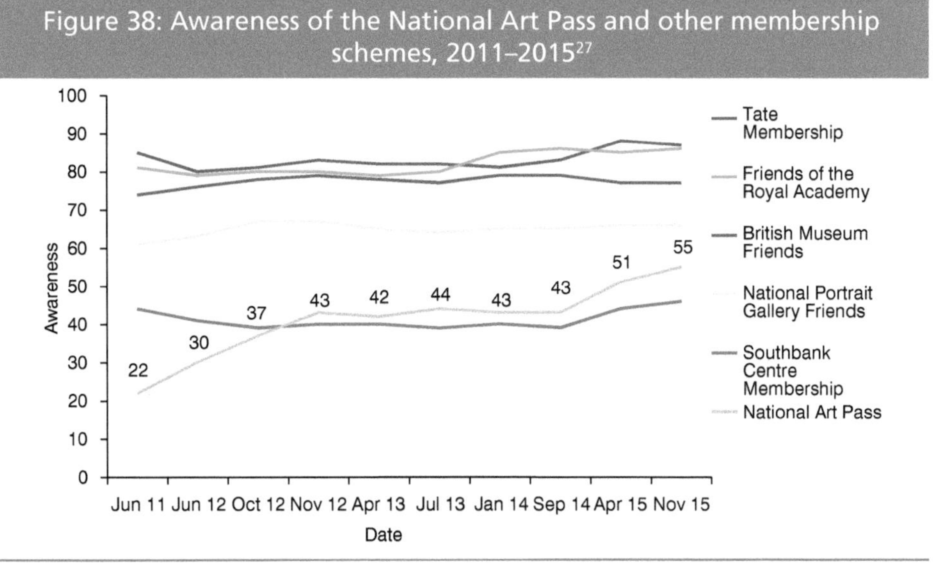

Furthermore, the overall proportion of museum and gallery visits coming from UK residents (the only visitors relevant to the Art Fund) actually dropped from 59%

in 2010–2011 to 53% in 2014–2015, and many prominent venues such as the Tate Galleries and the National Gallery saw a significant drop in domestic visitors.[28]

Calculating ROI

Taking the (pre-campaign) 2010 figure of 5,547 new members per year as the benchmark, we can calculate the profit upswing attributable to this campaign by multiplying the incremental members added each year by the average lifetime profit contribution per member.

This gives us a *total incremental profit of £12.9m* (Table 1).

Table 1: Membership and revenues

	New members	Benchmark	Incremental members	Average lifetime net profit contribution per member	Incremental revenue per member
2011	13,339	5,547	7,792	£236	£1,838,912
2012	12,701	5,547	7,154	£266	£1,902,964
2013	16,093	5,547	10,546	£291	£3,068,886
2014	15,861	5,547	10,314	£288	£2,970,432
2015	15,207	5,547	9,660	£322	£3,110,520
Total incremental profit					£12,891,714

Note that this is *pure profit rather than revenue*, as the cost of all forms of marketing has already been removed from the member contribution figures.

The marketing budgets per year are shown in Table 2.

Table 2: Marketing budget by year

	Marketing spend
2011	£745,000
2012	£451,533
2013	£515,155
2014	£732,898
2015	£721,699
Total	£3,166,285

With a total media cost of £3,166,285, we can calculate the ROI as incremental profit / marketing spend = £12,891,714/£3,166,285 = **£4.07 for every £1 spent.**

Conclusion

This paper demonstrates the power of framing and the value of a long-term approach to brand building.

In the era of 'always on' marketing, it serves as a reminder that less can still be more. £12.9m incremental profit has been achieved with a disarmingly simple media plan, crucially developed *alongside* the creative work, rather than either side of it.

The past five years have also seen a step-change in the self-perception of the Art Fund. It is no coincidence that the company's five-year 'marketing-led era' (after 100 years of purpose-led tin-rattling) coincided with a bold move from Millais House in sleepy South Kensington to state of the art headquarters between Central Saint Martins and Google in King's Cross.

Figure 39: Artworks retained or acquired with assistance of the Art Fund

Fifty per cent of employees now rate the Art Fund as 'one of the best' places to work, compared to 27% as recently as 2013. Whilst this kind of marketing effect is difficult to quantify in ROI terms, its significance should not be overlooked.

We now think of ourselves as an e-tailer, not simply a charity.
Carolyn Young, Director of Marketing, Art Fund

Finally, the Art Fund's purpose (saving art for the nation) has been well served by the creation and successful marketing of the National Art Pass. The £12.9m extra profit has helped museums and galleries to acquire or retain an astonishing range of art since 2011, which might otherwise have been lost.[29]

Notes

1. Source: The National Council for Voluntary Organisations.
2. Source: Art Fund internal data.
3. Total memberships fell by over 2,300 between 2006 and 2010 (Source: Art Fund internal data).
4. Source: Charities Aid Foundation, UK Giving 2014 report.
5. Source: The Charity Commission.
6. Source: The National Council for Voluntary Organisations.
7. Source: The Impact of the Cuts on Museums, The Museum Association, July 2011.
8. Source: Art Fund Strategic Plan 2011–2014.
9. Source: Muse Membership Qualitative Debrief, 2010.
10. https://www.youtube.com/watch?v=jhYmGx9q7v4.
11. https://www.youtube.com/watch?v=cMN8iQ7dLaI.
12. This chapter covers similar ground to the 2012 IPA paper, 'Art Fund: Never Without Art'.
13. Source: Muse Membership Research Qualitative Debrief, 2010.
14. Source: Muse Membership Research Qualitative Debrief, 2010.
15. Source: Muse Segmentation.
16. The average annual media budget during this phase (2012–2015) was £605,321.
17. During the period January 2012–April 2015, total marketing spend was £2,048,536 and total spend on press and outdoor advertising was £1,464,268 (71.5%).
18. Source: Department for Culture, Media & Sport, 2015.
19. Source: Visit Britain, 2015.
20. Whilst the National Art Pass offered its holders 50% off key exhibitions at these locations, many people were happy to visit the permanent collections, which were free to all.
21. Total revenue per year excludes a small number of one-off items, such as the profit generated from the disposal of a fixed asset in 2012, and special appeals, in order to better compare revenues over the six years in question.
22. The Consumer Prices Index was significantly lower in December 2015 than in December 2010 (Source: Office for National Statistics).
23. Source: Muse Brand Tracking. Q. Which of the following are you aware of…? (Tick all that apply).
24. Source: Muse Brand Tracking. Q. Have you read, heard or noticed anything about the National Art Pass recently in any of the following ways....? (Tick all that apply).
25. Source: Muse Brand Tracking. Q. Which of the following descriptions best fits your understanding of The Art Fund? (Tick all that apply).
26. Source: Muse Brand Tracking. Q. Which of the following brands do you consider to be a reliable and valuable source of information for people wishing to visit museums, galleries and other cultural attractions? (Tick all that apply).
27. Source: Muse Brand Tracking. Q. Which of the following are you aware of…? (Tick all that apply).
28. UK visits to these galleries fell by 20% between 2008/09 and 2014/15. Source: Department for Culture and Sport.
29. The works shown are, in order, 'Portrait of Mademoiselle Claus' (Manet), 'Self Portrait' (van Dyck), 'Still Life under the Lamp' (Picasso), 'The Kongouro from New Holland' (Stubbs), 'Salisbury Cathedral from the Meadows' (Constable).

Direct Line

Direct Line: we solve problems

By Carl Bratton and Ann Constantine, Direct Line Group; Nic Pietersma, Ebiquity
Contributing authors: Adrian Brook, MediaCom; Wez Eathorne, Hall & Partners; Richard Huntington, Saatchi & Saatchi
Credited companies: Direct Line Group; Bonamy Finch; Closer to Brands; Flamingo; SkyIQ; Truth

Summary

This paper outlines how a new brand idea can be a driving force behind an organisation's creative execution, proposition development, and operational improvement. Faced with share losses to price comparison websites and competitor brands, Direct Line adopted 'hassle free insurance that just works "as guaranteed"' as a principle to organise its way of working and win back consumer trust and business. In addition to changing its offers, customer service and website, Direct Line deployed Winston Wolf – Harvey Keitel's fixer character from *Pulp Fiction* – in its advertising as an archetypical solver of problems with efficiency and courtesy. This case demonstrates that the advertising campaign increased volumes of both car and home insurance quotes, and staunched the decline in the insurer's policies. The overall campaign net profit return was estimated at £1.22 for every £1 invested.

Editor's Comment

Faced with an ambitious task of turning the brand around, this case documented an extremely well-considered comeback that transformed the business from the inside out.

Client Comment

Ann Constantine, Head of Insight and Effectiveness, Direct Line

The launch of 'fixer' heralded a new way of working for Direct Line and a revitalised view of the role brand has to play and ultimately the value it can deliver for us as a business.

During recent years, while we had been cutting inefficient spend correctly, arguably we had gone too far leading to decisions being made through a short-term lens only.

Changing consumer perceptions and ultimately behaviours in what is considered to be a mature market, was always going to be a slow burn. The creative platform would need time to bed in and for consumers to resonate with the propositions.

But in this relatively short space of time, we have seen significant traction across not just our brand metrics but also across our commercials with a consistent and continual upward trajectory. Consequently our attitude and approach to how we measure and evaluate the impact of brand has evolved into using a broader range of tools and techniques to supplement testing and econometrics, ultimately providing richer commercial insight to marketing and the business.

Introduction

An archetype can be defined as an unconsciously known 'pattern of behaviours that, once discovered, helps people better understand themselves and others'.

Stories make use of archetypes to conjure familiar characters seemingly from thin air. The best film scripts can introduce a character and two hours later you feel like you have known them your whole life. The audience instinctively understands the archetypal roles of Hero, Villain, Traitor and Best Friend.

The best stories also have memorable secondary characters. Archetypes that move the plot along; without detracting from the central storyline. the Sage. the Joker. the Fixer.

Quentin Tarantino's *Pulp Fiction* character, Winston Wolf, is the embodiment of the Fixer. He comes into the story, fixes a problem, and then leaves.

Quickly and efficiently.

This is the story of how Direct Line discovered its archetype, rebooted the brand and reversed five years of commercial and brand decline.

Figure 1: Harvey Keitel as Winston Wolf

The backstory

Figure 2: The journey from 1985 to price comparison websites

Jules: The path of the righteous man is beset on all sides...

In 1985 Direct Line revolutionised insurance by cutting out the middle-man. We were famous for taking cost out of insurance. The direct revolution propelled us to market leader inside 12 years, so that by 1997 we were insuring 1 in 10 private cars.[1]

When Direct Line Group floated in the October 2012 IPO, the fundamentals of the business were healthy. We had a large customer base and cash flow was stable. In terms of 'in-force policies' in 2012, Direct Line was still one of the largest direct insurers in the UK for car and home insurance (Tables 1 and 2).[2]

Table 1: Car insurance

	Market share %
Aviva / NU	8.3%
Direct Line	7.7%
Admiral	6.9%
Liverpool V.	6.8%
Tesco	5.2%

Table 2: Home insurance

	Market share %
Aviva	7.0%
Halifax	6.1%
Direct Line	5.5%
Lloyds	4.7%
Churchill	4.7%

But as a business, we had an urgent problem to solve. The marketing model that we had effectively invented in the 1980s, direct response insurance, was broken. Price comparison websites (PCWs) had changed the face of insurance (Figure 3).

Figure 3: Search interest index – Direct Line and major PCW brands

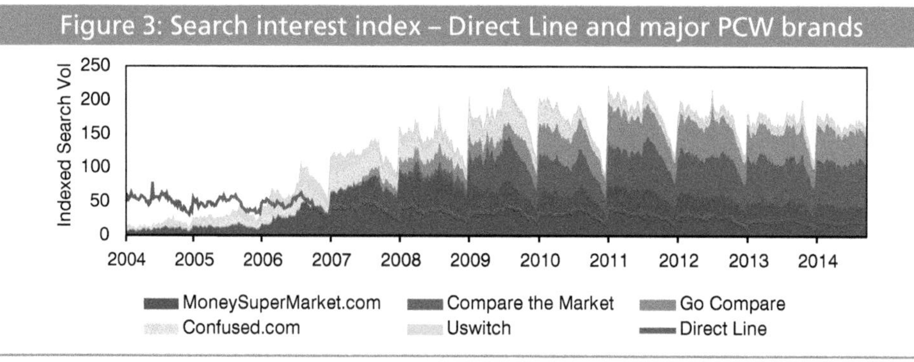

Source: Google Trends. March 2016

In 2005 Direct Line had more search volume than the top five PCWs combined. By 2007, Money Supermarket alone had more search volume than Direct Line.[3]

The market data tell a similar story. The 'direct' component (not sold through PCWs) of the car insurance market effectively halved, falling from c. 40% online share to c. 20% between 2009 and 2016.[4]

PCWs didn't just steal market share. They also put the middle-man back into insurance, put pressure on margins, added to transaction costs, reduced loyalty and commoditised the product (Figure 4).

Figure 4: 'Direct' share of web sales

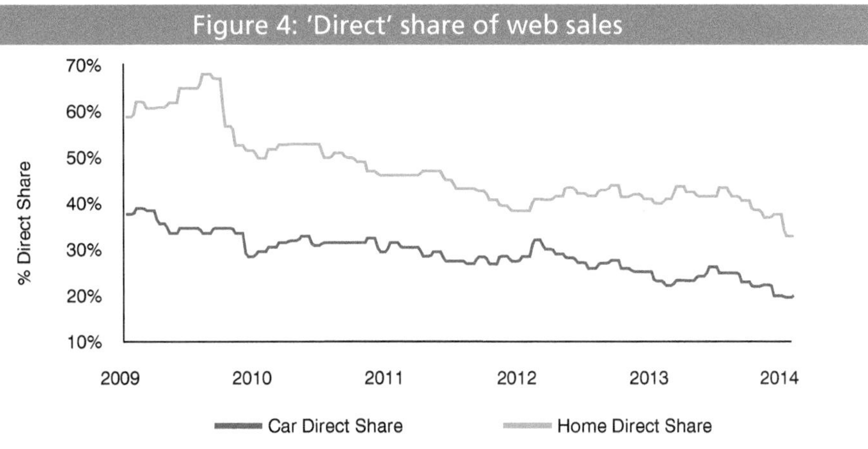

Source: Syndicated sales data. Original data chain-link adjusted for peer group

This technologically-led revolution was a challenge for all insurers, but it was a specific threat to Direct Line because the centre of gravity for our brand had always been 'going direct'.

The scale of the challenge was immense. In effect, PCWs broke Direct Line's business model.

Our quotes and sales (or 'new business') was reliably and predictably in decline year after year. We had a declining share of a declining market (Figure 5).[5]

Figure 5: Annual quote volumes (index and scale adjusted)

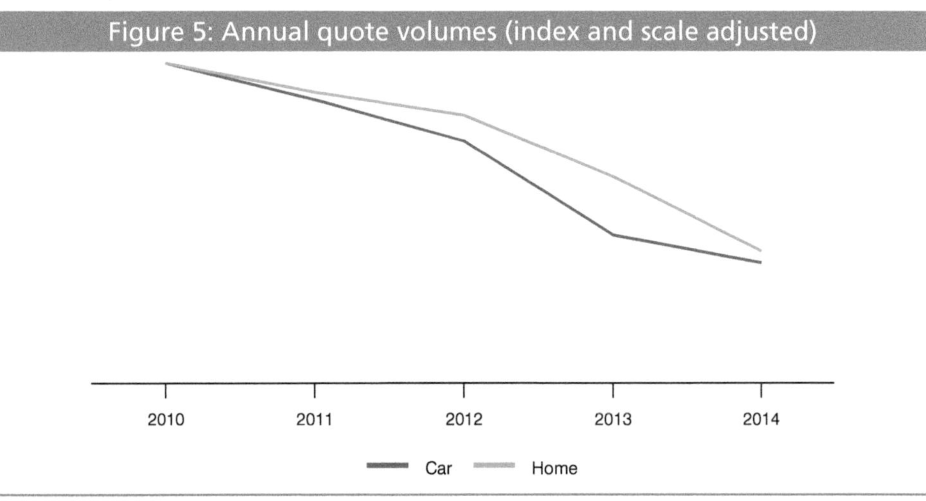

Source: DLG internal data

Declining brand in a distrusted category

Figure 6: Declining brand in a distrusted category

Jules: If my answers scare you, you should cease asking scary questions.

It would have been very easy for us to look at PCWs and conclude we just had a ‘technology problem’. But we weren’t just losing ground to PCWs; we were losing ground to direct insurers too. We saw this reflected in ‘branded search’ data – Direct Line went from the uncontested leader in 2004 to part of the pack by 2014 (Figure 7).

Figure 7: Search interest index for various insurance brands

Google Search Interest Indexed

Direct Line, Aviva/NU, Churchill, Liverpool Victoria, More Than

Source: Google Trends. Search data from 2004 to 2014.

By the first half of 2014, preference scores for Direct Line and a number of competitors sat between 10% and 12% – indicating that we had become just another member of a commoditised and undifferentiated competitor set (Figure 8).

Figure 8: Preference range of larger car insurance brands

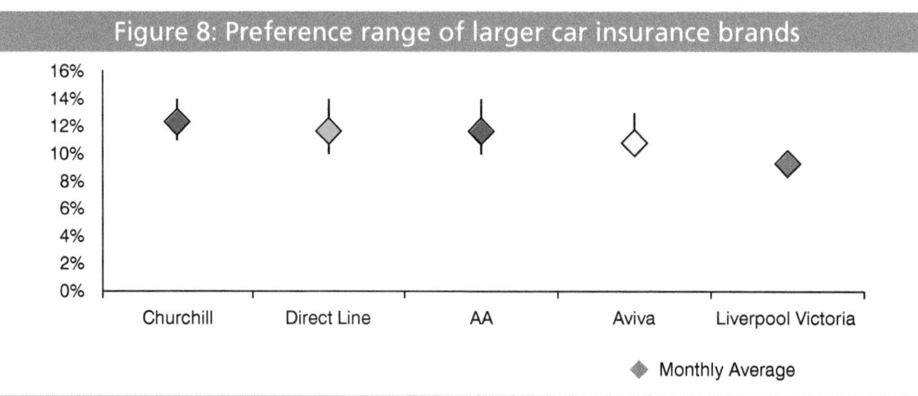

Our brand tracking identified a decline in many key metrics. Car insurance spontaneous awareness fell by 10% and consideration fell by 15% between 2012 and 2014 (Figure 9).[6]

Figure 9: Spontaneous brand total mentions

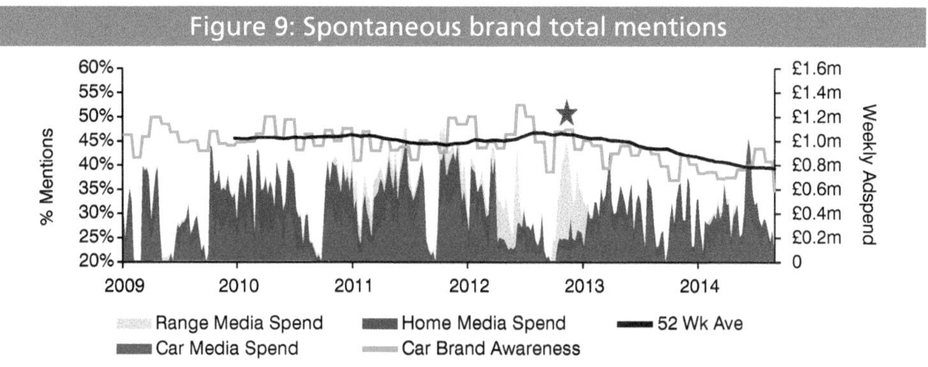

Source: Hall & Partners brand tracking survey data. Ebiquity Portfolio spend estimates for Direct Line inc. TV, Radio, Press, Outdoor & Cinema

The decline over this period can in part be explained by reduced above-the-line ad spend from 2013 (see above). But it also aligns with the launch of our 2012 'Take the Direct Line' creative platform (starred in Figure 9).

The 2012 creative platform was an attempt to update the look and feel of the Direct Line brand and stem the decline we were seeing in our commercial KPIs. We wanted to present ourselves to the world as a slick, modern business. We wanted to demonstrate scale. It needed to make us look 'big'. See the transcript in Figure 10.

Figure 10: 'Take the Direct Line'

With over 6000 of us across the UK, as well as specialists ready to secure your home or business, be there after severe weather, get you back on the road and even help protect your pet, we're here when you need us. **Take the direct line.**

Last year, we put over 300 thousand motorists back on the road and made sure they didn't lose out if it wasn't their fault. We protect their no claims discount when their cars were vandalised or hit by an uninsured driver. And right now, if you call us or visit us online, all new customers will get 15% off car and van insurance. **Take the direct line.**

However the message that Direct Line is 'big' doesn't really convey a benefit to the consumer. Nothing about the creative was disruptive. Some of the executions were simply communicating price signals, but for car insurance the price signals were particularly weak with only 10% to 20% discount on offer.[7]

Our biggest 'brand' concern was a significant fall in distinctiveness. One Hall & Partners respondent summed it up rather well: *'It's just the usual, bland, boring car insurance ad'*.[8]

This was of critical importance to us. We had gone from the consumer champion known for 'cutting out the middle-man' to an undifferentiated brand in a deeply distrusted industry (Figure 11).

Figure 11: Percentage of UK consumers citing complete or moderate trust

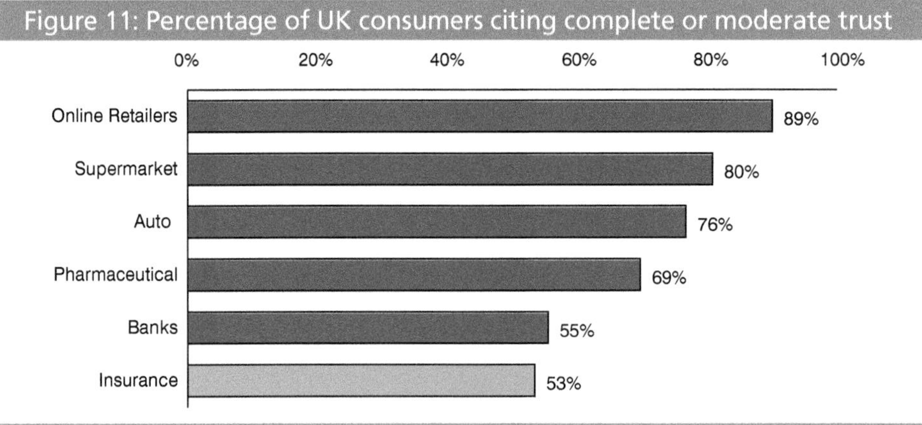

Source: Ernst & Young. Global Consumer Insurance Survey 2014.

The product had become commoditised and the momentum was against direct brands. Unless we could differentiate our brand and rebuild trust with the consumer, we couldn't reasonably expect consumers to choose us over any cheaper competitor.

We didn't just have an advertising problem or indeed a marketing problem. In fact, there was a problem with the brand itself. Our 'go direct' *raison d'être* was no longer meaningful or sufficient.

Yes, we needed to rethink the creative. But to stem the decline we also needed to rethink our identity, our propositions, how we did business. Direct Line, in its current form, was no longer sustainable.

So we got to work finding a solution.

The insight behind Fixer

Figure 12: The insight behind Fixer

Mr Wolf: Let's get down to brass tacks, gentleman. If I was informed correctly, the clock is ticking, is that right, Jimmie?

Direct Line has always had a strong commitment to evidence-based decision-making; using both qualitative and quantitative methods. The 2014 reboot, or the 'Fixer reboot' as it became known internally, was initially driven by focus group research[9] which identified the most effective brand territory that the new Direct Line brand could feasibly occupy.

The qualitative research pointed us towards a group of people who were within reach for the Direct Line brand. This attitudinal group tend to be assertive and look for a product that they can be confident in, that is flexible and that offers good value. These consumers are time-poor and they resent having to spend their time on insurance. They plan ahead. They want control over their affairs, but they also want reduced complexity. They want insurance that will just fix the problem and let them get back on track with their lives (Figure 13).

Figure 13: Target audience strategy

Control
Know what will happen, reassured you are covered, able to influence

Give me confidence	For me, on my own terms	Make it efficient	Provide good value
Transparency	Tailored / Personal	Ease	
Simplicity	Flexible	Speed	
Fairness	Expertise		

Source: Truth

Efficiency and simplicity were considered the most achievable 'ways in' to this target audience. For most consumers insurance is a commodity, but this audience is sufficiently motivated to pay an 'acceptable' premium[10] for a product that frees them from the unnecessary worry and hassle that surrounds insurance.

We needed to identify whether this strategy made sense in terms of the potential size of the market. To do this we created a market segmentation model based on consumer's attitude to risk and price.[11] Our bulls-eye target audience was aged 25–54 years old, met our income criteria and fell into both the 'control' mindset and agreed with the statement 'it's important to be well insured for everything'. The bulls-eye was about 2.8m individuals (or 3.9m excluding the age criteria).

We now knew what our core target audience looked like, but we still needed a brand position that would play well to a wider audience – we are, after all, a mass market brand. Hall & Partners tested the brand position *'hassle-free insurance that just works'* and found it had almost universal appeal across all key demographic groups.[12] Crucially, this was a relatively untapped area with no competitors yet synonymous with hassle-free insurance. No other brand owned this space.

Walking the walk

Figure 14: Walking the walk

Mr Wolf: Just because you are a character doesn't mean you have character.

In a given year only 10% of car policy holders claim. For home the figure is 20%.[13] Most consumers don't experience the 'quality' of their insurance most of the time. We needed to carefully rethink our propositions to land the Fixer message in the public mind.

We used survey data and econometrics to identify inefficiencies in our proposition mix. The evidence suggested that 'multicar discount'[14] had about half the impact/appeal of our 'write-off replacement' proposition.[15] We also knew that price propositions such as 'no claims discount' or 'free months' have high appeal and drive volume, but they do very little to advance or differentiate the brand.[16]

So we knew what not to do.

Looking forward, we wanted a proposition that would shout 'hassle-free insurance that just works'. Our research suggested that 7 out of 10 complaints related to timescales of settling a claim or failure to keep customers informed.[17]

We undertook the creation of a pipeline of new propositions, the first new proposition being: 'your car fixed in *seven days* or we pay you *£10* a day until the job is done'. We felt that this was the right way to launch the Reboot. What we liked about this proposition is that it acts as a proof point to the efficiency of our service. No other insurer automatically provides goodwill payments. It wasn't at the very top of the table in terms of appeal scores,[18] but we liked what it said about us. Home insurance had a similar *:* 'claims settled in *8 hours*' promise.

Here's the bit we're most proud of ... in order to 'walk the walk' we kicked off a significant operational change programme that saw the number of repairs completed within seven days jump from 35% to 70%.[19]

To 'signal' the quality of our insurance we also restructured our call centres so that cross-brand DLG agents became dedicated Direct Line Fixers. We cancelled amendment fees. We made our website easier to use.

For the first time in a long time we knew what we wanted to be, we knew our role in the world. We knew our archetype. We're Fixers, we put things right when they go wrong. We take the worry and hassle out of insurance. When we put the creative out to pitch, this was the insight that formed the brief (Figure 15).

Figure 15: The Creative Brief

The Brief in a Nutshell

Background

Insurance has become a deeply distrusted industry as it has become commoditised. With a lack of differentiation between brands, customers have reacted by buying increasingly on price. And some insurers have reacted by stripping out costs and service, hiding charges and exclusions, and only marketing price – all feeding further commoditisation and distrust. This has meant an increased use of price comparison sites, at the expense of the direct channel. Direct Line remains famous, but it has become more challenging to engage and connect with customers. We have been working hard to build technology and propositions over the last 2 years, and in 2014 we want to launch them with a new campaign that gives the brand new meaning.

Our ambition

To lead another insurance revolution, and become the clear market leader once again. To become the most trusted insurance brand by delivering on our brand promise. To build a genuinely mutually rewarding relationship with our customers, allowing us to grow our customer franchise and meet their wider insurance needs. To give consumers a compelling reason to come direct once again.

Target Audience and Consumer Insight

We are a mass market brand, targeted at mid to high affluence consumers. These customers have more things to protect and highly value their financial security and lifestyle. But with their busy lives they also want to avoid fuss and hassle. In the other parts of their life, they pay for high performance, and value the role technology plays in making their life easier. While they might not be directly "interested" in insurance, and want to minimise the time they spend dealing with it, they care deeply about its performance too – they have a very real worry that, at the worst possible moment, when they need help most, their insurer will let them down. They believe that when they desperately want help to get their life back on track, we'll be a hassle to deal with, try to get out of paying out, and leave them exposed, when our very job is to protect them and their family. Insurance is fundamentally a promise to be there, to offer financial protection and put life back to normal. But with only 10% of people making a claim each year, how do they know we will deliver? Insurance is a category without trust because consumers don't believe the promise.

The Direct Line Brand Benefit

We will take the worry and hassle out of properly insuring you and your family. Guaranteed.

The execution

Figure 16: The execution

Jules: We should have shotguns for this kind of deal.

This wasn't just a new creative, this was a new identity. We put the 'Fixer' brief out to pitch. We wanted a bold and brave agency that would match us step for step in pushing the boundaries.

The creative execution

Saatchi & Saatchi argued that PCWs had simplified decision-making in insurance to the point where the only things that people cared about were price and cover at the point of purchase. But what about performance at the point of need? The creative strategy needed to change the conversation to get around the communications eclipse that PCWs had created (Figure 17).

Figure 17: Consumer perceptions

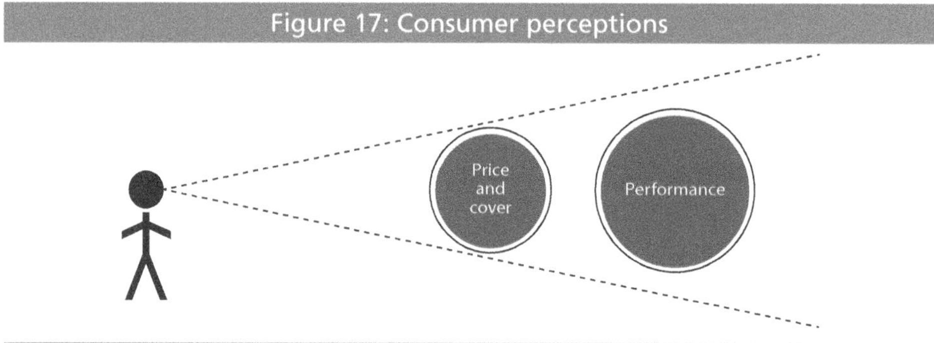

By repositioning Direct Line as 'high-performance insurance', the campaign aimed to return the category back to a conversation about insurance's fundamental role – fixing problems and getting life back on track.

Initially, Saatchi & Saatchi pitched using the concept of 'Hero' (think Super Mario rescuing the Princess). But this wasn't quite right. The moment of inspiration struck for Saatchi when they were crammed into a tiny lift with our marketing team. *We've been looking at the wrong type of Hero. You want to be Winston Wolf from Pulp Fiction.*

To us he was a superb parallel for the way great insurance works – a call away, knows exactly what to do, executes it without fuss, puts things right and gets out of your life.

At first sight the idea of signing up a gangland 'cleaner' as the brand spokesman for an insurance company seemed foolhardy in the extreme. However, while he caused a sharp intake of breath, most focus groups felt that if Mr Wolf was on their side their problems would be fixed – with efficiency, speed and courtesy.

We took the campaign to 800 respondents for pre-testing and benchmarked the results against a pre-flight testing database of 3,259 creatives. The results were overwhelmingly positive (Figures 18 and 19).[20]

Figure 18: Fixer Preflight Testing

Fixer campaign performance

1 Brand linkage is 20% higher than the average of all ads tracked to date

2 Top 5% most salient campaigns ever evaluated

3 Top 4% most involving campaigns ever evaluated

4 Top 25% most persuasive campaigns ever evaluated

5 Top 2% performing campaigns in increasing brand consideration

Hall & Partners

Source: Hall & Partners preflight testing.

The media execution

TV was crucial for delivering the impact the campaign would need. MediaCom launched with *X Factor* as the programme delivered the highest reach (8m) and was best positioned to generate buzz. It was the first show of the season for *X Factor* – we owned the night by flighting car, home and landlord ads in consecutive breaks. The strategy was to generate buzz and cut-through rather than efficient reach. The fact that Direct Line was 'trending on Twitter' on the night suggests we achieved this.

Following the initial phase, the goal shifted from generating buzz to supporting each product as efficiently as possible. MediaCom aimed to hit our target audience three to four times within a month. Monthly TV spend was phased to take advantage of seasonal patterns within the insurance market.[21] Patterns in the search data indicated that the first and last week of month, as well as Sundays to Thursdays, are peak periods for insurance. Our TV laydown mirrored this.

Whilst TV ensured that we reached a broad audience, adding a seven-week cinema campaign to the launch helped target a highly engaged and desirable audience. It also leveraged the fantastic 'cinematic' property we had in Tarantino's Mr Wolf (Figure 20).

Figure 19: Examples of Fixer creative

Winston Wolf, I'm here to help and this is your car called Randy, correct? Yeah, and I'd like to get my hands on whoever did this. **I can make them disappear.** Disappear? **I mean the dents. Now Laura, do me a favour. Send your photographs to my people, they'll take the car in and fix it within seven days or someone will pay.** What? **Direct Line will pay you £10 a day until the job is done.**

You're Dave, Right? Winston Wolf, I fix problems. May I come in? Sure. **You must be Lucy. I understand your computer, TV and bike have been stolen, right?** Right. **And you've sent photos of these items to Direct Line?** Yeah. **Then if all is good, replacements will be ready to send within 8 hours.** Great! **Now Lucy, there are people out there who can make sure this never happens to you again.** What will they do? **Fit a burglar alarm.**

Winston Wolf, I solve problems. You're Mike right? Yeah. **About your car, it's a total write-off, correct?** 100%. **Don't worry, Direct Line will find you another one like it, or even an upgrade.** Really? **Really. Unless you'd like to get paid off.** Look, thanks, I'd rather you found me another car. **Good enough, Mike. We just need to dispose of the body then.**

Jenny. Winston Wolf, I fix problems. Good, I've got one. **You were making chocolate fudge cake when a little accident caused damage to your mobile.** Yes. **And to Roger the rabbit. You have Direct Line Home Plus insurance so your phone can be replaced or you can have cash. Your call, but not on that obviously.** Can you send me a new one? **Sure. Now your daughter Connie comes home at 3.30 in the pm, correct? Uh-huh. That gives us 40 minutes to get the fudge out of Rog.**

Figure 20: Multimedia campaign launch

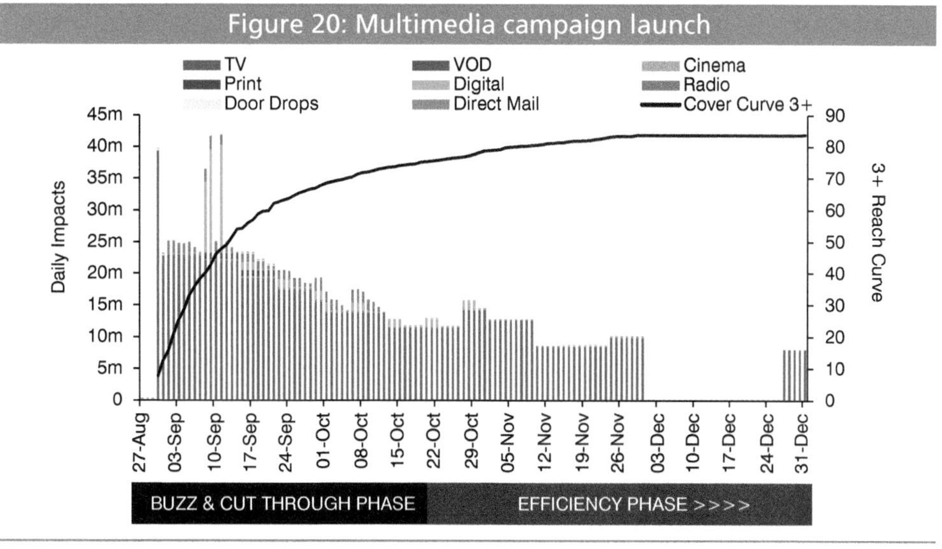

Digital

Our new digital strategy was rooted in the attitudinal research and would make more use of social and content marketing. In brief the digital launch had three strands:

- Social VOD: 'How To...' videos on YouTube featuring Winston Wolf and side-kick Billy solving everyday problems like getting rid of red wine stains. Resulting in 1.7m views at a 15% completion rate (vs. an industry benchmark of 12%[22]).
- Guardian Fixology: A content partnership microsite featuring 100 fixes to everyday problems. Seen by 600k people in the first three months of the campaign.
- Buzzfeed: Animated gifs featuring people who are 'totally on it'. Resulting in 200k views.

Between TV, cinema, digital and press we reached 85% of the population within the first month of the campaign.

Finding the budget for reboot

Figure 21: Finding the budget for reboot

Pumpkin: Okay people, I'm going to go 'round and collect your wallets. Don't talk, just toss 'em in the bag. We clear?

Our marketing budget has been reduced considerably as part of our continual focus on costs since DLG's IPO in 2012. Annual Direct Line marketing spend has fallen from £71m to £38m between 2011 and 2015.[23] We had to do more with less. To achieve this we undertook a long-term testing programme with a commercial focus on driving efficiency and cutting budget (Figure 22).

Figure 22: Annual Direct Line marketing budget – all products

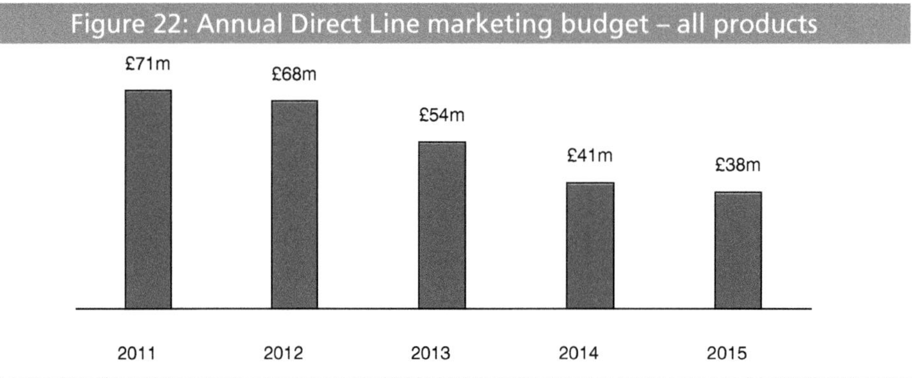

Source: DLG internal data. 2011 to 2015.

Testing programme

Geo-testing was used to 'fill the gaps' for media lines where traditional econometrics is considered less robust. The programme demonstrated that leaflets were only recovering about 55% of their cost so we reduced annual spend by **£11.4m** or *–97%* between 2011 and 2015.

We also found that online tracking painted an overly positive picture of conventional banner advertising. As a result we significantly reduced annual investment by **£1.4m** or *–50%* between 2012 and 2014. We fundamentally adjusted our digital strategy going into the Reboot.[24]

Matchback analysis

Control cells were used to measure the net response delivered by CRM media such as direct mail (DM) and email. We use a GLM propensity model to score and prioritise mailing prospects. There are significant differences in efficiency between the best and the worst candidates. The analysis suggests that the top quartile cost per sale for home is under £50, while the bottom quartile is over £200. Similarly, for car we identified that the top third cost per sale was £89, compared to £290 for the bottom third. As a result of this programme we were able to reduce the annual DM budget by **£2.3m** or *–51%* between 2011 and 2015.

DRTV reductions

We reduced DRTV spend by **£6.2m** or *–60%* between 2011 and 2015. This was informed by diminishing returns analysis from the econometric modelling. Reach and frequency analysis conducted in partnership with Sky IQ also identified that DRTV was contributing towards an excessive average monthly household frequency of 21+ compared to PCWs, which sat in the 9–12 range.[25]

The evidence

Figure 23: The evidence

Lance: Well, you're giving her an injection of adrenaline straight to her heart.

...

Vince: What happens after that?

Lance: I'm curious about that myself.

Commercial KPIs

Delivering new quote volume is seen as the key marketing KPI. To understand whether the Fixer Reboot worked, this is where we need to start.

Figure 24: Car insurance quotes YOY growth

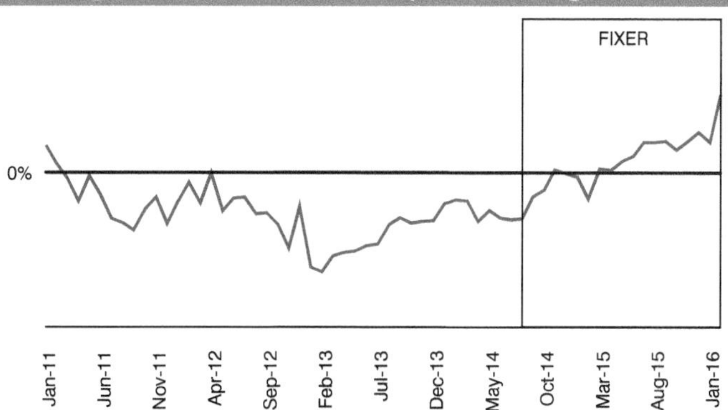

Source: DLG internal

Figure 25: Home insurance quotes YOY growth

Source: DLG internal

Whilst the rate of decline improved immediately, it took about six months to fully bed in and move us to positive growth.

By February 2016 we had sustained positive YOY growth in car insurance quotes for 12 consecutive months. Overall, we saw 10% growth over this 12-month period. Home insurance data tell a similar story: 16% growth over the same period.[26] One of the advantages of starting with quote volume is that it is not influenced by price,[27] so this KPI automatically 'controls' for competitiveness.

Total 'in-force' policies (IFPs) are influenced by price position, so unlike quote volume it is not a particularly clean metric for evaluating marketing.

Nonetheless, it is too important for us to overlook altogether. By February 2016 we had halted five consecutive years of decline (Figure 26).

Figure 26: 'In-force' policy YOY growth

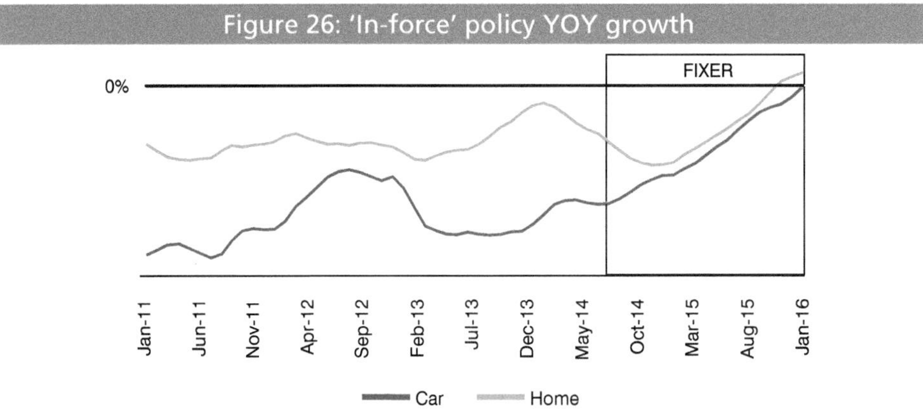

Source: DLG internal data. 2011 to 2015.

Econometric results & ROI

Although looking at quotes as a KPI inherently controls for competitiveness, it does not control for market movements or levels of ad spend. To do this we need to refer to the econometric results. The Fixer brand TV delivered significantly greater impact per 100 TVRs than the creative used in the previous 12 months (Figure 27).

Figure 27: Percentage quote uplift per 100 TVRs

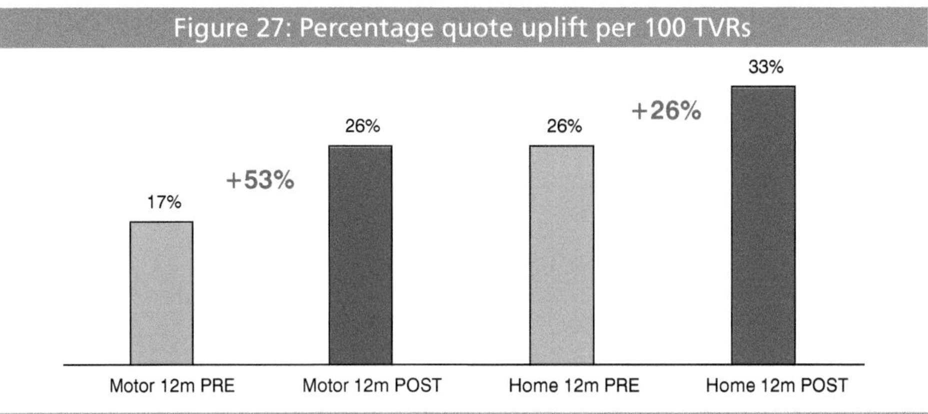

Source: Ebiquity econometrics March 2016

These improved TV uplifts[28] translate into a compelling set of results in terms of ROI.

The econometric analysis indicates that BRTV ROI was **£1.28 for car and £1.05 for home** in the 12 months since Reboot. Assuming constant 2015 TV costs, we achieved a *40% fall in cost per sale for car insurance TV advertising and a 10% fall for home.*

On the wider marketing budget[29] we achieved an ROI **£1.22 overall** – which breaks down into **£1.42** for car insurance and **£0.97** for home.

These ROI's factor in car-to-home halo effects and vice-versa. They do not factor in halo effects to pet, landlord, tradesman, breakdown, life, travel insurance etc. This ROI is calculated using a 10-year lifetime value or LTV but does not otherwise include any so-called 'long-term multipliers'.

Controlling for other factors

There are some other positive factors that have improved our performance since the Fixer Reboot in September 2014. This section outlines these factors and explains how we have controlled for them.

Market and pricing

At the top line the market was flat YOY in the 12 months to September 2015 for car insurance and –1.9% for home insurance.[30] The insurance premium tax change (IPT) implemented in November 2015 appears to have driven increased volume,[31] but our performance had improved before this.

The percentage uplift per 100 TVRs shown above comes from an econometric model that uses both Google Trends and syndicated sales data to control for the impact of market dynamics on quote volume.

It should be noted that we gained new business market share without any significant price change. In the six months to October 2015 our YOY market share for online car sales rose from 19% to 21% while our average sold premium declined by around 1%, compared to a market decline of 1.8%. Our home market share rose from 16% to 17% while our average sold premium declined by 7.8%, compared to a market decline of 9.7%.[32]

Price changes in insurance can be complex to consider because of composition effects,[33] but based on the data we are confident that the gains are not driven by a step change in pricing.[34]

Telematics

Direct Line ramped up its telematics or 'black box' offering in January 2015. This product uses GPS and accelerometer data to gauge driver risk and reward careful driving. This is a popular option for younger drivers. The telematics contribution is controlled for explicitly in the econometric model, which suggests that it accounts for only 37% of the gains in quote volume.

If we look at growth by sub-segment we can see that telematics is not the only growth factor. Telematics uptake is predictably concentrated in our younger driver segment and multicar households.[35] However, if we look at new business quote volume for car consumers aged 35+ it is clear that we are still up 10% YOY in the six months to October 2015 (Figure 28).

Figure 28: Telematics weekly quote volume

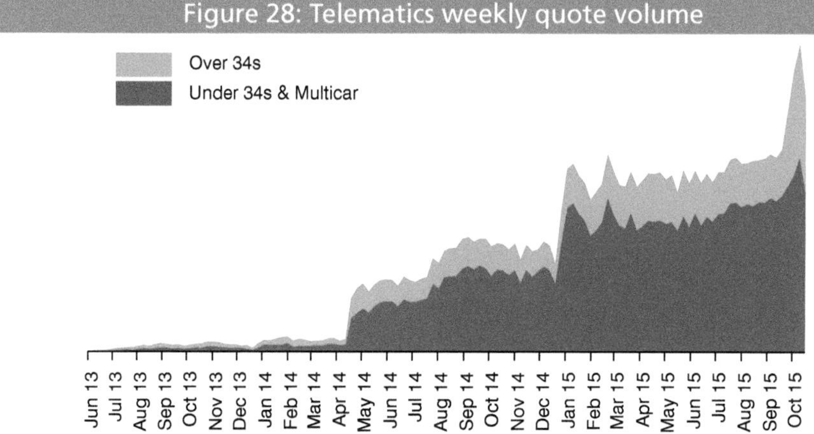

Source: DLG internal date March 2016

PPC cost per click

PPC cost per click fell 14% YOY in the 12 months to October 2015 for car and increased 5% for home. These are controlled for in the econometric model which factors in total click volume.[36]

Brand resurgence

Prior to the Reboot we saw that Direct Line was in decline both in terms of awareness and consideration. One of the aims of the Fixer campaign was to stem the decline in these key metrics. Looking at Figures 29 and 30 it is clear that we achieved this.

However, stemming the decline in awareness and consideration was never the only concern for us. *We were also worried about what people thought of us.*

The gains in preference told us that the campaign was working. People were getting the message that Direct Line offer a better product or 'hassle-free insurance that just works'.

Car insurance preference increased by 23% in the 12 months pre- to post-Fixer Reboot.[37] Preference for our home insurance improved by 39%.[38]

After one year, Direct Line was once again the clear market leader in terms of preference, scoring 15% for car (vs. 12% for the second rank brand) (Figure 31) and 14% for home (vs 12% for the second rank brand).

This was achieved with 20% fewer TV rating points.

Figure 29: Car insurance brand tracking and TVRs

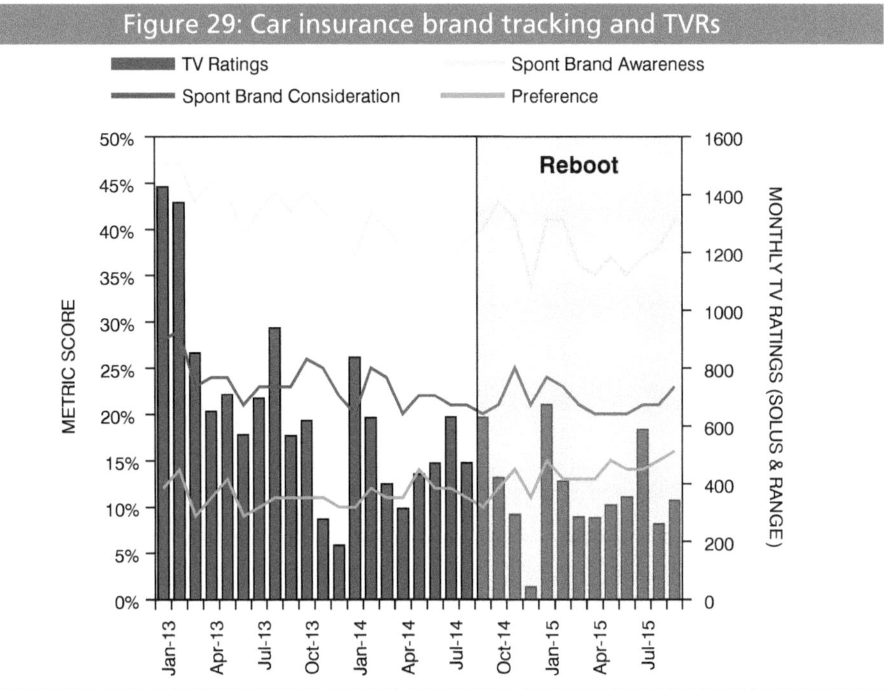

Source: Hall & Partners brand tracking. TV are All Adult 30 sec equivalent sourced from BARB/DDS

Figure 30: Home insurance brand tracking and TVRs

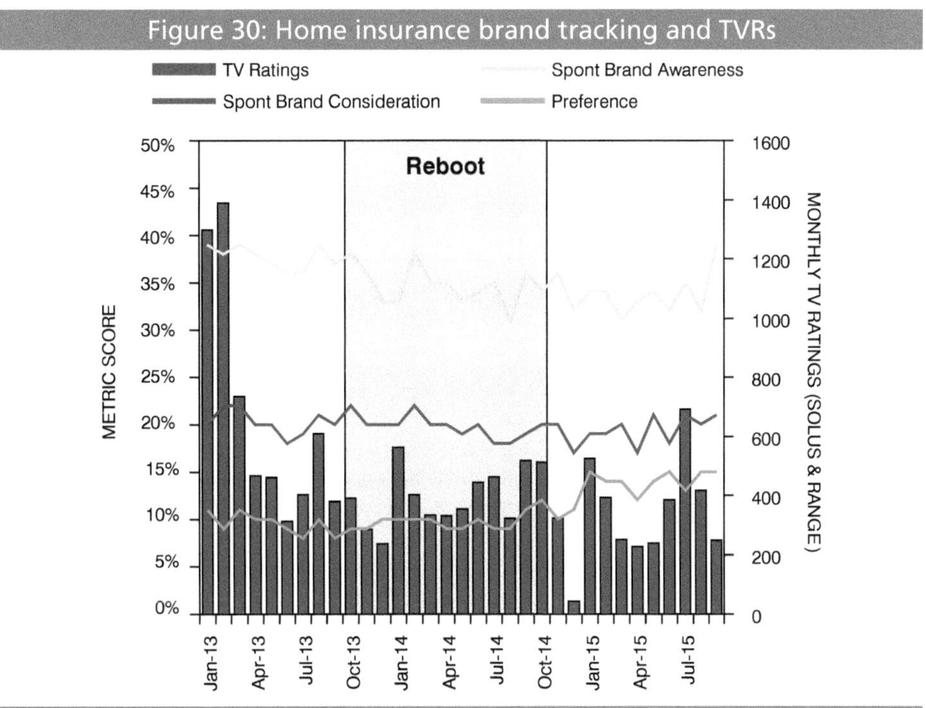

Source: Hall & Partners brand tracking. TV are All Adult 30 sec equivalent sourced from BARB/DDS

Figure 31: Preference for larger car insurance brands

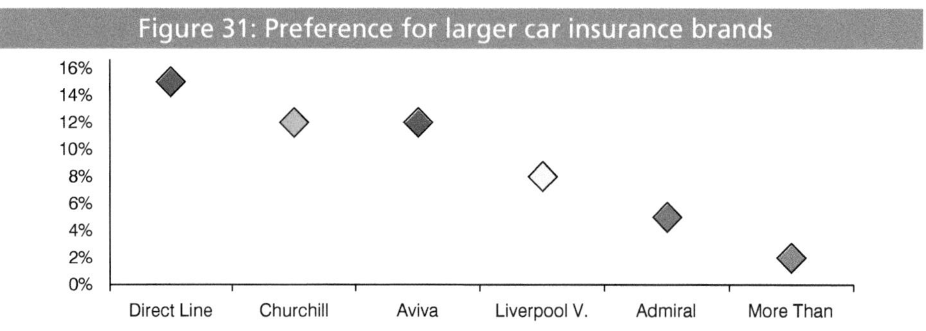

Source: Hall & Partners brand tracking. 3m Rolling. 'If price were equal, who would you prefer to use for car insurance?'

The reason preference jumped up is that we managed to fundamentally shift the consumers' perception of the quality of the insurance provided by DLG – we genuinely landed the message of 'high-performance' insurance and shifted the conversation away from price and cover at the point of purchase and towards performance at the point of need (Figure 32).

Figure 32: YouGov Brand Index quality score (net)

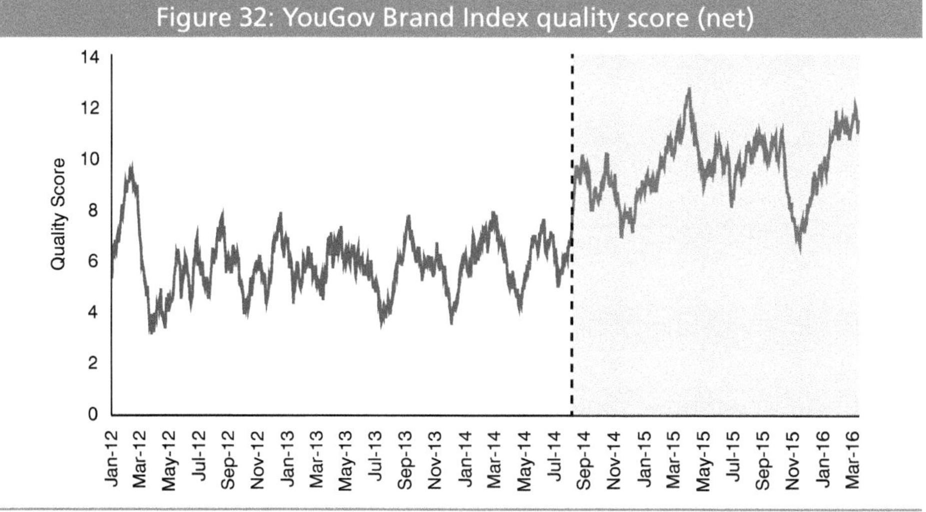

Source: YouGov BrandIndex. Net Quality Score. January 2012 to Mar 2016. 30 day rolling.

The Fixer Reboot changed how people saw us. The two statements we identified as absolutely core to our strategy were *'easy to deal with'* and *'takes care of your insurance so you can go on with your life'*. These saw a 13% and a 22% improvement, respectively. The majority of our brand metrics saw significant improvement (Figure 33).

Figure 33: Metric shift – six months to mid-Sept 2015 (after Reboot) versus six months running up to Reboot

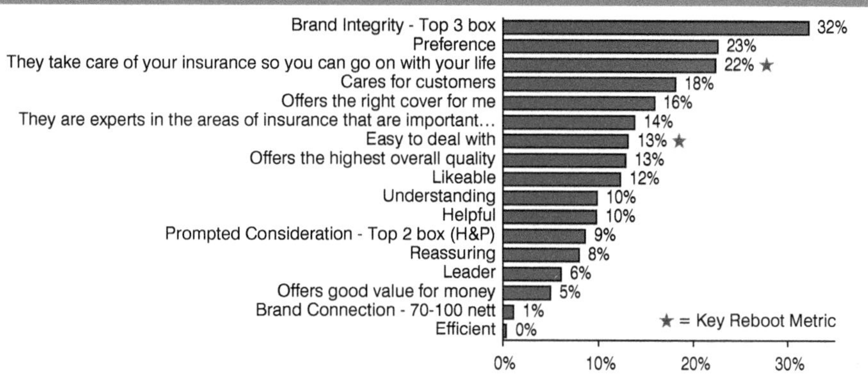

Source: Hall & Partners brand tracking.

The radar graph in Figure 34 illustrates how the Fixer campaign drove a holistic improvement of the Direct Line brand.[39]

Figure 34: Radar graph of Direct Line brand improvement

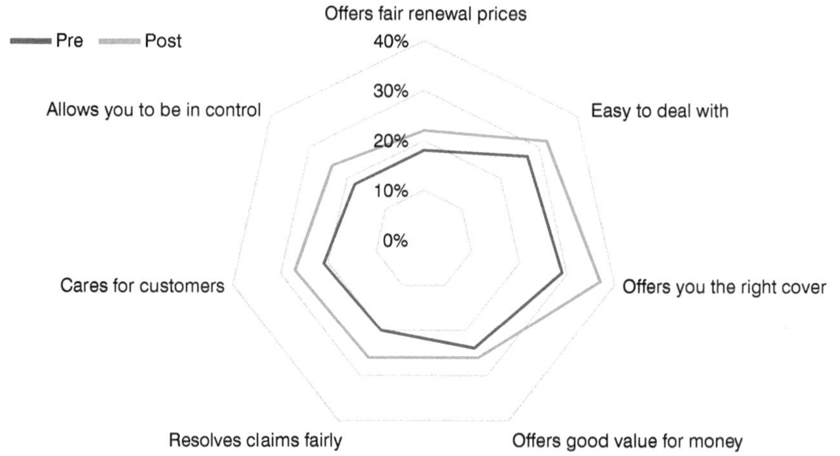

Source: Hall & Partners brand tracking

In addition, recasting ourselves as 'Fixers' has helped Direct Line take the No. 1 spot in a UK/USA *Harvard Business Review*[40] study on companies that 'get Twitter' and respond to customers with empathy. Net Promotor Score rose by 20% with 12 months of the Fixer Reboot.[41] DLG's share price is up by 10%.[42]

And so on.

The evidence from the brand health data, taken together with the econometric results and improved top line performance, together make a compelling case for the effectiveness of the Fixer Reboot.

Conclusion

Figure 35: Conclusion

Vince: I think we oughta leave now.
Lance: That's probably a good idea.

This is not the story of a plucky start-up that had a great idea and against all odds conquered the world. If anything, Direct Line were on the other side of that coin. This is the story of a once-great business that was a heartbeat away from catastrophe. A business that withstood a tidal wave of disruptive technology in the form of PCWs.

We took an uncompromising look at the evidence and identified a fundamental problem with our brand. We used a broad set of research tools to look back and identify what wasn't working anymore. And then we looked forward and identified what could work in the future.

This paper is meant to showcase excellence in strategy, creative and research – but more importantly we have shown how a business can reinvent itself around an idea.

We have a new *raison d'être*. We're Fixers. This has become the organising principle of our business. Once we discovered our archetype, we knew what to do next.

Notes

1. Source: Based on a comparison of internal data and Office of National Statistic Vehicle Registration by Keepership for 1997 (VEH0202).
2. Source: Consumer Intelligence. Data for 12 months ending December 2012. Sample size 12,184 for home and 12,208 for motor.
3. Source: Google Insights 2004–2016.
4. Based on syndicated sales data. The provider of this data cannot be quoted because of the terms and conditions of our contract.
5. Syndicated sales data. 2010 to 2014.
6. Hall & Partners brand tracking survey data. Dates for comparison are October–December 2012 and June–August 2014. Awareness fell from 8.3% to 7.4%. Consideration fell from 25.3% to 21.4%. These metrics had been stable for a number of years prior.
7. For car insurance. Direct Line home insurance was running higher discounts of in excess of 30%.
8. Source: Hall & Partners. September 2013.
9. We worked with a number of strategic and qualitative research partners including Closer to Brands, Truth and Flamingo.
10. The size of this 'acceptable premium' was measured through Hall & Partners conjoint analysis.
11. In partnership with Bonamy Finch.
12. Hall & Partners Market Mapping. March 2014.
13. DLG internal data. 2014.
14. DLG internal data. 2014.
15. 'If your car's a write off, we'll find a replacement car like yours or choose a cash settlement or pay for an upgrade'. This proposition built on trust and service perceptions and performed well both in testing and econometrics and so was kept in place for the Fixer Reboot (with a new creative wrapper).
16. Based on Hall & Partners proposition testing. September 2015. Out of a sample of 86 brand/proposition combinations we found that the average 'uniqueness' score for pure price propositions (including discount, cashback and 'from' price) would fall in the bottom quartile.
17. Source: DLG Complaints data, 12m to November 2013.

18. It was still much stronger than average. 56% appeal score versus 46% average across 35 propositions in Wave 1. Hall & Partners proposition testing. September 2015.
19. The so-called LEAN programme included a new system called ActiveWeb to monitor garage performance against the seven-day target. A new damage imaging system allowed us to speed up claims and hit our seven-day/eight-hour commitment.
20. Hall & Partners pre-flight testing client database for the five years to August 2014.
21. Seasonal optimisation was calculated by Ebiquity to leverage peak seasonality in the insurance market and take advantage of lower TV cost months.
22. Source: MediaCom. April 2014.
23. This includes all major media lines, but excludes creative and overhead.
24. We employ Ebiquity as a partner for our geo-testing programme.
25. Sky IQ Viewing analysis presented February 2014.
26. It must be noted that floods in December 2015 did deliver additional volume – but the product was in growth from May onwards.
27. Consumers do not know your price point until after they have quoted.
28. The uplifts shown represent a quote volume weighted average of all risk segments across phone and web. Adstocks are normalised to 0% retention rate.
29. Affiliates, DRTV, Dual Doordrops, Home BRTV, Motor BRTV, Multiproduct, Multiproduct Doordrops, PPC Product, Range BRTV, Range National Press, Range OOH, Range Radio, Solus Advertorial, Solus Direct Mail, Solus Doordrops, Solus National Press, Solus OOH, Solus Press Inserts, Solus Radio, Solus Specialist Press.
30. Syndicated sales data. Published January 2016.
31. Syndicated sales data. Car +7.5% and home +9.3% YOY for November 2015 to January 2016.
32. Market price change estimates are based on data from a 3600 person panel from Consumer Intelligence.
33. Becoming more competitive for a higher risk segment can paradoxically make your sold average policy premium increase.
34. For car insurance, a sales weighted Within risk segment price index shows an average price decline less than 1% ahead of the market (–2.7% vs –1.8%) comparing 12m pre- and post-reboot. By the same measure for home insurance our price actually increased vs. the market by 5.6% (–4.1% vs. –9.7%).
35. These groups accounted for about 75% of telematics quotes in 2015.
36. Unless otherwise stated PPC refers to generic or product PPC, e.g. 'best car insurance'. Brand PPC ('direct line car insurance') is considered to be endogenous and is excluded from analysis.
37. Source: Hall & Partners. Actual values from 11.3% to 13.8%.
38. Source: Hall & Partners. Actual values from 9.6% to 13.3%.
39. Hall & Partners comparison of April–June 2014 vs. August–October 2015. Sample size 1720 pre and 1427 post.
40. '50 Companies that Get Twitter – and 50 That Don't' https://hbr.org/2015/04/the-best-and-worst-corporate-tweeters?utm_campaign=Socialflow&utm_source=Socialflow&utm_medium=Tweet
41. Source: DLG internal data. Post-claim satisfaction survey as of September 2015.
42. Google Finance. Compares 29 August 2014 to 1 April 2016.

Guinness

An effectiveness story *Made Of More*

By Rory Gallery and Lilian Sor, AMV BBDO
Contributing authors: Alison Falconer, Diageo; David Hartley, Data2Decisions; Craig Mawdsley, AMV BBDO
Credited companies: AMV BBDO; Carat

Summary

By committing long-term to a brand idea, *Made of More,* Guinness defied significant challenges in the UK and Irish markets, and created an effective global communications platform. Guinness built on the qualified success of its early iterations of *Made of More* to develop films which more effectively communicated the brand's distinctiveness and salience. This includes films such as 'Wheelchair basketball' and 'Sapeurs' that told stories of individuals making bold choices and displaying character. The strategy delivered improving returns, and was estimated to have delivered an overall profit ROI of £3.88 for every £1 invested (almost twice the category norm).

Editor's Comment

The *Made of More* brand platform yielded strong business results over time. The case did a very good job of discounting all other factors, so that the judges were left in no doubt as to the effectiveness of the idea.

Client Comment
Alison Falconer, Global Planning Director, Guinness & Beer, Diageo

The *Made of More* Campaign has been an invaluable learning process for many reasons.

Creativity: *Made of More* is a global idea. This paper outlines the European work since this is where we had the best data available at the time of writing to allow us to demonstrate how the campaign has worked (to the standards of the IPA). However, the conceptual learnings that have been outlined in the paper have been applied to bring the Guinness purpose to life across the world.

We've learnt how to use the power that's always been embedded into Guinness' distinctiveness to attract and engage, by celebrating those with character, integrity and confident self-expression, and groups that live life on their own terms. These concepts shape all our briefs globally. We've harnessed the executional learnings around areas like tone, story-telling and authenticity.

There is not some kind of straightjacket model of what Guinness work should be, but we and the agency are better aware of what helps us play the tunes we want to play. And we will continue to test and iterate. There's no merit in standing still.

Scale: We have a robust case for spending on Guinness. A good idea, well executed, works. The proven ROI means that we can secure the media budgets required to give Guinness the vivid year-round salience it needs to thrive.

Effectiveness: The rugby executions in particular provide us with a powerful model of how a deep human insight that connects to the brand's purpose gives us cut-through and resonance on screen. We're getting better at activating rugby every year and Guinness is using that example to shape other work such as football activations in Africa, southeast Asia and Caribbean and ultimately make them more effective.

Introduction

This is Guinness's story of how a creatively successful idea, *Made of More,* enabled the brand to defy significant business challenges in the British and Irish market that in turn, led to a profit return on investment (PROI) of £3.88 for every £1 spent (the highest recorded PROI within the beer category in IPA history).

In 2012, the beer category was on shaky ground. An economic crisis had hit Great Britain and Ireland, changing traditional drinking habits that were reducing on-trade beer sales – Guinness's heartland. The proliferation of craft beers, the emergence of cheaper beers and the continued doggedness of their established competitors meant that Guinness was operating in the most competitive environment they had ever faced. And to add to the complexity of the situation, we now needed to navigate these challenges in Great Britain and Ireland with a new global strategy and creative idea.

This isn't just a story of growth in a complex environment. It's a story of grit, perseverance and dedication to unlocking the power of a new creative platform over a number of years, leading to an extremely effective period for the Guinness brand.

It's a story of a brand *Made of More.*

A bit about the 'black stuff'

Guinness is a dark stout beer that originated in 1759 in the brewery of Arthur Guinness at St. James's Gate, Dublin, Ireland (Figure 1). It's brewed in almost 60 countries and is available in over 150.

Figure 1: St James's Gate, the home of Guinness

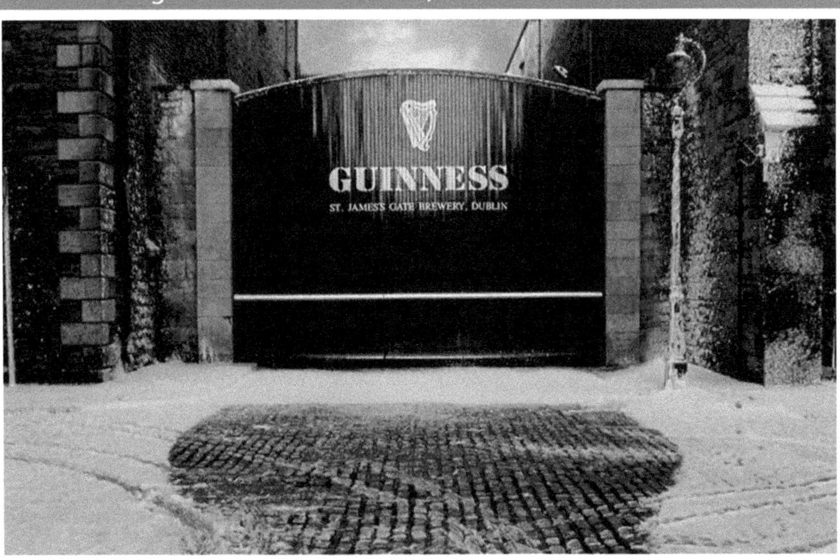

In communications, Guinness had traditionally focused on dramatising its various product truths.

For its first ever ad published in a national newspaper, Guinness used the slogan 'Guinness is Good For You' based on perceived medicinal benefits of the drink (Figure 2).

Figure 2: Guinness's first published advertisement in a national newspaper

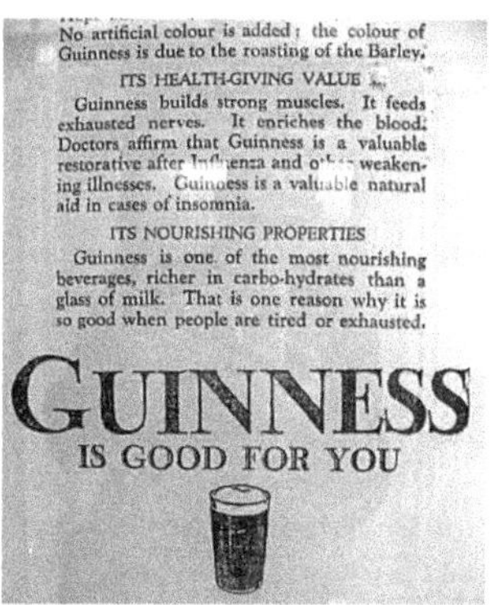

This meant that communications often differed by market as Guinness has different products and formats across the world (Figure 3). For example, in Europe and America it is mainly Guinness Draught (the famous pint with the creamy head), whereas in Africa and South East Asia, Guinness predominantly sells bottles of Foreign Extra Stout – a stronger tasting stout with a higher alcohol level, created to survive the long shipping trips when it was first exported.

Figure 3: International products

The move to one global brand positioning

Previously, the work we had been doing had focused on what made the Guinness product great in each market. This meant we were supporting no fewer than five different positioning statements globally. However, given the economic landscape, we needed to increase the effectiveness and efficiency of our communications around the world.

Creating one global platform would allow us to create communications of greater quality.

The strategic approach

A new approach was devised for Guinness that would see communications move away from solely focusing on the drink and, instead, focus on the shared attitude between the Guinness brand, the Guinness product and the Guinness drinker. The strategy was based on three truths:

A bold brand

As a company, Guinness has always been a brand with a bold outlook on life. The founder Arthur Guinness made a bold choice to sign a 9,000-year lease of his Dublin brewery, and most notably, decided to brew a dark stout when everyone else was brewing ale (Figure 4).

Figure 4: The great man himself, Arthur Guinness

A bold beer

Guinness is a unique drink. It is a black stout rather than a golden lager or ale. Guinness is bold in look, and has more taste and character than other beers.

A bold consumer

Through global research, we identified an aspirational consumer attitude amongst our beer drinkers. They are those in life who don't just want to follow the crowd, but instead make bold choices and carve their own path. They are people with more to them, who desire experiences and brands with more depth and substance.

This led us to our global strategic idea (Figure 5).

Guinness is a bold beer for those who like to make bold choices in life

Figure 5: Global brand purpose

Creative Idea

In turn, this led to the creation of *Made of More* (Figure 6).

This wasn't just a line.

It wasn't just our creative idea.

It was a shared attitude that connected the Guinness brand, Guinness product and Guinness consumer in many disparate markets.

Figure 6: *Made of More*

Implementing a global idea in Great Britain and Ireland

The first markets to launch *Made of More* were the territories Guinness defines as Great Britain and Ireland.[1] This paper tracks the evolution and success of the idea in these markets from launch (September 2012) to the most recent econometric data (June 2015).

We weren't having the luck of the Irish

As we prepared to launch our new brand platform in Britain and Ireland, Guinness faced a number of complex challenges.

Challenge 1: Our pub heartland was under threat

The collapse of the Celtic Tiger[2] and the Irish economy led to the fall of major financial institutions, failing businesses and huge emigration. It eventually led to an IMF[3] bailout (Figure 7).

Figure 7: Ajai Chopra, of the IMF, passes a beggar on his way to discuss the IMF's bailout with the Irish Government

The British economy wasn't much better off and it experienced a double dip recession in 2012.[4]

As a consequence of the economic climate, drinking habits were changing. Consumers were going out less than ever before, leading to a decline in beer sales (Figure 8).[5]

Figure 8: Beer sales decline 2011–2012

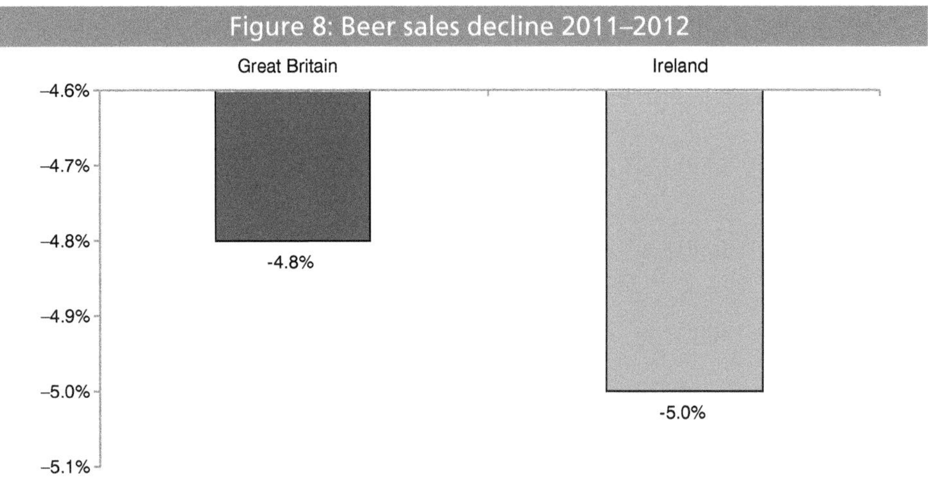

Source: *USA Today* and *Daily Telegraph*

The decline in beer sales meant many pubs across Britain and Ireland were closing (Figures 9 and 10).

Figure 9: Number of pubs in Great Britain 2008–2012

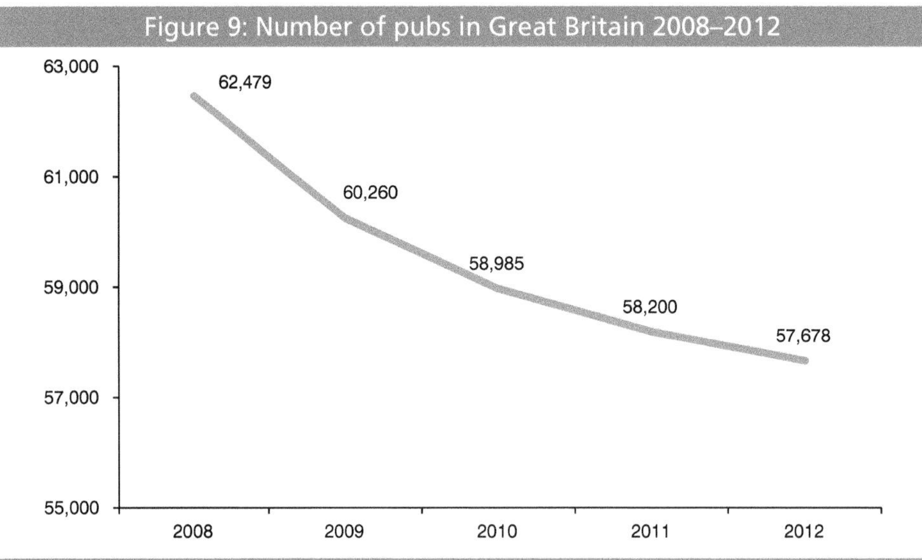

Source: Camra

Figure 10: Number of pubs in Ireland 2007–2012

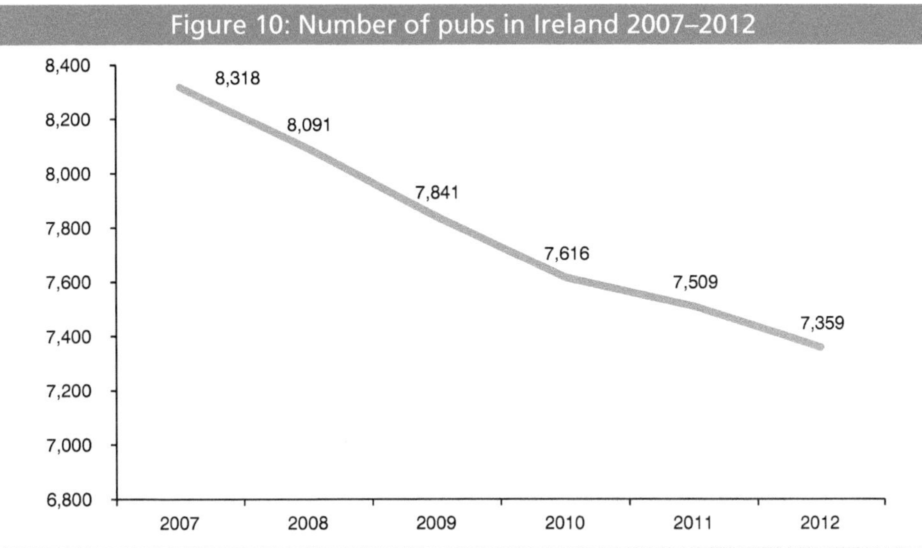

Source: Irish Revenue Commission

This was a huge problem for Guinness given that most of its volume comes from pub sales (Figure 11).

Figure 11: Guinness pub/in-home (on-trade vs off-trade) split

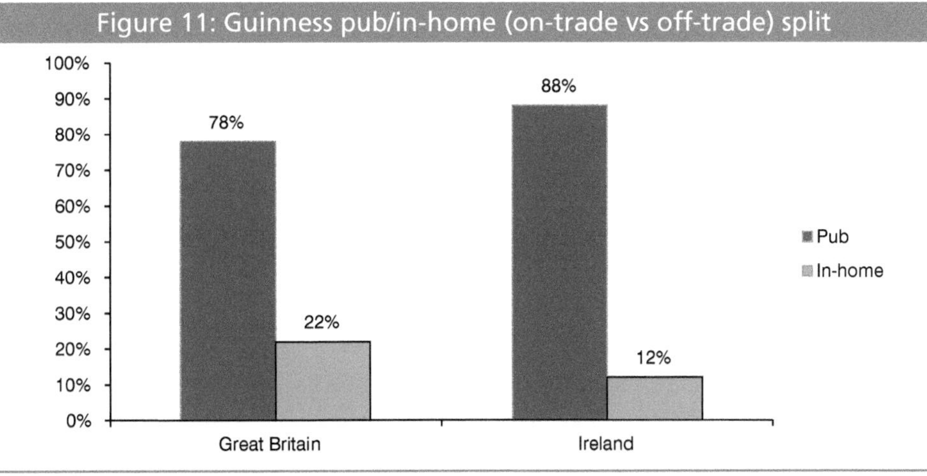

Source: Nielsen and Data2Decisions

The decline in on-trade sales hit Guinness harder than other beer brands. In Britain and Ireland, Guinness is a drink that most people consider to be best enjoyed in the pub rather than at home. And data was showing that on-trade stout[6] sales were declining ahead of the beer market (Figure 12).[7]

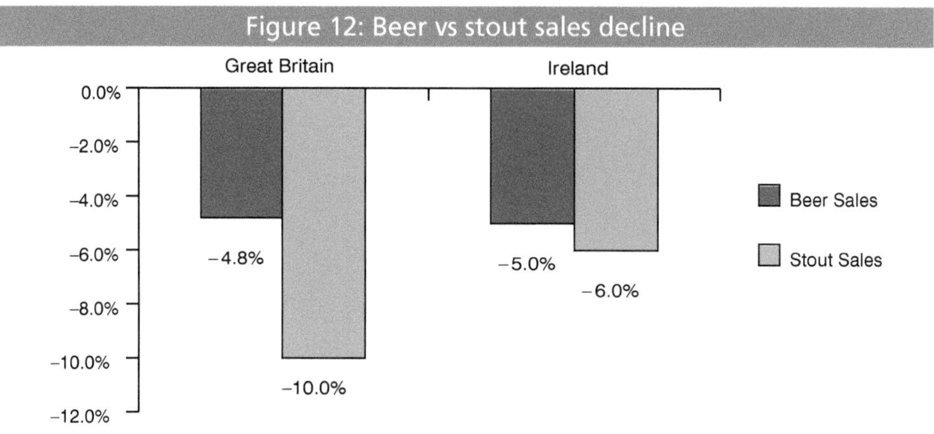

Source: *USA Today, Daily Telegraph, Research & Markets, Morning Advertiser*

Challenge 2: An increasingly competitive environment

Guinness was also facing huge competition. Consumers were now seeking cheaper beer options.

> *In Ireland, consumers wanted cheaper alternatives and pubs were willing to oblige. This meant that Guinness faced more competition in pubs. In the UK, cheaper ale and beer options were beginning to attract price-sensitive consumers.*
> Head of Global Consumer Planning and Innovation Director, Guinness

Craft beer had begun to emerge as a threat. In 2012, the craft beer market was still relatively small in Britain (1.9%) and Ireland (0.3% volume).[8] However, even at this early stage it was obvious from the quick growth of craft beers in the USA[9] that Guinness (and their competitors alike) would need to address this threat.[10] For a beer like Guinness, positioned as a more sophisticated alternative to lager, this explosion in interesting, progressive beers could have started to make our product feel less unique.

Finally, the beer market was full of established players who were all battling for revenue and profit in tough market conditions.

Challenge 3: We had to treat Britain and Ireland as one market

Historically, different communications answered the different needs of both Britain and Ireland. They were in very different places regarding consumption and attitudes to the black stuff.[11] In Ireland, Guinness was a fabric brand that was the undisputed number one player. In Britain, Guinness was admired but it didn't hold the same status.[12]

> *Imagine Guinness was a football team at the World Cup. You may admire their skills and enjoy watching them. But they would matter more to you if you were from the country. That sums up the difference between Guinness's relationship with Ireland and Britain.*
> Head of Global Consumer Planning and Innovation Director, Guinness

We were now tasked with developing one set of creative work and assets under *Made of More* that could work in Britain and Ireland.

Our Objectives

Market forces meant that Guinness couldn't rely on category growth to reach targets.

Our strategic options were limited.

One answer would have been to go after in-home occasions.

But Guinness's 'pub heritage' and the fact the in-home market is simply not as profitable ensured that winning the battle in the on-trade became the strategic priority. Our objectives were as follows:

1. Deliver cultural traction and creative brilliance for Guinness Draught...

In *The Long and the Short of It: Balancing the short and long-term effects of marketing*,[13] it has been proved that creatively awarded campaigns are 11 times more efficient than non-awarded campaigns. Guinness is a firm believer in the power of creativity. In this instance, creativity wasn't an output, it was an objective.

2. That results in brand fame that improves brand affinity...

Given the competitive landscape, we would need to see improved saliency and ensure our key affinity statements were moving in the right direction.

3. That decreases price sensitivity...

In the face of rising cost, reduced consumer price sensitivity is needed to maintain revenue growth and would help stem the long-term decline Guinness had seen over the years in value share.

4. That in turn improves the ROI for Guinness.

Ultimately, we wanted to increase the efficiency of our return on investment versus pre-*Made of More* work and see a more profitable return than our competitors.

The work: *Made of More* 1.0

Our first iteration of *Made of More* wasn't unlike the first iPhone operating system.

Novel, innovative, but not perfect.

We launched the platform with two films – 'Cloud' and 'Clock'. Strategically, the work was designed to establish the *Made of More* belief that making bold choices can have extraordinary consequences. The stories followed inanimate objects that choose to break their constraints (Figures 13 and 14).

Figure 13: 'Cloud'

In this commercial we see a lone cloud adventure around a city.

We open on a small cloud detaching itself from the main body, drifting towards an urban coastline.

VO: The cloud came from the sea. He was not like other clouds. The wind could not command him.

The cloud envelops a set of low hanging traffic lights and passes an office, where a worker looks round as it passes.

VO: The more he saw, the more he did. And the more he did, the more he became.

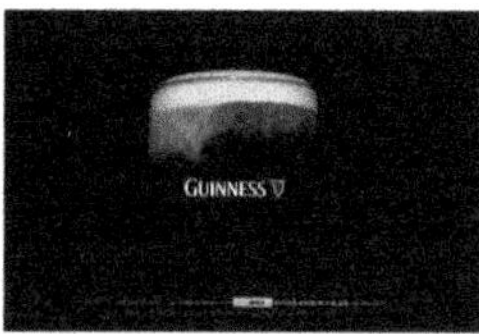

We see a warehouse on fire, with a team of fireman trying to tackle the flames. The cloud floats over it and releases a torrent of rain, extinguishing the blaze.

You see, he wasn't just a cloud. He was a cloud Made of More.

The cloud floats back out to sea before we cut to a view of the pint.

Title: Guinness. Made of More.

Online at http://bit.ly/1MtDmvF

Figure 14: 'Clock'

In this commercial we see what a clock 'Made of More' can do.

We open on the inside of a giant town clock, which we see is overlooking a town square in the early 1900s.

VO: At 8:24 precisely, I had an idea. Could I be more than just an everyday tick-tock kind of clock? Why let time drag, when I could make it fly?

Suddenly the clockworks speed up and we see a cobbler look delighted as his whole days' work disappears in front of him in seconds.

A fire breaks out in the town square, causing imminent danger to all and burning a man's house down in the process.

To give a second chance, my seconds could spin backwards.

The clock stops, and the action starts going in reverse - mirroring the hands on the clock. A man grabs a bucket of water and puts the fire out before it starts taking control.

And imagine if I could make precious moments less...momentary.

War heroes return home and are greeted by their loved ones who have been waiting for years to see them.

Because in the end we have a choice:

Do we settle for ordinary or do we strive to be Made of More.

Online at http://bit.ly/1V0JJZS

The work was supported with outdoor and press activity (Figure 15).

Figure 15: Outdoor and press activity

Our first set of learnings

The work told a beautiful story of making a bolder choice. But research revealed the news every strategist has nightmares about. It confirmed that the idea was not the unmitigated success we'd hoped for. It showed that we'd succeeded in captivating our audience to a certain extent. But there was one flaw that we hadn't envisaged. Though we had landed the thought of *Made of More* with some, most were unclear as to why Guinness had chosen to talk about being *Made of More.* Whilst both films saw a positive ROI, only 'Clock' in Ireland saw an improvement versus our pre-*Made of More* return on investment (Figures 16 and 17).

Figures 16 and 17 refer to both revenue ROIs (RSV ROI) and profit ROIs (PROI).

Figure 16: Great Britain – *Made of More* ROI

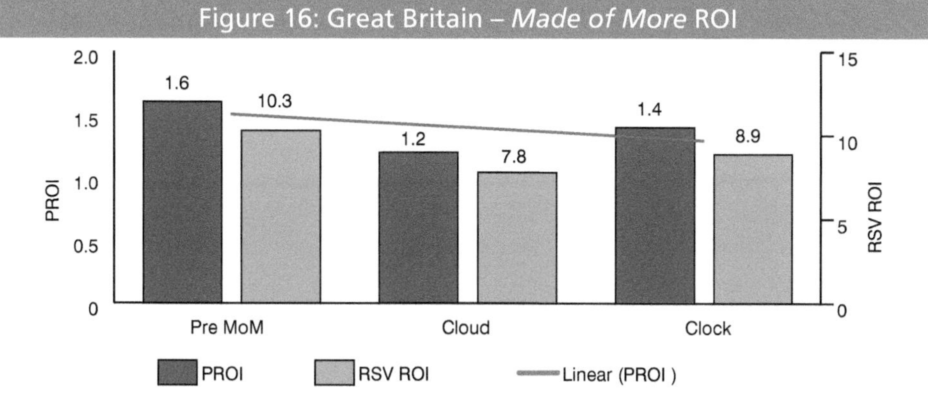

Source: Data2Decisions econometric modelling

Figure 17: Ireland – *Made of More* ROI

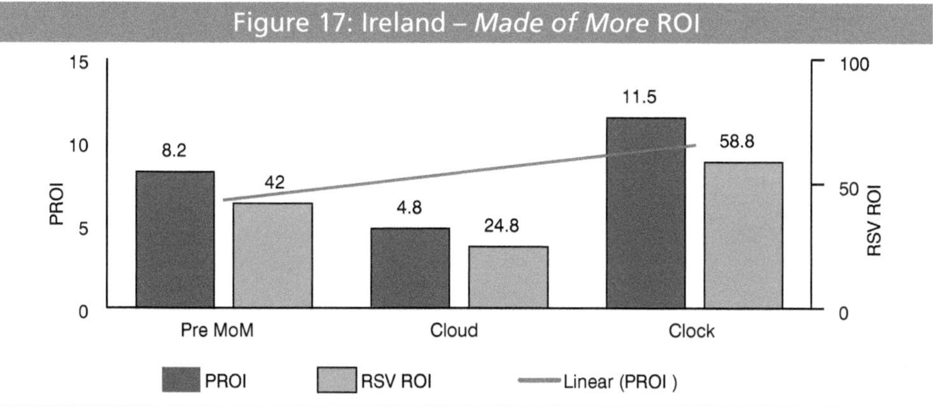

Source: Data2Decisions econometric modelling

We could have panicked

Thankfully, we didn't. We had faith in the strategic thinking behind *Made of More*, so we convinced all involved to press on. We discovered that to take *Made of More* forward, we might first need to go back a step.

If we really wanted to inspire consumers to carve their own path and make bold choices in life, we ought to back that up with our own intrinsic story of why Guinness is in fact a bold beer.

Made of More 2.0

Guinness is unquestionably a unique and bold drink.

As it is being poured, nitrogen bubbles slowly and gracefully ripple through the drink, leaving it with a dynamic surge.

The elemental power of the surge ensures that no other beer looks or tastes quite like a Guinness. The boldness of the surge gives it more character, more taste, more depth and more soul.

We set a clear new direction. If Guinness wanted to inspire others to be *Made of More*, our next round of work needed to help link the unique characteristics that made Guinness *Made of More* with the attitude we were celebrating.

The work, known as 'Surge', established the distinctiveness of Guinness in a way that had not been seen before, using the waves of the ocean to reflect the unique surge in every glass. Here, we successfully demonstrated how the philosophy Guinness celebrated in life is apparent within every single drink of Guinness (Figures 18 and 19).

Figure 18: 'Surge'

This commercial shows waves swirling to illustrate the Guinness surge.

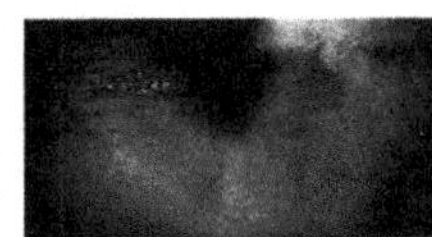
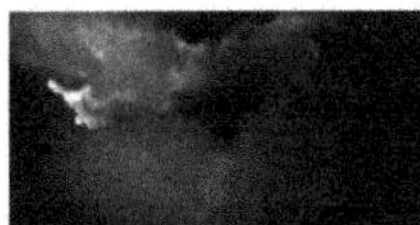

Black and white footage filmed on an underwater camera immerses the viewer in the sea. We see a wave begin to break overhead.

VO: Out of the depths it comes.

Swirling and surging, before at last it settles.

The wave surges and swirls, filling the screen. The visual is reminiscent of the Guinness pint. Finally, the water settles and becomes still.

Created like no other.

Guinness, Made of More

Online at http://bit.ly/1VoiuJu

Figure 19: Outdoor and press activity

A step closer to success

From 'Surge' came good news – consumers understood and liked the work, and comprehension around *Made of More* had improved. We were making progress. We saw higher ROIs in both markets compared to our pre-*Made of More* ROI (Figures 20 and 21).

Figure 20: Great Britain – *Made of More* ROI

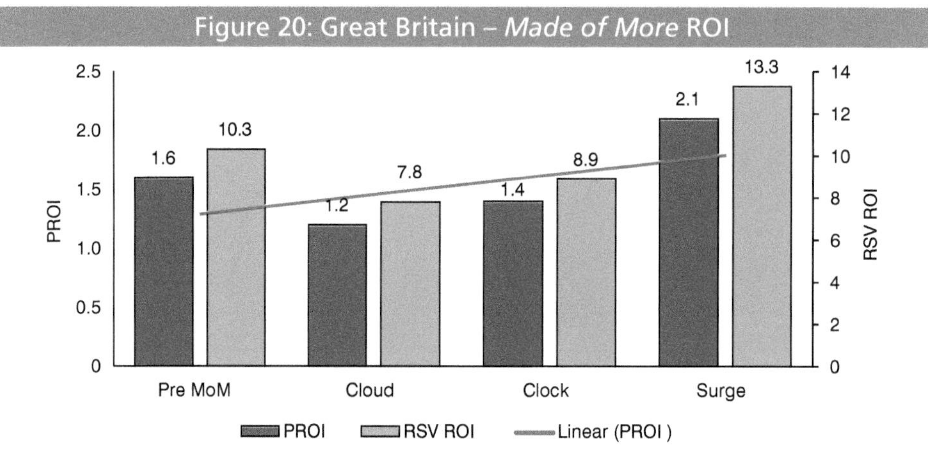

Source: Data2Decisions econometric modelling

Figure 21: Ireland – *Made of More* ROI

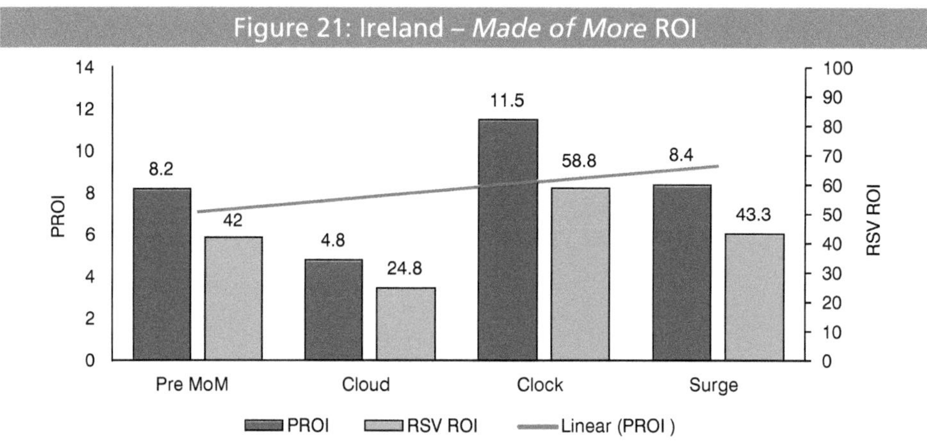

Source: Data2Decisions econometric modelling

But there was room for improvement. Projective research techniques uncovered something interesting about the work to date. All our initial iterations of *Made of More* had used inanimate objects, animals and metaphors to explain our idea. Our research found that these metaphors were bereft of certain Guinness brand characteristics our audience had come to expect, such as humanity, character and communion.

Our next iteration of *Made of More* needed a greater injection of the soul and spirit for which Guinness was known and loved.

Made of More 3.0: celebrating stories of those who have carved their own path

To ensure our work was more character-filled and less distant, we made the decision to celebrate people who shared our brand philosophy. These human stories would strengthen the perception of Guinness by telling stories of humanity, character and communion – the values the brand and product clearly held but hadn't been talking about. Coupled with that it would allow us to inject the warm tone of voice and 'twinkle in the eye' personality that Guinness communications were famous for.

We created a film about a group of friends, telling a story about their weekly, energy-packed game of wheelchair basketball. At the end of the game, all the friends unexpectedly stand and walk away from their wheelchairs, revealing that only one of the players is wheelchair-bound. The others are playing out of loyalty and dedication to their friend in the ultimate show of communion (Figure 22).

Figure 22: 'Basketball'

This commercial is about the importance of friendship and solidarity.

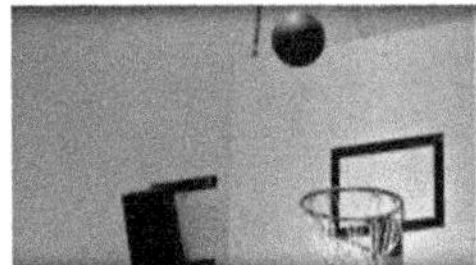

We see a group of men in wheelchairs playing a basketball game in a gymnasium.

VO: Dedication.

Loyalty.

Friendship.

At the end of the game, all the men get out of their wheelchair and stand up, except one. We realise that he is the only one who is disabled, but his friends have all borrowed wheelchairs to play basketball with him.

The choices we make reveal the true nature of our character.

The men go to a bar to enjoy a Guinness together.

Guinness, Made of More

Online at http://bit.ly/1ow44s8

We followed this with a TV ad and online documentary that told the story of the 'Sapeurs' – a real group of men who form 'The Society of the Elegant Persons of the Congo'.

Ordinary people by day, by night the gentlemen dress to the nines in flamboyant suits, coming together to bring joy to their community. Through their attitude and style, they demonstrate that no matter the circumstances you face, you can always choose to be bolder in life (Figures 23 and 24).

Figure 23: 'Sapeurs'

Ths commercial is about a real-life group of people in the Congo, known as the Sapeurs.

We begin in a typical African sugar cane field, being burnt for harvest. Then we cut to a man on the street pushing a wheelbarrow. We see more of these Sapeurs in their places of work and then mov into their homes, where they wash their hard days off them.

VO: In life, you cannot always choose what you do,

But you can always choose who you are.

These men have spirit. We see them putting on different clothes – a smart tie, a fedora etc. More Sapeurs emerge from different places and start to make their separate journeys somewhere.

We are the Sapeurs, the Society of Elegant Persons of the Congo.

We realise that the gentlemen have all made their way to the same tavern. A Sapeur rises from out of his seat and takes centre stage, dancing to the music and showing off his individual style.

You see my friends, with every brace and every cufflink we say:

I am the master of my fate,
I am the captain of my soul.

Guinness 'Made Of More'

Online at http://bit.ly/1meFEOw

Figure 24: 'Sapeurs' documentary

Online at http://bit.ly/LeGmO5

Our resolve to continually improve our understanding and delivery of *Made of More* paid off, with ROI's significantly improving in both markets (Figures 25 and 26).

Figure 25: Great Britain – *Made of More* ROI

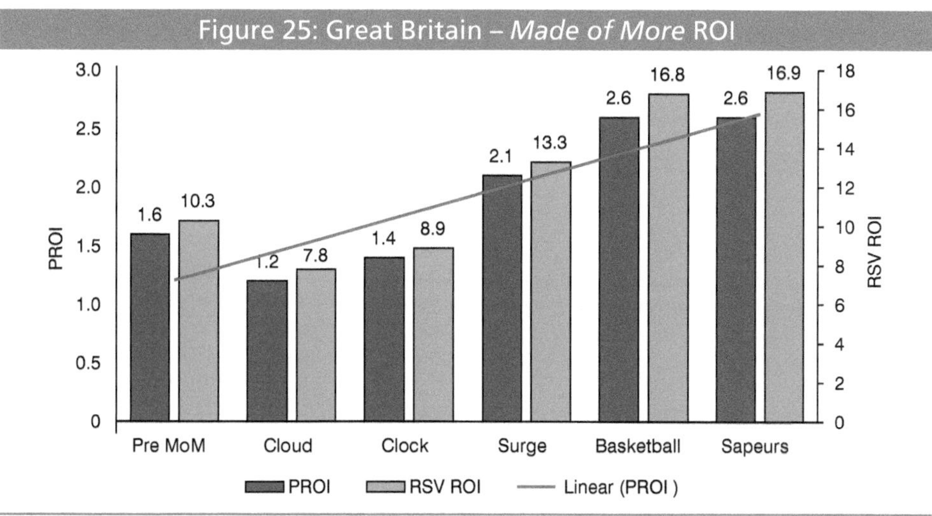

Source: Data2Decisions econometric modelling

Figure 26: Ireland – *Made of More* ROI

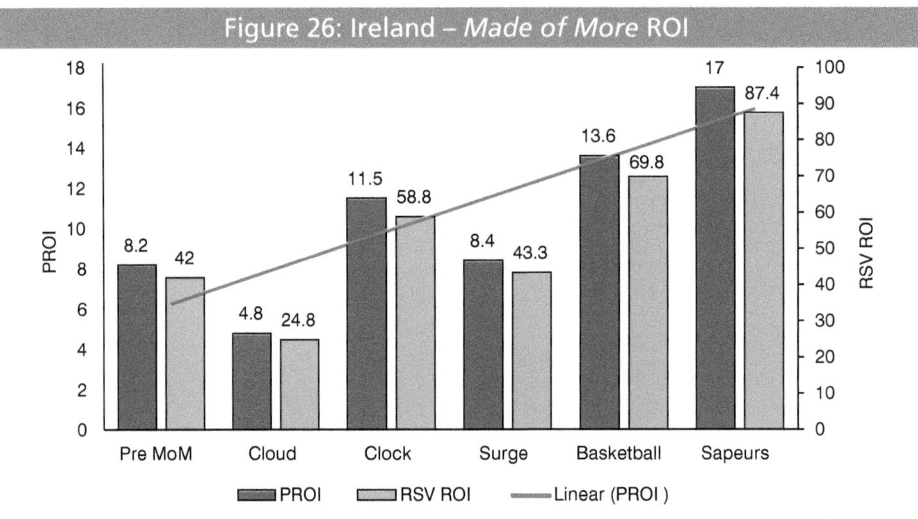

Source: Data2Decisions econometric modelling

Figure 27: The Sapeurs celebrate their impressive ROIs

Made of More 4.0

Guinness' next major project was to create communications for their rugby sponsorship. We had learned that delivering *Made of More* through human stories was particularly powerful. For rugby, we developed four films, one for each of the participating home nations (England, Ireland, Scotland and Wales), with every film tapping into the sporting team pride of each country (Figures 28–31).

Figure 28: 'Jonny Wilkinson – Loved By All, Even the French!'

This commercial shows how rugby legend Jonny Wilkinson is the 'humble hero' of Toulon.

We see the citizens of Toulon going about their everyday lives. French-speakers are filmed expressing praise and admiration; their words are translated by on-screen titles.

Titles: He gave back life and passion to the people.

We'd never seen his like before

When he goes in to a restaurant... people start standing up and clapping.

He's like an artist, like a singer... like a poet, like a writer...

He inspires us to become better.

He arrived in Toulon... his body a little broken.

Because of his injuries... everyone had their doubts.

But he was dedicated... body and soul.

We see groups of people making their way to a rugby game, bearing flags and banners.

Humility. Courage. Solidarity.

He was a gentleman.

He never played dirty, not once.

The perfect man.

He's the heart of the town. He's in our hearts.

All I want to say is... Thank you, Sir Jonny.

We see Jonny on the pitch at the Stade Mayol, the crowd cheering and clapping.

JONNY WILKINSON
Humble hero, loved by the English.
Adored by the French.

Guinness. Made of More

Online at http://bit.ly/10lorf6

Figure 29: 'David and Goliath'

This commercial is about the historic Munster victory over the All Blacks in 1978.

We open on archive footage of Limerick City, as anticipation builds for the rugby game.

VO: One team dominates the game of rugby. The All Blacks.

We see the Munster team waiting nervously in the changing room. We cut to the pitch, where the All Blacks perform their intimidating haka.

Rivals surrender before a ball is even kicked.

And that's your fate today, the Munster team was told.

The game gets underway; we hear commentary documenting the action.

But none of them listened; not even their smallest player.

With a single tackle, he stopped Goliath, dead.

We witness Seamus Dennison's famous tackle on Stu Wilson. The tone changes, as Munster begin to fight back.

And every Irishman grew twelve feet taller.

The crowd cheer as the Munster team make history, beating the mighty All Blacks.

Titles:
31 October 1978
The day 15 brave Munster men
beat the unbeatable.

Guinness. Made of More

Online at http://bit.ly/1BHNuKP

Figure 30: 'Mind Over Matter'

This commercial is about how Welsh rugby player Shane Williams defied critics who said he was too small to play rugby.

We see a rugby team walking through the tunnel and out onto the pitch.

VO: Strength. Size. Power.

These are the things a man needs to play rugby.

The team line up to sing the anthem. We see Shane Williams, dwarfed by his teammates.

And you have none of these, Williams, they said.

But they were wrong.

We see footage of Shane scoring tries, outrunning the opposition. His teammates congratulate him and crowd go wild.

It was the size of his heart.

The power of his ambition.

The strength of his character.

SHANE WILLIAMS
87 caps. 58 tries.
And "too small to play rugby".

Guinness, Made of More

Online at http://bit.ly/1sjDb67

Figure 31: 'Irrepressible Spirit'

This commercial tells the story of how the 'Voice of Rugby', Bill McLaren, became a commentator.

We see archive footage of a hospital ward, where tuberculosis sufferers are being tended to by nurses.

VO: To be told: "You have tuberculosis; you'll never play rugby again" on the eve of playing for your country would break most people.

We see a photograph of a young Bill McLaren, standing alongside his rugby teammates.

But not Bill McLaren. He started commentating on the hospital ping pong, to make the others smile, he said.

We hear Bill McLaren's voice and see photographs of him in the hospital, followed by footage of ping pong matches and hospital patients smiling and laughing.

And in doing so, found a way back to the game he loved.

We see footage of Bill McLaren in the commentator's box, turning out his famous witticisms and catchphrases as he observes the action on the pitch. The crowd cheer, showing their admiration.

Titles:
BILL MCLAREN
The irrepressible "voice of rugby".
And ping pong.

Guinness. Made of More

Online at http://bit.ly/1HfeTn6

A grand slam

Again, we continued to see work that delivered ROIs that were significantly higher than work that ran prior to the development of *Made of More* (Figures 32 and 33).

Figure 32: Great Britain – *Made of More* ROI

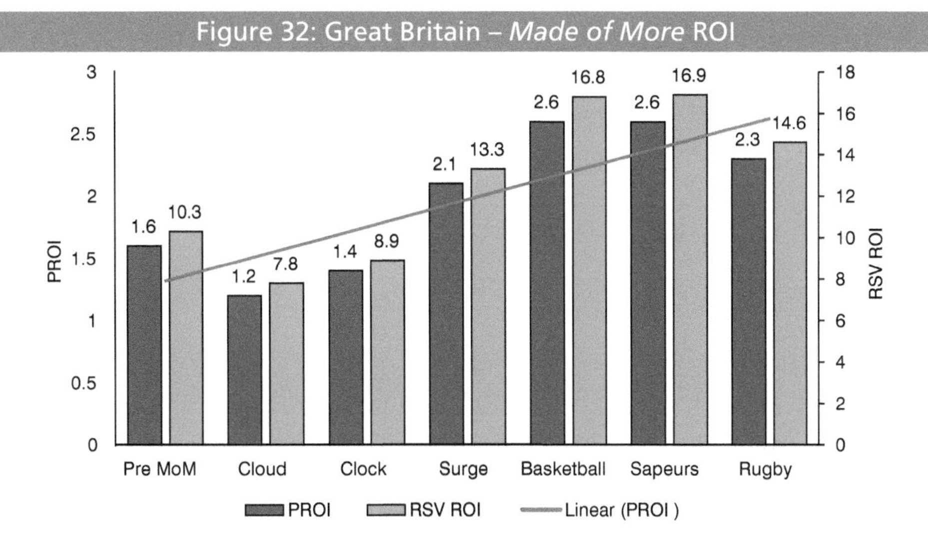

Source: Data2Decisions econometric modelling

Figure 33: Ireland – *Made of More* ROI

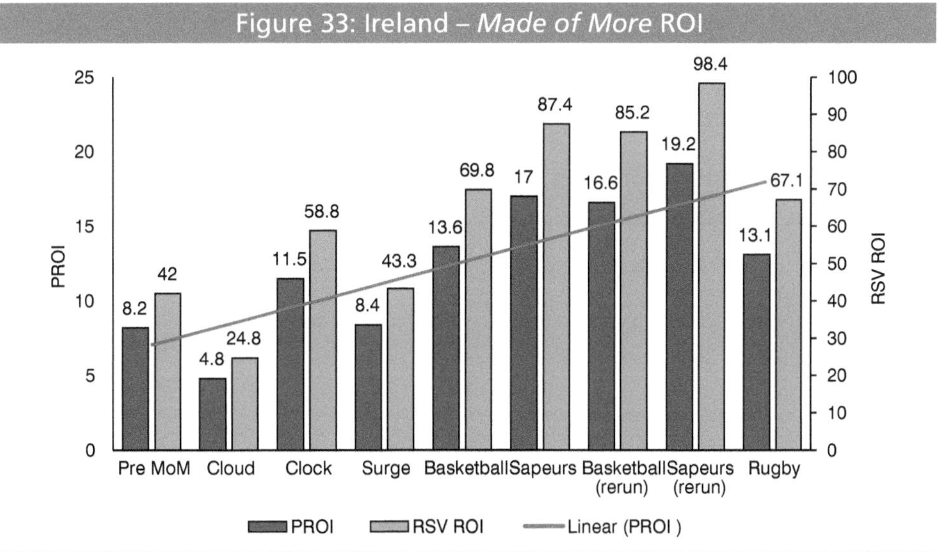

Source: Data2Decisions econometric modelling

A return on investment *Made of More*

The econometrics clearly evidence that a commitment to a long-term strategy and a creatively brave idea has paid off over time. As we honed our creative approach we saw a steady build in ROIs until eventually we were delivering ROIs up to *1.6 times* as effective in Great Britain and *2.3 times* as effective in Ireland as pre-*Made of More* campaigns.

Revisiting our objectives

1. Did we deliver the cultural traction and creative brilliance that Guinness has become known for?

Yes we did.

People loved the work

Qualitative research demonstrated the popularity of our work:

'Cloud'

'The usual distinctive, arty mini-film I expect from Guinness advertising.'

'It gave a deeper impression of the character of the drink.'

'It highlights the fact that Guinness is not the same as other brands, it is unique.'

'The cloud was so clever an idea, so different from other adverts.'

Millward Brown post-test evaluation

'Clock'

'Outstanding and the brand strives for more.'

'Distinctive.'

'Guinness is a special brand.'

'The clock and the ambition to be more than a normal bloke in the street. Excellent.'

Millward Brown post-test evaluation

'Surge'

'Guinness is cool – dark, complex, and ads are always clever and provoking.'

'Epic – almost neoclassical sense of art.'

'Every Guinness is unique – very striking.'

'Makes me really think how good the brand is.'

Millward Brown post-test evaluation

'Basketball'

'I think it is original and shows how much friendship is worth.'

'The theme of equality and friendship is powerful.'

'It is unusual and fits the brand well.'

'It's the type of advertising I expect of Guinness.'

Millward Brown post-test evaluation

'Sapeurs'

'I liked the characters featured as they felt warm and interesting.'

'This is quite unique and special.'

'The sense of style and care with which the advert was made – in that sense very reminiscent of other Guinness advertising.'

'It is good to be different and to stand out – be proud.'

Millward Brown post-test evaluation

'Rugby'

'If you think back to famous Guinness ads this fits with that, there's that kind of story, that passion behind it – these are Guinness ads no doubt.'

'You can see the emotion immediately and that draws you in.'

'You almost don't need to know what country it's set in, it's the story of a team doing the impossible.'

Millward Brown post-test evaluation

It's an idea that has landed in culture

'Surge' was picked up by influential surf magazines including *Transworld Surf*, *Stab Magazine* and *Club Of The Waves* (Figure 34).

Figure 34: *Surf* magazine

'Basketball' received scores of earned PR with the Huffington Post noting that 'we don't often give advertisers free promotion, but this Guinness commercial had us utterly captivated'.

Figure 35: Online press

The Guinness sales team were inundated with calls requesting permission to hold their own 'Sapeurs' nights in pubs. Radio shows and newspaper articles proactively ran spots and column inches discussing the fortunes of the Sapeurs. And the word 'Sapeurs' actually became part of everyday conversations with people using it to describe particularly fashionable gentlemen (Figures 36 and 37).

Figure 36: Irish rugby pundit George Hook is called out on Facebook for his fashionable dress sense

Figure 37: BBC Radio 4 took an in-depth look at the Sapeurs

The Democratic Republic of Style

By Mike Wendling
BBC News

14 March 2016 Magazine

When you got dressed this morning, how much thought did you put into your clothes? Probably not as much as a group of young men in

In today's Magazine

For the rugby work, Millward Brown found that 66% of consumers who had seen the films said they would talk about them with friends (versus 46% norm). Google reported that one film even had a paid-to-earned ratio of views of 1:1 (that is, the film had an equal percentage of paid views to earned views).

It was even tweeted about by influential rugby players including Dylan Hartley, the now captain of England (Figure 38).

Figure 38: Dylan Hartley tweet

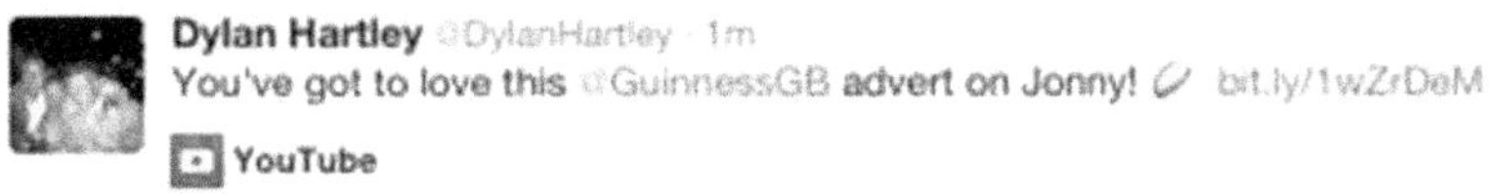

Dylan Hartley @DylanHartley · 1m
You've got to love this @GuinnessGB advert on Jonny! bit.ly/1wZrDeM
YouTube

People were interested in finding out more about *Made of More*

People were interested in the backstories of the work. For example, the making of the 'Surge' work has received over 500,000 views with no media support behind it (Figure 39).

Figure 39: The making of 'Surge'

Created Like No Other: Making of Guinness Surge Advert in Tahiti | Guinness 2013

There were over 1.7 million views of the Sapeurs' back story in an online documentary (Figure 40).

Figure 40: 'Sapeurs' back story

People parodied our work

A number of groups, including a university fashion society parodied the film (Figure 41).

Figure 41: 'The Dappers'

It even helped someone sell a book

Post the launch of the 'David and Goliath' rugby film, a book written about the Munster vs All Blacks 1978 game had to go back into print to meet a sudden upsurge in people requesting it (Figure 42).

Figure 42: Alan English, author of *Stand Up and Fight*, tweets his thanks to Guinness

Award juries around the world loved the work

In total, the *Made of More* work detailed in this paper has received 102 creative awards including wins at all of the major international award festivals. The work featured in this case study has won 10 Cannes Lions.

Sapeurs was the fourth most awarded film in the world in 2014.[14] The same year, Diageo (the owner of the Guinness brand) was awarded *Campaign* magazine's Advertiser of the Year with Guinness cited as a key reason for victory. Recently, Guinness was awarded *Advertiser of Excellence* at the BTAA for its great work over the years (Figure 43).[15]

Figure 43: *Campaign's* Advertiser of the Year

2. Did we see an increase in brand fame and affinity to the Guinness brand?

Yes we did.

Our cultural traction and creative success enabled us to achieve this objective. In a more competitive environment, saliency was key. Brand fame can be evidenced in improvements between pre and post campaign dips (Figure 44).

Figure 44: Salience

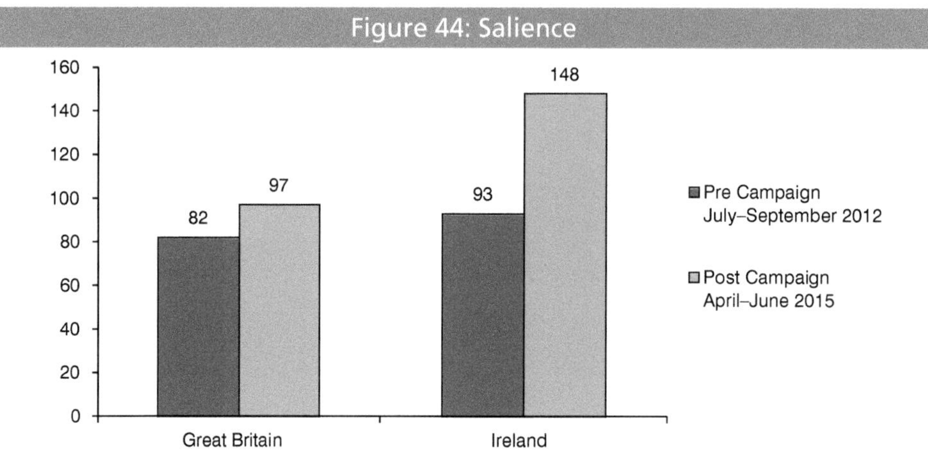

Source: Millward Brown
Note these figures are measured as indices rather than percentages and are benchmarked against the category average.

In order to stave off the threat posed by competitors, it was important to be seen as more distinctive than the rest of the category. Both markets saw an uplift (Figure 45).

Figure 45: Guinness is a distinctive brand

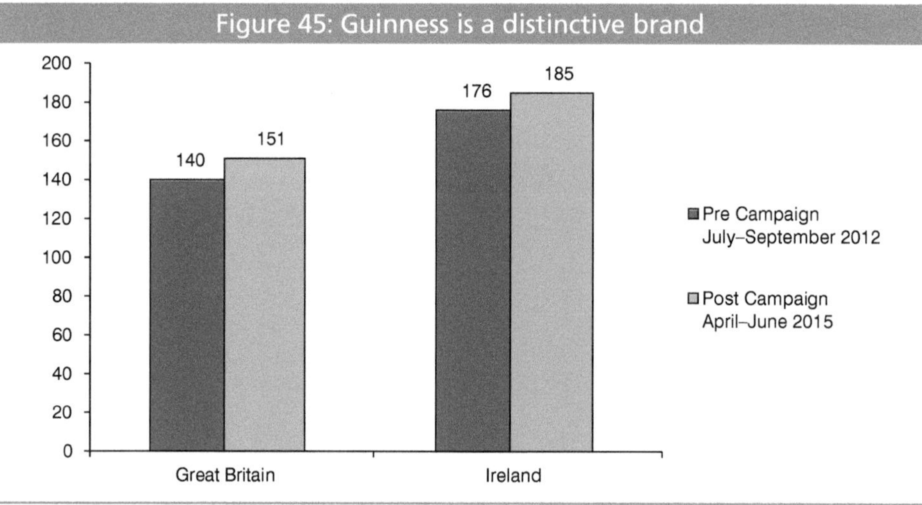

Source: Millward Brown
Note these figures are measured as indices rather than percentages and are benchmarked against the category average.

Guinness also saw a significant increase in pre and post campaign dips in both markets across the metric 'Guinness is a brand that is leading the way' (Figure 46).

Figure 46: Guinness is a brand that is leading the way

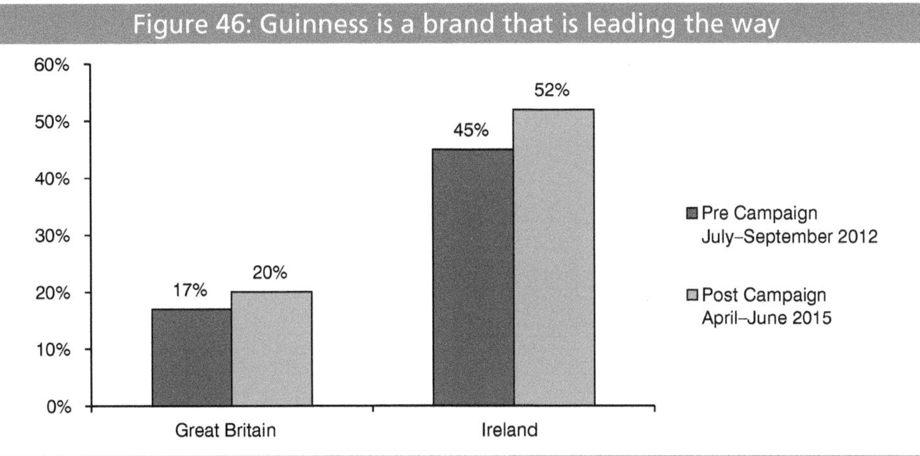

Source: Millward Brown
Note these figures are measured as percentages.

3. Did we see a decrease in price sensitivity?

The price of Guinness in bars and pubs has been increasing constantly over the past four years (Figure 47).[16]

Figure 47: Price per pint, Guinness Draught, on-trade

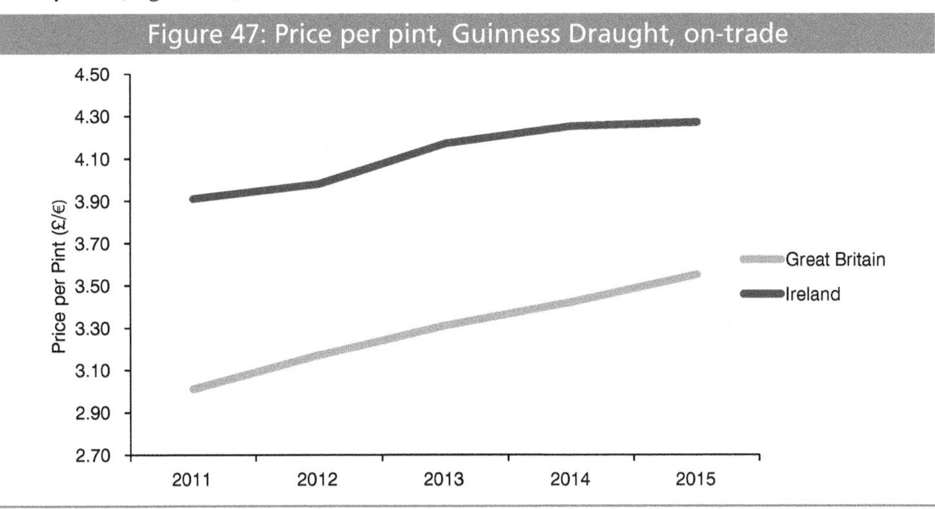

Source: Nielsen / CGA

By 2014, Guinness started to see significant drops in price elasticity in both Great Britain and Ireland (Figure 48).[17]

Figure 48: Price elasticity, Guinness Draught, on-trade

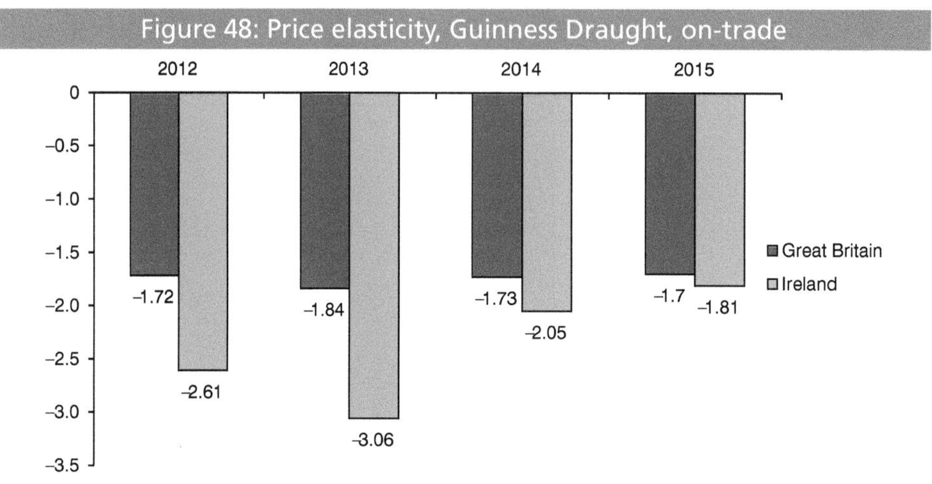

Source: Data2Decisions econometric modelling

Years of decline were turned around as we developed *Made of More*. Value share decline was arrested in 2014 (Figure 49).[18]

Figure 49: Guinness Draught, on-trade value share (%)

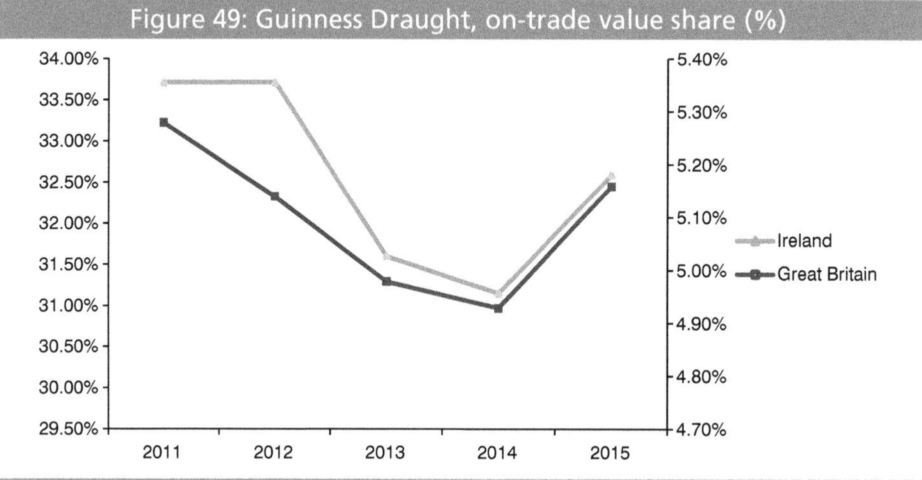

Source: Nielsen / CGA & Diageo internal sales data

The reduction in price sensitivity also helped us to stem long-term decline in volume in GB, and we saw an upturn in fortunes in Ireland (Figures 50 and 51).

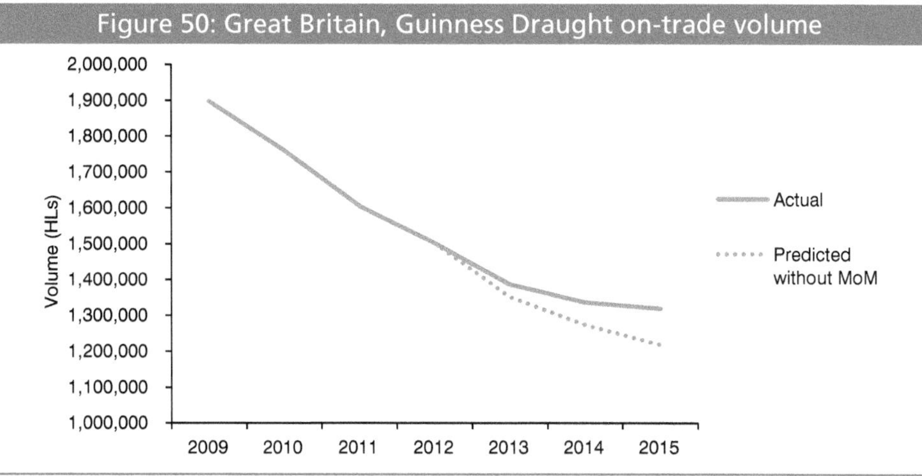

Source: CGA, Nielsen, internal Diageo sales and Data2Decisions econometric models

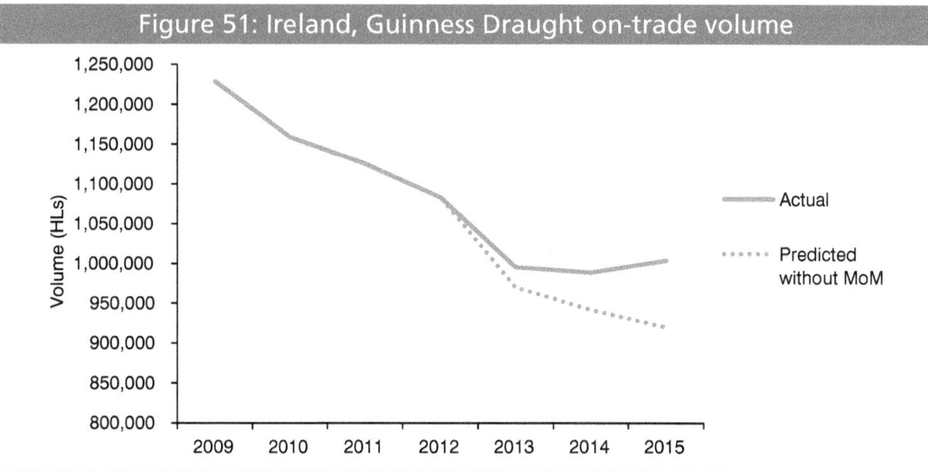

Source: CGA, Nielsen, internal Diageo sales and Data2Decisions econometric models

4. Did we see an improved ROI for Guinness?

Data2Decisions has conducted econometric modelling on the effect of the campaign.

Revenue ROI

Our revenue ROI is £19.90 per £1 spent.

This is significantly higher than our pre-*Made of More* campaign average revenue ROI (£12.01) (Figure 52).

Figure 52 Pre vs post *Made of More* revenue ROI

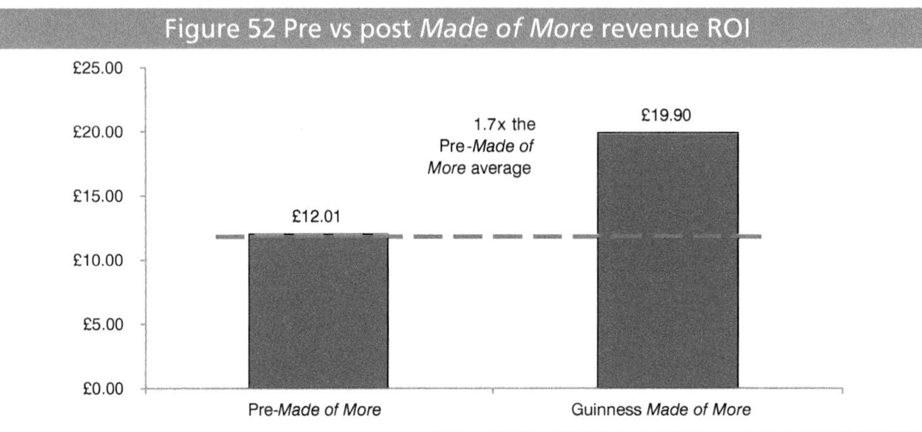

Source: Data2Decisions econometric modelling

This is the second highest recorded Revenue ROI for a beer brand in the IPA awards – behind only the Foster's 2014 Grand Prix winning campaign (Table 1).

Table 1: Revenue ROI by brand

Brand	Year	Revenue ROI
Fosters	2014	£32.00
Guinness	2016	£19.90
Stella Artois	2000	£12.00
Budweiser	2002	£6.00
Bud Ice	1998	£5.00
Stella Artois	1996	£5.00
Marston's Pedigree	1994	£4.00
Stella Artois	1992	£2.00

Source: WARC/IPA

Profit ROI

We didn't just generate extra revenue. We saw an incredible improvement in profit ROI (partly due to our strategic decision to focus communications on the profitable on-trade sector).

Overall, *Made of More* delivered a profit ROI 66% higher than campaigns prior to its introduction.

The total profit ROI is £3.88 per £1 spent.

This is significantly higher than our pre *Made of More* campaign average profit ROI (£2.34) (Figure 53).

Figure 53: Pre vs post *Made of More* profit ROI

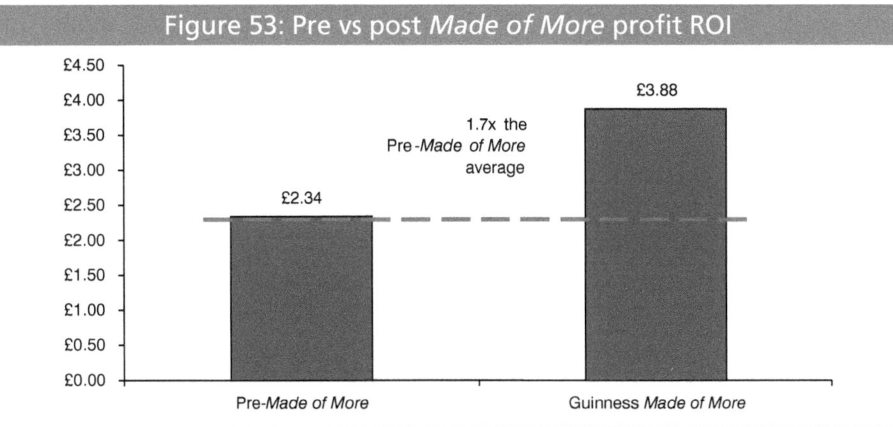

Source: Data2Decisions econometric modelling

To put this performance in context against the category benchmark, this campaign significantly outperforms profit ROIs from other beer brands in Data2Decisions database, with a *PROI 1.8 times the category norm* (Figure 54). Rather than having parity with the category, we performed significantly better.[19]

Figure 54: Guinness profit ROI vs category

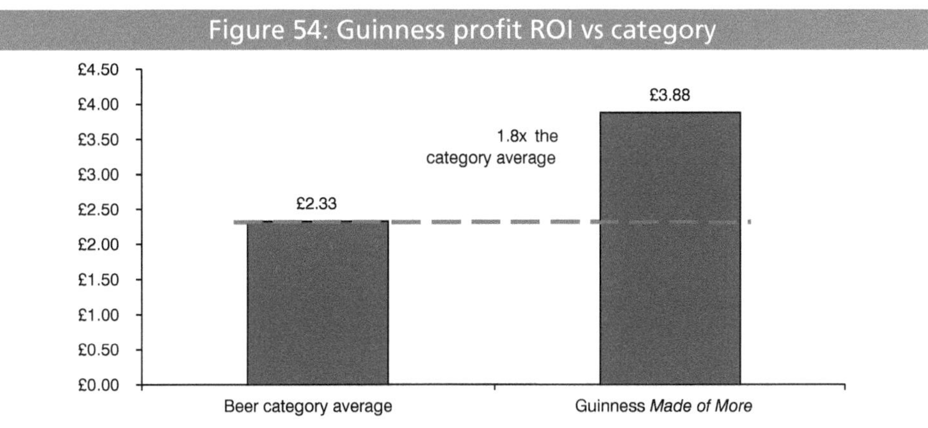

Source: Data2Decisions database

This makes us the most profitable beer campaign in the history of the IPA awards (Table 2).

Table 2: Profit ROI by brand

Brand	Year	Profit ROI
Guinness	2016	£3.88
Carling Black Label	1996	£2.08
Stella Artois	1992	£1.92
Marston's Pedigree	1994	£1.64
Marston's Low C	1994	£1.29
Tribute Ale	2009	£1.16

Source: WARC/IPA

Discounting other factors

Econometric modelling conducted by Data2Decisions has isolated the effect of the communications when calculating the ROI. This section demonstrates how none of the other key sales' drivers could have been responsible for the turnaround in commercial results for Guinness.

Price

Our work has improved the price elasticity of Guinness. The price index of Guinness versus the rest of the market has been consistent over the period in both markets (Figure 55).

Figure 55: Guinness Draught price index vs market average

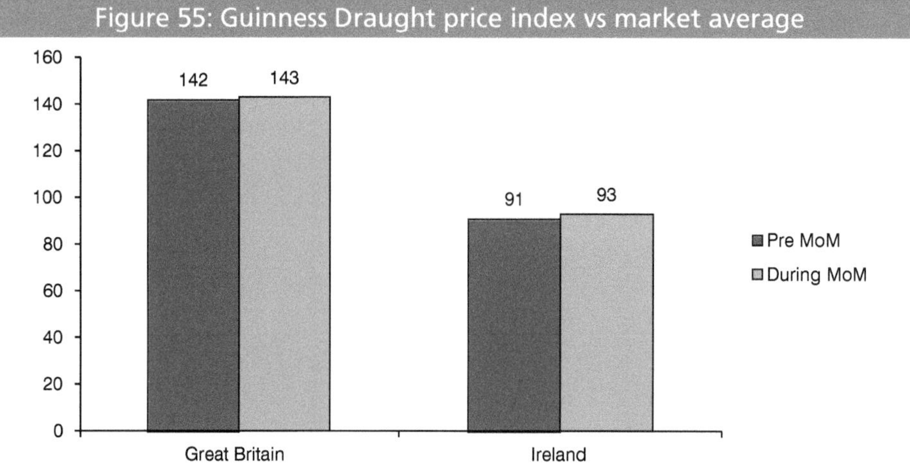

Source: Nielsen / CGA

Promotions

Given the complexity of promotions, along with the huge range of Guinness SKUs sold in the off-trade across both markets, we have excluded the impact this campaign may have had on this channel. However, it is highly likely that our work has also contributed to sales in the off-trade channel. Due to alcohol restrictions, promotion in the on-trade in alcohol is minimal and therefore not a factor.

Product

Guinness launched a range of new products over the period in question including a range of new porters, a golden ale and a new lager. We have not included sales from these new products as part of our volume sales, value share or ROI calculations, even though undoubtedly the *Made of More* campaign will have driven additional sales for these products.

Distribution

Distribution in Ireland has remained steady, but declined in Britain (partly due to the growth of craft beer). If anything, distribution has applied negative pressure on sales and market share (Figure 56).

Figure 56: Guinness Draught on-trade WTD distribution

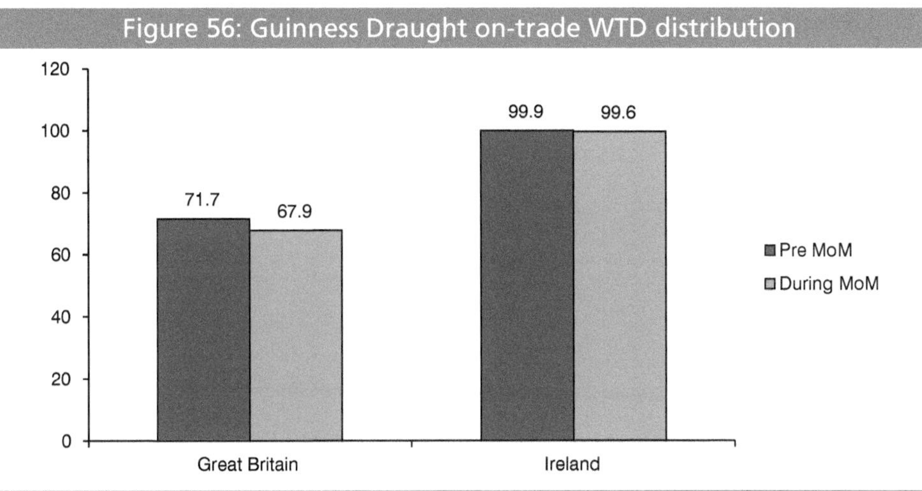

Source: Nielsen / CGA

Number of pubs

Success cannot be attributed to a growth in the number of pubs. Pub numbers actually declined in both markets (Figures 57 and 58).

Figure 57: Number of pubs in Great Britain 2008–2015

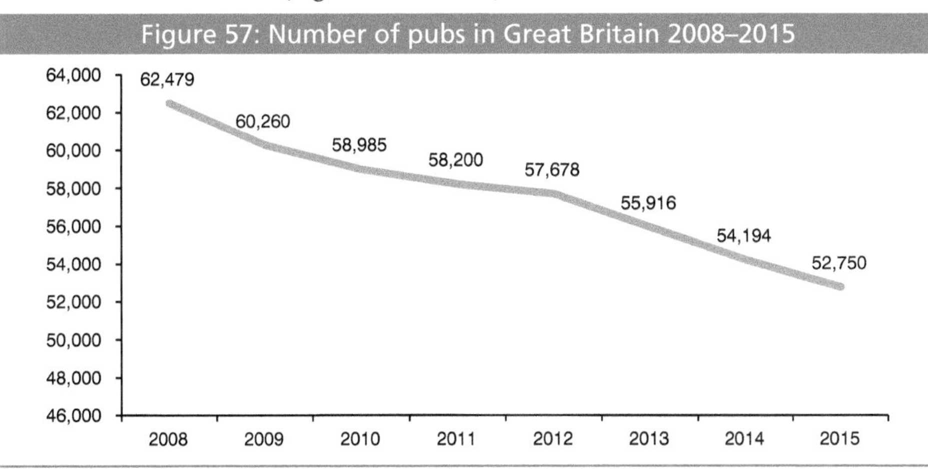

Source: Camra

Figure 58: Number of pubs in Ireland 2007–2015

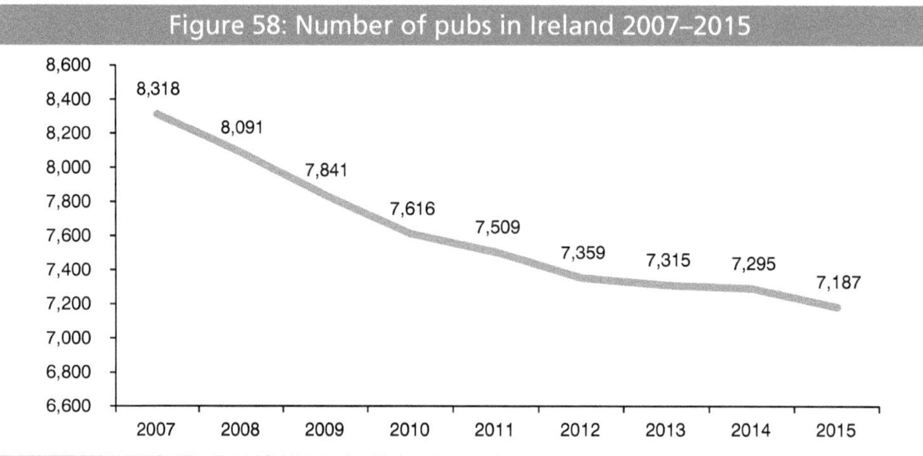

Source: Irish Revenue Commission

Economy

The effect of any economic growth (and beer trends driven by the economy) has been captured in the econometric model.

Spend Level/Share of voice

Whilst media spend for both Guinness and other beer brands fluctuated over the campaign period there was no sustained share of voice advantage for Guinness during the campaign (Figure 59).

Figure 59: Guinness share of voice

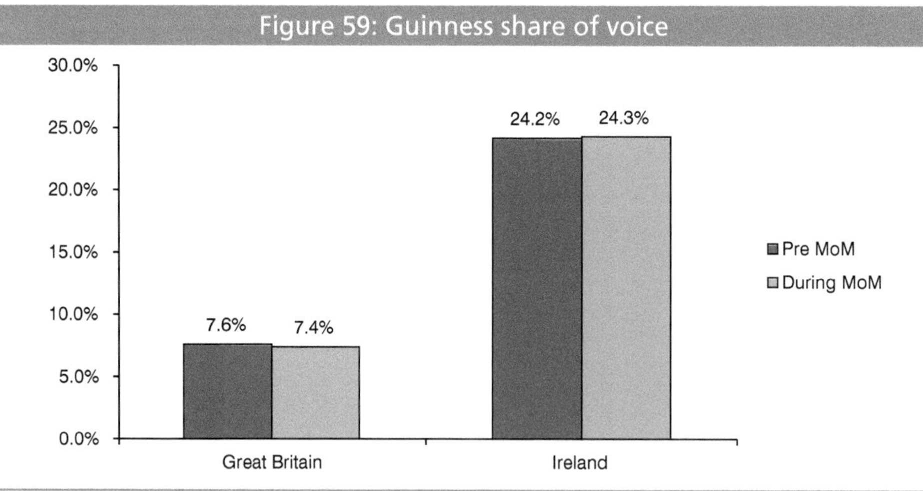

Source: Nielsen Ad Dynamix / Carat

Weather

Weather does influence Guinness sales over time. The effect of this is measured in the econometric model. Perhaps unsurprisingly, colder weather drives an increase in

Guinness sales whilst warmer weather dampens Guinness sales as consumers tend to switch to other options like lager. On average, over the period, temperatures were actually slightly higher in both markets and therefore putting downward pressure on Guinness market share (Figure 60).

Figure 60: Average temperatures

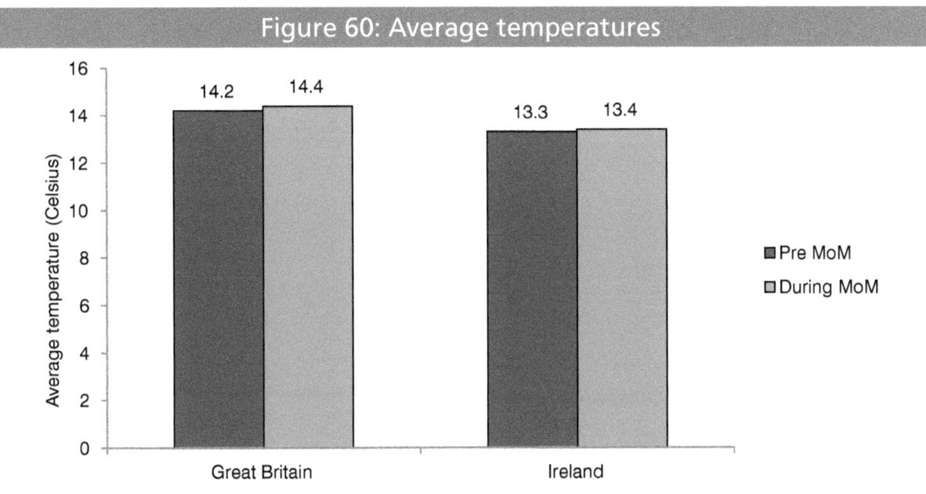

Source: Weather Underground

Conclusion

Made of More has not only continued the Guinness tradition of creating memorable and magical advertising, but has helped the business face a multitude of macro challenges in both Britain and Ireland. It took a tenacious team that had the grit and willingness to test and learn along the way to help reveal the power of *Made of More.*

Together, we've built a rich bank of learnings that have been used in Guinness markets worldwide. *Made of More* has now successfully been deployed around the world, winning a swag of awards in our sister markets of Africa, America and Asia.

It proves that sticking to an idea and taking an iterative approach really does pay off in the longer term.

Guinness has the highest recorded profit return on investment within the beer category in IPA history (£3.88 for every £1 spent).

Sláinte to that.[20]

Notes

1. For the purposes of this paper, Great Britain is defined as being England, Wales and Scotland, whereas Ireland refers to both the Republic of Ireland and Northern Ireland.
2. The Celtic Tiger was a period of unprecedented economic growth in Ireland. It began around 1995, and ensured Ireland at one point became one of the wealthiest countries in Europe. This came to a dramatic end in 2008 and the effects are still being felt today.
3. International Monetary Fund.
4. 'UK lurches back into recession', http://www.thisismoney.co.uk/money/news/article-2134870/UK-lurches-recession-0-2-GDP-fall-signals-double-dip.html

5. Data comes from: 'Euro crisis even staggers Irish pubs', http://www.usatoday.com/story/news/world/2012/09/25/ireland-economy-pubs/1588187/&British; 'Beer sales plummet', http://www.telegraph.co.uk/finance/newsbysector/retailandconsumer/9626126/British-beer-sales-plummet.html.
6. Guinness is a stout. However, their main competition is the beer category (lagers and ales).
7. This segment is also made up of stouts such as Murphy's and Beamish. The Irish statistics come from Research and Markets. http://www.researchandmarkets.com/reports/2238319/ireland_beer_market_insights_2012. The British statistics come from: 'Outlook is black as Guinness sales fall'. http://www.morningadvertiser.co.uk/Drinks-Brands-News/Outlook-is-black-as-Guinness-sales-fall
8. 'Brewing up a storm: craft beer sales continue to climb', http://www.bighospitality.co.uk/Trends-Reports/Brewing-up-a-storm-Craft-beer-sales-continue-to-climb; 'Mintel reviews the Irish drinks market', http://www.bordbia.ie/industry/manufacturers/insight/alerts/Pages/MintelreviewstheIrishdrinksmarket.aspx?year=2013&wk=4
9. In the USA, by 2012, the craft beer market held 6.5% share of total beer volume. http://www.brewersassociation.org/press-releases/brewers-association-craft-continues-to-brew-growth/
10. And we were proven to be right. According to CGA strategies, the craft beer category is now growing at a rate of 79% per year.
11. Guinness is often referred to as a 'pint of the black stuff'.
12. In the results section of this paper, it is worth bearing this in mind as the results in Ireland versus Great Britain reflect the maturity of the brand and the relationship it has with its drinkers in each market.
13. Peter Field and Les Binet (2013) *The Long and the Short of It: Balancing the short and long-term effects of marketing*, London: IPA.
14. Gunn Report 2014.
15. The sources for these can be found at http://www.campaignlive.co.uk/news/1326028/&http://www.britisharrows.com/awards-2016/winners/
16. This trend is likely to continue (not just for Guinness but for the entire beer market) as pub and bar owners continue to pass on rising costs directly to consumers as well as higher tax measures on alcohol being a real possibility.
17. The incremental revenue and profit that was generated from this drop in price sensitivity is not directly included in our ROI calculations and, perhaps more importantly, the safeguard against future sales degradation in the face of rising prices is not included either. So it is fair to say that the ROIs calculated in this paper and their potential long-term benefits could be substantially higher.
18. Value share had also been in decline for a number of years prior to 2011. However, the specific breakdown of the on-trade versus off-trade is not available.
19. Our pre *Made of More* ROI was only £0.01 higher than the category average.
20. How the Irish like to toast their drinks.

GOLD AWARD

Macmillan Cancer Support

Making sure no one faces cancer alone, today or tomorrow

By Andrew Perkins, VCCP
Contributing authors: Henry Bilson and Matt Butler, VCCP; Carly Wilson, Macmillan Cancer Support
Credited companies: VCCP; Macmillan Cancer Support

Summary

This paper tells the story of how Macmillan Cancer Support achieved record fundraising income at a new level of efficiency. The 'Not alone' campaign helped Macmillan achieve £96.7m of additional income from fundraising alone, even before adding in the financial benefits of the improvement in Macmillan's brand metrics and in its influence as an organisation. The profit ROMI was estimated to be about £2.40 for every £1 invested. 'Not alone' also helped more people access Macmillan services, and informed corporate partnership and government policy. This was all achieved by launching a simple, striking and irrefutable idea that no one should face cancer alone, a thought which encouraged those living with cancer to get support, and others to give support.

Editor's comment

The task faced was complex with a number of different audiences needing to be appealed to. The judges admired how a single insight had pulled all these audiences together to produce a campaign with exceptionally strong results.

Client Comment

Carly Wilson, Head of Brand Advertising and Campaign Integration, Macmillan Cancer Support

'Not alone' enabled Macmillan to achieve a new level of integration, not only in our brand communications but also across fundraising, services and partnerships. In a complex organisation like Macmillan, that meant the brand team working more closely with the wider organisation to educate on the idea behind the campaign, and demonstrate its value.

The campaign also increased the level of emotional intensity in our communications. This meant working with VCCP closely to ensure we always did this in a way that was sympathetic and never gratuitous. We had to be ruthless guardians of the Macmillan brand, and ensure that we always kept the interests of people living with, and affected by, cancer at the heart of our behaviour. The increased impact our advertising delivered also meant we needed to be prepared for an increased scale and intensity in feedback from the public.

'Not alone' opened up new opportunities to communicate: we created new experiential campaigns like our 'Isolation box', new calls to action like our 'Reach out' campaign, and new tools, such as The Source, to help people overcome issues of isolation.

These innovations involved working with teams across Macmillan, and helped us become better prepared for a future in which our support is delivered in more diverse, and often more indirect ways.

And finally, 'Not alone' required more complex comms planning than previous campaigns, and so meant that we worked in a more integrated way with our colleagues and agencies, involving VCCP, PHD and our research partners like The Nursery in more collaborative up-front planning, campaign development and campaign evaluation.

Introduction

Previous IPA Effectiveness Awards papers from the world of not-for-profit have tended to demonstrate payback either in terms of fundraising, or the financial benefits (usually to the taxpayer) of a social behavioural change.

This paper attempts, we think for the first time, to do both: to demonstrate how a single idea, brought to life in advertising and far beyond, has driven record improvements in fundraising income, while at the same time creating behaviour changes at individual right up to government level that will deliver lasting benefits to society as a whole.

This attempt is undertaken not to make life hard for the authors (or indeed readers) of this paper, but simply because this properly reflects the objectives of the campaign as they were originally set: to inspire millions of people to get involved – either by giving the help they can or, if they are affected by cancer, to get the help they need.

We'll start with the story behind that brief.

The story behind the brief

In 2010, there were two million people in the UK living with cancer. That figure is expected to double by 2030.[1]

This presents an enormous challenge as to how cancer care will be delivered: it won't just happen in hospitals, clinics and surgeries, but in homes, high streets and online. We will all need to get more active in helping each other live with cancer.

And it's Macmillan that occupies what you might call the 'living with cancer' space. Cancer Research UK and others research cures and treatments, while Marie Curie and local hospices focus on palliative care (looking after people who are dying). Macmillan deals with everything in between. Nurses of course, but also other medical professionals,[2] a helpline, information services, grants and benefits advice, an online community, public policy and research, and acting as a critical friend of the NHS, working with multiple services partners to redesign and radically improve the way cancer care is delivered across the UK. They are there for people with a cancer diagnosis, and everyone who loves them. And all of this is 99% funded through voluntary contributions. Unlike many large national charities, Macmillan neither runs high street shops, nor receives any significant government funding.

It's a diverse, nuanced response to the highly varied challenges facing people living with cancer. And as those lives change, Macmillan needs to change too. For over 100 years, it has provided care and support for people living with cancer and their loved ones. It's testament to the extraordinary commitment of its people that it has become one of the UK's most loved and dependable charities.

But by 2010, with recession biting, Macmillan was finding it harder to grow at anything like the rate required. Nine hundred people a day were being diagnosed with cancer, but after three years of strong fundraising growth, income grew just 1.6% in 2009.

Nowhere near enough to fund the services required.

A refresh in 2008 had given the brand a new appeal and consistency, as evidenced in campaigns like 'Good day' in 2010, that brought to life the challenges of living with cancer daily across print, TV and digital (Figure 1).

Figure 1: Good Day campaign 2010

In 2011 and 2012 'Every step of the way' highlighted the range of services Macmillan offer (Figure 2).

Figure 2: Every Step campaign 2011–2012

But at the end of 2012 Macmillan made the decision to take a new approach. While recent campaigns had been more successful, it was felt that a step change was required for the organisation to continue to meet the demands of people affected by cancer today and tomorrow.

That meant:

- increasing the number of people who get support from Macmillan when they need it, from calling one of the specialists on the support line, going online, or walking into information services;
- increasing the number who give support and increase the value of their donations;[3]
- but also expanding what giving can mean: volunteering, campaigning for change, sharing your experience with someone who needs it, being there for someone in your life.[4]

This was encapsulated by the phrase at the core of the brief Macmillan gave to agencies in a competitive pitch: *inspire millions to get involved.*

Responding to the brief

VCCP was lucky enough to be chosen as one of those agencies to pitch, and identified five major challenges to answering the brief:

1. Macmillan is diverse. The brand has never had an equivalent of 'Together we'll beat cancer' to succinctly capture why it exists, why you should give.
2. Unlike other charity brands, such as Cancer Research UK, the majority of Macmillan's ad spend has focused on *get support*, rather than *give support* messages. And because Macmillan is seen as such a rock, particularly thanks to its nurses, this risked leaving the brand lacking the perceived urgency needed for fundraising.
3. To increase urgency, the obvious response is to increase emotional intensity. But we could never let the drive for income result in us frightening or demeaning anyone, or preventing anyone seeking our help. A harrowing ad might raise money in the short term, but at what cost to people living with a diagnosis today? There is a balancing act between touching hearts while not gratuitously playing on emotions.
4. To spend effectively, we needed a single campaign to work for both audiences, and both calls to action. It must make people give support. But it must also encourage people to get support.
5. It couldn't be just advertising. Macmillan is active in so many ways, from fundraising events to social research, from working with corporate partners to influencing government and NHS policy. We needed, if possible, an idea that would have a positive effect on this broader world.

This was a new approach in the charity sector, and it required us to be completely authentic in what we said: a superficial advertising conceit would not be enough.

We needed an insight that would ring true in four ways (Figure 3):

1. People living with cancer, or caring for someone who is, would have to see something of themselves in the work we created.
2. Equally, people unaffected by cancer would have to be moved to do something.

3. Macmillan would have to be able to show how they could help tackle the issues we dramatised.
4. To really inspire millions, everyone would have to see how they could contribute to the cause and the charity: we would need to help everyone feel a part of the We in *We Are Macmillan.*

Figure 3: Four ways the insight needed to ring true

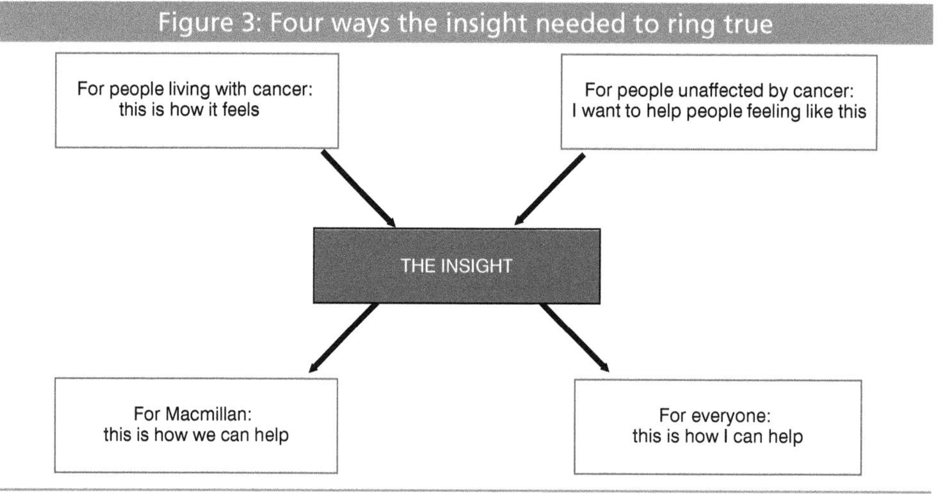

Finding the insight

A grandfather refusing help with pain relief.

His step-daughter caught between anguish and frustration.

A single mum trying to shield her child from what she's going through.

An old lady who goes to gruelling chemotherapy sessions alone.

A husband who doesn't know how to touch his wife any more.

A teenager who can't sleep.

A friend who doesn't know the right words to say, and so says nothing.

Nine hundred people a day diagnosed with cancer. The thousands who love them.

Every story intensely personal, refracted through different families, different friends. How do we find a single thought to, not just express, but dignify and empathise that spread of human emotion and experience?

We read and re-read the research. We did our own focus groups with people living with cancer. (Unforgettable. The most moving, of course, would you believe also the most joyful, the funniest?)

We talked about our own experiences. And one thing kept coming back:

Despite the fact that cancer will directly or indirectly affect most of us, too often it can feel like you're facing it alone, whether you are living with a diagnosis or caring for someone who is.

Figure 4: Quotes around loneliness from those diagnosed with or affected by cancer

Source: Macmillan and VCCP Qualitative Research

It can be the physical effects of treatment; friends and family finding it hard to talk; missing work or school; having less money to do things you normally would. It can come from feeling treated as a condition rather than a person, or just not knowing where to turn.

Untold stories of feeling alone.

And this is the one thing Macmillan can do, and that you can do.

We can't take away pain.

We can't take away the fear, the sadness, the tiredness, the anger.

We can't make it go away, or ever promise we can.

But we can all help someone feel less alone.

Research showed that the idea of being alone was universal, was moving, but, crucially, uplifting too. Because it implied that you didn't need to be a superhero to help someone. You just needed to be you (Figure 5).

Figure 5: Quotes around support from those diagnosed with or affected by cancer

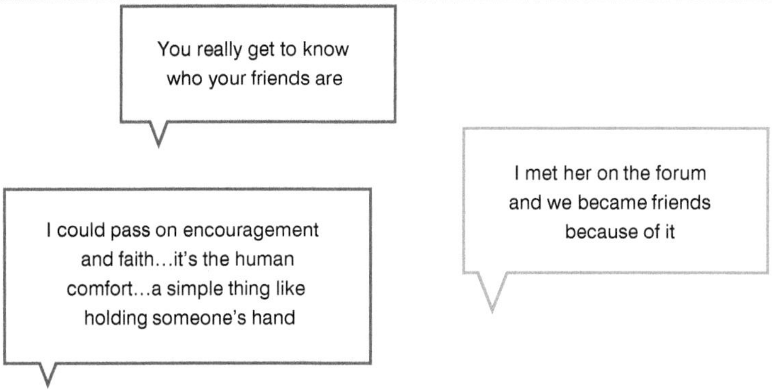

Source: Macmillan and VCCP Qualitative Research

From this we developed a simple, striking and irrefutable idea for Macmillan that summed up the purpose of the organisation, tapped into a universal feeling about a cancer experience, and, crucially, contained something that everyone could do to help.

NO ONE SHOULD FACE CANCER ALONE

Bringing the idea to life

Broadcast

We launched in February 2013 with PR around a new research report, *Facing the Fight Alone* that brought widespread news coverage. Our ATL campaign broke nationally on TV with the ad ‘Falling’, out of home, and digital, with two calls to action, to ‘Give help’ by donating, or ‘Get help’ by contacting us (Figures 6 and 7).

In 2014 we ran ‘Thank you’, to inspire millions by showing how their support felt to someone living with cancer, and educate on the wider services Macmillan offer (Figure 8).

And in 2015 we launched Loneliest Place with two executions: ‘Blizzard’ focused on the support our nurses provide, while ‘Mist’ encouraged people to be there for loved ones who needed them (Figure 9 and 10).

Fundraising

In fundraising, we reorganised around what the customer wants and needs, ensuring we had clear understanding of who our current and prospective supporters are and how they behave.

In individual marketing, ‘Not alone’ messaging was integrated into our DM, and has proved our most effective pack to date. Our Christmas appeal told a family’s story that really resonated with our supporters, and we launched the UK’s first text to enter raffle, and now have 100,000 playing the weekly lottery.

In events, ‘World’s biggest coffee morning’ continues to go from strength to strength, while we’ve launched successful new events for a new, younger audience: *Night In, Go Sober, Brave the Shave.* Challenge events were helped by redesigned pages on the website, and a new Regional Challenge Events Team. And ‘Not alone’ messaging translated across merchandising (Figure 12).

Figure 6: 'Falling' TV ad, February 2013

So we've had your test results back from the lab and I'm sorry to have to tell you that, it's not good news. It's cancer.

What we're going to... (muffled speech)
In the meantime do you have any questions?

I don't think so.

(Music plays)

Today, 889 people will be hit with the news they have cancer. Then it will hit everyone that loves them.

No one should face cancer alone.

With your support, no one will.

Figure 7: Print advertising, February 2013

Figure 8: 'Thank you' TV ad, February 2014

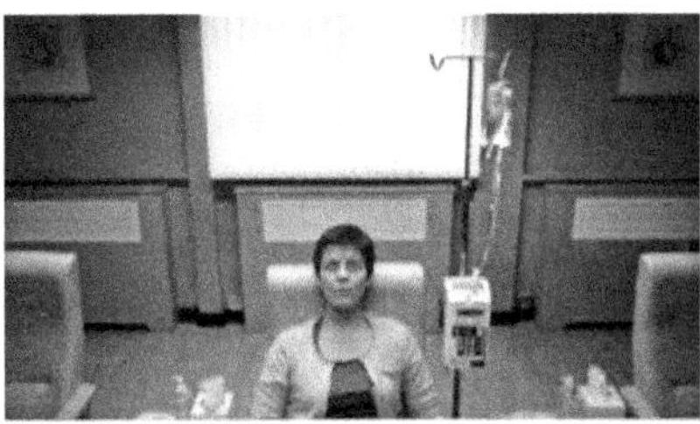

(Lights buzzing and machines beeping)

"Mum, thank you for not just saying "everything will be okay"

"Mark, thanks for not talking with my husband. I hate how hard this is for him."

"Sam Jenkins from Stoke. Thanks for putting change in the bucket this morning."

"And Tim, You're helping so many people"

"Ben. You've been a really brave boy while Mummy's not feeling well"

"Nicki. Thank you for helping me find a way to tell my son I have cancer"

No one should face cancer alone but we just can't be there for everyone and urgently need you to support our nurses and other vital services. Please text FIVE to 70550 and donate £5 today.

Figure 9: 'Blizzard' TV ad, 2015

(Storm sounds)

(Storm sounds)

Are you okay David?

Yeah.

Good, this way.

Cancer can be the loneliest place. If you're living with cancer or someone who is, our help line is here for you, for information, advice or a chat. Call us free on 0808 808 00 00

Figure 10: 'Mist' TV ad, February 2013

(Storm sounds)

(Storm sounds)

(Storm and footsteps sounds)

(Hieavy breathing sound)

(Raining sounds)

Are you okay Claire?

Yeah.

Cancer can be the loneliest place, do something amazing and reach out to a friend or loved one with cancer today. For advice and inspiration visit macmillan.org.uk/reachout.

Our outdoor mixed impactful brand advertising with more detailed service advice, particularly around our financial support.

Figure 11: Outdoor activity 2015

Figure 12: Sample of fundraising activity 2013–2015

Engagement

Every campaign is now deepened online through powerful case studies, research and information on how to get involved (Figure 13).

Figure 13: Sample of 'Not alone' content 2015

OUR NOT ALONE CAMPAIGN

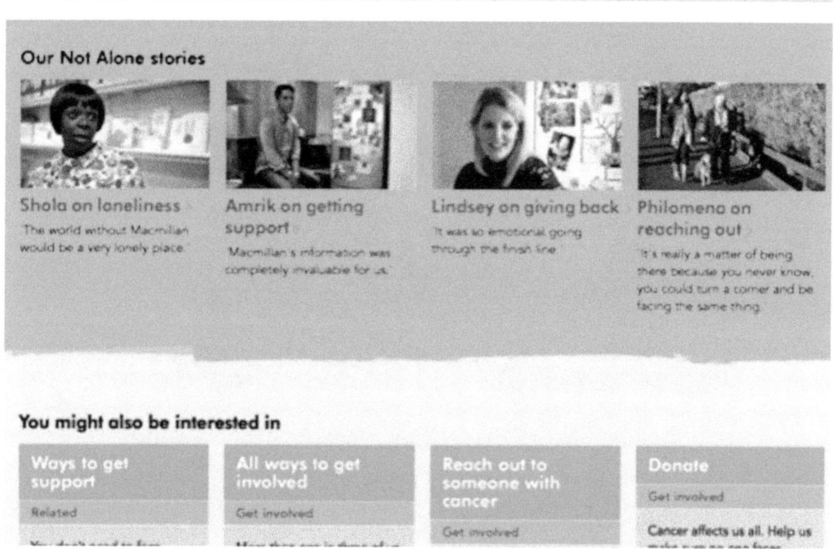

Source: http://www.macmillan.org.uk/about-us/what-we-do/our-ambition/not-alone-campaign.html?origin=homepagecarousel

Social media enables us to share the campaign, and encourage people to talk about their experiences (Figure 14).

Figure 14: Sample of social activity 2013

In December 2014, we create a new way to give help, when 'Not alone' was translated into a new digital service – The Source – where everyone can share simple tips and advice on helping people affected by cancer (Figure 15).

Figure 15: The Source, https://source.macmillan.org.uk

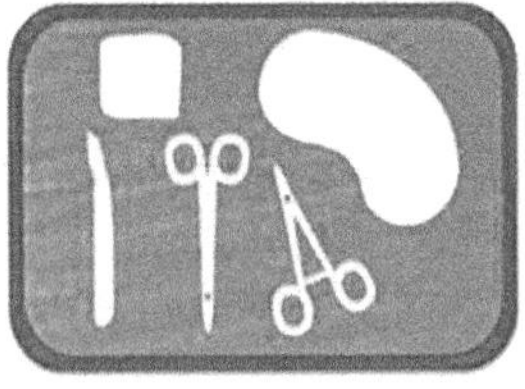

In Spring 2015 we toured an isolation box around major train stations, giving people the chance to experience the sensation of isolation in a crowded place (Figure 16).

Figure 16: Coverage of 'Isolation box' in *Time Out*, February 2015

There's an 'Isolation Box' in Paddington station

Posted at 5:00 pm, February 11, 2015 in News

If you happen to have walked through Paddington station today (Feb 11) you may have noticed an incongruous illuminated glass box in the middle of all the commuters. The rather moving 'Isolation Box' is part of Macmillan Cancer Support's latest 'Not Alone' campaign to raise awareness of the loneliness and isolation felt by cancer sufferers.

Partnerships

Our partnership with Boots gives us presence across 2,500 high streets, a new opportunity to make sure that no one faces cancer alone but giving Macmillan high street presence for the first time.

As well as 2,000 specially trained pharmacists, there are now 300 trained Boots Macmillan beauty advisors, who can help to boost the confidence of those living with cancer, crucial in helping reduce the social isolation effects of cancer diagnosis and treatment (Figure 17).

Figure 17: Boots and Macmillan partnership

The results

In this section we will show that Macmillan Cancer Support has, in recent years, achieved unprecedented success: helping record numbers of people, greatly extending its influence, and enjoying a growth in fundraising income unequalled among the large UK charities.

And we will show how the 'Not alone' campaign contributed to those results.

Large charities inhabit complex ecosystems, and health charities in particular create interesting relationships between individuals and organisations. In Macmillan's case, while it's voluntary income that enables people to be supported, very often those who have been helped by Macmillan who go on to become fundraisers, volunteers and in some cases influencers of corporate charity partnerships.

In addition, Macmillan's ability to support people affected by cancer is crucially dependent on its relationship with other healthcare professionals, and with policy makers.

If advertising is to truly deliver value for an organisation, it must go beyond the obvious direct effects of support and income, to exert a wider influence through creating greater brand equity.

The model in Figure 18 attempts to capture this complex web of influences. So, in this section we will measure payback in three ways:

First, and most conventionally, we will show how the campaign directly and indirectly grew fundraising income.

Second, we will show how the campaign meant more people living with or affected by cancer were helped by Macmillan.

Finally, we will attempt to draw out some of the wider ways in which 'Not alone' paid back to society as a whole, from creating informal networks of support, to improving relationships with other healthcare professionals, to influencing government policy.

But to start with, we will show how Not Alone set a new level of sustained advertising impact in the category, and improved brand equity.

Figure 18: The wider impact of the 'Not alone' campaign

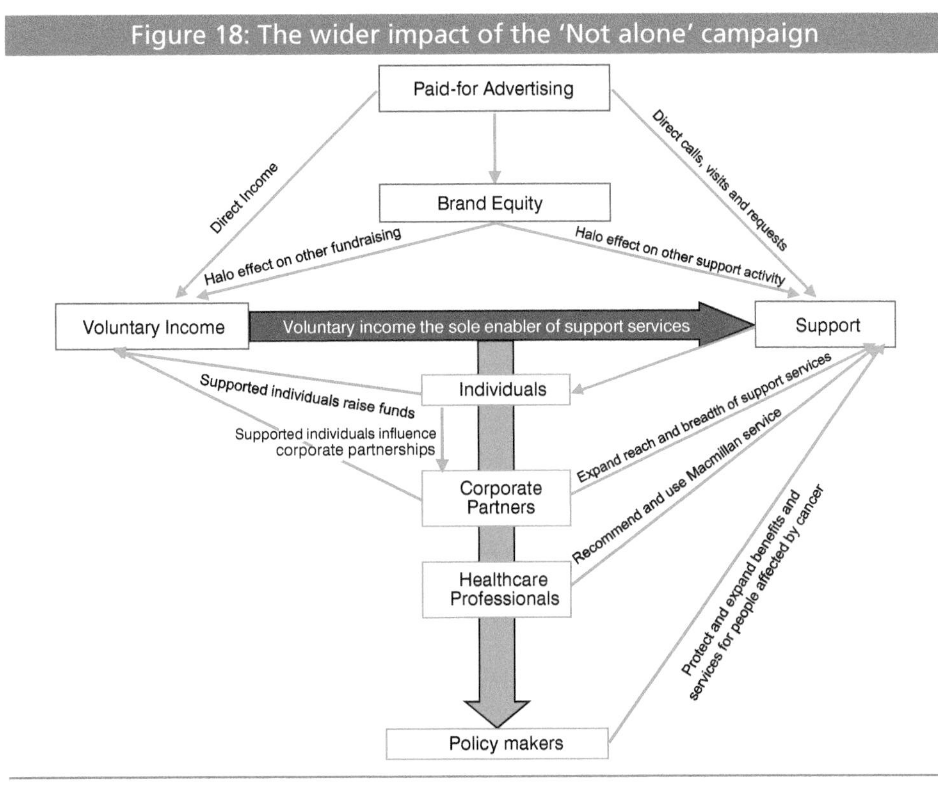

1. A more impactful advertising campaign

TV Advertising recognition

Our TV advertising recognition end-of-year target in our first year was 40%.[5] We hit 52% in our first wave, and 63% by year-end, significantly outperforming any previous Macmillan adverts (Figure 19).

Figure 19: TV advertising peak recognition: 'Falling' vs previous Macmillan ads 2010–2012

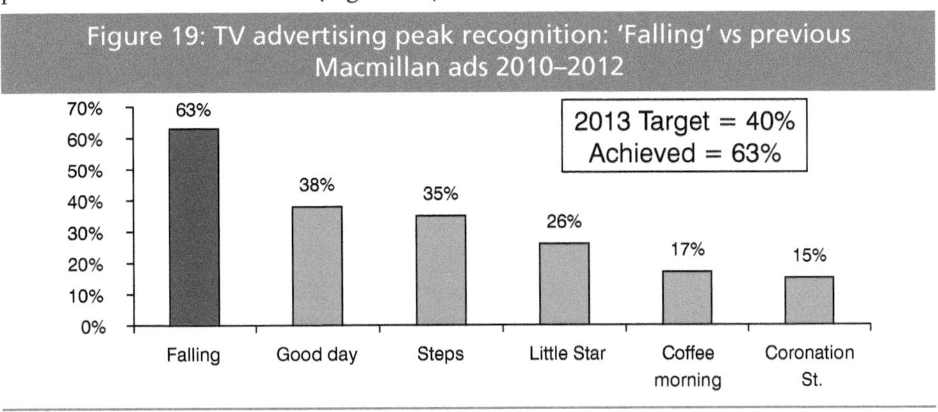

Source: Nursery tracking, 2012–2013

Over the last three years, we have consistently achieved the highest recognition scores among major cancer charity advertisers (Figure 20).[6]

Figure 20: TV advertising peak recognition: 'Falling' vs competitor ads 2013–2016

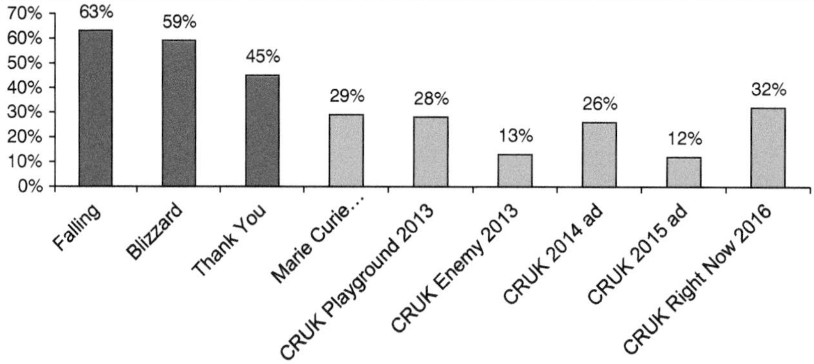

70%
60%
50%
40%
30%
20%
10%
0%
63%
59%
45%
29%
28%
13%
26%
12%
32%
Falling
Blizzard
Thank You
Marie Curie…
CRUK Playground 2013
CRUK Enemy 2013
CRUK 2014 ad
CRUK 2015 ad
CRUK Right Now 2016

Source: Nursery tracking 2013–2016

We are increasingly getting significant impact from our outdoor advertising (Figure 21).

Figure 21: Print advertising peak recognition 2013–2016

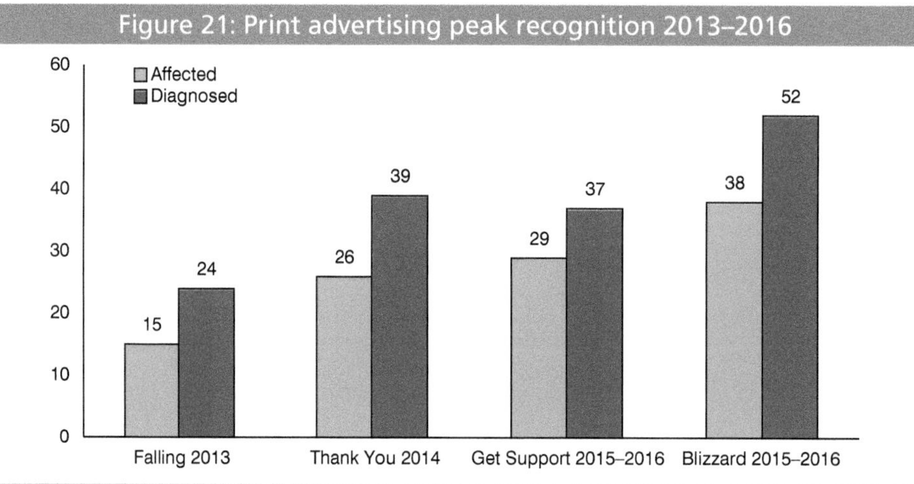

60
50
40
30
20
10
0
Affected
Diagnosed
15
24
26
39
29
37
38
52
Falling 2013
Thank You 2014
Get Support 2015–2016
Blizzard 2015–2016

Source: Nursery tracking 2013–2016

Advertising diagnostics

We consistently find that our advertising is moving, powerful and memorable, regularly getting more than two thirds of our 'Affected' to 'strongly' or 'very strongly agree' to the following statements and, on the occasions we have tracked it, outscoring other cancer charity advertising (Table 1).

Table 1: Top 2 box agreements

Top 2 box (6–7/7) agreement	Falling	Thank You	Blizzard	Mist	CRUK 2014	CRUK 2015–2016	Average difference Macmillan vs CRUK
It's a moving ad	67	69	64	67	51	n/a	+16
It's a powerful ad	77	69	75	69	59	59	+13
It's a memorable ad	62	n/a	59	57	n/a	48	+11

Source: Nursery tracking 2013–2016

Crucially, we don't gratuitously generate impact, but authentically capture the emotions of living with cancer. This can be seen in the extent to which those 'Affected', and particularly 'Diagnosed', feel they can relate to our ads (Figure 22).

Figure 22: Very strongly agreeing or strongly agreeing with the statement 'I can relate to the ad'

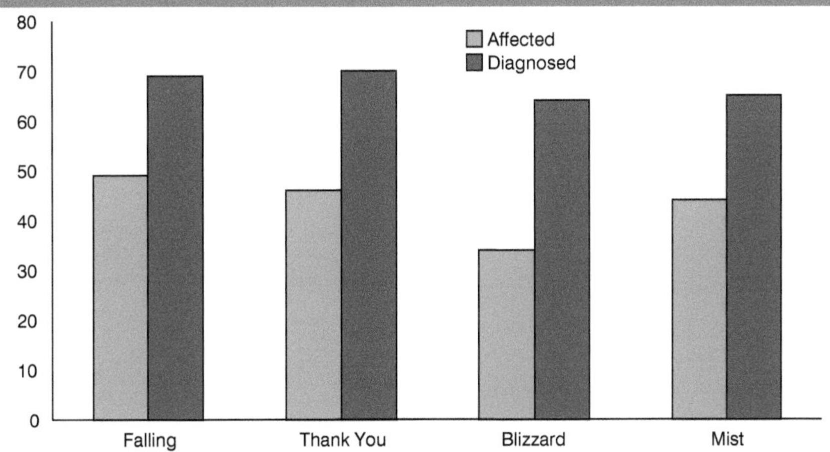

Source: Nursery tracking 2013–16

We also see this qualitatively, in the very often moving response we see on our social channels (Figures 23 and 24).

Figure 23: YouTube comments on 'Falling' ad

Sean wyatt 1 year ago

Hi, I was dianosed with cancer in November 12 and this was exactly how I felt with hearing my dianosis. I am a 44 year old mans man and this advert had me sobbing like a baby. So powerful and moving.

Suki Gallagher 1 year ago

When I was told I had Cancer it felt like someone had pressed the fast forward button on my life. This is advert captures that feeling and how blessed we are to be able to rely on MacMillan Cancer Support - thank you x

Figure 24: Facebook comments on 'Falling' ad 2013

One of the less obvious advantages of a strong and admired advertising campaign is that it allows us to generate additional free media space. A number of outdoor media owners kindly donate excess inventory, and as the campaign has built momentum and fame, we've been able to increase the equivalent media value of the spaces we receive (Table 2 and Figure 25).

Table 2: Value of free media space

	2013	**2014**	**2015**
Value of free outdoor media space (NB. This is market rate, not rate card)	£3,600,792	£4,368,681	£7,013,368

Source: Macmillan

Figure 25: Coverage of free media space

Signature Outdoor supports Macmillan's 2015 Not Alone campaign

MARCH 6TH, 2015

Signature Outdoor pledged their support to Macmillan Cancer Support's Not Alone campaign in January and February 2015.

Carrying the message 'Cancer can be the loneliest place ...', the campaign ran across a selection Signature's Mega 6 Sheets delivering over 3.5 million impacts per two-week period and broadcasting Macmillan's Not Alone message throughout Birmingham.

Lucy Peterson, Macmillan Brand Officer said "*We're delighted with our campaign through Signature's Mega 6 sheets portfolio. The panels are in strong, eye-catching roadside locations and allow us to reach large numbers of people with our message that cancer can be the loneliest place, so we need the public's support to fund our vital services for people affected by cancer.*"

Source: http://www.signatureoutdoor.co.uk/news/signature-outdoor-supports-macmillans-2015-not-alone-campaign/

2. A more powerful brand

Since the launch of the campaign in February 2013, Macmillan has become a more visible, more talked about brand.

The NFP Charity Awareness Monitor shows that, against a broad trend of declining awareness of big national charities, Macmillan grew (Figure 26).

Figure 26: Changes in brand awareness 2012–2015 – Macmillan vs all major UK charities

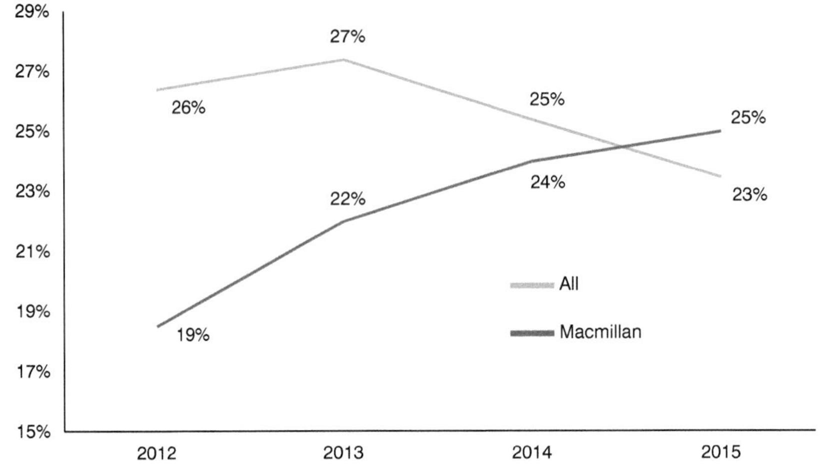

Source: Charity Awareness Monitor/ NFPSynergy 2012–2015

Of the top five brands by the end of the period, Macmillan was the only one to show significant growth (Figure 27).

Figure 27: Changes in brand awareness 2012–2015 (indexed vs 2012)

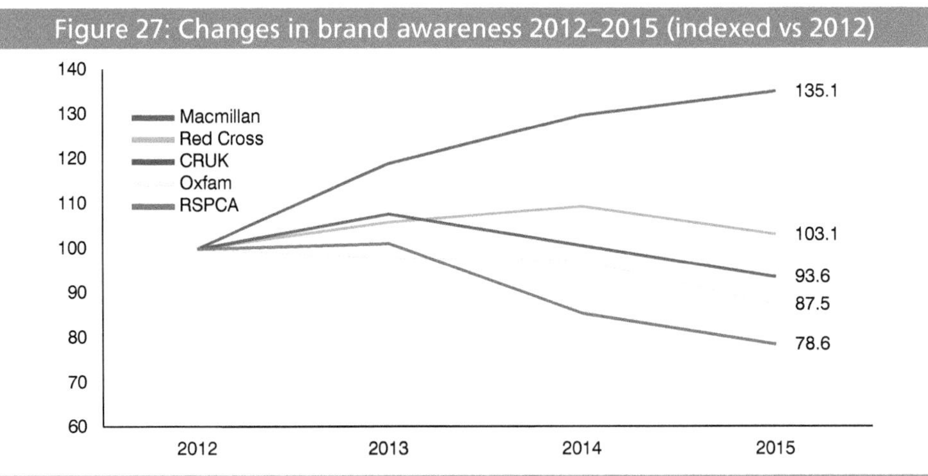

Source: Charity Awareness Monitor/ NFPSynergy 2012–2015

Indeed, of the top 10 brands tracked in the Charity Awareness Monitor, Macmillan is the only brand to have improved its ranking, from eighth to joint fourth (Table 3).

Table 3: Charity Awareness Monitor ranking

	2012	2013	2014	2015	Change in rank 2012–2015
1	Oxfam	Oxfam	Oxfam	Oxfam	=
2	Cancer Research UK	Cancer Research UK	Cancer Research UK	Cancer Research UK	=
3	RSPCA	RSPCA	RSPCA	RSPCA	=
4	British Red Cross	British Red Cross	British Red Cross	**Macmillan (=4)**	**+ 4**
5	British Heart Foundation	British Heart Foundation	**Macmillan**	British Red Cross (+4)	– 1
6	NSPCC	NSPCC	British Heart Foundation	British Heart Foundation	– 1
7	Barnados	**Macmillan**	NSPCC	NSPCC	– 1
8	**Macmillan**	Barnados	Barnados	Barnados	– 1
9	Save the Children	Save the Children	Save the Children	Save the Children	=
10	Marie Curie	Marie Curie	Marie Curie	Marie Curie	=

Source: Charity Awareness Monitor/ NFPSynergy 2012–15

This momentum behind the brand can be seen in the fact that Macmillan was YouGov Charity Index charity brand of the year 2013, 2014 and 2015, based on buzz scores: the public's positive perceptions of charities across impression, value, quality, reputation, satisfaction and recommendation metrics (Figure 28).

Figure 28: YouGov Charity Index 2013–15

Macmillan Cancer Support tops YouGov's 2015 CharityIndex rankings

For the third year in succession, Macmillan Cancer Support was the UK's top charity brand, new analysis from YouGov's CharityIndex finds.

Source: https://yougov.co.uk/news/2016/02/01/macmillan-cancer-support-tops-yougovs-2015-charity/

We were also Third Sector's Brand Index Brand of the Year in 2013, and second placed in 2015, and Marketing Society's Brand of the Year in 2014.

Finally, in 2015 we were placed no.5 in the Guardian Influential Brands poll.[7]

A stronger brand among healthcare professionals

The public sentiment around Macmillan is reflected in improved perceptions among healthcare professionals. This is a crucial audience for the brand to ensure that those who need our help are more likely to be recommended our services (Figures 29 and 30, Table 4).

Figure 29: Awareness of Macmillan in the area of cancer care has increased significantly amongst GPs

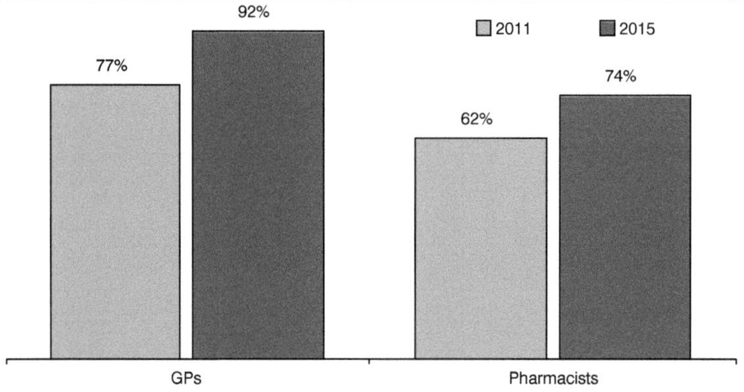

	2011	2015
GPs	77%	92%
Pharmacists	62%	74%

Source: Nursery healthcare professionals tracking 2011–15

Figure 30: Likelihood to recommend has increased since 2011 amongst GPs and pharmacists

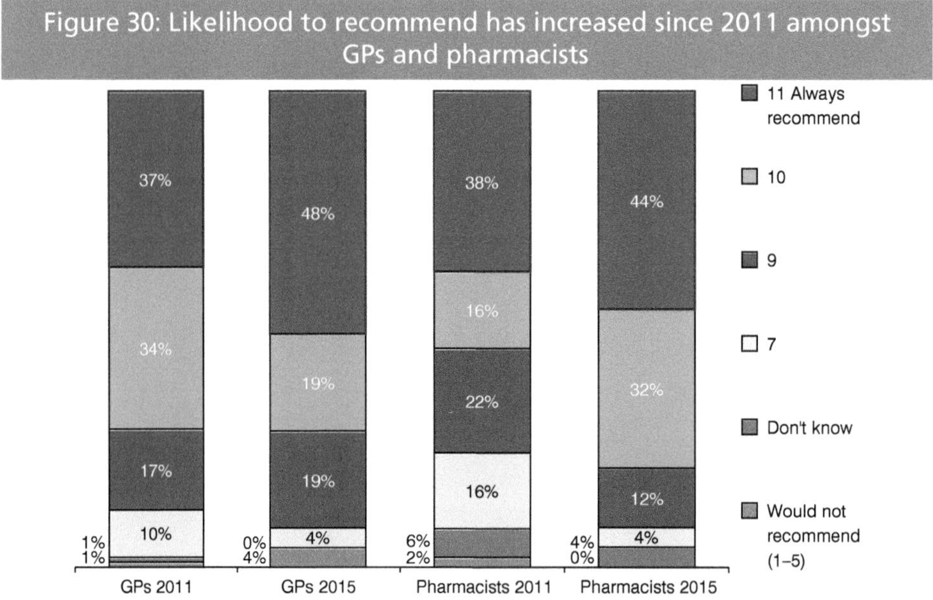

Source: Nursery Healthcare professionals tracking 2011–2015

Table 4: GP associations with Macmillan

Among GPs, associations with Macmillan by statement	2011	2015	Shift
They offer support at all stages from diagnosis to beyond treatment	46%	56%	+10%
They are easy to contact	37%	46%	+9%
Macmillan is a brand name that would reassure patients	39%	44%	+5%
They offer services that no other charity does	20%	23%	+3%

Source: Nursery Healthcare professionals tracking 2011–2015

3. Unprecedented income growth

Since the launch of the campaign, Macmillan has seen a growth in voluntary income unprecedented either in its own history, or among other major UK charities. For the period 2013–2014 for which audited data is available for the 12 biggest UK charities by voluntary income, Macmillan saw both the largest absolute growth, and the biggest percentage change in income (Table 5).

Table 5: Fundraising income 2012–2014

	2012	2013	2014	Growth 2012–14	Change 2012–14
Macmillan	**152.0**	**185.7**	**215.2**	**63.2**	**41.6%**
Great Ormond Street	58.9	62.2	81.2	22.3	38.0%
British Red Cross	109.6	128.3	140.5	30.9	28.2%
RNLI	153.3	170.1	190.1	36.8	24.0%
Marie Curie	76.2	83.6	91.1	14.9	19.6%
Cancer Research UK	364.3	388.8	415.6	51.3	14.1%
Salvation Army	101.8	100.3	114.6	12.9	12.6%
BHF	92.6	95.4	102.3	9.7	10.5%
Save the Children	121.4	144.0	128.9	7.5	6.2%
NSPCC	120.5	117.3	117.7	–2.8	–2.3%
Comic Relief	75.2	96.4	73.0	–2.2	–2.9%
Oxfam	129.7	111.5	118.3	–11.4	–8.8%
ALL (excluding Macmillan)				15.5	16%

Source: cited charities' annual reports

When we include the 2015 figures (where published data is available at time of writing) the picture is even more striking. Macmillan's growth in income is by some margin the greatest: more than double that of any other individual charity, and more than four times the average of the other brands (Table 6).

Table 6: Fundraising income 2012–2015

	2012	2013	2014	2015	Growth 2012–2015	Change 2012–2015
Macmillan	**152.0**	**185.7**	**215.2**	**226.0**	**74.0**	**48.7%**
BHF	92.6	95.4	102.3	114.0	21.4	23.1%
Marie Curie	76.2	83.6	91.1	92.1	15.9	20.9%
Cancer Research UK	364.3	388.8	415.6	430.6	66.3	18.2%
Great Ormond Street	58.9	62.2	81.2	67.4	8.5	14.5%
NSPCC	120.5	117.3	117.7	119.2	–1.3	–1.0%
Oxfam	129.7	111.5	118.3	124.8	–4.9	–3.8%
ALL (EXC. Macmillan)					17.6	0.12

Source: Cited charities' annual reports

And 'Not alone' has proved more efficient than previous campaigns. Over the period of the campaign, our share of voluntary income has grown, while our share of voice has slightly fallen (Table 7).

Table 7: Share of income vs share of voice 2012–2014

	2012	2013–2014
Share of voice (top 10 brands)	18.80%	18.20%
Share of income	11.50%	13.60%

Source: Cited charities' annual reports, Nielsen

The strength of the Macmillan brand has enabled it to improve fundraising across a range of audiences, and from both traditional and new sources.

Corporate partnerships have more than doubled in value since 2013, after a dip in 2012. They include the likes of Home Retail Group, which has raised £1.5m for Macmillan since the start of our partnership in March 2015, almost all of which is employee fundraising (Figure 31).

Figure 31: Income from corporate partnerships 2011–2015

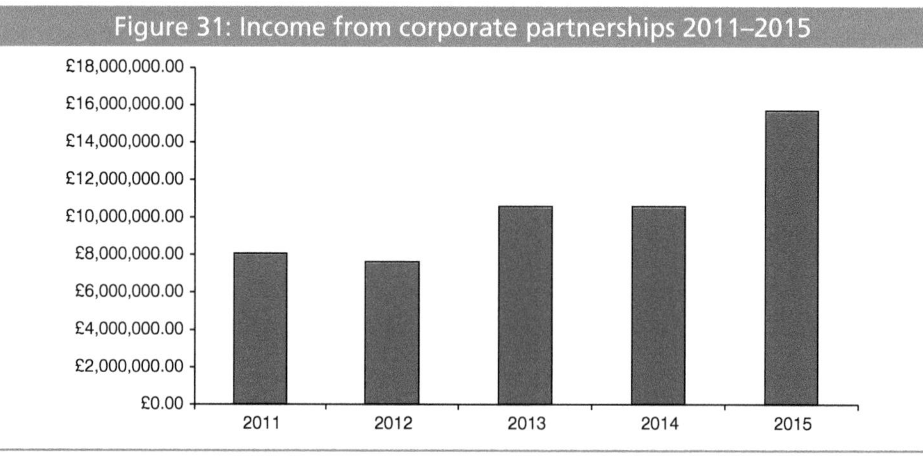

Source: Macmillan

'World's biggest coffee morning' enjoyed a spectacular 25th birthday in 2015, raising a record £26.9m, while the newer 'Brave the shave' campaign generated £4.4m against a target of £740k.

So the strongest advertising in category and in the brand's history has driven unprecedented brand momentum, and enabled the organisation to generate record income.

And this has been achieved with a more efficient spend on fundraising, with the proportion of costs to income lower since the campaign launched (Table 8).

Table 8: Income vs fundraising costs 2012–2014

	2012	2013	2014
Income	152.7	186.9	215.2
Fundraising costs[1]	50.307	58.07	68.4
Costs as % of income	32.9	31.4	31.7

1 This is the figure for total fundraising costs, everything from DM to merchandising and the administration of events and partnerships

So in the first two years since the launch of 'Not alone', we have generated £96.7m incremental income from an additional investment of £27.6m.

This equates to a ROMI for fundraising alone of 2.4:1.

But as discussed above, fundraising is only part of the picture.

4. More people helped in more ways

As fundraising grows, so does support. Macmillan is reaching more people than ever before, a record 5.8m in 2015, of a record spend on services of £144 million, enabled by the sustained growth in income. Most of these people used multiple sources of Macmillan support.

Visitors to macmillan.org.uk have grown strongly since the campaign launched in February 2013, after a dip in H2 2012.[9] There were almost 5.4m unique users to the site in 2015 (Figure 32).

Social metrics for Macmillan are not a vanity metric, but genuine delivery on our promise that no one should face cancer alone.

Facebook followers have grown to 602k, and our main Twitter account has 460k followers. Our Online Community helped 75,000 people a month in 2015, while the campaign platform The Source received 98,000 visits.[10]

The number of Macmillan Professionals posts increased by 12% to over 8,000.

In 2015 our nurses reached over 590k people, and in total we had 6,265 healthcare professional posts.

The value of these interactions, while of course immense to the individuals concerned, is not possible to quantify financially.

But our financial support is.

Figure 32: Macmillan.org.uk users 2012–2015

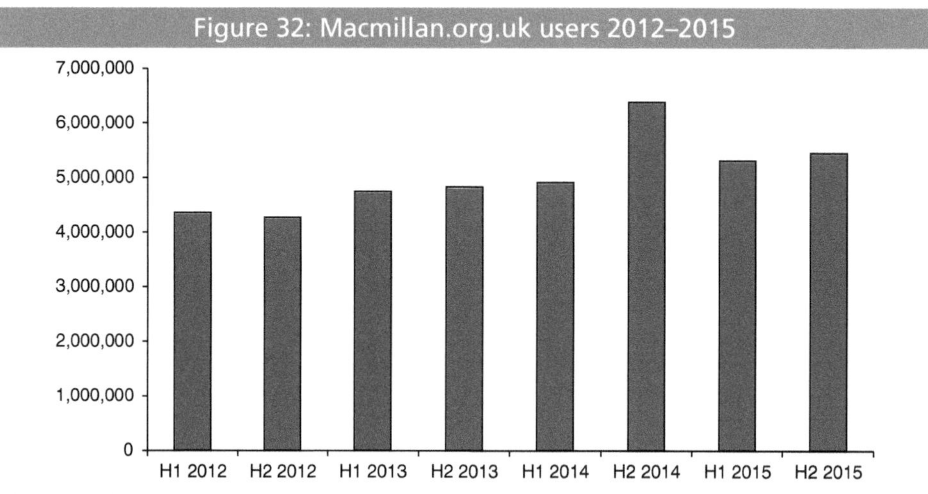

Source: Google Analytics

Over the period of the campaign, Macmillan Financial Support grew annually:

- Benefits advice schemes reached over 68k people, 5% more than 2014. These helped people to gain over £211m in benefits, up £20m from before 'Not alone' launched.
- The Welfare Rights Team reached 22k people, 7% more than 2014, and helped people to access £55.98m in benefits. That is up £17.4m from before 'Not alone', and a cumulative £35.88m since the campaign launched.[11]

Table 9: Welfare Rights Team performance

£m accessed	2012	2013	2014	2015	Total incremental value delivered
Welfare Rights Team help	38.6	44	51.7	55.98	£35.88

Source: Macmillan internal data

5. The wider impact of 'Not alone' on society

Finally, the increased status of the brand has enabled Macmillan to make a wider impact on society.

As we have shown, our *partnerships* have increased their levels of fundraising. But more than that, from our idea of 'Not alone', partnerships are starting to change the face of cancer support.

Our Boots partnership has given cancer support a new place on the high street, with both pharmacy and beauty support, and was recently voted the second most admired charity–corporate partnership. Most importantly, it means every Boots is able to help us fulfil the promise that no one should face cancer alone.

Figure 33: C & E Corporate NGO Partnerships Barometer 2015

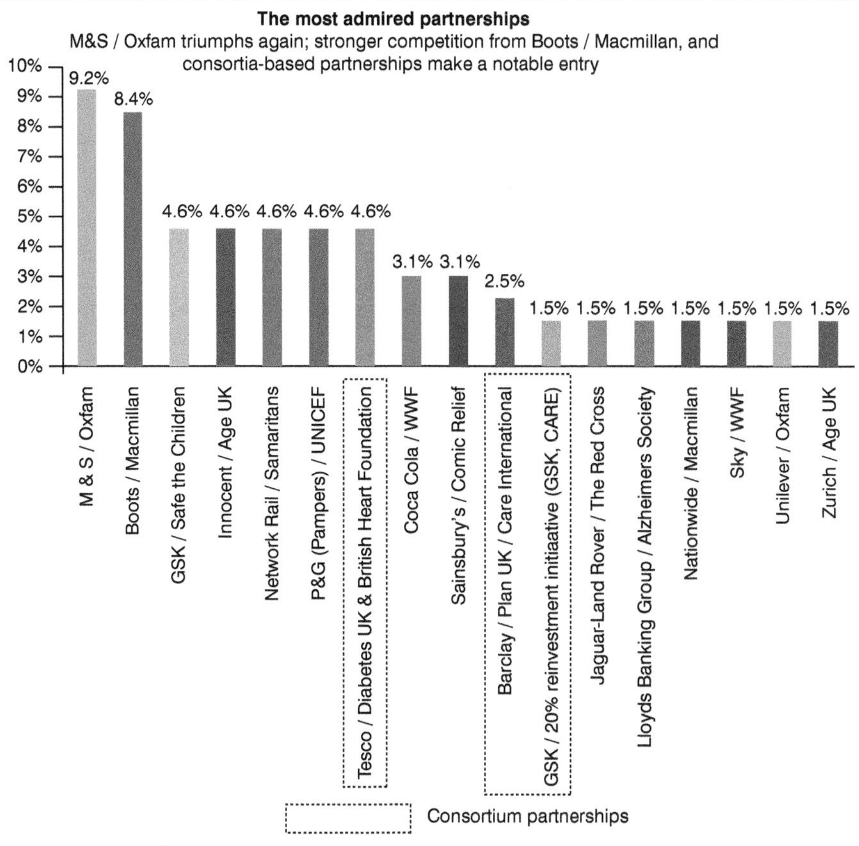

What other corporate–NGO partnerships do you admire and whay? [Respondents could list up to three starting with their most admired]. Source: http://www.candeadvisory.com/barometer

Our partnership with Nationwide will mean fewer people face the financial costs of cancer alone. A pilot rolled out nationally in 2015 to help prevent financial problems for customers who are affected by cancer, with an end-to-end service to support existing customers with their finances after a cancer diagnosis. We helped Nationwide set up a specialist team who have been trained and empowered to make decisions.

Our stronger voice in society has strengthened our ability to *influence major government policy.*

Macmillan successfully campaigned for personal independence payment waiting times to fall to the recommended 11 weeks and to 7 days for those with a terminal illness, down from lengthy delays in 2014–15. Before this, some people with cancer had even died before receiving their payment.

Macmillan influenced cancer strategy for England to include their priorities (improving patient experience, workforce, five-year living with and beyond cancer programme, funded cancer alliances – bringing key partners to drive improvement at a local level).

The Macmillan at Work service continued to help employers provide the right support for employees affected by cancer, keeping them in work, or getting them back as soon as possible. The programme engaged 1,900 new organisations. Over 3,000 are now signed up.

End of Life Care: Progressing well. Macmillan Specialist Care at home cited as best practice in the Choice Review, and both the Choice Review and the Health Select Committee strongly recommended Macmillan's call to provide free social care at end of life.

The General Election campaign – 'Time to choose' – managed to get all three of Macmillan's campaign calls into the main parties' manifestos.

There is the impact to society of tackling isolation among those living with cancer. Evidence cited in *Facing the Fight Alone* report of 2013 drew attention to the fact that feelings of isolation can have a clinical impact[12] which ultimately affects the costs to the NHS and society as a whole of cancer:

- In 2006, a study by US epidemiologist Candyce Kroenke and her colleagues suggested that women who were most socially isolated before they were diagnosed with breast cancer were twice as likely to die from the disease as women with the strongest social network.
- In 2012, research by another team of US scientists suggested that women with ovarian cancer who had the most supportive social relationships lived for at least a year longer on average than those without support.

Conclusion

Over the last three years, Macmillan has delivered outstanding income growth, and helped more people than ever before, in a greater variety of ways. It has become a more influential brand, and used that influence to change the way governments and businesses are operating to help people living with and affected by cancer.

No one should face cancer alone, as a creative idea and a strategic platform has enabled Macmillan to better prepare the UK for the challenges nearly all of us will have to encounter at some point in our lives.

In a world where one-off viral fundraising campaigns get the lion's share of publicity, it's still vital for charities to build long-term, predictable revenue to properly invest in the services that people truly need. So that, whatever happens, we will be able to say that no one will face cancer alone.

Figure 34: No one should face cancer alone

Notes

1. Through a combination of an ageing population, improved diagnosis and treatment, and changing lifestyles. Indeed today, the figure already stands at 2.5m.
2. Including doctors, radiographers, dietitians, occupational therapists and more.
3. Through individual spontaneous giving, direct debits, legacy giving, and participation in fundraising events like 'World's biggest coffee morning', as well as through corporate fundraising.
4. This isn't just nice to have. In the changing care world outlined above, cancer support needs to be something provided by friends, neighbours, colleagues, family, and concerned strangers, as much as by healthcare professionals.
5. Our target for most metrics is against those 'Affected' by cancer. We also track among those 'Unaffected' and 'Diagnosed'. As a broad rule, most measures broadly follow the same pattern, with lower scores for 'Unaffected', and higher scores for 'Diagnosed'. The 'Affected' audience is judged to be the best proxy for overall success, since it is a reasonably broad target (there are around 17m people in the UK affected by cancer in some way).
6. Due to budget restrictions we don't track every single competitor TV ad, but we believe we have covered a reflective spread.
7. http://theguardianinfluentialbrands.com/.
8. This is the figure for total fundraising costs, everything from DM to merchandising and the administration of events and partnerships.
9. The spike in H2 2014 was driven by 'Ice bucket challenge'.
10. All data source: Macmillan internal data.
11. All financial support data: Macmillan annual reports and internal data.
12. http://www.macmillan.org.uk/documents/aboutus/mac13970_isolated_cancer_patients_media_reportfinal.pdf.

Narellan Pools

Diving into big data for Narellan Pools

By Luke Brown, AFFINITY
Contributing authors: Adam Shar and Angela Smith, AFFINITY
Credited company: AFFINITY

Summary

Narellan Pools is an Australian pool builder. In a market experiencing declining home affordability, increased debt, and a shift towards higher density urban living, company sales were in long-term decline. A shift towards digital helped reverse this decline. This case outlines how the business then accelerated its growth by exploiting a 'big data' insight about the exact time when prospective pool buyers were most likely to convert into sales. A strategy activated marketing whenever this window of opportunity opened and turned it off at less propitious times. The approach increased leads by 11%, and sales by 23% on a media budget cut by a third. The incremental revenue ROI was $54 for every $1 invested.[1]

Editor's Comment

On a tiny budget, the judges applauded the clever use of data and analytics married with strong creative to ensure minimum media wastage and maximum ROI.

Client Comment
Chris Meyer, Managing Director, Narellan Pools

To be honest, I don't really understand everything that AFFINITY do, but I understand the results. The results delivered by AFFINITY for Narellan Pools created a significant increase on our enquiries, a radical increase on our sales and a record-breaking increase on our profitability.

What AFFINITY has actually managed to do is become a strong partner with Narellan Pools – by diving deep into our business activities and getting a true understanding of how our potential customers tick. AFFINITY showed me that it all comes down to building trust for your agency through a strong partnership. As the icing on the cake, I can't believe AFFINITY couldn't even spend our entire budget to create the results they delivered.

I can't remember a time as a client when we were handed back 30 per cent of our media budget by an agency to create groundbreaking results. It just goes to show, if you're brave enough to trust your agency with new and innovative digital and data strategies, you can really stand out from the pack and reap the rewards.

Introduction

If you've read many previous IPA papers you may have been left with a sense that to be effective, you need to spend millions of dollars, pounds or euros on both marketing and measurement to first achieve and then prove effectiveness.

The majority of papers use measures such as awareness, brand consideration tracking research and econometric modelling. But due to their expense, these methodologies are beyond the reach of many businesses. Whilst all of these measures can be important, they're not always necessary to create and demonstrate effectiveness from your marketing investment.

This paper sets out a case that you don't need millions of dollars, pounds or euros to create truly effective marketing. We argue that the most important thing required to deliver effectiveness is smarter, relevant thinking which is accessible on any budget, in any category.

We won't be dazzling you with a big name car brand, bank or chocolate bar. We'll be detailing our approach and success with a swimming pool brand, yes, a pool brand. And chances are you've never read an effectiveness paper in this category and we're certain you've not heard of the brand. Irrespective, the results should speak for themselves.

Narellan Pools (Narellan) is one of Australia's largest pool builders. By mining their first-party and third-party data we unearthed a consumer-targeting nirvana: identification of the exact moment of tipping-point from consideration to sale. As a result of our activity in 2015, we increased leads by 11%, and increased sales by 23% whilst decreasing their media spend by 30%. Overall, delivering an incremental ROI of 54:1.

This paper demonstrates that often it's not just what you say or how you say it, but *when* you say it that's important. Our aim is to demonstrate to other smaller businesses with commensurately smaller budgets that you don't need to spend millions to make your business thrive. Relevance and context will always trump the size of investment.

Background

Australia is the driest continent on earth,[2] so once the 'Australian Dream'[3] of home ownership has been realised, for many Australians buying a pool has traditionally been high on the priority list of what to achieve next.

Narellan is one of Australia's largest pool builders. It's a franchisee-based business that operates in 49 different defined regional and metro centres. Collectively they sell thousands of pools every year and the average sale price is approximately $50,000.[1]

Unfortunately there have been strong headwinds for the pool industry in the last few years making selling a pool harder. These include demographic shifts, housing affordability and a big rise in competition.[4]

Demographic shifts

As for many countries around the world, in Australia there's a significant trend toward higher density living as people strive to live closer to cities. Twenty years ago there were nearly 3.5 houses for every apartment, but the last Australian census in 2012 found there were just 1.6 houses to every apartment.[5] Experts believe this ratio is likely to be 1:1 in the census carried out this year (2016). This trend means the pool-buying market has literally halved from 1992 to 2011 (Figure 1).

Figure 1: Denser living – ratio of detached house to medium and high density dwellings

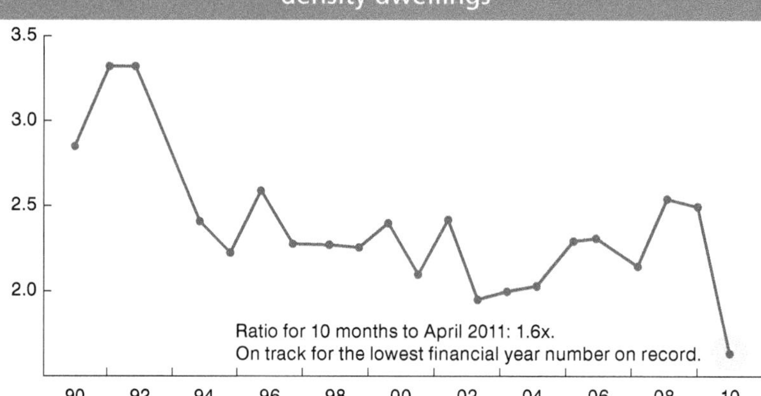

Housing affordability

The second trend is that home rental vs home ownership is increasing not only due to lifestyle choices but because of housing affordability.

Recent growth in housing prices is greatly exceeding the growth of household income and is the worst it has been in decades.[6]

In 2014 the IMF Global Housing Index showed Australia was the third most expensive country globally in which to buy a house[7] (Figure 2). So with more Australians renting their homes than ever before in our history, the opportunity for major household improvement vendors is increasingly diminishing.

Household debt

For those able to purchase a home however, with more income going to purchase their house and service the debt, there's less money left over to improve their homes. This is demonstrated by the proportion of Australian household debt to GDP reaching an all-time high (Figure 3).[8]

Figure 2: Australia real housing sector indices 1986–2014

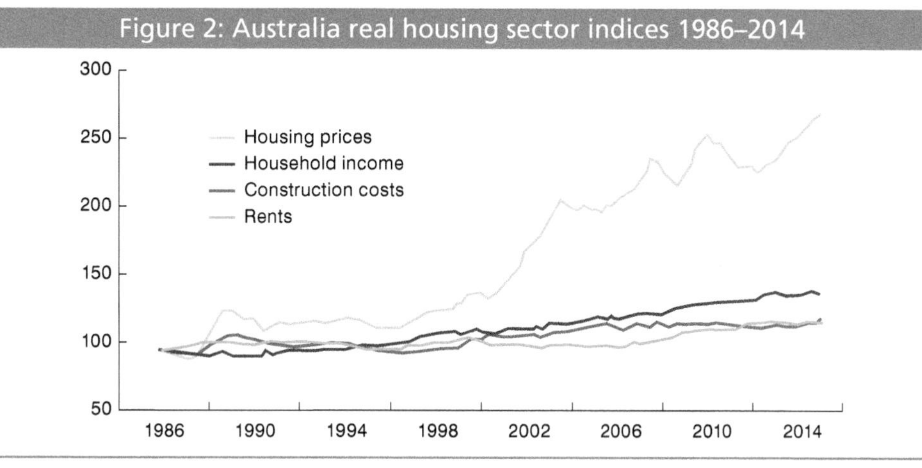

Figure 3: Household debt (% of GDP)

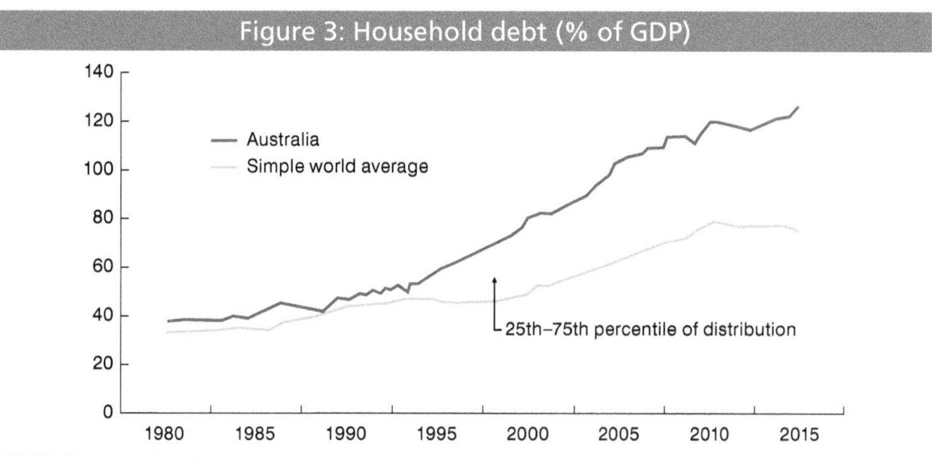

The culmination of demographic shifts in housing, affordability and household debt means that we started our journey with Narellan with a pool market in serious decline.

Declining interest in pool ownership

These trends are borne out with behavioural data reflecting a declining interest in pools. Using Google Trends Data we found fewer people in Australia are searching for the keyword term 'pool builder' based on an aggregated year-on-year view for the past three years.[9]

Increased competition

In addition to a shrinking pool-buyer market, the cost of entry to being a pool builder has substantially dropped thanks to the effect of Google.

The accessibility of Google AdWords has been a great leveller for many small businesses. Accordingly, we've seen a 100% increase in pool builder keywords in cost per click (CPC) per region since 2011. Many new, small solo operators have found it lucrative to promote themselves as pool providers with many generalist builders turning to pools to supplement their incomes.

In regional areas, Narellan have gone from being one of only one or two pool builders in their territory to now competing with as many as 28 different providers in just under five years. As solo operators these providers are in a position to further increase competition by easily undercutting Narellan's pricing.

To put the element of competitive hyper-fragmentation in perspective, by 2015 there were 247 different pool builder providers competing with 70% of all sales across Narellan's 49 regions.[10]

A stagnating market

IBIS World estimates that the pool industry revenue has only grown by an annualised 1.3% over the last five years.[4] This growth rate is nearly half that of inflation over the same period, meaning that the market has been stagnating and tending toward a slight decline.[11]

A business in decline

As a result of these factors, Narellan's sales have essentially declined year-on-year for the last seven years (Figure 4).

Figure 4: Narellan Pools index of total sales 2007–2013

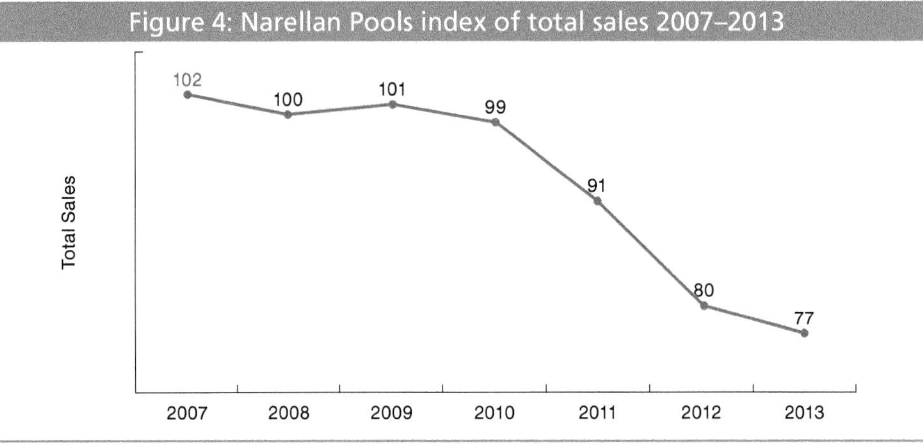

Objectives

We were initially appointed in 2013 to help Narellan turn sales around for 2014. Our brief was to arrest the decline and over time bring sales back to 2008 levels. Narellan's 2008 media spend was in excess of $900,000. In 2014 only $495,000 was allocated to media in response to the pressure of declining sales. Prior to our appointment, Narellan had deployed a traditional media strategy focused around mass awareness channels of TV and print with search rounding out the rest.

We started our engagement by implementing a digitally-led media strategy focused on performance media. With less people in the market we realised we had to make Narellan's investment count.

Leads, not just awareness, are the lifeblood for a company such as Narellan and during this period we increased these to the highest level in seven years – up 21% year-on-year, with sales increasing by 35%. Based on feedback from the franchisees, we knew the leads we drove in 2014 were more qualified than those of previous years. Over the course of 2014 we helped deliver one of the highest ever sales results for Narellan and certainly reversed their downward sales performance. The results of 2014 are not the focus of this paper but help set the scene for the challenge set out for what came next.

It was on the basis of the strong results of the previous year that Narellan set us an ambitious target in 2015 to increase leads by a further 10% and conversion to sales by 5%. We smashed both.

We knew that after a year of optimisation, the digital strategy from 2014 had reached maximum usefulness and would not deliver on our new increased objectives. We calculated there was a possibility of no more than a 2–3% additional efficiency gain in leads over and above our 2014 performance through digital optimisation.

Despite being a highly seasonal market, with more pools sold during summer than winter, a substantial media budget would be required to establish a constant presence during the key selling period. To give perspective, spreading Narellan's $495,000 media spend over 49 different territories, translates to just over $10,000, per territory, per annum.

We needed to radically change things up to deliver on our client's challenging objectives.

Strategy

Our first step in developing our strategy was to talk to pool buyers to gain a deeper understanding of drivers of pool purchase coupled with an aim to identify a tipping point to sale using Narellan's first-party data.

Creativity and innovation

After conducting qualitative research[12] with recent Narellan pool buyers we found that the aspiration of their first 'dive-in moment' in their own pool is one of the most powerful motivators for buying. So we crafted creative around this insight, celebrating the moment of the first dive on a shoestring budget.

Meanwhile, our data team went to work to find insights that would best utilise Narellan Pools' limited media spend. Understanding this was a lead-generation driven category, our focus was on maximising conversion. So, our goal was to identify the all-important tipping point for when people shift from wanting a pool to actually purchasing a pool – and we unearthed something amazing.

Our first task was to do a full CRM audit where we identified the average path to sale was between three to nine months.

Whilst there we saw the expected seasonal uplift in leads in warmer months, we also found that there were some interesting and unexplained changes in behaviour.

On some days within the focus months there were pronounced increases in leads, as well as massive spikes in conversion of those leads with no clear causation for either (Figure 5).

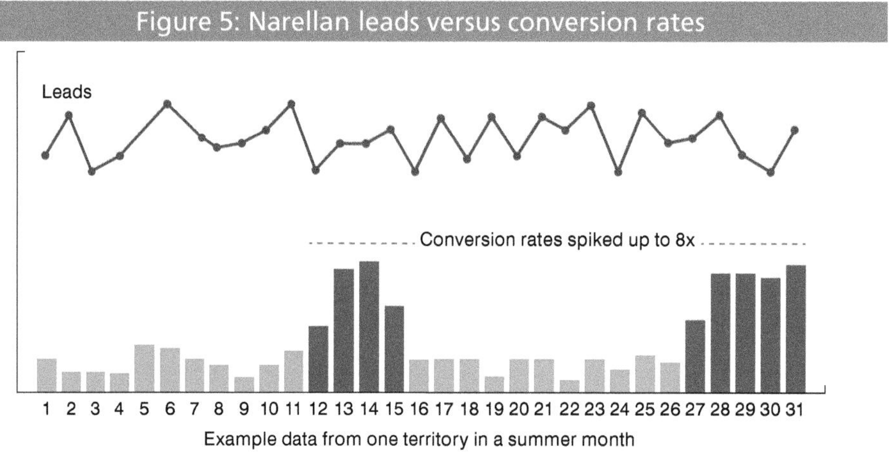

Figure 5: Narellan leads versus conversion rates

So we'd discovered an unexplained anomaly – conversion rates were spiking up to 800% on certain days in each month for a period of up to four days. We had to find out why.

We started by overlaying Narellan's first-party data including leads, sales, conversion rates, marketing and promotional plans along with website analytics such as traffic, time on site and visit to enquiry conversion rates. We then further compared this with third-party data including consumer confidence, interest rates, CPI, building approvals, search volumes for pool quotes and related keywords and weather.

This data was mapped over a five-year period. We undertook an intensive process to gather and compile the data into a structured format ready to analyse. In total this amounted to over seven terabytes of data and resulted in data tables with over 100 million rows.

We analysed the data across all 49 territories where we found that temperature was *the* important determinant in successful lead generations and conversion to sales. But the eureka moment was in the detail. Temperature being higher on a given day or across a month did not in itself affect leads and conversions.

We discovered that if the temperature was higher than the *mean monthly rolling average* for more than two consecutive days, we saw a spike in sales conversion rates (Figure 6).

To be clear, the temperature effect wasn't creating pool buyers that hadn't been thinking of buying a pool previously. It simply acted as the tipping point for taking the next critical step in their path to purchase: picking up the phone or making a web enquiry for a quote.

Figure 6: Narellan conversion rates overlaid with weather

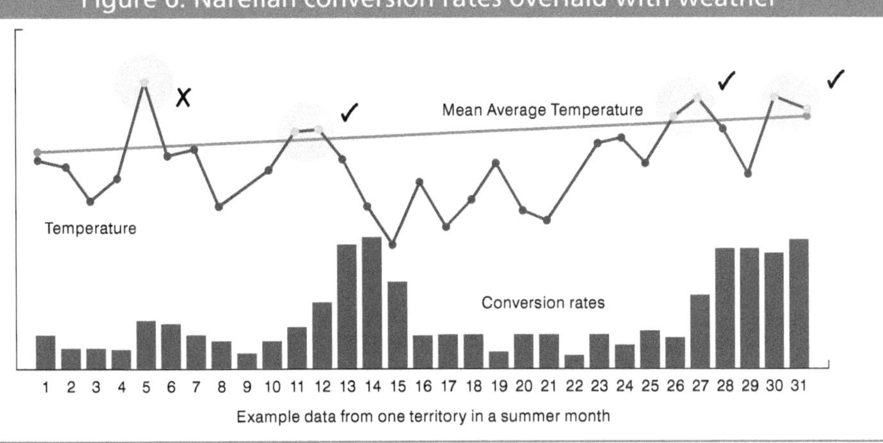

Not only were we seeing more leads, the quality of these leads were significantly higher. When we analysed the Narellan CRM data, we found that leads coming through under these conditions were up to 800% more likely to buy a pool from Narellan. We also found that these leads had a considerably shorter buying path or latency. Finally, we observed the increase in quality and conversion phenomenon lasted for a total period of four days, inclusive of the second day over the mean average temperature. Our findings support what most sales people already intuitively know – that all leads are not created equal.

Through our intensive analytical approach, we'd found our advertising nirvana and could deliver true context marketing. We had defined the exact tipping point for highly qualified intending pool purchasers. Now we had to action this data insight.

Execution

Knowing that qualified potential pool purchasers were more likely to act every time these specific temperature conditions occurred, we delivered our 'dive-in moment' creative message. If the specific temperature conditions were met in any of our 49 targeted regions, we activated the media spend for our creative campaign which included pre-roll video, banners, search and social. How did we do this?

We created rules in our programmatic buying tools to set the campaign live (see Figure 7) based on the following:

- If the temperature yesterday was higher than the mean monthly rolling average temperature
- And the forecast/real-time temperature for today is higher than the mean monthly rolling temperature
- Set campaign live and turn off after four days, unless the conditions were met again in that period.

Figure 7: Narellan conversion rates, temperature and campaign activation overlay

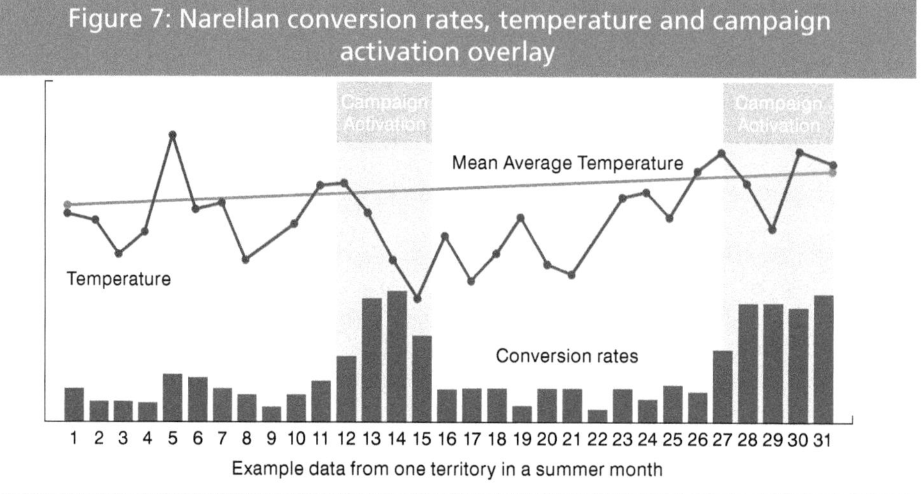

To deliver this, we built an innovative and intricate weather-polling app to seamlessly feed forecast real-time temperature data from 49 different regions into our real-time buying platforms. We then hacked programmatic buying tools to activate spend, only when our specific conditions were met.

Turning the campaign on *and off* in real-time based on specific weather conditions – so that we only ran advertising when we'd have the greatest effect – is, to our knowledge, a world first.

By spending only when these conditions were met, we delivered some unprecedented results for Narellan.

Results

Despite being asked to deliver a 10% increase in target in the context of a diminished market size, less media spend and increased competition, we smashed our goals.

We increased direct leads by 11% and increased sales by 23% year-on-year (a whopping 360% of our goal). In 2015 we helped Narellan deliver its highest sales result in over a decade (Figure 8).

Not only that but by spending only when the conditions were met meant that we couldn't spend all of Narellan's media budget – we were able to reduce the overall media spend by 30% (Table 1).

Table 1: Objectives and results

	Objectives for 2015	Result for 2015
Increase leads	10%	11%
Increase sales	5%	23%
Media spend	0%	–30%

Figure 8: Narellan Pools index of total sales 2007–2015

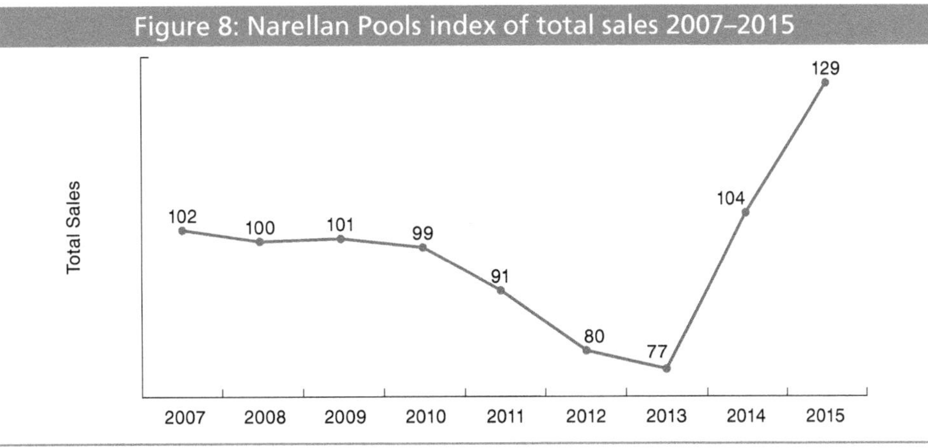

This campaign generated a ROI of 54:1 in incremental sales. Yes, that's a $54 return for every $1 dollar spent.

Discounting other factors

Promotion

There were no price reductions in 2015. Across 2014 and 2015 similar incentives and tactics were used with identical finance offers running November–December in both periods.

Distribution

There was also no increase or change within the franchisee base or coverage for Narellan.

Media spend

The effectiveness of our insight was not due to an increase in media budget. Rather, our insight was able to deliver a reduction in budget spend. Overall media spend[13] decreased 30% year-on-year, and was nearly three times less than invested four years ago (Table 2).

Table 2: Narellan Pools media spend

Year	2011	2012	2013	2014	2015
Index	100	97	91	57	40

Market growth

Market growth was not a factor. As we've demonstrated earlier the market was actually in decline in real terms.[4, 11]

Product

There were no new product innovations, extensions or other changes to the Narellan product during the period in question.

Competition

As outlined in the 'background' section, there was a significant increase in direct competition for leads and sales over the period as well as commensurate clutter and confusion in an increasingly fragmented market.

How does this compare to other IPA winners?

Looking through other recent winning IPA papers we couldn't find a direct comparison in this category, so we included a broad range of categories to draw comparison with. They're ranked by return and range from 32 to 1.1, which puts into perspective how spectacular the performance of providing a return of 54:1 in incremental revenue actually is.

Table 3: ROI results from previous IPA papers

Brand	Category	IPA Year	Revenue generated per $/£/€
Narellan Pools	Swimming pools	2016	54
Fosters	Beer	2014	32
Morrisons	Grocery	2009	21.57
Virgin Atlantic	Travel	2012	15.66
Travelocity	Travel	2005	5.6
Waitrose	Grocery	2007	5.57
Swinton	Insurance	2010	4.31
KFC	Food	2008	4.3
Dacia	Automotive	2014	4
BT: Broadband	Telecommunications	2010	3.36
Cadbury Wispa	Confectionary	2010	3.32
British Gas	Utility	2012	1.82
Mercedes-Benz	Automotive	2014	1.1

Conclusion

With so much against us, we had to dig into data to find a smarter solution. Defining our intent to action tipping point meant we could spend at and around the optimal moment in time. We were able to speak to fewer, but more qualified, people and in turn spend less of our client's money and sell more product.

With this paper we hope to have demonstrated you don't need millions of dollars to deliver remarkable results, and that a different approach to thinking and finding actionable insights is available to brands big, small, famous and obscure.

Acknowledgement

We'd like to thank the team at Narellan Pools for their courage to allow us to try something so new and different and for trusting us to deliver when the stakes for a smaller business are always so high.

Notes

1. All amounts are expressed in Australian dollars.
2. http://www.australia.gov.au/about-australia/our-country/our-natural-environment
3. https://en.wikipedia.org/wiki/Australian_Dream
4. *Swimming Pool and Spa Equipment Stores Market Research Report*, IBIS World – July 2015
5. http://www.afr.com/real-estate/residential/the-new-australian-dream-own-an-apartment-20110615-iccwe
6. Australian real housing indices 2Q86–2Q15 – Variant Perception
7. IMF Global Housing Index 2014
8. Australian household debt 1980–2015 – Variant Perception
9. Google Trends Data – 2013–2015 Key Word: Pool Builder
10. Count of competitors per Narellan's 49 regions aggregated into brands and estimated market share
11. Consumer Price Index 2012–2015, Reserve Bank of Australia January 2016
12. Agency Research
13. Media spend excluding GST

Save the Children

Making embarrassing knitwear into something to be proud of

By Toby Harrison and Ben Worden, adam&eveDDB
Contributing authors: Les Binet, adam&eveDDB
Credited company: adam&eveDDB

Summary

In the wake of the financial crisis, 2012 was one of the toughest times to be a charity. With Brits giving less, and more charities competing for every pound, Save the Children needed to find a way to engage new supporters. Pulling on a thread of culture, Save the Children took a guilty pleasure (festive pullovers), and turned it into a powerful fundraising and support-generating machine. From a tiny meme to a mass movement, Christmas Jumper Day became part of the fabric of Christmas. It generated a category-beating profit ROI between 2012 and 2014 of £3.31 for every £1 invested.

Editor's Comment

The judges were impressed by how this idea unlocked a new audience along with new partnerships for the charity, and drove profitable growth over a number of years.

Client Comment

Kate Hewitt, Head of Marketing Communications, Save the Children

It is hard to dispute the positive effect that the 'Christmas Jumper Day' has had for Save the Children. Both engaging and effective, the idea has not only galvanised our staff and volunteers, but also allowed our organisation to broaden its relationship with a wide section of the public. All this, whilst becoming a regular fixture of the festive season.

As effective and as engaging as it may be, 'Christmas Jumper Day' is not a revolutionary piece of thinking, and this perhaps is the cleverness of it all. Whilst there is a definite charm to the idea, 'Christmas Jumper Day' is the product of sensible and practical thinking.

The main learning we have taken from this campaign was, rather than trying to 'magic a behaviour out of thin air' creatively, we instead found one that existed and gave it a shape and form that would fit our needs. Looking carefully at culture first and then grounding it in honest, considered common sense, is what we believe has led to its success.

Introduction

This paper outlines Save the Children UK's campaign for 'Christmas Jumper Day'. It covers the campaign's first three years of activity from 2012–2014 and its effects.

This is a story of how Save the Children built a fund-raising machine, connected with a new generation, and created a cultural institution that's now the fabric of Christmas.

This paper is about how the most potent cultural movements aren't created, but are harnessed instead. How big ideas should ask for very little, and most importantly ... how a little bit of fun can go a very long way.

The business background

In over 120 countries, Save the Children run programmes dealing with the survival, health, hunger, poverty, education and protection of children. It's important work that touches the lives of over 17 million children a year, and due to the scale of the operation, is very costly too. Like a select few charities, Save the Children carry out two streams of work that rely upon the public in different ways.

1. Delivering aid

Save the Children's 'on-ground' activity has a direct and immediate influence on the children of the world. In emergency situations they are often the first 'on site', delivering vital humanitarian aid. Their experience, professionalism and sheer force of will have made them a formidable aid organisation. But aid costs money, and donations are what enable them to deliver help where it is needed most.

2. Creating influence

There is another side to the organisation that is equally powerful – their campaigning arm. Through lobbying and campaigning, Save the Children create influence that affects the way the world treats children. Critical to this is Save the Children's ability to mobilise a faithful group of what they call 'supporters' (registered individuals who have opted-in) who they can lean on when they need to generate this influence.

Donations + support = sustainable help

Whilst fundraising is of critical importance, there are times when the power of their supporters can do more than money can: Save the Children are masters of using public outcry and well-targeted support to generate action from recalcitrant governments or authorities that need 'motivation'. For example, demonstrations of the public's will, such as a million texts in support of aid for Syria, can persuade the Treasury to unlock £10m in foreign aid funds. On these occasions, supporters are worth their weight in sterling.

Charity in context

It was tough times for charity

Like almost every other business sector, the global financial crisis had a detrimental effect on the charity category. Between 2010 and 2012, the total amount given to charity decreased by 22% (Figure 1).

Figure 1: UK charitable giving (£bn adjusted for inflation) 2010–2012

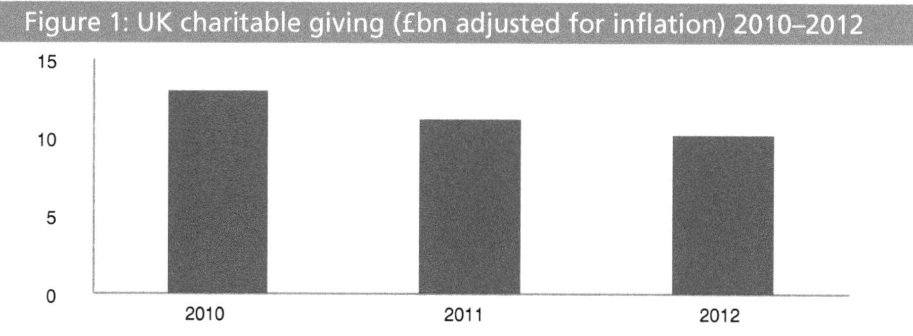

Source: CAF *UK Giving Report* 2014

More hands reaching out

4,448 new organisations were added to the register of charities in the UK in 2010. However, in 2012 that number grew to 6,661 – a 16% raise YOY. There was less money, and more mouths to feed (Figure 2).

Figure 2: UK registered charities, 2009–2014

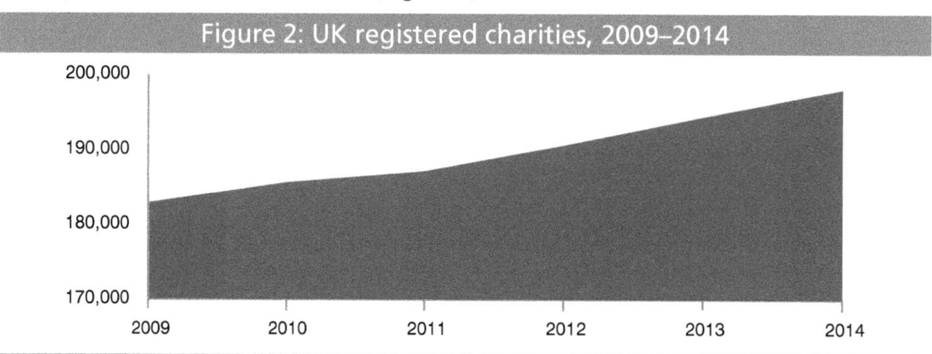

Source: NVCO 2014

The category was struggling, and Save the Children had their own issues too.

1. TV taking the strain

Traditionally, Save the Children used DRTV campaigns showcasing the plight of children to secure funds and supporters. This model had been used for many years, as the organisation's primary fund-raising tool. Whilst it delivers necessary funds and supporters, a supplementary programme was needed to meet the demands of the organisation.

2. Churn increasing

In times of crisis, support is strong – but issue-focused. The 2010 East Africa emergency and 2011 tsunami in Japan had swelled the number of donations and supporters for Save the Children. However, this influx of support was tied to those specific causes, meaning the churn rate was very high (Figure 3).

Figure 3: Save the Children supporter churn rate, 2009–2011

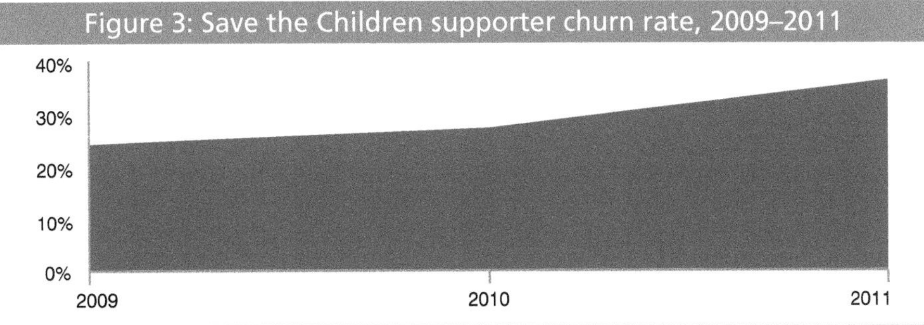

Source: Save the Children 2009–2011

3. Ageing support

Across the category, just 7% of the donor base contributes over 45% of the funds. And it was the same for Save the Children. They primarily focused on retirees who wanted to 'give a little back'. These altruistic and affluent 'active givers' delivered the greatest quantity of 'unrestricted' donations – money that Save the Children could spend as they saw fit. Whilst they were valuable, the inconvenient truth was that they were getting old. Inevitably, this 'active giver' segment would reduce over time, meaning the organisation's reliance upon them would become an issue.

4. Shock tactics no longer shocking

Whilst the 'child in plight' model of communication (Figure 4) would enrage 'active givers' into action, this type of shock and awe communications couldn't be relied on to engage everyone. Research conducted by OnePoll indicated that over 47% of the public said 'shocking images' did not make them likely to donate or support a cause.[1]

Figure 4: Save the Children 'No child born to die' DRTV ad 2011

The task

Bring in new blood

With high churn, a maturing supporter base, and their tried and tested model of marketing failing to connect with a younger audience, Save the Children recognised they needed to supplement their current model. Critical to this task was building a relationship with a new audience.

It is important to understand that whilst most charities just want money, Save the Children also needed to grow their number of supporters. This is significant because of the two-fold way (donors + supporters) Save the Children operates. Each 'registered supporter' who has opted-in, is someone Save the Children has the permission to contact to ask for help, whether that be for fund-raising or to lend their voice in support of a campaigning issue.

A direct relationship fulfils both needs of Save the Children; it provides a low-cost channel to acquire new funds, and creates an easier way to mobilise the support system ... but getting people to register their support is tremendously difficult.

Campaign objectives

In 2012 adam&eveDDB were tasked to create an initiative that would invite mass participation in the brand, giving Save the Children the broadest prospect pool to secure new registered supporters and opening the door for long-term campaigning and fund-raising potential:

- The year one target was to deliver an activation that 40,000 people would participate in, with an aim to register 500 new supporters as the primary goal.
- A fundraising goal of £100,000 was also attached to the initiative for the first year.

These targets were particularly ambitious. Save the Children had looked at other participation programmes to find lofty, but realistic benchmarks. For participation, Macmillan, Cancer UK and Movember had all generated good success, with Movember's growth swelling to 44,520 people by its third year in the UK.

The fundraising requirement was feasible, but no less tough. Established events such as Macmillan's bike ride had raised £100,000, however this was by the event's twenty-second year, which coincidentally, was also Macmillan's centenary.

The audience

Finding the new supporter

To create a change in their behaviour, adam&eveDDB looked to better understand the 'passive giver'. Younger, urban and poorer, they may have been 'passive' in their relationship to charity; however, in other parts of their lives they were anything but. They were highly social and deeply engaged with their communities and friends. But when it came to charity, they wanted a 'lighter' and more casual relationship.

Not because they didn't care, but because at their life stage, they just wanted a more positive and convenient way to 'do their bit' ... if and when it suited them.

To build a relationship with this group, the 'enrage' approach wouldn't work. Their young lives were filled with socialising and enjoying the fun to be had. They certainly didn't have time for the arduous, worthy or sad. To engage them, a lighter touch was needed.

The big insight into this audience wasn't genius, it was just common sense. Like most young people in the prime of their lives, 'passive givers' were more interested in having fun, than doing good. If Save the Children was to connect with them, they needed to do things differently...

A new approach

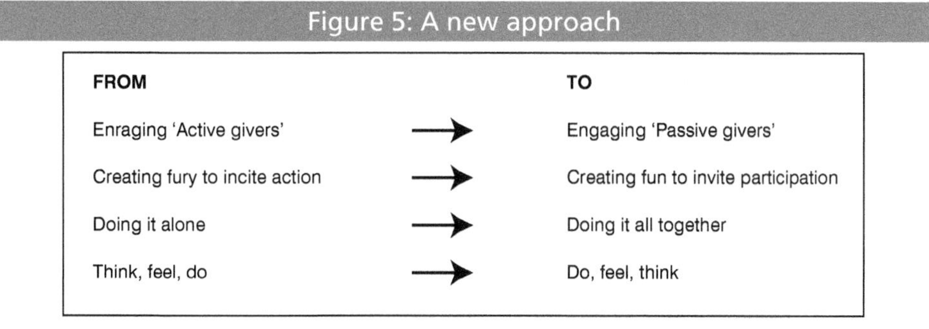

Figure 5: A new approach

FROM		TO
Enraging 'Active givers'	→	Engaging 'Passive givers'
Creating fury to incite action	→	Creating fun to invite participation
Doing it alone	→	Doing it all together
Think, feel, do	→	Do, feel, think

To connect with this new audience, adam&eveDDB and Save the Children agreed to flip the traditional model. Instead of starting with the cause and using this as a negative trigger to create action, the opposite approach was taken.

The challenge was clear

Create a fun and contagious activity in the summer of 2012 that anyone could participate in, with the lowest possible barrier to entry.

It was a tough environment to compete in

Standing out in the summer of 2012 was difficult, especially with the Olympics, European Championships, Sport Relief and even the Diamond Jubilee all vying for the public's attention. So adam&eveDDB and Save the Children chose to focus on Christmas. It is a charitable time of year, and more importantly, a permissible opportunity for passive givers to engage in a fun participation programme.

Aiming to capture the spirit of excitement about the forthcoming Christmas, the date of 14 December was decided upon. As the last full school day of the year, people would be 'demob' happy and far more willing to do something fun.

The critical thread

Looking at other successful participation programmes, one thing was clear: with limited funds, it was a much bigger task to get people to adopt an 'invented' behaviour.

The smarter choice was for Save the Children to take something from culture, and then give it a shape and form they could make their own.

Knitting together a big idea

adam&eveDDB's idea was to take a festive guilty pleasure and create permissibility for the nation to indulge in it – together. It was simple, charming, had a low barrier to entry and was fun (Figure 6).

Figure 6: 'Christmas Jumper Day'

The idea: make the world better in a sweater

In retrospect, it seems strange to think Christmas Jumpers haven't always been a 'thing', but before Friday 14 December 2012, that was the case. This changed when the people of the UK were urged to come to school or work in their most garish, ghastly or gorgeous Christmas garments ... something they all secretly loved and wanted to do. People were able to collectively participate in something, that cost £1 for children and £2 for adults, that made them feel good, did good and they could enjoy together.

How it was planned to work

The idea was strong, and had the potential to satisfy Save the Children's objectives. If it worked as expected, the organisation would see a rise in the number of donors (albeit with smaller amounts) and through the experience, they would hope to convert participants into supporters.

The role for communications was critical: *get the public engaged.* Clearly, there was a fun meme in Christmas Jumpers, but it needed to be shaped and formed in a way that culture could adopt and embrace. To effectively engineer this 'social movement' two things were needed:

- People on the ground that could cheerlead the activity and serve as our media.
- A sense that the movement was already happening.

... all with a very limited budget of £95,000.

The 3-part communications strategy

1. Identify the influential

Specific schools and workplaces (Figure 7) were identified for the initiative due to their fun environment and employees' influence.

Figure 7: Companies with influential employees

Within each of these, influential 'organisers' (teachers and office managers) were targeted to act as promoters for the event on Save the Children's behalf. Mailers and full-page ads in teaching publications (Figure 8) would drive sign-ups.

2. Inspire and inform

To inspire 'passive givers', fun Christmas Jumper Day packs (Figure 9) were sent as a follow up, informing them of how they could organise others to join in with them. The tonality of these communications was very important. They needed to assure the audience that Christmas Jumper Day was an event that felt right for them, and conveniently could do some good for the world.

3. This is happening

For the movement to take off, there needed to be a perception that the 'woolly revolution' was already happening. Two weeks prior to the big day, Save the Children surrounded people on their way to work/school with material that made the campaign feel bigger than it was. The organisation leveraged ambassadors (Figure 10) to promote the event using their own social channels to show-off their festive knitwear.

Figure 8: *The Teacher* and *Ofsted Magazine*

12 cover feature

Class teacher Olly Bloom gives one member's view

MAKE THE **WORLD** BETTER WITH A **SWEATER**

Get everyone in your school to wear a woolly wonder and donate £1 to help change children's lives.

Tinsel up school jumpers, rescue Granny's homemade knitwear, or flaunt your best festive pullovers.

Register now for your free Christmas Jumper Day Kit on **020 7012 6400** or **savethechildren.org.uk/jumpers**

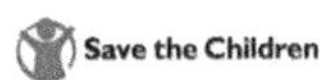

MAKE THE **WORLD** BETTER WITH A **SWEATER**

Get everyone in your school to wear a woolly wonder and donate £1 to help change children's lives.

Tinsel up school jumpers, rescue Granny's homemade knitwear, or flaunt your best festive pullovers.

Register now for your free Christmas Jumper Day Kit on **020 7012 6400** or **savethechildren.org.uk/jumpers**

International

Defending children's rights

Arab women teachers together

Figure 9: Christmas Jumper Day packs

Figure 10: Save the Children ambassadors and organic reach through influential companies

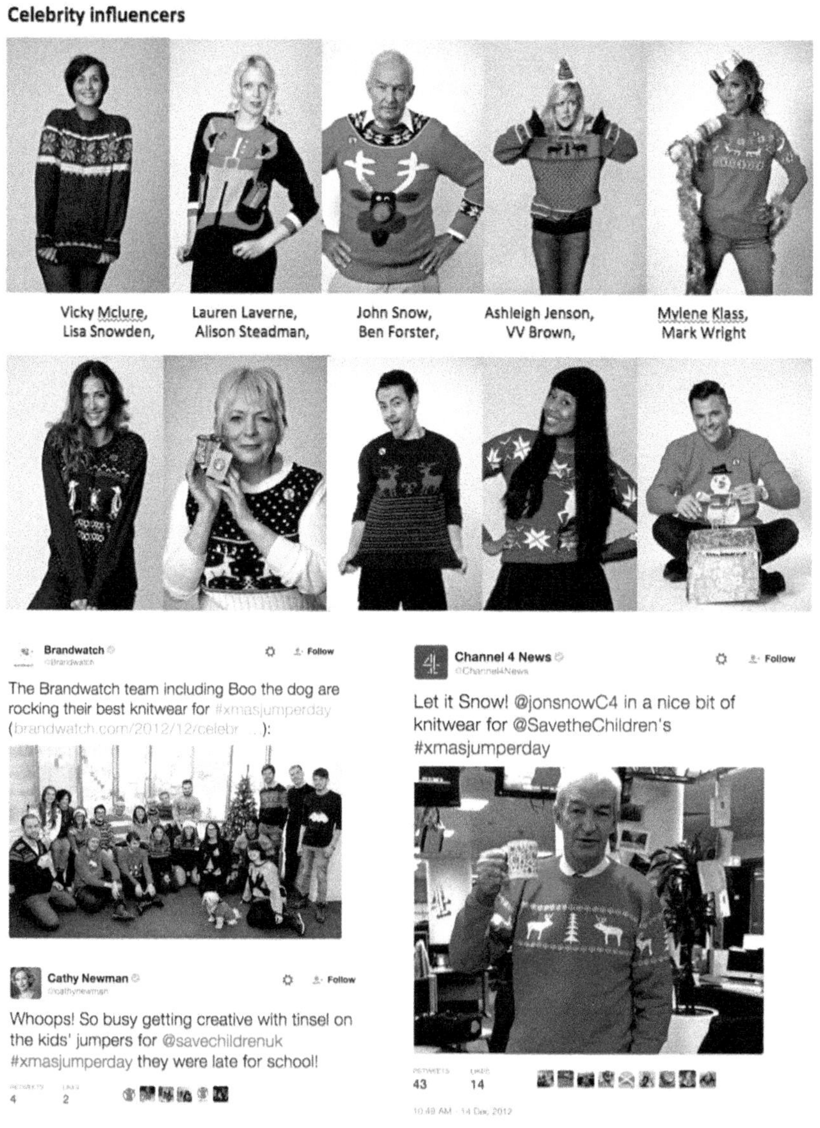

Building to a crescendo, online display, transit and a print media partnership with *Time Out* would augment this organic reach.

The public's support for Christmas Jumper Day was fervent and highly visible. Kicking-off with Samantha Cameron (Figure 11), hundreds of thousands of Brits donned festive knitwear, becoming human advertising for the initiative (Figure 12).

Figure 11: Samantha Cameron poses with schoolchildren on the steps of Number 10

Figure 12: Participant photos from social media

The 'selfie' generation extended the impact digitally, with #ChristmasJumperDay trending across social networks.

A common bond between wearers even broke down social barriers, with reports of participants actively speaking to other Christmas jumper wearers they didn't know on the Tube! Even the Old Bailey was touched by the activity (Figure 13).

Figure 13: Christmas Jumper Day at the Old Bailey

Ruth Mosalski @ruthmosalski · 14 Dec 2012
At least one person in the court building today is taking part in #xmasjumperday. Jury foreman, in a green number, just delivered a verdict.

Figure 14: 2012 activity

Activity partners

Workplace sign-up DM mailers

Print and digital display

Outdoor at Westfield Point and Shepherd's Bush

How Christmas Jumper Day worked: year 1

1. Participation

The goal was to get 40,000 people to participate in Christmas Jumper Day.

On 14 December 2012, 402,999 people wore their Christmas Jumpers with pride: *More than 10 times the target* (Figure 15).

Figure 15: Christmas Jumper Day 2012 – participants vs target

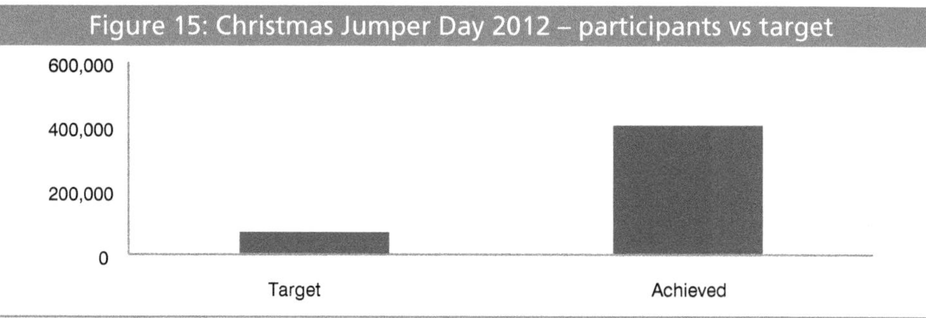

Source: Save the Children

2. New supporters

With supporters so critical to the future success of Save the Children, it was essential that amongst the participants, 500 new supporters be recruited.

5,709 new supporters were recruited: *again, more than 10 times the target,* delivering 5% of Save the Children's annual supporter target of 100,000 in *one fell swoop* (Figure 16).

Figure 16: Christmas Jumper Day 2012 – new supporters vs target

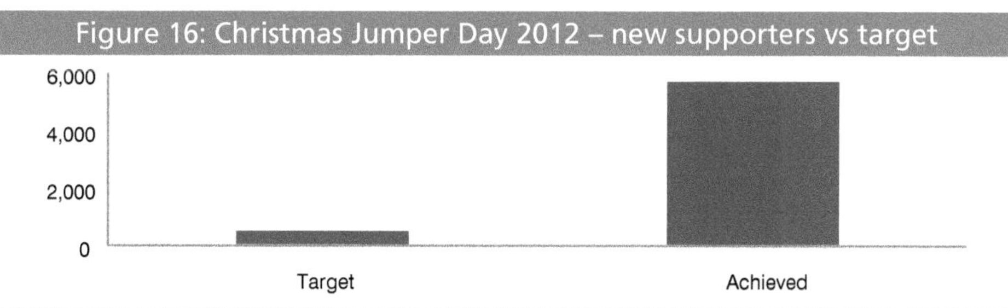

Source: Save the Children

3. Donations

Additionally, the target of £100,000 in donations was smashed.

Christmas Jumper Day brought in £360,000 – *three and a half times the target* (Figure 17).

Figure 17: Christmas Jumper Day 2012 – donations vs target

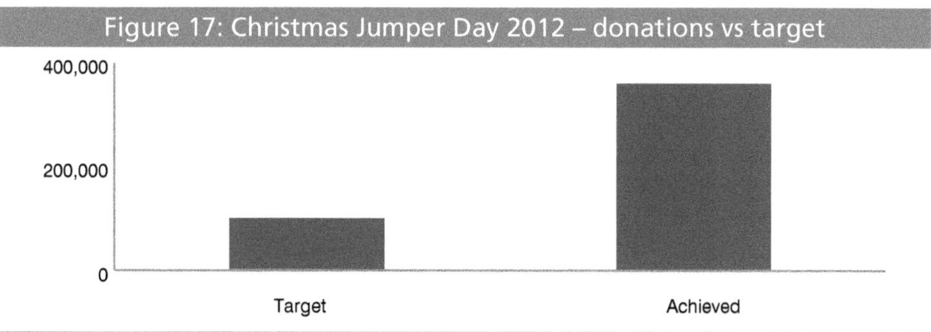

Source: Save the Children

4. Exposure

To extend the reach of the activity beyond participants, Save the Children hoped to expose an additional 70,000 people to the brand, thus increasing consideration for the organisation.

With PR value from earned media equating to over **£1.4m**, and *with over 40m impressions*[2] across social media of #christmasjumperday, the impact for the brand was huge, surpassing the objective with ease.

5. Communication that registered supporters

The effect of the communications was considerable. Even though organic word of mouth is the second most effective communication for securing supporters, this could be attributed to the targeted materials that were delivered to key influencers. Excluding telemarketing, the communications account for all the other large effects (Figure 18).

Figure 18: Christmas Jumper Day 2012 – drivers of registration

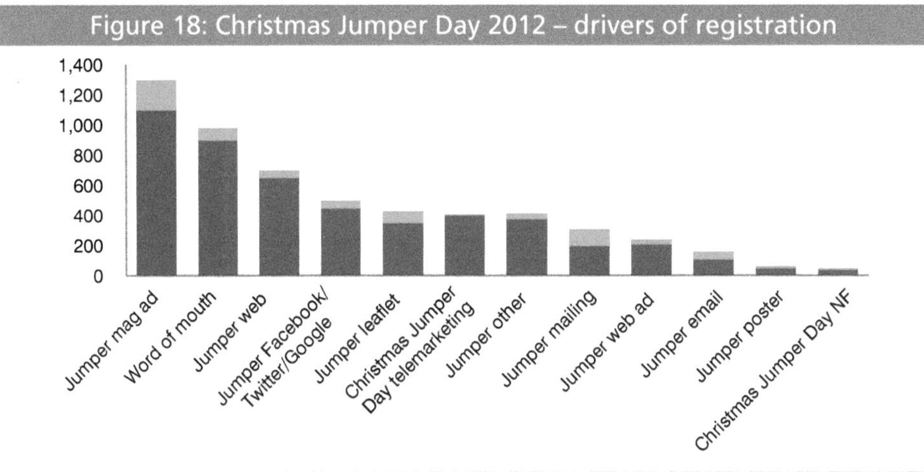

Source: Save the Children participant survey 2012

6. The cost of success

All of the activity for year one was delivered with a budget of just **£95,403**.

Christmas Jumper Day 2012 generated a net profit of **£220,189**. However to calculate a profit ROI it is necessary to account for the fact that Save the Children spends 12p in every £1 generating the funds, leaving 88p to be spent on making a real difference to the lives of children.

Deducting this 12% running cost from the revenue generated by Christmas Jumper Day 2012 results in a bona-fide *profit ROI of £3.31:1.*

Unsurprisingly, the decision was made to make Christmas Jumper Day an annual event.

And in years 2 & 3, things got bigger and better

Figure 19: 2013 Activity

Year 2 – 2013
Budget: £363,936
Media used: Print – Metro
Guardian, Big Issue, Evening Standard, TimeOut, Independent & i, Stylist and Stylist.co.uk
Emerald Street Newsletter
OOH – Tube card panels
Train card panels
Digital – Social video
DM

Activity partners

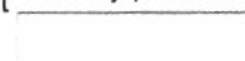

Workplace sign-up DM mailers

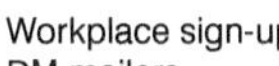

Print and OOH

Digital display

PR placement

'The Killing' does Christmas Jumper Day social video

Figure 20: 2014 Activity

Year 3 – 2014
Budget: £1,256,281
Media used: Print – Metro
TimeOut, Stylist, Shortlist, Evening Standard, Big Issue, Manchester Evening New, Birmingham Mail,Liverpool Echo, The Sun Scotland
DM, SMS, and EDM – School and workplace mailers
OOH – Tube card panels
Train card panels
TV – DRTV

Social media

Print and OOH

DRTV ad

School and workplace mailers

Harry Enfield 'whatever's' comfortable' social video spoof

How Christmas Jumper Day worked: years 2 & 3

1. A nationwide event, with millions of people taking part

The success of Christmas Jumper Day 2012 laid the foundations for future success. The fame earned in 2012 helped to ensure mass participation in 2013, and the number of 'sweater wearers' would eventually reach 4 million in 2014 (Figure 21).

Figure 21: Christmas Jumper Day participation, 2012–2014

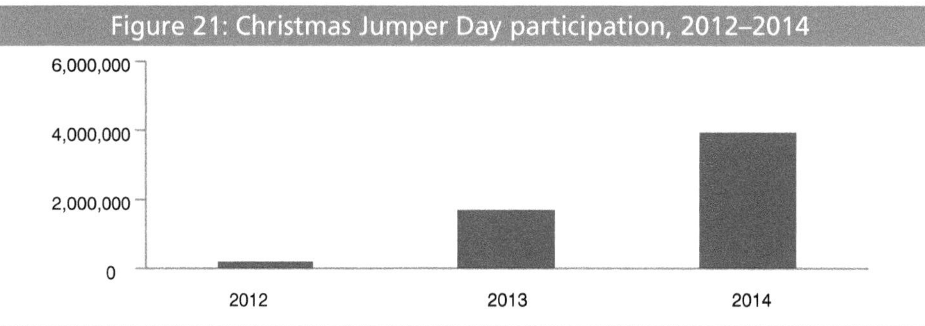

Source: Save the Children

2. Earned media snowballed

With celebrity involvement from the likes of Samantha Cameron, Richard Branson and Usain Bolt, press coverage increased (Figure 22), delivering PR worth £7.7m in 2013 and £15m in 2014, helping to ensure even greater awareness of Save the Children amongst a younger audience.

Figure 22: Christmas Jumper Day press coverage – number of articles

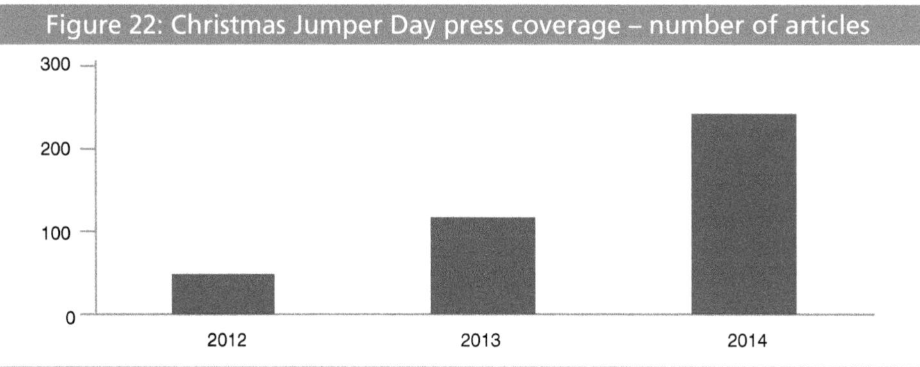

Source: Factiva

3. Donations increased in line with participation

After the runaway success of Christmas Jumper Day 2012, more ambitious targets were set for 2013 (£979,865) and 2014 (£3.5m). Once again, Christmas Jumper Day surpassed expectations, generating £1.3m and £4.2m in years two and three (Figure 23).

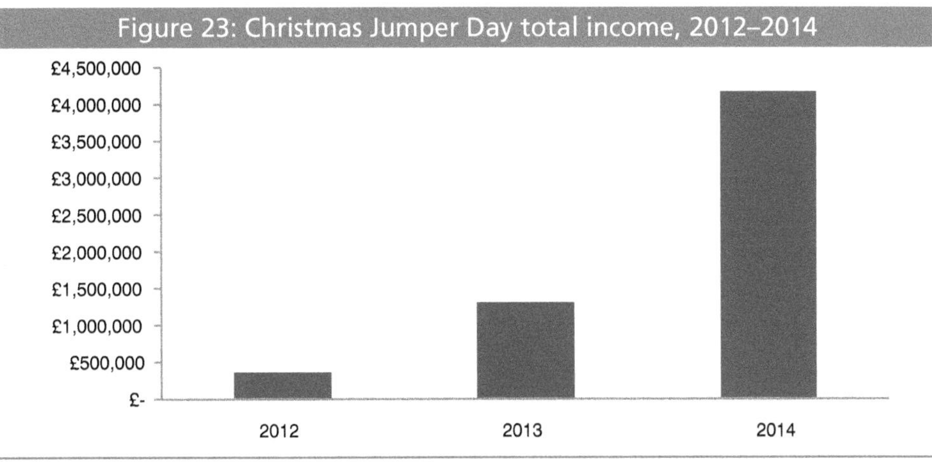
Figure 23: Christmas Jumper Day total income, 2012–2014

Source: Save the Children

4. Christmas Jumper Day is the single most effective way to engage supporters

In the second year, supporter numbers increased by 21,233. However, by 2014, Christmas Jumper Day engaged even greater numbers of new supporters, bringing in a grand total of 50,579 (Figure 24).

Figure 24: Christmas Jumper Day new supporter recruitment, 2012–2014

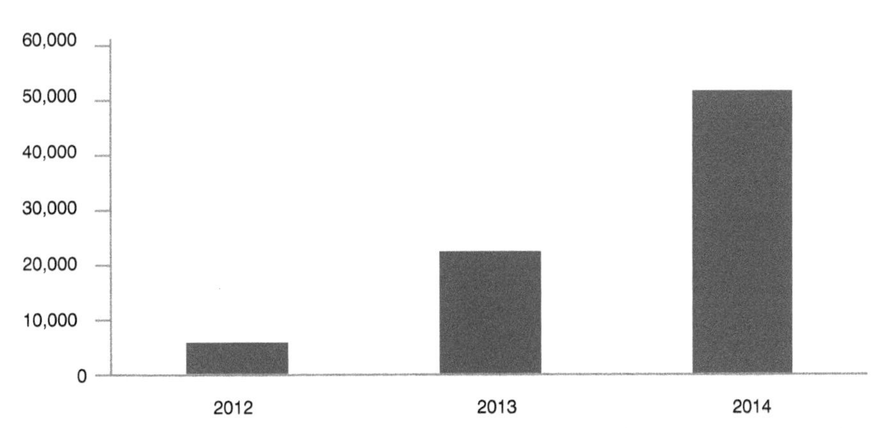

Source: Save the Children

What began as a means to bring in 500 new supporters had now become the primary driver of engagement for the organisation.

5. Building success at scale

2012 demonstrated the power of Christmas Jumper Day to drive participation, engagement, fund-raising and supporter recruitment. Yet, in 2013 and 2014 brand engagement, income, and supporter numbers driven by Christmas Jumper Day grew exponentially. As a fundraising activity alone, it was Britain's fastest growing activity.[3]

As the event grew in scale, so did the costs to make it happen. However, this increase in overheads did not sacrifice the profitability of the venture (Figure 25).

Figure 25: Christmas Jumper Day costs vs income, 2012–2014

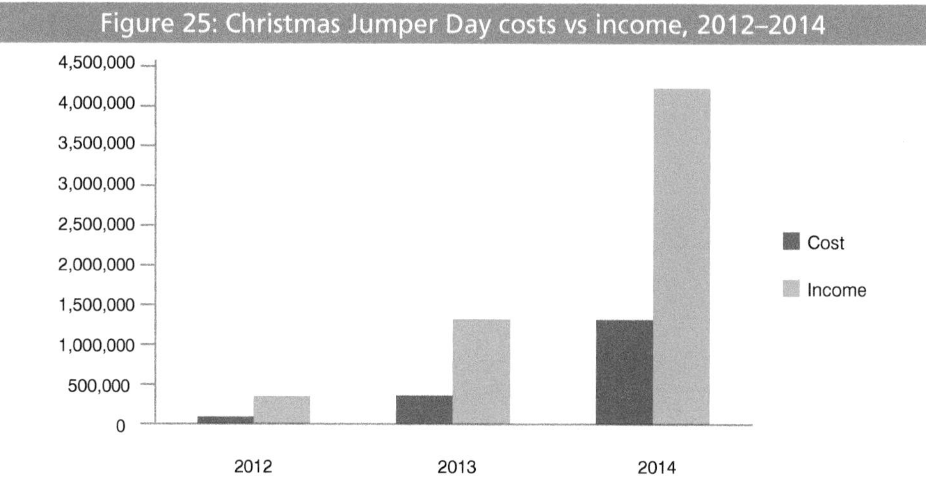

Source: Save the Children

6. ROI stability

Christmas Jumper Day grew in a sustainable way. Profit and return on investment remained at an average 3.4:1 over the three years covered by this paper (Table 1).

Table 1: Christmas Jumper Day profit analysis

	2012	2013	2014	Total
Media spend	£95,403	£363,936	£1,256,281	£1,715,620
Donations generated	£360,356	£1,305,907	£4,170,000	£5,836,263
Overheads	£44,764	£155,356	£448,072	£648,192
Net income (ex overheads)	£315,592	£1,150,551	£3,721,928	£5,188,071
Income per £1 spent on ads	**£3.31**	**£3.16**	**£2.96**	**£3.02**
Net profit	£220,189	£786,615	£2,465,647	£3,472,451
ROMI	231%	216%	196%	202%

Source: Save the Children

In just three years Christmas Jumper Day had become not just an institution, but also a fund-raising and engagement machine. And in just a single event, it secured a significant number of a totally new type of supporter for the organisation.

7. The human profit

In 2014, Christmas Jumper Day raised £2.4m. To put this in context, that could deliver life-saving treatments to 1.04 million children suffering from illnesses such as diarrhoea and malaria, two major killers amongst the under-5s in some of the poorest parts of the world.[4]

An idea that did more

Christmas Jumper Day wasn't just a 'flash in the pan' idea. Whilst it has been very effective at providing access to new donors and securing fundraising, it has also enabled Save the Children as an organisation to open up new revenue streams and operate more efficiently.

Partnerships

Christmas Jumper Day allowed Save the Children to broker powerful partnerships with other businesses such as ASDA, Costa Coffee, Pets at Home, Primark and more recently ITV. These partnerships greatly increased the scale and exposure of the idea (and in the case of ASDA allowed people to buy Christmas Jumpers and make an instant donation), therefore increasing the opportunity for people to participate and contribute (Figure 26).

Idea adoption

The simplicity and power of the idea has made it easy for other national offices to adopt Christmas Jumper Day...(the UK, Iceland, Canada and the US have run a Christmas Jumper Day programme) with the only barrier to entry being the temperature at Christmas time. Apparently this is not an issue in Iceland.

Tying up the loose ends

Christmas Jumper Day is a tremendously effective single body of activity. In order to attribute the results directly to the activation, it has benefited from having a specific Christmas Jumper Day channel, allowing Save the Children to isolate its results from other activity. Therefore, all figures regarding results are independent of any other mechanics, channels or recruitment techniques employed by Save the Children during this time.[5]

However, in order to accurately attribute the effects of Christmas Jumper Day, it is important to discount certain other factors.

Was it other activity?

There were no other similar campaigns in market from Save the Children that would have boosted participation or donations to Christmas Jumper Day. Additionally, the nature of other communications from Save the Children wasn't of any comparable model. This was the very communication that had not connected with the younger audience previously, so it is fair to assume there was no 'ad-stock' residue that Christmas Jumper Day was leveraging.

Were there any disasters that the public were responding to?

Whilst there were no major disasters or crises that would incentivise participation in 2012, Typhoon Haiyan struck the Philippines in 2013. A separate appeal for this

Figure 26: Christmas Jumper Day partnerships

Pick up a Christmas jumper and support Save the Children!

This Christmas we're working with Save The Children to 'make the world better with a sweater' and help disadvantaged children living in the UK.

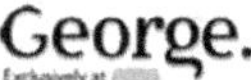

cause raised £3.7m and channelled the funds directly to the cause. In 2014, there were no significant disasters.

Did Christmas Jumper Day benefit from an absence of competitors?

There was no withdrawal of a competitive activity or event. Christmas Jumper Day did not benefit from the absence of any other notable event, as all major 'mass participation' charity events continued as per the previous calendar year. If anything, Christmas competitive activity increased.

Was it the weather?

Seasonality and timing did not adversely benefit the campaign. Christmas Jumper Day fell on the same day (the last full working day/school day before Christmas) each year. On Friday 14 December 2012 it was 9 degrees Celsius, Friday 13 December 2013 it was 13 degrees and Friday 12 December 2014 it was again 9 degrees. Therefore it was not considerably colder, forcing people to don more Christmas knitwear.[6]

Was there an increase in spending overall?

Whilst other charities greatly increased their spending over 2012–2014, Save the Children's spend only marginally increased (Table 2).

Table 2: Growth in charities total media spend 2012–2014

	2012 Spend	2013 Spend	2014 Spend	Percentage Increase
Cancer Research UK	£10.89m	£16.19m	£24.99m	129.4%
Macmillan	£17.23m	£20.01m	£24.32m	41.1%
The Red Cross	£10.37m	£13.19m	£13.67m	31.8%
Save the Children	£13.64m	£15.48m	£15.20m	11.4%

Was it a more Christmassy Christmas?

The Christmas of 2012 was not considerably more happy or festive than in previous years. In fact, GFK's consumer confidence index had slipped to –29 in December. This was only 4 points difference (–33) to the same time in 2011.[7]

Weaving a conclusion

Behaviour change is a Holy Grail for any organisation. It is a rare and sacred thing, because creating change is incredibly hard. There must be both a tangible reason and clear reward for people if they are going to change what they currently do. In Christmas Jumper Day, Save the Children mobilised a completely new audience to raise funds and deliver support for the organisation by having cheap, easy fun. Deconstructing how they achieved this, the great learning of this campaign is that behavioural change is not created – it is shaped.

Rather than trying to create a movement, Save the Children instead found one that already existed, but it was nascent, and needed a public vote of permissibility. adam&eveDDB and Save the Children recognised what others didn't: that Christmas jumpers were a sleeping giant – a guilty pleasure that people were desperate to indulge in, but had no good reason to commit to.

Christmas Jumper Day made knitwear not only a badge of honour, but also a positive force of change. It had a low barrier to entry, it was fun, sociable and the way it was introduced to the world lacked the heavy-handedness of traditional charity campaigns.

Considering its small price tag of £1.7m, Christmas Jumper Day is a big marketing idea. However, the learning in this paper is how communications took a meme and turned it into a movement, by giving shape and form to a behaviour that both the organisation could harness and culture could embrace. Save the Children did this by flipping the model and the way they engaged an audience. From leveraging fury, to encouraging fun allowed them to connect a new audience to an idea that has consistently delivered one of the most significant ROIs for the category in IPA history (Figure 27).

Figure 27: Benchmarking – most effective charity campaigns (ROMI)

Source: IPA DataBank

Notes

1. Source: 'Shock tactics – do they work' by Kate Magee, *PR Week*, 8 December 2011.
2. Source: Save the Children Media and PR calculations. Developed in association with JAA media.
3. Source: Massive – Top 20 mass participation charity league 2013.
4. Source: Save the Children annual report 2014.
5. NB: This paper does not include 2015 activity where Christmas Jumper Day was associated with ITV's 'Text Santa' activity. As this mechanic was shared across multiple charity partners, it has made it impossible to isolate and directly attribute the effect of Christmas Jumper Day within the results.
6. Source: London Heathrow Airport weather reports: available at http://www.weatheronline.co.uk/weather/maps/city.
7. Source: GFK consumer confidence index UK Period 2010–2015.

Snickers

Thinking like a Hollywood blockbuster

By Elly Fenlon, AMV BBDO
Contributing authors: Matt Boulter, Dan Burdett and Clarence Mak, Mars Confectionery – Snickers; Michael Magee, Mars Chocolate UK; Catriona Collins, Katy Talikowska and Will Whalley, AMV BBDO
Credited Companies: AMV BBDO; Data2Decisions; Nielsen; MediaCom

Summary

This is the story of how a single film, featuring Rowan Atkinson's Mr Bean character as a bumbling Kung Fu artist, became globally famous; connecting with 1.85bn people worldwide, and driving over $70m in incremental sales for Snickers, the chocolate brand. Inspired by Hollywood blockbusters, the initiative reframed the brand's established 'You're not you when you're hungry' idea to keep Snickers relevant in a world increasingly concerned about sugar and snacking. By airing in up to 60 markets, the film created economies of scale and saved production costs. In markets in which the film ran, Snickers reversed share declines and outperformed territories not showing the film. Overall, the brand surpassed its category in both sales value and volume growth. Globally, the revenue return was estimated at US $10.65 for every US $1 invested.

Editor's Comment

The judges were impressed both with the scale of the ambition to produce a single idea that could run across multiple markets, and by the scale of the results.

Client Comment

Matt Boulter, UK Brand Director, Snickers

'You're not you when you're hungry' has been a fantastic campaign for Snickers. Its development over the past six years shows how a universal insight based on human truth can be incredibly powerful for brand communications across geographies and that the clearer the insight the greater scope there is for great work. 'Bean Kung Fu' is a wonderful example of this – it has connected with people all over the globe, pushing the boundaries of YNYWYH, whilst delivering against the human truth at the heart of the campaign idea.

The process of creating 'Bean Kung Fu' showed the importance of being brave in our communication. 'Bean Kung Fu' did not follow all the rules of what traditionally made a successful YNYWYH ad but in some ways this is also why it was so successful. The business results and economies of scale ultimately gained all over the globe proved that bringing the campaign to life in this new way was a risk worth taking.

Ultimately, I think 'Bean Kung Fu' has taught us that it's a good thing if the initial idea excites but also scares you a bit! And to then bring that big idea to market takes real trust and respect between you and your agency partners. It has given us real faith in the principle that if you believe in something – work together and do everything you can to make it happen as it will be worth it in the end!

This is the story of how a single film with a bumbling Kung Fu artist connected with 1.85 billion people in over 60 countries, driving over $70 million in sales.

It's hard work selling chocolate bars. Even one as successful as Snickers.

'You're not you when you're hungry' (YNYWYH) was formulated as a response to hard times in 2009, where global share of value sales dramatically dropped, and competitors were encroaching on Snickers' position as the world's biggest chocolate bar. The strategy originated in a desire for a more focused approach to communications, and the logic that the way to arrest global[1] decline would be through a united strategy across all markets. The full story of the development is covered in a previous winning IPA entry 'You're not you when you're hungry' from 2012.

To recap briefly, the idea was built on a simple but powerful universal insight: that there is an unspoken code of conduct that must be abided by in order to stay part of the male pack. Being hungry can endanger your ability to abide by the code of conduct that keeps you as 'one of the guys'. Whether you become irritable, weak, or dopey, there are certain universal symptoms of hunger that can stop a guy from keeping to the code. Snickers is the solution: as a filling, peanut-packed bar, Snickers can sort out hunger and restore your place in the pack.

The simplicity of the idea and universality of its insight meant widespread adoption by Snickers' many local markets, and in the years since launch YNYWYH carved out worldwide fame and business success via locally produced executions. YNYWYH helped Snickers regain global market share of $376.3 million between 2009 and 2011, with the launch ad 'Game' creating 400 million media impressions and becoming the most successful Superbowl ad at the time.

However, 2014 saw new headwinds. The global chocolate confectionery category only just managed to maintain volumes in a world increasingly concerned about sugar intake and bombarded by alternative snack options. Snickers' unfashionable format as a heavy duty 'bar' performed even worse than the category, with a 1.59% drop in volumes (representing around 60 million Snickers bars), meaning that value market share growth fell by 1.81%.

It was clear that in a changing consumer environment, we needed to re-think how we framed YNYWYH.

The new vision

We needed to drive sales in order to regain market share. We knew that achieving this in the chocolate category meant increasing penetration. Our analysis of the IPA databank from our previous IPA paper showed that campaigns targeting penetration were more likely to achieve our goals (Table 1).

> *Fame is not simply about generating brand awareness ... It is about building word-of-mouth advocacy for the brand – getting it talked about, creating authority for the brand and the sense that it is making most of the running in the category.*
>
> Peter Field, *Marketing in the Era of Accountability*

Table 1: Campaigns targeting penetration have a demonstrably bigger effect on both sales and market share

Percentage reporting very large business effect on:	Average on all campaigns reporting hard evidence	Campaigns aiming to increase penetration
Sales	45%	62% (+++)
Market share	25%	35% (+++)
Profit	23%	31% (++)
Penetration	23%	46%
Loyalty	7%	7%
Price sensitivity	4%	5%
Any measure	55%	77%(+++)

There are plenty of chocolate bars competing at the shelf so increasing penetration means being the most salient. Since everyone knows Snickers, our goal isn't about brand awareness but about delivering brand fame. Being famous is our single most important metric as it means being talked about by a higher proportion of those people who currently don't care about us. We know this dynamic means fame can deliver significantly and exponentially in terms of market share gains.

YNYWYH is, in many ways, the perfect tool to deliver fame in today's fractured, fragmented media landscape. Not one big idea, but a coherent framework for the creation of many smaller ones. A framework that creates momentum as consumers pick it up to use as their own – largely driven through the use of local celebrities in order to drive buzz and relevance. It is like an open source software for a global community to participate in, share with their peers, and implement in the most relevant way to them (Figure 1).

Figure 1: Examples of Snickers ads

However in 2014, with category-wide decline especially affecting the UK, Russia and Australia, we needed to evolve our construct to match our changing business environment. Our existing strategy relied on local celebrities, but we found a critical insight that inspired us to explore a different approach. Analysis of YNYWYH activity showed a correlation between talent fee and effectiveness (Figure 2).

Figure 2: Correlation between talent fee and effectiveness

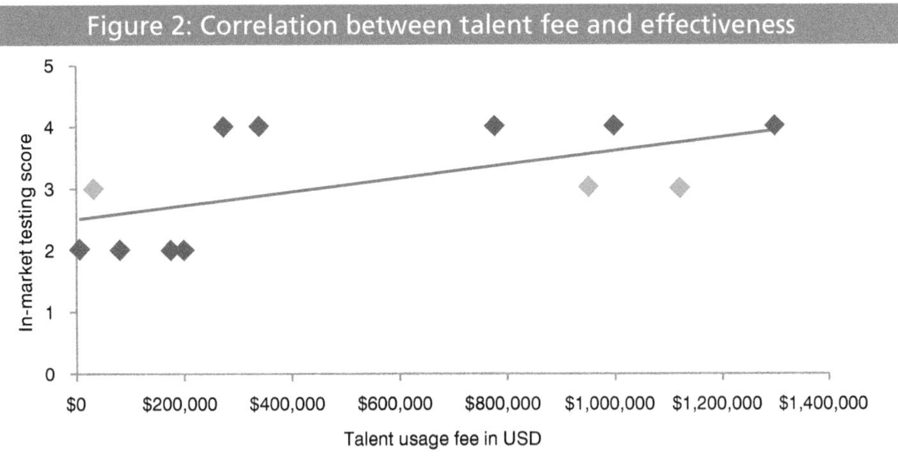

Source: AMV analysis

Though this may seem obvious, 'you get what you pay for', it raises serious challenges for any brand, maybe even more so for a family company such as Mars. The organisation would need to take a leap of faith and make a significant investment in what many believe to be 'non-working' spend. However if we could find a single celebrity who commanded relevance and buzz across multiple markets, then we could fund the project by planning for scale.

A plan was born. We would complement the existing YNYWYH platform by adding a 'blockbuster' at the head of our 'long tail' of local, relevant and organic activity: a single execution that could tackle the divergent issues facing a range of markets. Crucially, it needed to help us in Russia, the UK and Australia, which were all suffering from significant sales decline for reasons which varied from economic trouble to distribution difficulty.

A different approach to global advertising

Initially we were hesitant about briefing in a global YNYWYH execution. We knew that copies informed by local insight tended to struggle outside their originating markets, as per the Ipsos ASI study in Figure 3.

So we looked outside of advertising for inspiration. Since our key objective was to create fame, we considered the biggest fame-driving industry in the world: Hollywood. The success of film franchises like Star Wars, the Jurassic Parks and Harry Potters showed us that efficacy is not always locally bound. So how do they do it? An analysis from *The Economist* recently attempted to break down the various factors determining their success at the box office (Figure 4).[2]

Figure 3: Only about 40% of ads perform identically between two markets in the same region

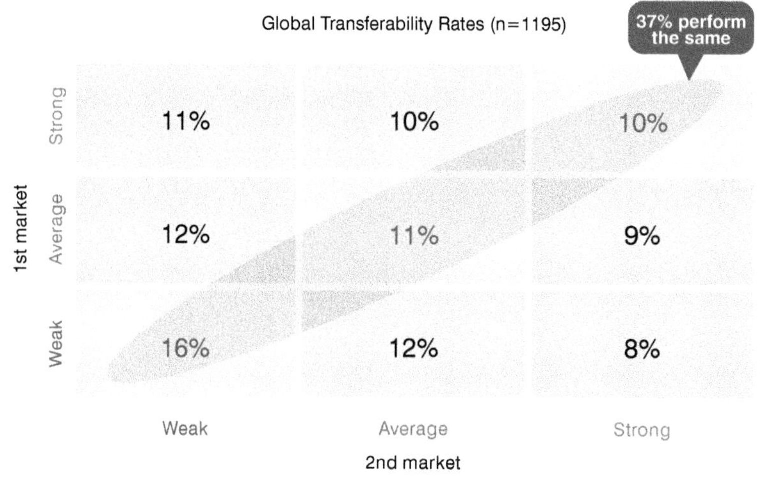

Source: Ipsos ASI Global Database of Intra-Regional Identical Ad Pairs Tested (n=1195)

Figure 4: Superheroes – super box office

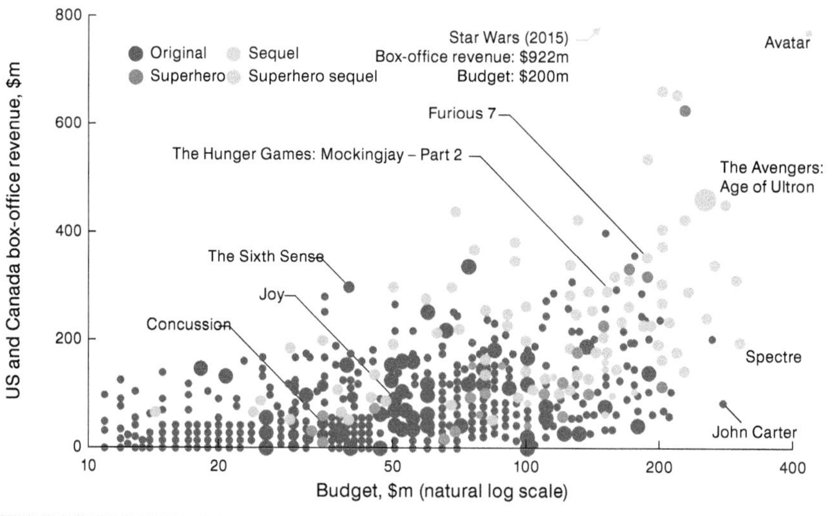

*Box office revenue from leading actors' non-sequel films over five previous years.
Source: *The Economist*.

Their analysis shows that films with more production budget usually create bigger box office, and to get the level of investment required, studios are relying ever more heavily on revitalising franchises that have proven track records.

Notably, a number of the more successful franchises operate within fantasy worlds. We theorised that by creating a new world for the story, films are more aspirational, exciting, and are more easily transferred across markets as they are equally relatable to everyone. We also considered how the hype and buzz around these films must have contributed to their success – especially the latest instalment of Star Wars.

This was our breakthrough: To create fame in very different markets, we would adopt the model of global entertainment, not advertising.

Bean Kung Fu – our big bet

Needing to create global fame, and a 'blockbuster' at the head of our long tail of organic and local activity, we naturally looked to the extensive and reliable reach of TV. Ideally to fill out the long tail our idea would translate online and locally, but first and foremost we needed to crack a film that would work in at least three markets with a celebrity who would be recognisable across country borders.

Enter Mr Bean. His last film *Holiday* was a worldwide box office success – taking millions of dollars in the Russian, Australian and UK box offices, amongst others.[3] Rowan Atkinson's hit TV show has been shown in over 200 countries, spawned two films, and two animated series.[4] His non-verbal humour made him instantly global, and his *schadenfreude* approach to comedy made Mr Bean the perfect character for a YNYWYH film.

Mr Bean's inimitable characteristics made him incongruous in most scenarios, but an ancient Chinese setting for the film was decided upon as the pinnacle of incongruity, as well as for its filmic 'blockbuster' associations.

To launch the final Bean Kung Fu film, we emulated as many Hollywood techniques as we could. In the UK we partnered with ITV to create teaser trailers, before airing a cinematic 60" cut of the film during the *X Factor*. Cinema spots were also booked to show off the film at its very best. Atkinson spoke at an internal conference, which boosted confidence within the business to take the film out to further markets. In China, we 'leaked' stories about Atkinson flying to Shanghai to film a new Kung Fu movie – with a signature new Kung Fu move – and he made an appearance on the popular 'Tonight 80s' talk show. Mr Bean's new Kung Fu move, the 'Fist of Hunger' was so popular it got parodied by the press and transcended into 'meme' status. We also launched four short 'prequels' online, which documented Mr Bean's Kung Fu training, to extend the experience for keen fans. We ensured that Rowan was involved in the scripting and production of these to make them as authentically 'Mr Bean' as possible.

The film launched in the UK in October 2014. By summer 2015 it was running in 49 markets,[5] and at time of writing it was in over 60 markets (and counting). A truly global film (Figure 5).

Figure 5: Bean Kung Fu

Overall results

With a world-class production we initially greatly exceeded the average budget per market for a Mars film. However the investment was quickly paid off with our design for scale approach. In Figure 6 we have spread the actual cost of Bean over all 49 markets it aired in through 2014 and 2015, and compared that figure to the average cost of a film per market.[6] We can see that by the time Bean had been aired in eight markets it was *already* creating return for the business purely through saving on production costs.[7]

Figure 6: The more markets Bean Kung Fu ran in, the more money we stood to save

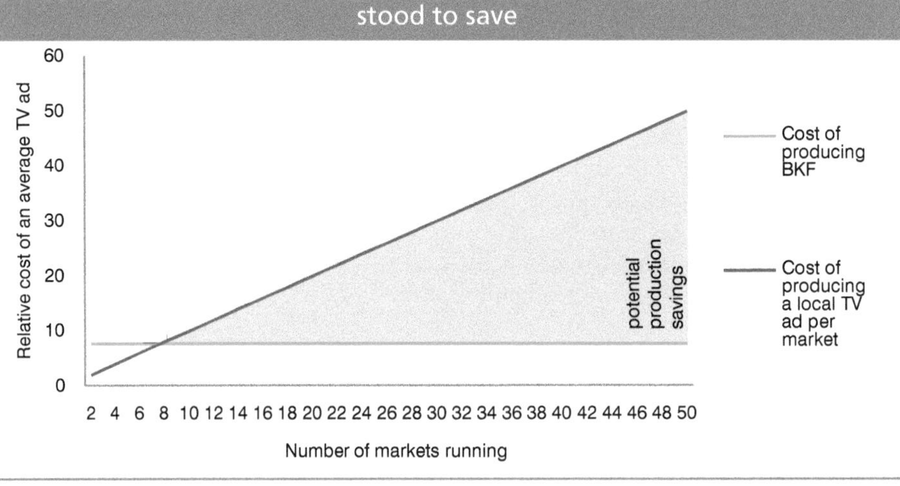

But the spot didn't just create economies of scale for Snickers. It also delivered on the harder business metric of market share. In 2015 the markets airing Bean collectively saw market share growth of 4.06%. Compare this to the markets that didn't air Bean (but were airing other copies) and we see a stark contrast in performance (Figure 7).

Figure 7: Markets running Bean Kung Fu had much greater propensity to grow value market share

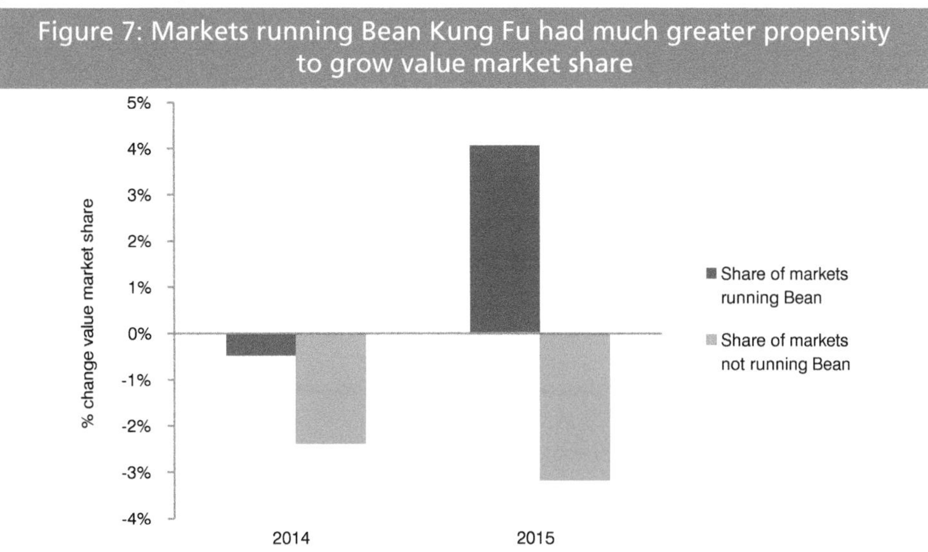

Particularly noteworthy is the fact that the markets that ran Bean were dropping share in 2014, so the growth we see in 2015 cannot just be a result of choosing to run it in growing markets. We also know that Bean's ability to create value share growth was not driven by any one market as we can see that it fulfilled its global objective in its performance across all markets (Figure 8).[8]

In 2015, in those same markets, Bean Kung Fu helped Snickers to grow volume sales by 5.38% (Figure 9), way ahead of the category. Value sales equally outpaced growth in the category at 9.91% (Figure 10).

Overall, the money saved and generated by Bean Kung Fu far outweighed its initial investment. It generated production savings of $14.1m and incremental sales of $71,061,500. Therefore, taking into account the production, incremental media, and global usage costs, coming to an impressive ROI of $10.65 – nearly $11 return for every $1 spent.[9]

Those non-working dollars were working very hard indeed.

As previously mentioned, there were three particularly problematic markets that inspired the development of a 'global' copy. The UK and Russia are two of Snickers' major markets and Australia is an important emerging market. All were experiencing difficulty– Russia and Australia both have historically struggled to make effective YNYWYH work, and the UK saw a dramatic loss of sales after reducing their multipack size from four to three bars.

We will now analyse the performance of Bean Kung Fu in these three problem markets in more detail.

Figure 8: Value sales post-campaign increase in 92% of markets

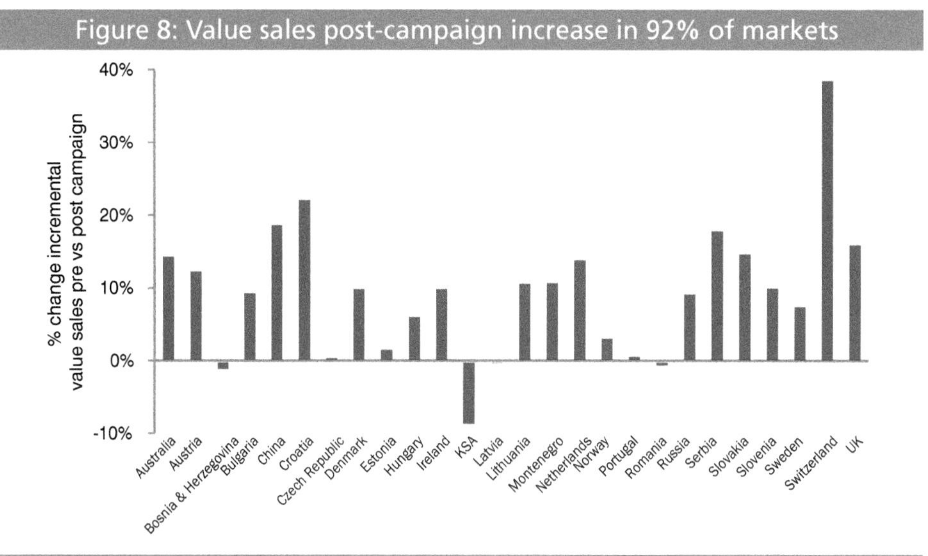

Figure 9: Total Bean value sales change YOY – volume

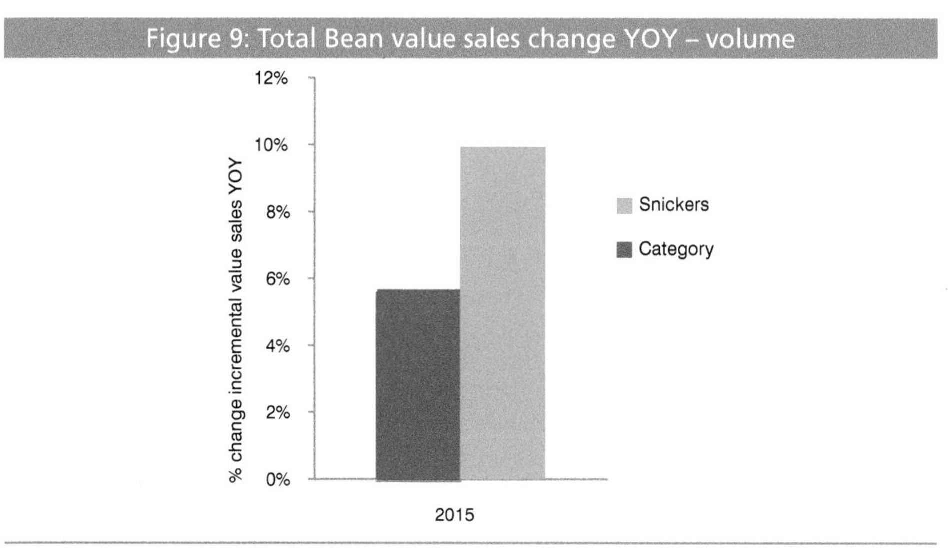

Figure 10: Total Bean value sales change YOY – growth

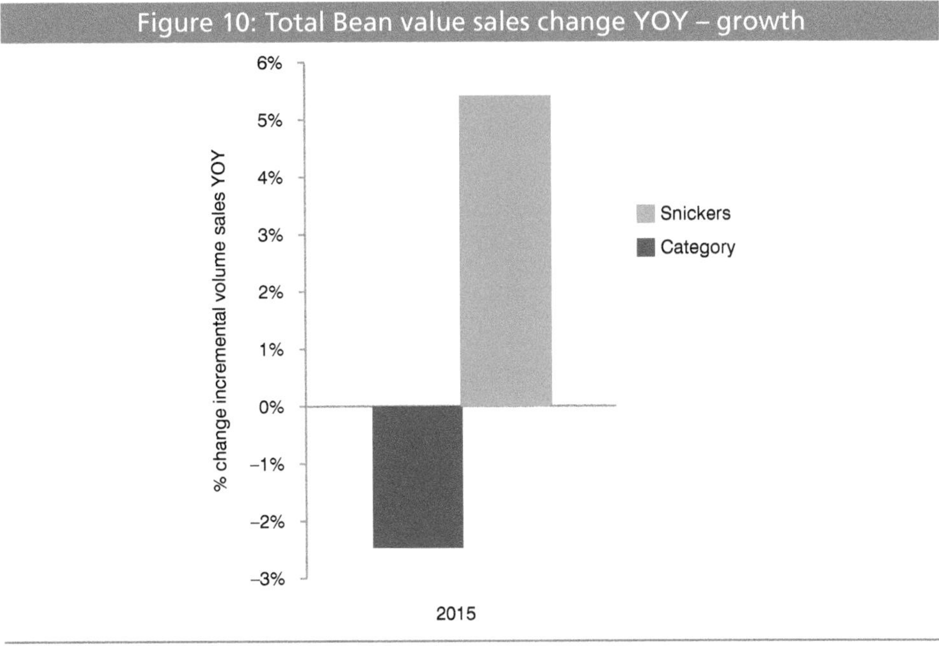

Market specific results – UK

In 2014, the UK urgently needed new work to drive fame. Volume sales were down 27% YOY due to the smaller multipack size, and supermarkets were heavily out-competing independent and convenience retailers (who represent a significant amount of Snickers' distribution). Having effective communications on air became vital.

Bean was the answer. In its first week the idea was already delivering against its objectives, as the online film and its 'prequels' received 7.4 million organic views, creating 174 million PR impressions.

But it was clearly not just creatively exciting.

Over the next few months we measured Bean's effectiveness using Mars' in-market testing system, which measures the effect of a TV copy on sales (we will provide more detail on the methodology later). Bean achieved the top rating of 4*, proving its commercial worth to the business. We also continued to monitor its impact on volume sales and market share (Figures 11 and 12).

Returning to our original metric of needing to create fame to drive penetration, we can also see that in 2015 penetration in the UK grew by 1.3% providing us with the definitive evidence of Bean's success (Table 2).

Table 2: UK penetration rates

	2014	2015	% uplift
UK penetration rate %	26.80%	28.10%	1.30%

Bean's continued ability to deliver on all fronts gave the business the confidence to roll out the campaign to further markets.

Figure 11: Snickers was struggling to make headway against competitors in 2014. Post-Bean volume sales increased and outgrew the category

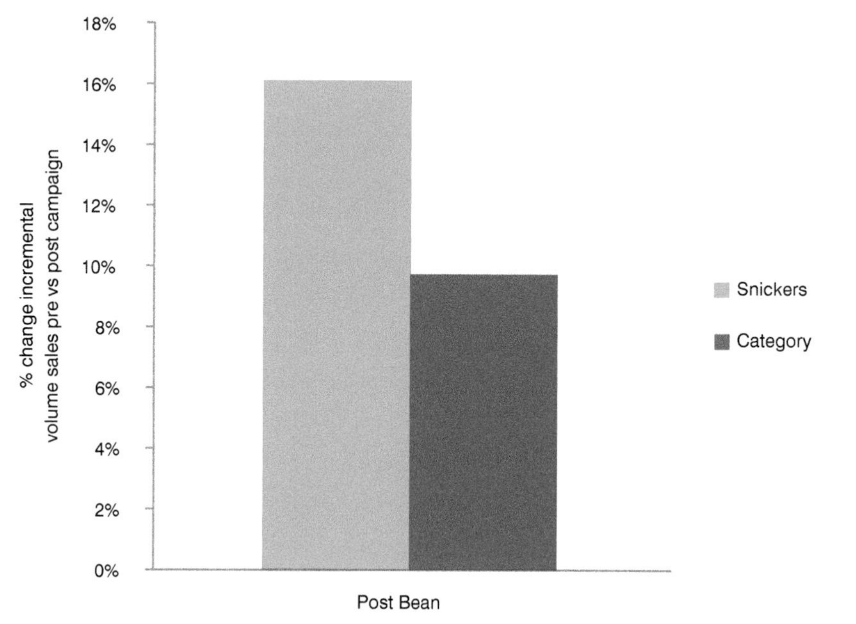

Figure 12: This growth helped to create a remarkable turnaround in value market share

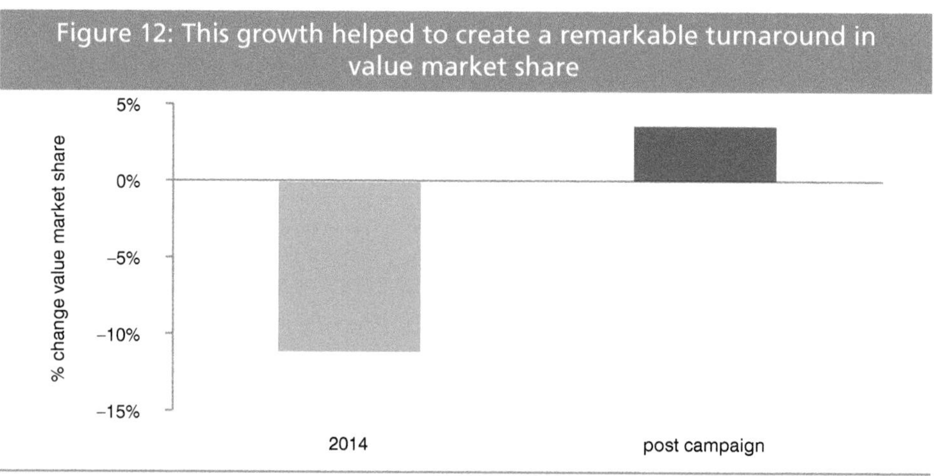

Market specific results – Russia & Australia

Both markets had been looking for a successful version of YNYWYH for five years. Local development, and even adapts of ads from other markets, had either failed in pre-testing or in market.

As one of Snickers' largest markets, it was business-critical that Russia had effective communications on air. But culturally, they struggled with typical YNYWYH adverts using the 'everyman' setting of locker rooms and football games, and 'banter' in scripts. They felt that Snickers needed to be more aspirational and desirable for Russian consumers to connect with it. Meanwhile they were experiencing hyperinflation due to a plummeting rouble.

In the six months after the campaign launched, Snickers successfully prevented volume sales from dropping with the category – which dropped five times as much in the same time period (Figure 13).

Figure 13: Russian incremental volume sales pre and post campaign

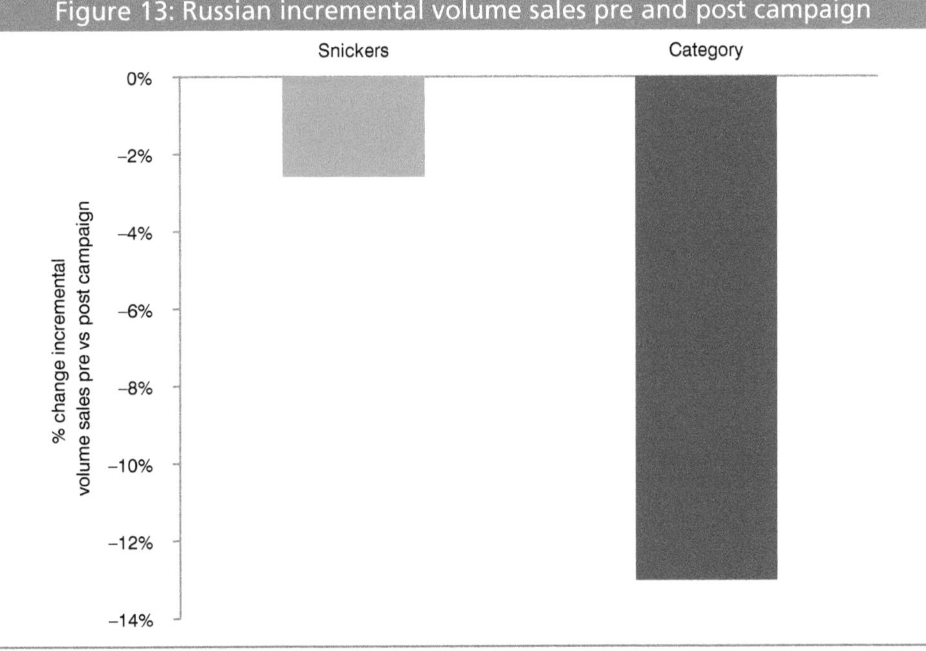

Bean's aspirational way of mimicking awe-inspiring martial arts films made it exciting and inspiring for consumers. It was tested twice through in-market testing; achieving the first-ever top rating for a Snickers ad in Russia, and repeating this success for a second time a few weeks afterwards. Overall, Russia saw an impressive 2.3% uplift in penetration, delivering on our key metric for this heavily fluctuating market (Table 3).

Table 3: Russian penetration rate

	2014	2015	% uplift
Russian penetration rate %	15.1%	17.4%	2.3%

Australia historically also struggled with YNYWYH. They felt it had failed to create fame as the celebrities used did not have high enough recognition in market, especially with adapted work brought across from other countries. The fame of Rowan Atkinson as Mr Bean finally led them to a commercially successful campaign. Bean was tested in-market again, achieving the first-ever pass rating for a Snickers ad in Australia. In the six months following launch, Australia saw an increase of 21% in volume sales, and a 14% increase in value sales.

Figure 14: The improved sales performance of Bean drove value market share post campaign

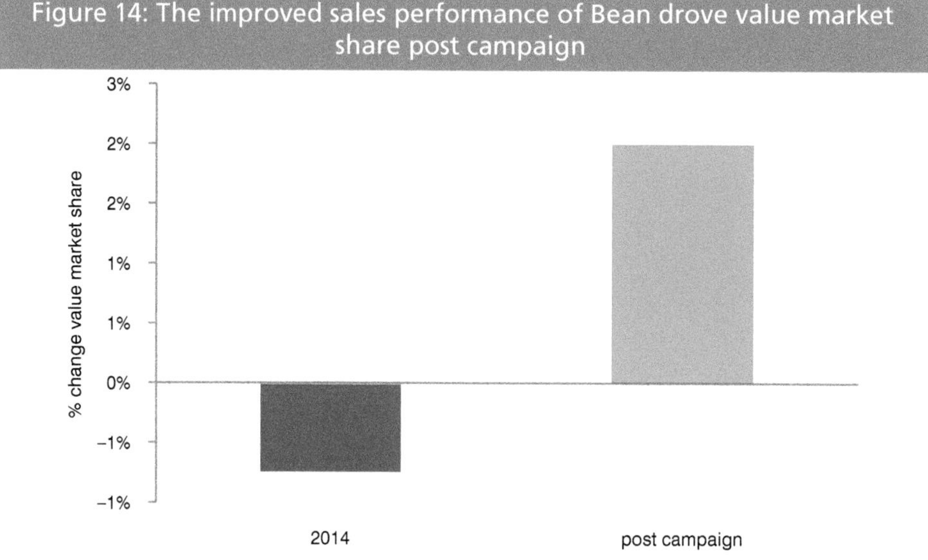

And to top it off, we saw encouraging uplift in penetration rates (Table 4).

Table 4: Australian penetration rates

	2014	2015	% uplift
Australian penetration rate %	20.60%	22.40%	1.80%

Controlling external variables

In-market testing

A number of times in this paper we have referred to Mars' in-market testing system being considered strong evidence for the business to believe that an advert is growing NSV for the brand. A quick methodology of the approach is laid out below to explain why it has such sway within the business, and to show how we are confident we can discount most external variables from the sales increases we have seen during Bean Kung Fu's campaign period.

To track advertising effectiveness, Mars use a measure called Advertising Value Index (AVI) based on single-source data. Using panels in key markets we track media and purchase behaviour and compare the difference in purchase behaviour of people exposed to our advertising (on TV or online video) versus people who have not been exposed to our advertising. This allows us to isolate the specific effect of advertising as all other factors in market are constant. The consumer panel is administered by an external data provider, but for confidentiality reasons the data analysis is done internally by Mars market research group based on a proprietary methodology. The approach was pioneered by Mars internally in the early 2000s, and has been refined over the years.

To report advertising effectiveness or AVI we use a 1–4* system. Our analysis demonstrates that a 4* copy aired with a typical Mars media plan results in approximately +10% of incremental sales during a given time period (compared to no advertising) and the impact of a 3* copy is about 7%. To put this in context, our analysis shows that only the top quintile of all ads measured across categories achieve 4* effectiveness.

So in the case of Bean Kung Fu, which was 3* in Australia, we know for certain that the advertising had a direct positive effect on net sales of as much as +7% NSV. In the UK and Russia where it measured 4* the effect could be as much as +10% NSV.

Distribution

Figure 15: Global distribution levels did not change significantly in markets airing Bean

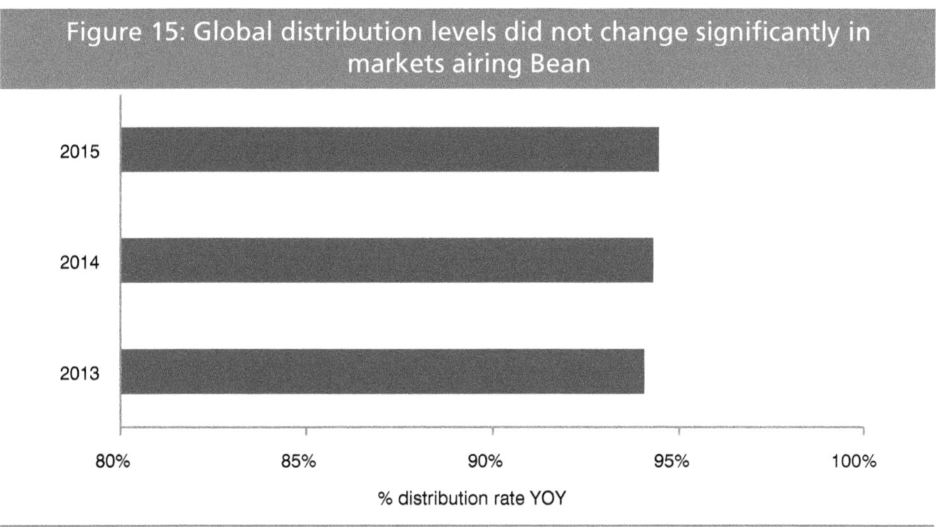

The respondents in our single-source testing panels are deliberately spread across each market to be nationally representative. Even though we can see here that there is no significant change in distribution for Snickers on a global level, we know there is no flux affecting our analysis of the performance of the advert, as the only variable tested in single-source is the participants' exposure to advertising.

Variant launches

In our key markets, we were able to analyse whether variant launches could have inflated Bean's apparent performance. As we can see from Table 5, no permanent variants were launched during the time of the Bean Kung Fu campaign. Most markets seasonally launch new SKUs for around five months per year. Whilst variants are a tried-and-tested way of boosting NSV, we know that these particular launches could not have been solely driving sales success during the campaign period due to our single-source testing. First, single-source testing is only measured against the purchase of normal Snickers bars, so any variants purchased would not inflate the reported success of Bean Kung Fu. Second, as respondents in our panels are nationally representative, any variant launch would affect respondents in both the control and test. Therefore the only variable separating the two groups is exposure to the Bean Kung Fu film.

Table 5: Variant launches

	2013	2014	2015
UK	Feb–April *More Caramel & More Nuts*	Oct–Dec *More Caramel, More Choc & More Nuts*	Aug–Dec *Snickers & Hazelnut*
Russia	Sep–Dec *Snickers Almond*	Sep–Dec *Sunflower Seeds*	Sep–Dec *Peanuts Rebellion*
Australia	Sep–Dec *Hazelnut*	Aug–Jan *Almond*	Jan–July *Max Caramel* Jul–Jan *Rocky Nut Rd*

Media spend

In keeping with Snickers' objectives of creating fame, share of voice is incredibly important to the brand and encourages an always-on media strategy. Therefore, we know that regardless of whether we had created Bean Kung Fu, Snickers would have had to run communications in the 'Bean' markets to keep up share of voice. This means that as a piece of communication in itself, Bean incurred very little additional media spend, as all TV, online video, and broadcaster VOD would have been booked already. The incremental media booked for Bean included cinema spots and video sponsorships, which account for 5% of the total media spend over the campaign period (Figure 16).[10]

Promotional spend (percentage sold on promotion)

The percentage of Snickers sold on promotion decreased YOY in the UK, and only marginally increased in Australia, showing that heavy discounting cannot be attributed to the business' success over the campaign period. In Russia we are unable to gather all the data required for such an analysis, but know that the percentage sold on promotion was very small over the beginning of 2015. Regardless, the same point stands for variant launches as it does for promotions in regards to single-source

Figure 16: Bean Kung Fu only required 5% incremental media to launch

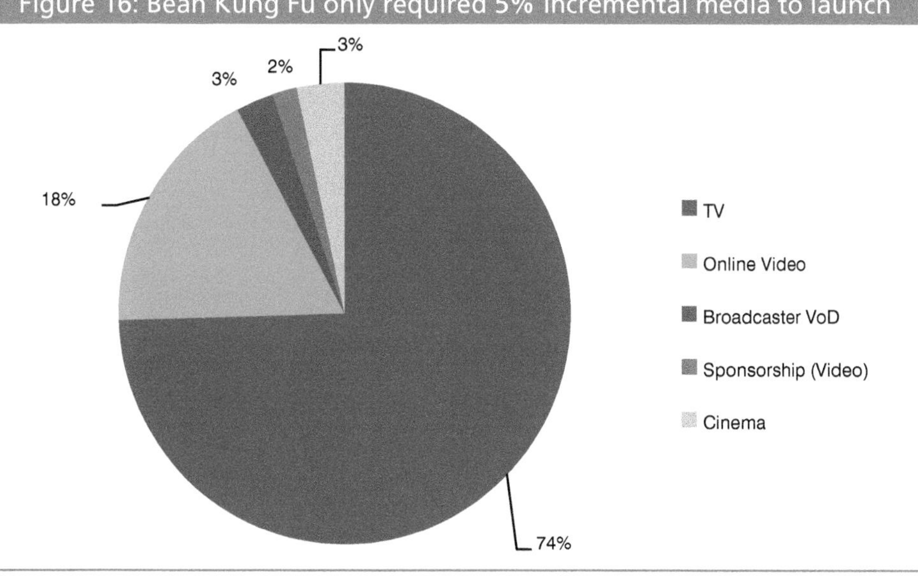

testing. All respondents, whether in the control or test group, would have been exposed to in-store promotions. Hence if we see a measurable difference in sales between the two groups we know we can attribute this to Bean Kung Fu, as this is the only variable between the samples.

Price

The price per unit of Snickers in the UK and Australia marginally changed during 2015, in both markets slightly increasing thereby showing that neither a spike in promotions nor a drop in base price caused the increase in sales of Snickers bars (Figure 17).

Figure 17: PPU increase in the UK and Australia was below 1%

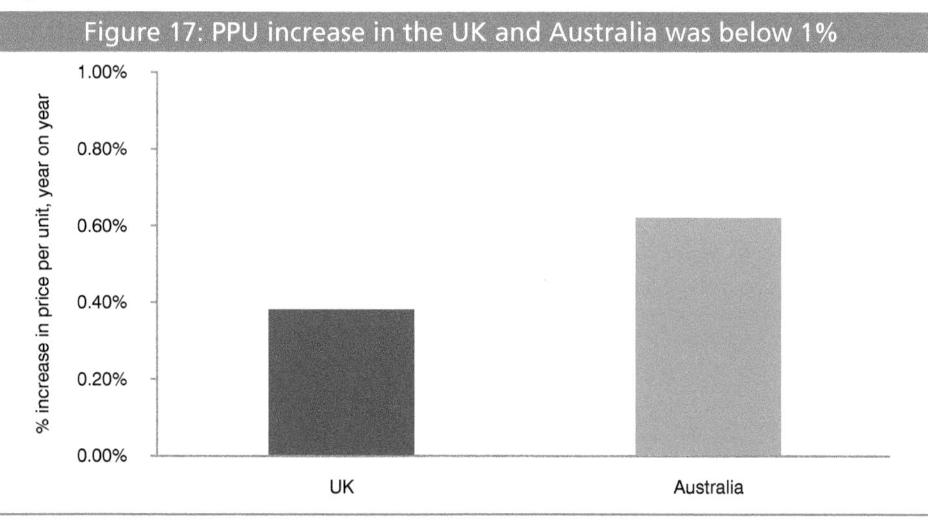

In Russia the same analysis is a little more difficult to do as their economy is currently experiencing hyperinflation, however we do see that base price did not drop (Figure 18).

Figure 18: Year on year, the absolute cost of Snickers rose 20%

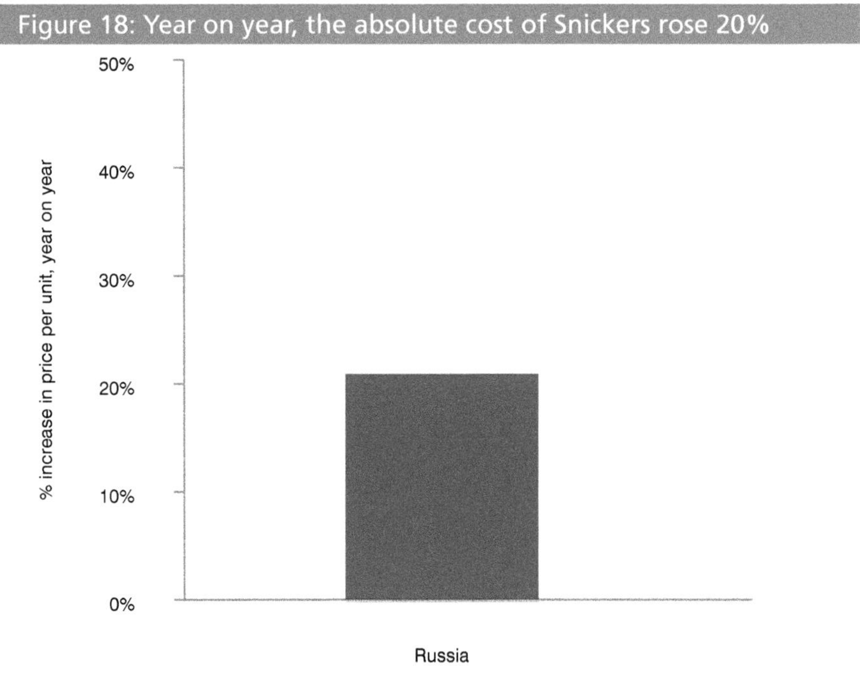

The worldwide economy

Whilst a number of the markets running Bean Kung Fu would have experienced economic growth during the campaign period, we can reasonably assert that the spread of markets was wide enough that this alone cannot have accounted for the additional sales gained versus markets that did not run Bean. To compare two major markets for Snickers, where economic growth or decline would significantly affect global sales, Russia (a Bean market) experienced economic decline of 3.8% in 2015 whereas the USA (a non-Bean market) experienced economic growth of 2%.[11]

Conclusions and learnings

Anybody worth their salt knows that the future of communications is in digital and using big data. Thanks to digital technology, marketing is getting more and more sophisticated: micro-targeting increases ad efficiency; programmatic buying increases ad effectiveness through real-time optimisation; and quicker, more cost-efficient production provides the ability to spread risk through numerous small ideas.

It seems the era of the Big Idea is dying out.

Modern marketing requires the flexibility, agility, and speed of digital to keep up with changing consumer interests and behaviours. In many ways, YNYWYH is the perfect creative tool for such an approach to communications, and it has enabled us to create a coherent portfolio of work globally that is diverse, driven by local insight, and effective.

In such an environment, it would have been second nature for Snickers to solve its multi-market issues through a stream of new local YNYWYH productions. But returning to the roots of Snickers' business strategy of using fame to drive penetration meant we had to make a counterintuitive decision. Creating work locally, with local budgets, would only ever make us famous locally. To drive the penetration we required in our critical markets, we needed work that would travel and make us famous globally. We had a 'Big Idea' in YNYWYH, now we needed a 'Big Film' to head it up.

Saving the business $14.1 million USD, and growing the value market share of participating markets by 4.06% overall, Bean Kung Fu became the most successful Snickers film ever made. It allowed Snickers to outperform the category, even in the most difficult business climate since the origination of the YNYWYH idea.

Our lesson: that there is still a place for 'Big Work' in today's brand portfolios.

Spending 'big bucks' upfront on non-working media may feel uncomfortable. But by being bolder and more ambitious, we can begin to tap into the behaviours of blockbuster entertainment and help our brands to flourish globally – trumping local fame, and paying big dividends.

Notes

1. As calculated from Nielsen data, covering the markets: Australia, Austria, Bosnia & Herzegovina, Brazil, Bulgaria, Canada, China, Croatia, Czech Republic, Denmark, Egypt, Estonia, France, Germany, Greece, Hong Kong, Hungary, India, Ireland, Italy, KSA, Latvia, Lithuania, Malaysia, Mexico, Montenegro, Netherlands, New Zealand, Norway, Philippines, Poland, Portugal, Puerto Rico, Romania, Russia, Serbia, Singapore, Slovakia, Slovenia, South Korea, Spain, Sweden, Switzerland, Taiwan, UK, Ukraine, and the USA.
2. http://www.economist.com/news/business/21693594-how-make-hit-film-silver-screen-playbook
3. http://www.imdb.com/title/tt0453451/news?year=2007
4. http://www.ibtimes.co.uk/mr-bean-video-rowan-atkinson-drives-around-london-celebrate-25-years-comedy-character-1518507
5. Market list: China, UK, Russia, Kazakhstan, Azerbaijan, Belarus, Australia, Albania, Austria, Bosnia & Herzegovina, Bulgaria, Croatia, Czech Republic, Denmark, Estonia, Finland, Hungary, Iceland, Ireland, Kosovo, Latvia, Lithuania, Macedonia, Montenegro, Norway, Portugal, Romania, Serbia, Slovakia, Slovenia, Sweden, Switzerland, Netherlands, South Africa, Lebanon, Syria, Turkey, Jordan, Cyprus, UAE, Bahrain, Kuwait, Oman, Qatar, Afghanistan, Iran, Iraq, Yemen and Saudi Arabia.
6. As calculated by Mars.
7. Whilst we cannot guarantee that every one of these markets would have produced its own TV spot, we do know that individual markets frequently create their own spots which do not travel outside of their market. Therefore this graph shows the greatest possible impact of using Bean Kung Fu in all 49 markets.
8. Summary of value sales performance from all Nielsen-tracked markets.
9. ROI = (production savings + incremental sales) / (production cost + talent cost + media spend).
10. Media spend data available in Australia, Austria, China, Croatia, Czech Republic, Gulf, Kazakhstan, KSA, Netherlands, Portugal, Russia, Slovakia, Switzerland, Turkey, and the United Kingdom.
11. GDP growth for USA and Russia last checked on tradingeconomics.com on 13 April 2015.

Speeding (New Zealand Transport Agency)

Mistakes

By Linda Major, Clemenger BBDO
Contributing authors: Matt Barnes, Clemenger BBDO; Paul Graham, New Zealand Transport Agency; Matt McNeil, OMD Wellington; Rachel Prince, New Zealand Transport Agency
Credited companies: Clemenger BBDO; OMD Wellington

Summary

Most speeding drivers believe they're skilled enough to exceed the limit; everyone else is the problem. This New Zealand anti-speeding film relied on this assumption for its impact, gaining international fame. More importantly, it created a conversation about speed amongst people who had stopped listening. In the first year after the campaign launched, average speeds on New Zealand roads fell by an average of 0.4km per hour, projected to reduce NZD 46m from the cost of accidents. Using a conservative estimate that 10 per cent of this saving was attributable to communications, the campaign is estimated to have returned NZD 1.6 for every NZD 1 invested.

Editor's Comment

This case united a brilliant insight with a strong use of channels. The judges were particularly excited by the breadth and scale of this campaign, and its ability to ignite a national debate around the subject of speeding.

Client Comment

Rachel Prince, Principal Advisor: Network User Behaviour, Access and Use Group

The major lesson learnt was to find something we can agree with our audience on, rather than fight against people's beliefs and blame them as we'd previously done.

'Mistakes' has only heightened our belief in the power of storytelling and using strong emotions to resonate with people. The emotional core of the story transcended many audiences, cultures and even languages – it was a universally recognised truth.

Our campaigns have always been research-led with thorough testing throughout the process. The success of 'Mistakes' has cemented our use of research in formulating briefs and rigorous audience testing at multiple stages of the creative process. We will continute to follow this approach.

Speeding is the number one road safety problem, and its reduction potential the most effective road safety strategy – global research models show that lowering mean speeds by just 1 km/h will result in 4–5% fewer road injuries and deaths.[1]

The problem we faced was that most speeders believe they're skilled enough to drive over the speed limit. And that it's everyone else who's the problem.

Instead of resisting that belief, we launched a campaign that supported it.

And it had an unprecedented effect.

The world shared it. Other countries asked to use it. The Gunn Report ranked it the third most-awarded film campaign in the world. TED Talks chose it as one of 10 'Ads Worth Spreading' in 2014.

More importantly, it created a new conversation about speed amongst people who had stopped listening.

By changing the discourse around speeding – agreeing for the first time with an audience we had blamed for almost 20 years – we reframed an undesirable behaviour.

While entrenched behaviour takes time to change, there is strong evidence that 'Mistakes' has started to influence behaviour on the road, with mean speeds falling to the lowest levels in 20 years in the two years following the launch of the campaign.

Speeding campaign history and challenges

The speed campaign was introduced in 1995 in New Zealand. For two decades it has followed a proven 'blueprint' for road safety advertising: high-impact ads that point the finger squarely at the speeding driver, leaving a disturbing image of what could go wrong.

This has often been the most graphic and unpleasant advertising on our screens.

Contrast this with the unadulterated sexiness of car advertising – which is in essence our competition; promising the thrill of speed, saluting the man alone in his car and feeding a very human craving to drive fast. Car manufacturers typically outspend our investment in anti-speed advertising by 60 to 1.[2] Add to this the weight of video games, motoring shows and films like *The Fast and the Furious,* all that glorify speed.

Despite such strong and direct competition to our 'slow down' message, historically, the speed campaign has been highly effective.

In the early years of the speed campaign it was unexpected and shocking, and the message was new. Average speeds dropped and speed-related crashes fell 37% in the first five years (Figure 1).[3]

But, in the last decade, the speed campaign has struggled to make further progress – with the number of crashes in 2013 on par with where we were in 2000.

Simply put, the 'easy wins' have been achieved. We've successfully focused on high-level speeding – people travelling 15–20km/h over the speed limit. Mean speeds have dropped a massive 6 km/h since the campaign began.[4]

It's now rare to see people driving at extreme speeds on our roads; speeds that most people agree are dangerous. On the open road only 4% of cars exceed the limit by more than 10km/h.[5]

As mean speeds drop, we're focusing more on 'moderate' speeding which, as the research models show, is still a serious cause of unnecessary crashes and casualties.

Figure 1: Speed-related crashes per 100,000 population

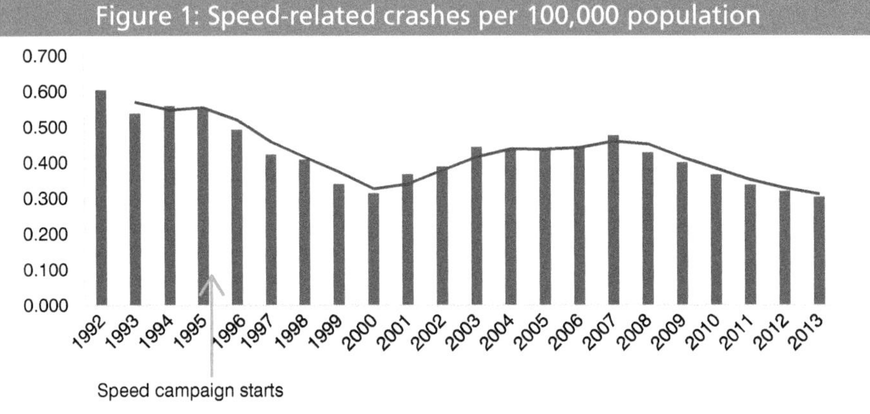

Making further progress is difficult because:

- Moderate speeding is a lot more common and normal
  - **One in four** drivers travel up to 10 km/h over the speed limit on the open road and **over half** travel this fast in urban areas.[6]
- Moderate speeding is a lot tougher to shift
  - Because people don't see the risk of their speed.
  - Because the perceptual gap between problem and desired behaviour is small.

To make matters worse, in New Zealand, moderate speeders are travelling within a generally accepted 'tolerance' level for speed. New Zealand police generally apply a 10km/h speed tolerance, which means drivers can escape a ticket if they're driving up to 10km/h over the limit. This is much higher than the 0 or 4km/h thresholds that many other countries enforce.

In fact, the speed tolerance is often seen as tacit endorsement for low-level speeding. As shown by the fact over half of road users define 'speeding' as '10km/h or more' over the speed limit.[7]

In other words, their own behaviour (moderate speeding) isn't *really* considered speeding.

Whilst still delivering results, the speed campaign was becoming less effective as people were becoming more immune to advertising, evidenced in the steady decline in free recall (Figure 2).[8]

Figure 2: Audience recall – all speed TVCs

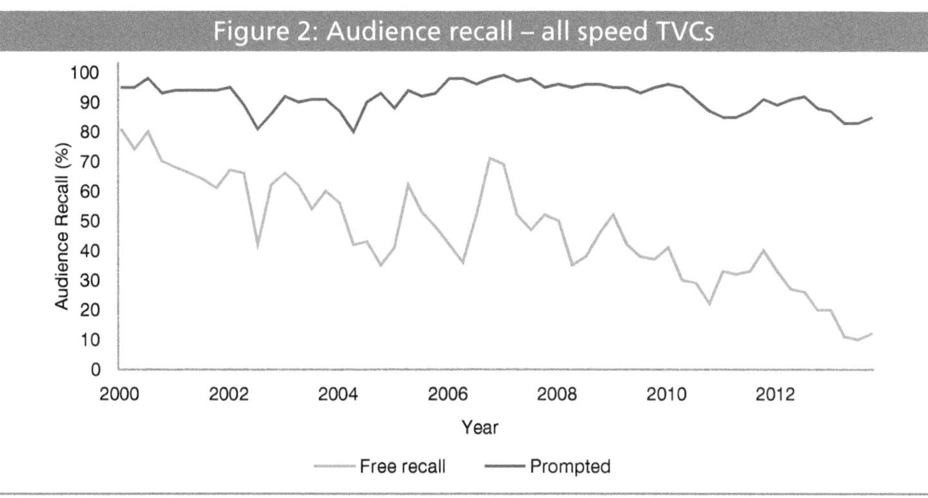

Whereas previously people saw it as a message for them, our research showed that people were opting out, arguing speed isn't the problem that it really is, or assuming the message was for someone else (Figure 3).

Figure 3: Example of social commentary

Roger Murray In reality if you look at the cause of most of the accidents you will find that speed is quite a way down the list behind Incompetence Inattention Alcohol and drugs . Even road conditions and construction is a problem. Too much is falsely blamed on speed I think.

Like · Reply · 👍 4 · 21 January at 10:31

Tragically, crash statistics tell a different story. Inappropriate speed is a factor in nearly a third of fatal crashes in New Zealand (Figure 4).[9]

Campaign objectives

Our work, ultimately, has a single goal: getting people to slow down.

Because irrespective of the cause of a crash, it's speed that determines the outcome – whether someone is killed, or walks away.

As already indicated, global evidence shows if we can reduce mean speeds by just 1 km/h the result will be 4–5% fewer deaths.[10]

This is a long-term game. Increases or decreases in mean speeds each year are usually in the 0.1–0.2km/h range.[11]

Over the two-year period (2014–2015), our specific objectives were to:

1. Increase compliance with the right speeds on urban streets and the open road *(behaviour change)* leading to fewer crashes.
2. Increase public intolerance of speeding *(reframe societal norms)*.

Figure 4: Percentage of crashes with speed as a factor

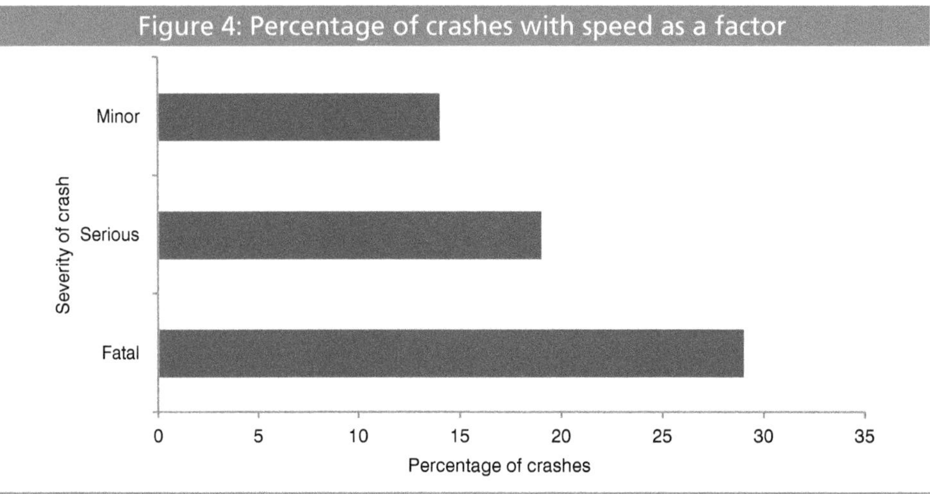

To drive these key metrics, specific advertising efficiency objectives were set, based on strongly performing speed ads:[12]

- *Unprompted recall of ≥ 15% within 6 months*: Unprompted recall is critical for road safety. Drivers need to freely recall the message when they're on the road, not just when prompted by a researcher.
- *Personal relevance of advertising of ≥ 50%:* This target is high for a product we would consider a 'grudge purchase'.
- *Correct message outtake:* The three highest messages relate to speed and its risks.

We also had an ambitious engagement and attitudinal goal: to change the conversation around speed. To do so we needed to:

- *Facilitate broader ownership of the problem* (measured through social monitoring).
- *Disarm conventional counter-arguments* (measured through social and news media monitoring).
- *Shift attitudes towards speed* (measured through ad tracking and attitudinal surveys).

Our core challenge

Twenty years of road safety advertising targeting 'perpetrators' had conditioned people to believe bad drivers cause road carnage; young, inexperienced 'hoons' and risk-takers who deserve to be targeted by the police.

Experienced drivers, on the other hand, believe they should be left alone. They rate their driving skills and believe they can speed safely. They argue it's everyone else who's the problem. They don't self-identify as 'bad drivers'.

We had to completely rethink how we had been talking about speed for 20 years to get *skilled* drivers to take notice and accept that this message is still for them.

The strategy

We're telling an old story.

For years we've crafted arguments to persuade people to slow down. We've used every tool in the trade: victims' stories, enforcement threats, and irrefutable laws of physics.

Speeding drivers are well-versed in the idea that 'the faster you go, the bigger the mess'. They get that speed affects time and distance needed to stop. They agree you need to adjust your speed for the conditions. They buy that the sudden stop will hurt.

But our greatest competition is the drivers' own experience.

Most of the time when we speed, nothing happens. Consequently our advertising has invited fierce argument from speeders and motoring commentators (Figure 5).

Figure 5: Example of motoring commentary

stuff National World Business Tech Sport Entertainment Life & Style
motoring
News Lifestyle Vehicles Road tests Customs & Classics Bikes Motorsport
Critics doubt effect of speed campaign

nzherald.co.nz Search for content...
National Opinion Business Tech World Olympics Sport Entertainment Lifestyle
National NZ Herald Focus Crime Politics Opinion Employment Health Insights
Ford wants $2m road safety TV ad written off

We studied media reports and social commentary over many years of speed advertising and they revealed the insight, in the audience's mind: *Speed* isn't the problem; it's bad driving (and 'I'm not a bad driver').[13]

Figure 6: Example of social commentary

Very well written. Bad idiot drivers are far more dangerous than speed. Standards of driving desperately need to improve. I see shocking decisions being made by some drivers every day.

Like · Reply · 6 · January 1 at 8:53pm · Edited

I think the speed limit should actually be increased and bad driving clamped down on. Especially: not indicating for 3 seconds before changing lanes, staying in a fast lane whilst not over-taking, cutting people off, tail-gating, not letting drivers in/speeding up rather. I see near crashes all the time because of what I just mentioned!!!

Like · Reply · 80 · November 26, 2013 at 10:25am

Although the audience disagreed, the crash statistics are clear: speed is our biggest problem. But we had nothing to gain by arguing with speeders' own experience.

So we looked for a truth all drivers can relate to, to start to reframe an undesirable behaviour.

People make mistakes

In life, mistakes are made often. Usually, we get to learn from them. But not when driving – the road is an exception. Even the smallest of mistakes on the road can cost us our life, or someone else's.

We had previously put the speeder front and centre in regards to blame.

What if we used the speeding driver's own bias – that it's all those idiot drivers out there who cause the problems on the road – and turned it back on them?

Because despite how good a driver you are, there is another irrefutable truth:

You can't control other *people's mistakes.*

When someone makes a mistake, your speed determines whether you can stop in time.

Whether someone is killed or walks away.

The big idea

Help people see that when they speed, other people's mistakes suddenly become their problem.

The creative and media approach

The core idea is to show 'good' drivers not what *they're* doing wrong but what might happen when someone else makes a mistake, to get them to reassess their belief that they can speed safely.

Figure 7: 'Mistakes' billboard

The creative story is an eye-opening depiction of the 'if only' moment for two drivers. They have both done something wrong. In the split-second before impact, the drivers get out of their cars and have a conversation.

They realise with mounting horror that there is nothing they can do. Because of his speed, the outcome has already been determined.

They walk back to their cars, and we share their sense of anguish and helplessness. The ad ends with a simple message: *Other people make mistakes. Slow down.*

The result is a harrowing and powerful commercial.

All without the need for blood and broken bodies. Without casting the speeding driver as the villain.

And leaving no room for denial.

Media approach

We needed to appeal broadly to New Zealanders and urge them to slow down – because moderate speeding behaviour is widespread. High reach and impact were important considerations.

Television remains the dominant channel to deliver video content to broad audiences in New Zealand. 'Mistakes' launched across television and the web in early January 2014 when the roads were busy following public holidays.

Our objective was also to change conversations about speed. We wanted our audience to consider their speeding through the eyes of others, so we selected channels that people consumed with others.

Cinema provided a high impact, targeted environment for reflection and a special 90-second version was created for the medium.

'Mistakes' was also placed, with appropriate editorial framing, into online environments where discussion is a regular feature. This enabled us to gain a deeper understanding of message interpretation and helped to fuel new conversations around the issue.

Figure 8: 'Mistakes' TVC storyboard

To view: https://www.youtube.com/watch?v=bvLaTupw-hk

It allowed the public to do our work for us – arguing it out amongst themselves and quickly jumping in to shut down counterarguments.

Tactical placement of billboards and radio reached drivers on the road, a successful method for prompting recall of the emotive story at 'point of use'.[14]

Table 1: Media spend by channel

	2014		2015	
Type of media	**Budget / media spend**	**% of overall budget**	**Budget / media spend**	**% of overall budget**
Television	NZ$ 1,561,760	79%	NZ$ 626,093	68%
On demand / pre-roll	NZ$ 5,044	0.5%	NZ$ 17,957	2%
Cinema	NZ$ 97,543	5%	NZ$ 0	0%
Digital / online facilitation	NZ$ 30,000	1.5%	NZ$ 36,927	4%
Billboards	NZ$ 113,252	6%	NZ$ 184,537	20%
Print	NZ$ 96,095	5%	NZ$ 57,052	6%
Radio	NZ$ 59,449	3%	NZ$ 0	0%
TOTAL	NZ$ 1,963,143		NZ$ 922,566	

Results

Behavioural impact

Our overarching objective was to get people to slow down, leading to a reduction in crashes.

As the major component of the 2014 speed campaign, 'Mistakes' contributed to a reduction in mean speeds and in the proportions of drivers exceeding the limits on both open and urban roads in 2014 (Figure 9). *These were the lowest levels achieved in 20 years.*[15]

Figure 9: Percentage of cars exceeding speed limit (2011–2015)

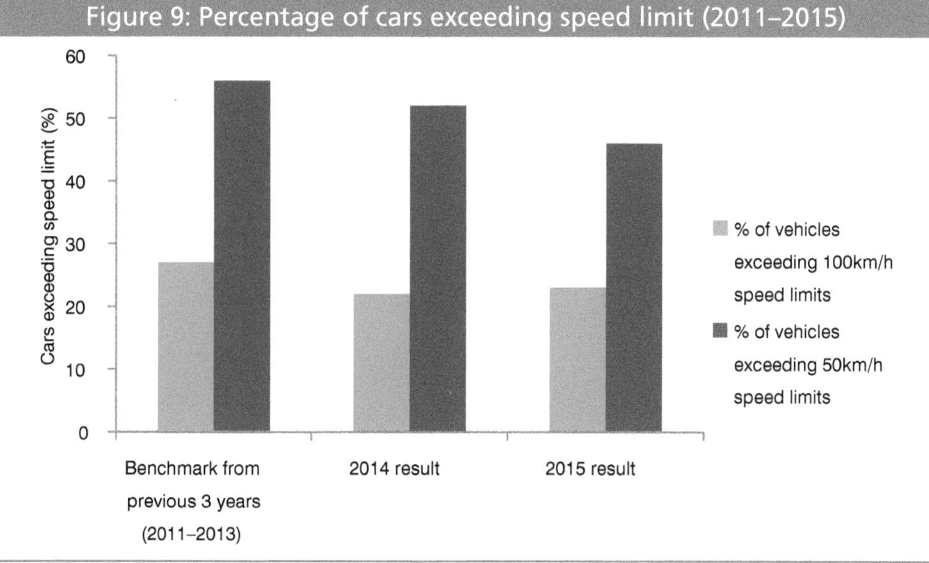

As noted previously, increases or decreases in mean speeds each year are usually in the 0.1–0.2km/h range. Mean speeds dropped by *0.4km/h* on the open road and *0.6km/h* in urban areas in 2014 alone.

Total crashes fell by *5%* over the same period – roughly double the decrease achieved in the preceding years (Figure 10).[16]

Against a backdrop of *4%* population growth and *279,000* more vehicles on the road compared to the previous year, and more kilometres travelled in 2014 than any other year (which the above graph isn't adjusted for) – we could reasonably expect an *increase* in total crashes in 2014.[17, 18]

Communication efficiency

Independent tracking[19] shows the campaign was highly efficient in communications terms, giving us confidence the advertising has contributed to the desired behaviour: people slowing down.

Figure 10: Total fatal and injury crashes per year (2011–2014)

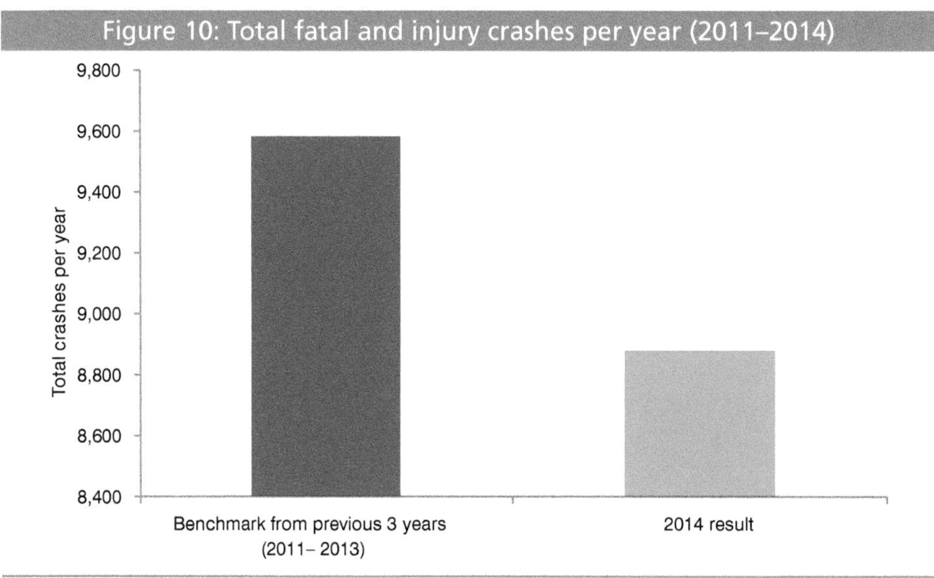

Note: 2015 data on total crashes not yet reported.

Objective 1: Advertising recall of ≥ 15% within 6 months (unprompted)

At 6 months, *unprompted recall reached 55%* and averaged 52% for the rest of 2014.

'Mistakes' is the first speed ad in 20 years to achieve 50% free recall (Figure 11).

Figure 11: Speed ads unprompted recall (2005–2015)

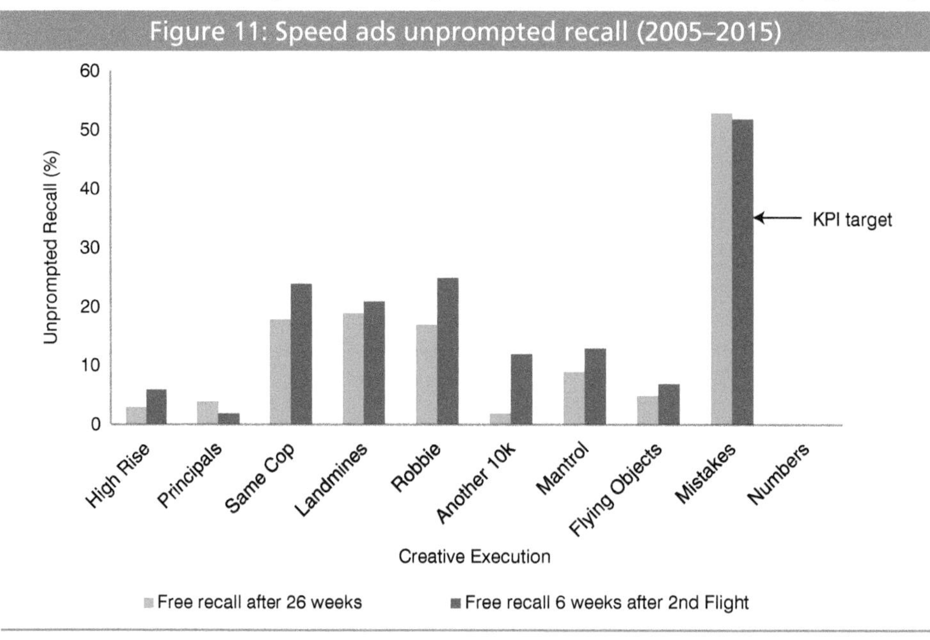

Objective 2: Advertising relevance of ≥ 50%

'Mistakes' achieved *75% relevance with its core target group*, well above the 50% benchmark for what we would consider a 'grudge purchase' (Figure 12).

Figure 12: Advertising relevance to target audience (2010–2015)

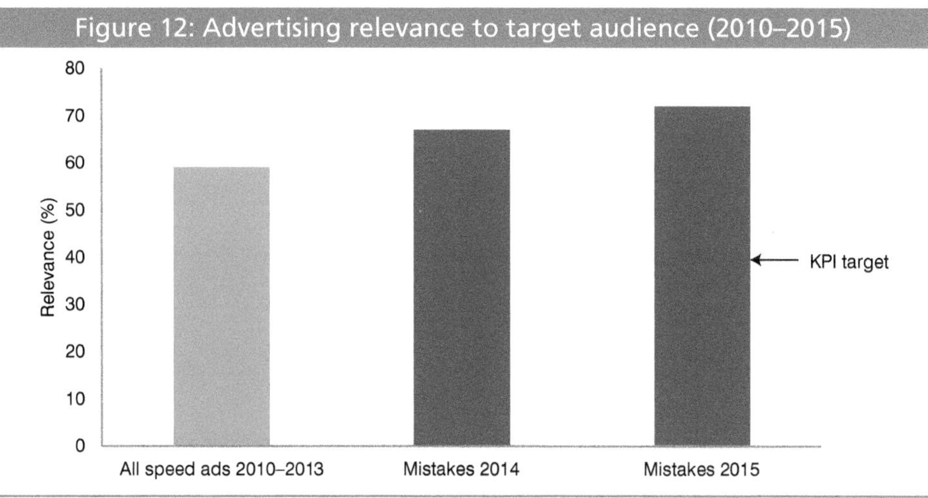

Objective 3: Top three messages are on brief

'Mistakes' achieved correct message interpretation: of the three message outtakes 'Slow down' was the most important, as that's the action we want people to take, and is the behavioural 'product' we want our audience to 'buy'. The two next highest messages attributed are the substantiation of why the audience should slow down (Figure 13).

Figure 13: 'Mistakes' main message interpretation

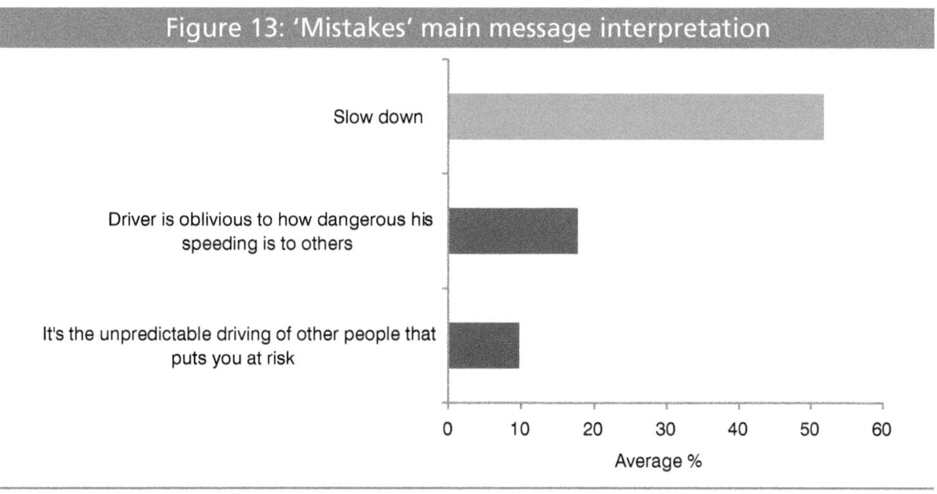

Engagement and attitudinal results

More than this, the campaign created exceptional levels of engagement, advocacy and strong indications of attitudinal shifts.

Objective 4: Create new conversations about speed, facilitating broader ownership of the problem.

'Mistakes' gave people a new reason to slow down and the conversation it generated was unprecedented.

The ad went viral on Day 1 – something no other social marketing ad in New Zealand had done.[20]

Within just one week, there were over 10 million views of 'Mistakes' across the world. On YouTube, over 6,000 comments have been posted and the video has a 98% 'like' rate (Figure 14).

Figure 14: 'Mistakes' on YouTube

A single post on a local police Facebook page attracted over 250,000 likes and shares, reaching 7 million people.

But what really makes its impact impressive is how 'Mistakes' has given a voice to a side of this argument that has been quiet for so long. By side-stepping blame and, for the first time, inviting speeders to be part of the conversation, 'Mistakes' has given people a reason to ask others to slow down – and to defend this position (Figure 15).

Figure 15: Examples of social commentary

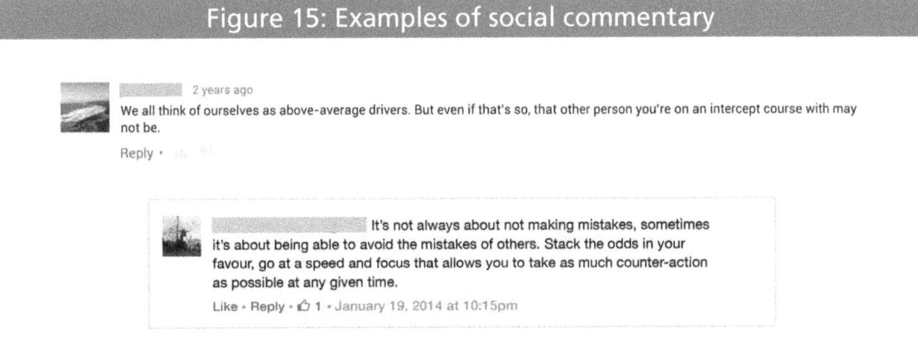

Objective 5: Disarm conventional counter-arguments

Previous speed campaigns – even those designed to stir up community concern and intolerance for speed – resulted often in speeders becoming more defensive and angry. But by acknowledging that they *are* good drivers, and asking them to allow for other people's mistakes, we won over and gained a new group of advocates who had previously been highly critical of our speed advertising.

For the first time, the motoring community praised the campaign and supported the message, writing about it and sharing it in their own communities (Figure 16).

Figure 16 : Examples of motoring community support

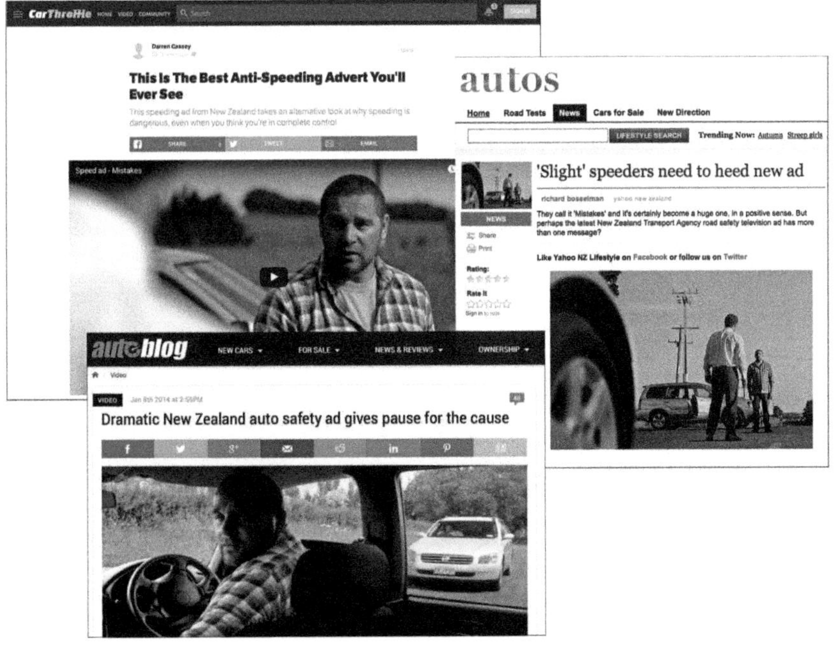

Mainstream media also picked up the message to advocate for slower speeds:

The simple truth is that even though there are good drivers with modern cars – who in an ideal world could cruise safely at higher speeds with relative impunity – they can't and shouldn't in New Zealand. That's because you simply can't trust people around you to do what they should, or for their cars to react the way a modern one can.

Figure 17: Example of shift in media discourse

Motoring

NO NEED FOR SPEED

There's a perfect storm of reasons why we don't deserve and won't get a higher open road speed limit in New Zealand, says Dave Moore.

"The simple truth is that even though there are good drivers with modern cars - who in an ideal world could cruise safely at higher speeds with relative impunity - they can't and shouldn't in New Zealand. That's because you simply can't trust people around you to do what they should, or for their cars to react the way a modern one can."

Objective 6: Shift attitudes towards speed

Attitude shifts are critical in helping to influence behaviour and public policy – tougher enforcement interventions are generally introduced with *majority public support behind them.*

After just three months of advertising, 73% of people said 'Mistakes' had changed their attitude, demonstrating we were indeed persuading people to look at this old problem through a new lens. This is the first time a highly recalled ad also shifted attitudes at a very high level – which is critical for widespread behaviour change (Figure 18).[21]

Online conversations also indicate attitudes are shifting. For the first time in the history of the speed campaign, people were openly accepting the message for themselves (Figure 19).

The thousands of comments posted have given us clear insight into what society thinks about speeding. The sentiment is overwhelmingly positive and on-message, with people readily jumping in to defend the 'slow down' outtake if someone tries to argue speed isn't the problem (Figure 20).

Figure 18: Likelihood to change attitude after seeing ads (2005–2015)

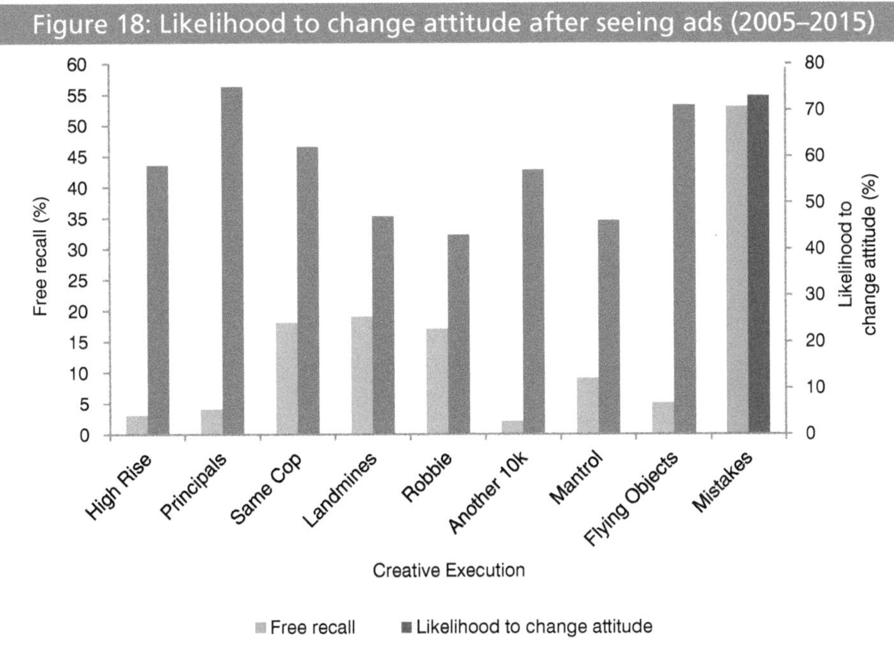

Figure 19: Social media examples of message acceptance

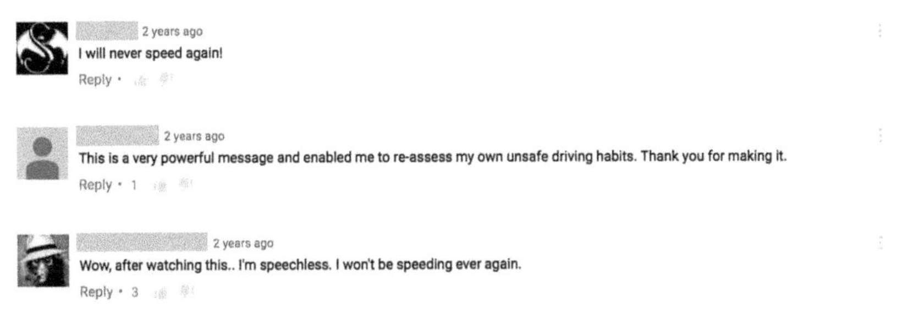

Figure 20: Example of social media counter arguments

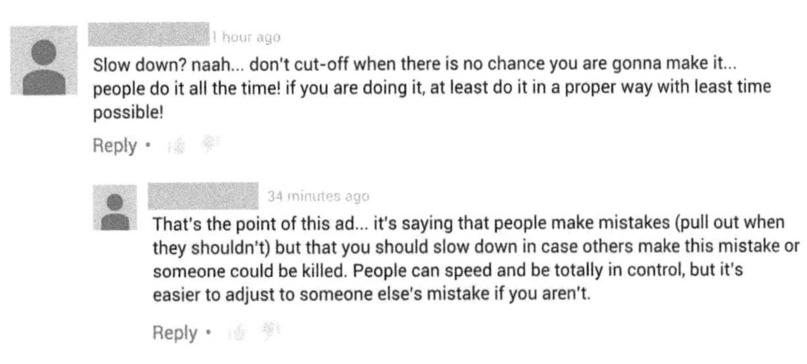

Calculating the value of speed reductions to society

The cost of road casualties is very high, both in economic and human terms, with thousands of families and communities affected every year.

Before the launch of 'Mistakes', the average casualty rate during 2011–2013 was 282 deaths and 12,300 injuries, with an average social cost of $3.997 billion per year.[22]

Research shows that lowering mean speeds on the open road by 1km/h results in 4–5% fewer deaths and 3% fewer injuries each year across the network.

We can therefore monetise a reduction in speed: each 1 km/h reduction in New Zealand is worth $45–56 million in reduced fatalities and $71 million in reduced injuries, a total of $116–127 million in reduced social costs.

Following the first year of 'Mistakes', our surveys showed average open road speeds had dropped by 0.4km/h.

Therefore in the first year of 'Mistakes', the advertising campaign has contributed to a reduction in social costs of at least 0.4 × $116 million = $46 million.

Even if the campaign takes credit for just a tenth of this reduction (to allow for some contribution from enforcement and engineering), the financial return is $4.6 million for an outlay of $2.8 million, in the first year alone.

That may be too conservative, however. There was little difference in policing in 2014 and 2015 compared to previous years (202,000 tickets per year during 2011–2013, 209,000 in 2014–2015[23]) so we could reasonably attribute a higher return from the advertising.

Discounting other factors

We can identify the impact 'Mistakes' clearly had on people in shifting entrenched attitudes towards speeding – through which we've also seen an impact on behaviour.

- We can confidently attribute awareness, social 'buzz' and cultural influence to the advertising campaign. 'Mistakes' was the only new speed marketing activity introduced in 2014. News media coverage was in response to the popularity of the campaign and massive viral reach (as outlined in the results section above).
- In terms of influencing behaviour change, as noted there was no significant change in the levels of police enforcement from previous years. Over holiday periods, the enforcement threshold was lowered to 4km/h over the limit, which is consistent with previous years.
- No other widespread speed initiatives were introduced in this period. The police did not blitz enforcement in response to the popularity of 'Mistakes'. This was a deliberate strategy to start to change long-held beliefs about speed and enforcement: from drivers being forced to comply with the law (slowing down temporarily to avoid a ticket) to voluntary, sustained compliance (slowing down for the sake of others).
- The impact of engineering (improvements in the road and vehicle infrastructure) is important but in its nature very gradualist and slow burn – impacts over a year or two are likely to be small.

- Economic factors also clearly have an impact on road crashes. Record high fuel prices saw a steady decline starting in early 2013, resulting in average kilometres travelled in New Zealand increasing by 68km per capita in 2014.[24] With more vehicles spending more time on the road, the collective risk increases so we could reasonably expect crashes to *increase* in the last 2 years. As we have seen, the opposite has been the case.

Summary

We broke the mould and in doing so gained unprecedented levels of public support for an issue people had stopped wanting to own. For the first time, we agreed with speeders and used their own argument to convince them to slow down. By inviting a moment of self-reflection and by *not* pointing the finger, we helped New Zealanders understand that the speed message was a message for them.

For everyone.

Leading the world

We didn't set out to change the world – just New Zealanders' behaviour and attitude toward speeding – but 'Mistakes' is now considered a breakthrough in speed advertising on a global scale, selected by the TED Foundation as one of 10 'Ads Worth Spreading' in 2014[25] and attracting the attention of international road safety organisations (Figure 21).

Figure 21: 'Mistakes' at TED

> *I am writing to say a huge congratulations on your new 'Mistakes' advertisement. It is really a landmark in global road safety … We have long grappled with how to communicate the safe system and speeding message but your ad delivers that message in such a powerful and moving way. This ad will truly make a difference to road safety around the world.*
>
> (Transport for New South Wales)

Figure 22: Examples of attention from international transport agencies

The 'Mistakes' story was picked up and discussed widely by news organisations around the world (Figure 23).

Figure 23: Examples of international media coverage

It is impossible to accurately track and value this coverage, but we can estimate a further US$20 million was invested in paid media in France, Italy, Australia and Iran, where 'Mistakes' was borrowed, re-made and run (Figures 24 and 25).

Figure 24: Storyboard of French 'Mistakes' remake

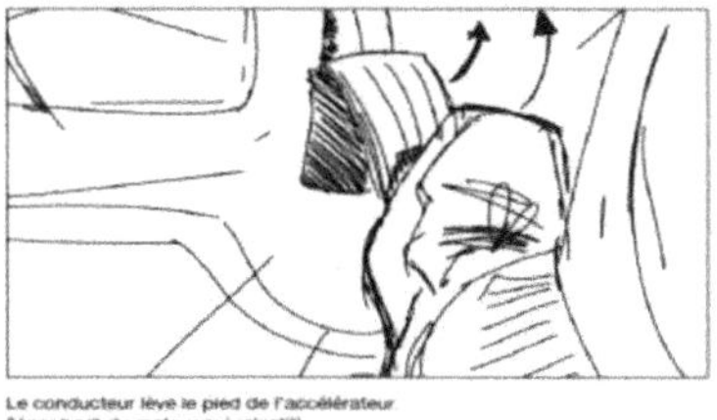

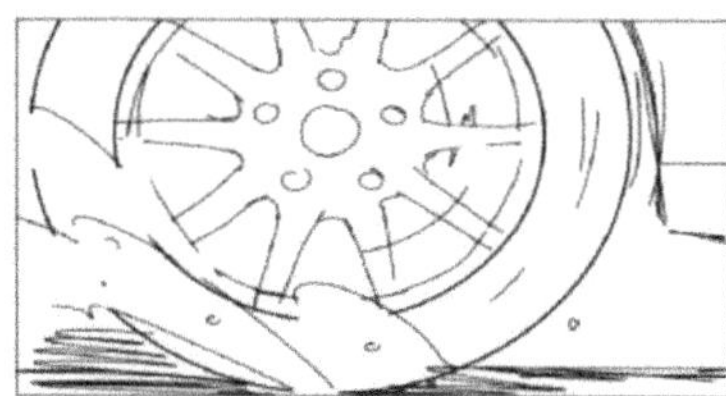

Figure 25: Storyboard of Iranian 'Mistakes' remake

People from other countries have independently translated 'Mistakes' into numerous languages, from Portuguese to Russian to Arabic, and re-posted it on YouTube. One translated version alone attracted over 2 million views.

Figure 26: 'Mistakes' in various languages

Although not the direct objective of this campaign, the core thought of 'Mistakes' has been shared and used to inspire speed campaigns all around the globe – arguably contributing to reductions in mean speeds outside of New Zealand as well as the powerful results here.

Behaviour change learning

This case presents a powerful approach for shifting entrenched attitudes and driving behaviour.

1. To reframe an undesirable behaviour, find a universal truth that all drivers can relate to.
2. Avoid fighting people's belief that they're a good driver.
3. Bypass blame to invite self-reflection.
4. Invoke a strong emotional response.

Notes

1. Source: World Health Organisation http://whqlibdoc.who.int/publications/2004/9241562609.pdf
2. Source: Nielsen ratecard data 2014
3. Source: Fatal and serious injury speed-related crashes. Source: Ministry of Transport road crash statistics
4. Source: Ministry of Transport Speed Survey, open road car speeds 1996–2013
5. Source: Ministry of Transport speed survey
6. Source: Ministry of Transport speed survey
7. Source: IPSOS Road Tracking survey
8. Source: Glasshouse Road Tracking survey 2000–2013
9. Source: http://www.transport.govt.nz/assets/Uploads/Research/Documents/Speed-2014.pdf

10. Source: World Health Organisation http://whqlibdoc.who.int/publications/2004/9241562609.pdf
11. Source: Ministry of Transport speed survey
12. Source: Glasshouse Consulting roadtrack reports and Agency/Client KPI reports: 2005–2015
13. Source: Safer Journeys consultation report, Agency qualitative research and Media monitoring
14. Source: Glasshouse Consulting: Historic correlation between free recall of message and exposure via billboards when run in parallel to TV
15. Source: Ministry of Transport speed survey
16. Source: Ministry of Transport: reported injury crashes 2014
17. Source: Statistics NZ
18. Source: NZ Transport Agency vehicle volume
19. Source: Glasshouse Consulting road safety tracking reports, 2014. This is a weekly monitor
20. Source: One News report, 9 January 2014
21. Source: Glasshouse Consulting road safety tracking, Q1 2014
22. Source: Ministry of Transport – Social Cost of Road Crashes
23. Source: NZ Police enforcement statistics
24. Source: http://www.transport.govt.nz/ourwork/tmif/transport-volume/tv003/
25. Source: http://www.ted.com/watch/ads-worth-spreading/mistakes

Stoptober

A radical new way to get England to quit smoking

By Jo Arden, 23red; Pete Buckley, MEC; Nick Hirst, adam&eveDDB, formerly Dare; Nigel Shardlow, Sandtable; Matthew Walmsley, Public Health England
Contributing authors: Gemma Cass, TNS BRMB; Annie Hau, Sandtable
Credited companies: 23red; Dare; EMO; Freuds; M4C; NOW; OgilvyOne; Sandtable; TNS BRMB; MEC London, Carat, M&C Saatchi; iris

Summary
Stoptober is a public health intervention created through marketing. It has been used to save thousands of lives in England and been adopted by clinicians internationally. Every October for four years the initiative challenged smokers to quit for 28 consecutive days from October 1, with the evidence-based promise that if they made it the whole way through, they would be five times more likely to quit forever. The campaign provided tools and messages to mobilise 'a herd' effect more typically seen in January when people start new health regimes. This case study provides evidence that Stoptober grew in impact – with 65,000 more quitters in Year 4 than Year 1 – and a total 1.5m quit attempts driven by the communications. The short-term ROMI was estimated at £2.85 for every £1 invested.

Editor's Comment
The judges admired this case for delivering strong results over a number of years despite the fact that the task became increasingly challenging, as the audience they needed to affect were the most 'committed smokers'.

Client Comment
Matthew Walmsley, Deputy Director Planning and Insight, Public Health England

'Stoptober' has rewritten the rule book on what works. Marketing has been deployed to tackle smoking for decades in the UK, but it has been dominated by health harm-based advertising. 'Stoptober' is different because it is a mass market health intervention wholly manufactured by marketing. It combines piercing smoker insight with behavioural economic thinking.

Not only is it highly effective in triggering quit attempts, it is endorsed by clinicians and academics. It has galvanised all 152 local authorities, and is now an established event in the public health calendar both in England and abroad.

Stoptober demonstrated the power of combining behavioural economics principles with marketing communications to create scale and galvanise an entire nation including the health system, commercial brands and news organisations around a single event.

Evaluation of public health behaviour change campaigns is always challenging. For Stoptober we utilised the latest in agent-based modelling to evidence effectiveness. For the first time, this approach allowed us to model an individual quit attempt, giving a much more granular view of impact than econometrics could ever achieve. Stoptober is a real achievement for public health marketing, and a credit to its effectiveness in driving behaviour change.

In 2012 we launched a product that would change the face of quitting smoking … and it wasn't an e-cigarette.

Stoptober is a marketing-manufactured health intervention, so effective at triggering quit attempts it's been published as a case study in a peer-reviewed academic journal, and is now being copied by clinicians globally.[1]

This paper tells the story of how it worked.

Smoking may feel like a relic of another age, but there are still over 8 million smokers in England, costing the NHS £2.7bn annually, and still the single biggest cause of preventable death.

Public Health England's (PHE) Tobacco Control programme aims to reduce prevalence by triggering as many quit attempts as possible across the smoking population.

But this was getting harder and the reduction in prevalence was slowing.

This paper explains how Stoptober helped us accelerate the reduction by:

- Directly stimulating an additional 1.5 million quit attempts
- Significantly increasing the success rates of those attempts
- Creating a completely new quitting season in October, which has become so big that it even rivals the traditional January quit season
- Transforming the perception of what it is to quit, from difficult and lonely, to achievable and popular for those involved
- Establishing an annual event in the NHS calendar which has the potential to influence smokers regardless of marketing budgets
- Revolutionising what social marketing can achieve, for all smokers, not just the easy targets.

Alongside this, we have invested in world-class evaluation. We have developed a revolutionary agent-based model to help us plan and evaluate campaigns. The model goes further than standard econometric models by capturing the heterogeneity of the smoking population in their response to the media, and the potentially overlapping effects that media has on smoking behaviour.[2, 3]

An almost impossible challenge

In 2011, Public Health England were set the target of reducing smoking prevalence from 21% in 2011 to 18.5% by 2015. This was ambitious; having fallen continually since the early 2000s, the fall in prevalence started to plateau between 2008 and 2011. Even assuming that our existing marketing campaigns would remain as effective as ever, we would still miss our prevalence targets by an estimated 250,000 smokers.

There were two big initiatives from outside of the marketing world that would help: e-cigarettes and the cigarette POS display ban. But while we were confident these would make up some of the shortfall, they were both as yet untested in a UK market. At the time, the health effects of e-cigs were far from clear, meaning we couldn't recommend,[4] or even rely on, e-cigarette usage to help us hit our goal. Social marketing would have to step up to get prevalence back on its downward track.

The task was two-fold:

1. Trigger as many quit attempts as possible
2. Ensure that as many as possible of those attempts would be successful.

But we faced significant challenges. First, our audience was becoming tougher.

The number of 'hardened smokers' was increasing

A higher proportion of smokers were resistant to help. In the face of huge price rises, a ban on smoking in public, successive and successful 'health harms' campaigns, and probable death (1 in every 2 smokers die of a tobacco-related disease if they continue to smoke), more smokers were saying they had no desire to quit – moving from 16% in August 2008 to 30% by October 2010.[5]

Motivation was low

Even among those smokers who wanted to quit, less than a fifth (16%) had any firm plan to do so. And troublingly, our marketing to date had been most successful at triggering quit attempts by the shrinking minority of smokers who already had an intention to quit.[6]

More disadvantaged smokers were struggling to stay quit

Although smokers from all backgrounds make roughly the same number of quit attempts, smokers from less affluent socio-economic groups (where prevalence is typically higher) were twice as likely to fail in their quit attempt when using quitting aids as more affluent smokers.[7] Most quit aids focused on helping smokers get over the chemical addiction – which takes about three days, no matter who you are. Smokers from poorer communities, though, are more likely to be subject to the 'psychological' factors that make it harder to quit and easy to relapse – for example, being surrounded by large numbers of other smokers.

These three barriers meant that, every year from 2007 to 2011, the number of quit attempts dropped. Rates moved from 42.5% of smokers making an attempt in the last 12 months in 2007, to 33.5% in 2011.[8] Worryingly, these quit attempts were also becoming less successful.

As if these audience barriers weren't enough, we had other challenges too.

Dramatically shrinking budgets

Under the Coalition Government's austerity agenda, all government marketing, including tobacco control advertising, was stopped across 2010 and reinstated at a much lower level. It was clear the future would be about delivering more with less.

Little room for incremental improvement

Years of highly successful smoking cessation campaigns had produced a finely tuned quit-making machine (winning a number of effectiveness awards).[9] It was hard to see how we would make these campaigns significantly more effective such that they would deliver hundreds of thousands more quit attempts, with no more budget.

And finally, we had a 'contextual' challenge – possibly the toughest of all.

We couldn't rely on January

The biggest natural season for quitting is the New Year; 40% higher than other months.[10] We already had highly effective activity happening in January. So we had to find a new window in the calendar. But running a campaign outside of January would mean we couldn't rely on the effects of January itself. There were two specific behavioural triggers we'd lose: the 'herd' effect (the sense that lots of other people are quitting too); and intention setting (people quit in January because the New Year gives them an arbitrary but clear start date to commit to. Outside January, we'd have no such date).

A new strategic approach

We needed a new strategy which would allow us to trigger more successful quit attempts among all smokers – including hardened or less motivated smokers and those from less affluent backgrounds.

The key strategic pillars for this new approach were as follows:

- Ask smokers to quit for a specific time to overcome that behavioural science showed smokers didn't make 'forever' quit attempts because they feared failure
- Talk to smokers in a completely different way: engaging with positivity, rather than hard-hitting imagery to give them a final push
- Provide a new range of tools to support their quit attempts
- Protect from further budget cuts by looking to create an 'austerity proof' solution
- Recreate the 'January effect', with two behavioural triggers:
  - The 'herd effect' – a sense that lots of other smokers were taking part (before a single one had signed up)
  - Creation of SMART goals (specific, measurable, achievable and realistic goals) – replicating the familiar 'on the first of January I will stop smoking'.

We decided not just to copy January, but to improve upon it. Whilst January provided a start point ('I will quit on New Year's Day'), it didn't provide a realistic goal ('I will make it through a month'). Whilst the feeling of everyone doing it is a good prompt for an initial action, it doesn't keep people on track day-to-day.

Creating a new January was a bold ambition and a significant departure from the well-established rhythm of the quitting year. But, if successful, it could create a life-saving culture change in quitting.

What we created

In keeping with our socially contagious, positively motivating behavioural triggers, we adopted a positively motivating tone of voice – in complete contrast to our own previous campaigns and those around the world.

The friendlier, welcoming tone of voice would be a breath of fresh air to smokers who felt hectored, helping us to cut through and engage.

The start point was not an ad, it was a programme. The programme, based on our behavioural triggers and built mostly from communications tools, was action-orientated, clear and inclusive. People needed to believe from the outset that it was on their side.

And so October became Stoptober; a positive, participative, mass quit attempt – the first of its kind anywhere in the world. Quitters were challenged to quit for 28 days from 1 October, with the (evidence-based) promise that if they made it the whole way through, they'd be 'five times more likely to quit'. The simplicity and lightness of the brand and the construct spoke to smokers who wanted to be treated as grown-ups. The barriers were lowered and people signed up in their thousands.

Stoptober has now run for four years, and whilst each year has a distinct theme, the core tenets remain the same:

1. Support tools

A free set of academically endorsed tools, designed to move the quitter's motivational system in the right direction during their quit attempt, not just to stimulate the first few days:

- A physical kit (Figure 1) including a 28-day quit calendar with motivational facts and tips to keep people on the right track
- An SMS support service offering daily tips and advice
- An app that helped quitters get through each smoke-free day.

Figure 1: Stoptober kit and app

2. Social media support groups

Inspired by the valuable support offered by local stop-smoking services, we used social as a virtual support group, using the power of the peer network to help smokers quit. We encouraged peer-to-peer support on Facebook and Twitter, posting frequent content to fuel what became a vibrant community of mutual support (Figure 2).

Figure 2: Selected Facebook and Twitter content and responses

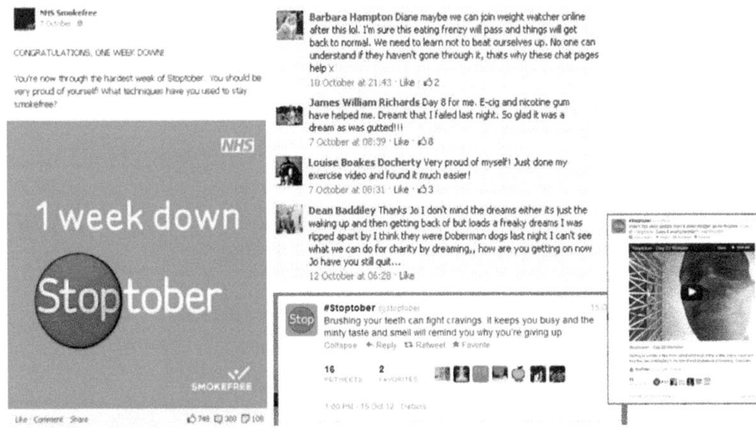

3. Grassroots and community activation

Stoptober galvanised the nation. Every single local authority (all 152) got involved and local stop-smoking services across the country wanted to be part of it and deliver localised activity under the Stoptober banner. A first for a public health campaign.

Commercial organisations enhanced Stoptober's pervasiveness by gifting retail space and briefing staff to help customers sign up.

Over 6000 pharmacies, from large chains like Tesco, ASDA, Superdrug and Lloyds Pharmacy, to high-street independents in communities of high prevalence took part in Stoptober. By 2015, this had risen to 9978 (or nearly 80% of all pharmacies in England).

And in 2012, 49 of England's largest employers, with 900,000 staff combined, launched workplace activity on the same day, encouraging staff to do it together. Tapping into groups of co-workers meant making a virtue of the natural copying behaviour seen with smokers at work. In 2012, this was the largest number of employers launching workplace health activity on the same day, a record we superseded in 2015 with 157 employers reaching 1.5 million people.

Figure 3: Selected local activation and coverage

4. Advertising

This had two distinct phases: 'Get me in' and 'Keep me in'.

The 'Get me in' phase (before 1 October) was designed to make Stoptober feel immediately popular and relevant to all adults regardless of whether they were a smoker or not, recognising that everyone was a potential supporter of a smoker who's trying to quit, be they a friend, family member or work colleague.

'Get me in' advertising was 'brand response' driving both fame and triggering immediate action.

Heavyweight TV created a sense of popularity by using real people to create the 'social contagion' effect we needed. In the first year we showed pre-recruited pilot participants taking part (Figure 4). In subsequent years we used real people from Year 1, before injecting yet more populism with well-known comedians from Year 3 onwards.

Figure 4: Screenshots from TV ads

The TV was supported by a combination of radio and paid social/digital display targeted directly at smokers, focusing on the benefits of signing up to Stoptober and reducing the steps to do so by using in-ad sign-up forms.

The second phase was 'keep me in' (after 1 October). This phase was designed to offer visible encouragement to quitters and their supporters. We did this by taking the unusual step of making the contents of our CRM programme public, using print and digital advertising. For example, 19 different print ads appeared in newspapers across the month containing messages to motivate quitters day by day – from alerting them to their newly reawakened taste buds, to telling them how much money they'd saved (Figure 5).

Figure 5: Selected support ads

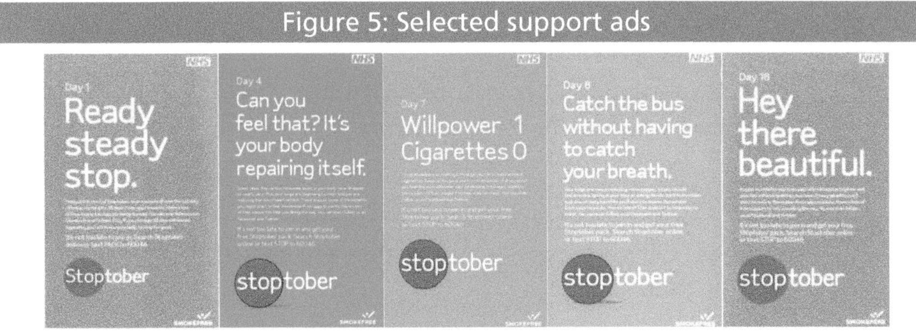

5. PR as popularity machine

Stoptober delivered unprecedented coverage for a smoking campaign which helped build a sense of scale and popularity.

Celebrities were recruited to coach 'super quitters'; celebrities seen smoking were sent Stoptober kits; and major columnists were targeted with collateral (Figure 6). (Even jokey responses were helpful: Caitlin Moran spoofed the idea of Stoptober with other ideas for themed months.)

Figure 6: Selected PR coverage

Evolving Stoptober year on year

We used insights to evolve or theme Stoptober in the following years:

- *Stoptober 2013* – we knew from the post-campaign research which support tools worked best, and we also knew that using two types of support (specifically the app and the physical kit) hugely increased people's chances of success.[11] So in Year 2 we changed the architecture of the Stoptober sign-up site to nudge more people into selecting that option. The result was that more people chose a multi-support option and more people stuck with the programme for longer.
- *Stoptober 2014* – we explored whether the levity of tone could be dialled up further. Consumer testing said it could. It was apparent that Stoptober had started to reset what people react to in quitting communications. This paved the way for the 2013 theme – comedy. We recruited Paddy McGuinness, Al

Murray, Dr Bob and Andi Osho to front the campaign and wove the 'swap fags for gags' thought through all communications.

- *Stoptober 2015* – since the launch of Stoptober, quitters had praised the personalised tools such as the app. Stoptober 2015 built on this, promising that 'this time it's personal'. Working with new comic talent (Bill Bailey, Al Murray, Shappi Khorsandi and Rhod Gilbert) to create virtual groups, participants were able to choose the comedian they most identified with and join their squad. Quitters' experience was then tailored to fit their preference as well as their habit.

Did it work?

Yes, it did.

By 2014 prevalence was at 18.5%, we had reached the 2015 target a year early (Figure 7).

Figure 7: Smoking prevelance (% of adult population smoking)

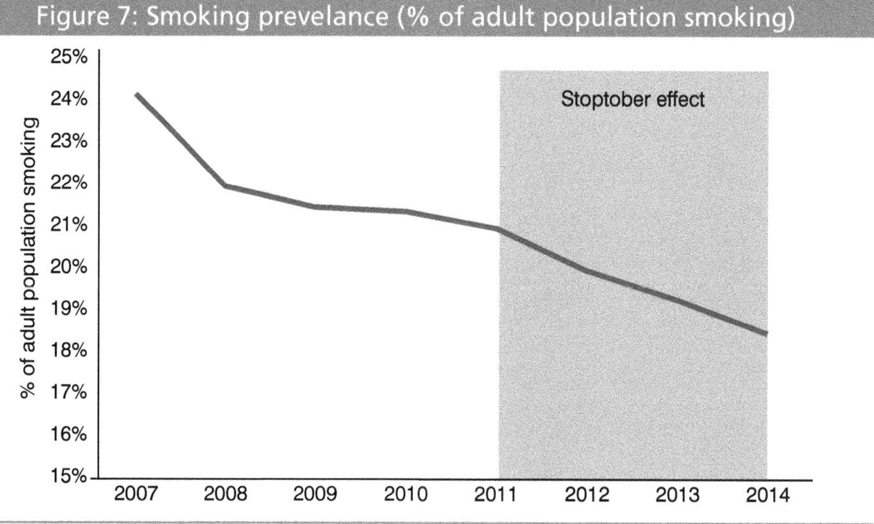

Source: UCL Smoking Toolkit Study

In real numbers, there are 70,000 fewer smokers today as a direct result of Stoptober. That's just shy of the full capacity of Old Trafford. (And, as many Stoptober 2015 participants are still in their first year, that figure is likely nearer 100,000.)

We used PHE's Tobacco Simulation Model (TSM), an agent-based model to determine the impact of Stoptober. TSM is a behavioural simulation that aims to support public health practitioners by providing a comprehensive, dynamic and interactive picture of the smoking system in England. TSM, developed in conjunction with UCL, is built using, and validated against, a variety of public and proprietary smoking data sets.

The simulation consists of a population of agents representative of the population of England who engage in realistic smoking-related behaviour, such as starting to smoke, quitting, and dying, and a 'world' in which they operate. This world includes the relevant external factors that affect their behaviour, such as advertising. When the simulation is run, agent behaviour is recorded over time. Each agent's decisions are tracked at the individual level. The population behaviour is the sum of all of the actions of the individual agents.

The model shows us that Stoptober was crucial in meeting our twofold challenge:

- Trigger as many quit attempts as possible
- Ensure that as many as possible of those attempts would be successful.

1. Trigger as many quit attempts as possible

The model shows that Stoptober directly drove 1.5m quit attempts across the four years. Stoptober has built-in effectiveness. And at an absolute level, overall, Stoptober has driven a greater number of quit attempts than previous campaigns (Figure 8).

Figure 8: Quit attempts driven directly by public health campaigns since 2012

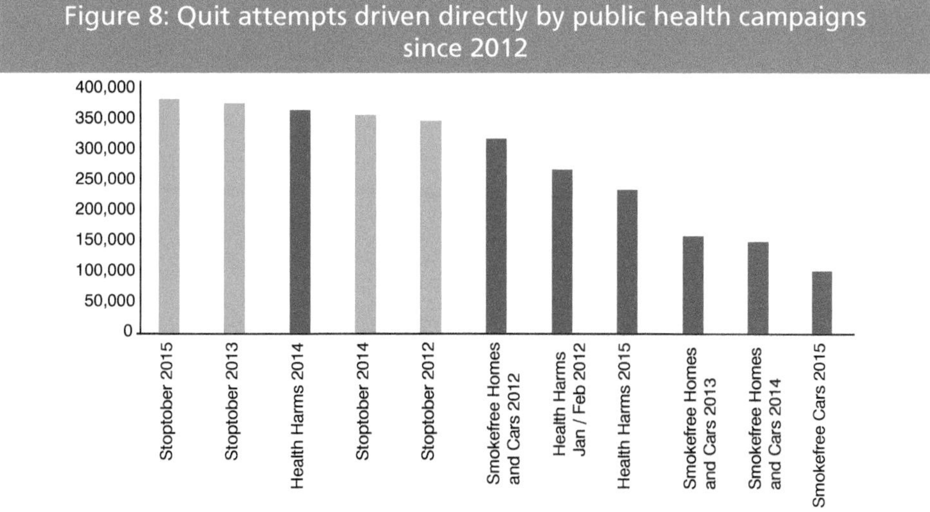

Source: PHE Tobacco Simulation Model

Whilst Stoptober's budget has been slightly higher than some previous quit activity, on average the cost per quit has improved on other Public Health England quitting campaigns, meaning Stoptober has grown mass whilst preserving efficiency (Figure 9).

Figure 9: Average cost per quit driven by PHE campaigns

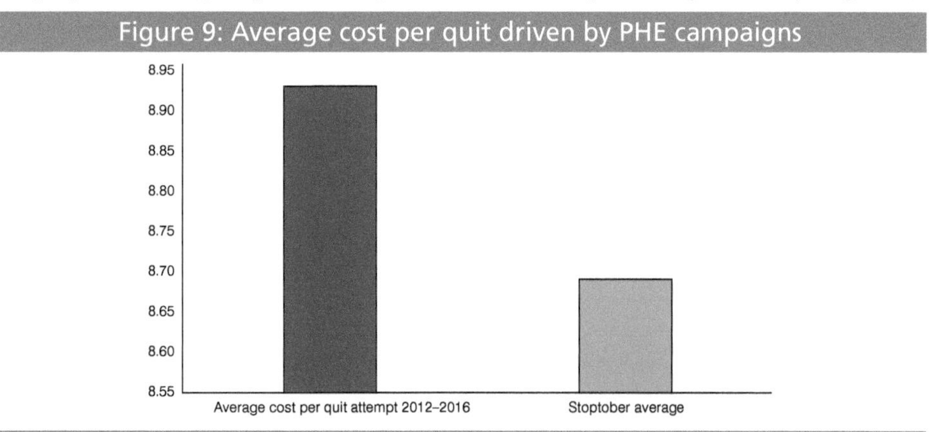

Source: PHE Tobacco Simulation Model

TNS tracking data corroborates the story: by 2015 an incredible 17% of smokers had claimed to have made a Stoptober quit attempt. Attempts have increased consistently across the four years even though Stoptober media spend remained roughly consistent at around £3m (Figure 10).

Figure 10: Smokers claiming to make a Stoptober-related quit attempt

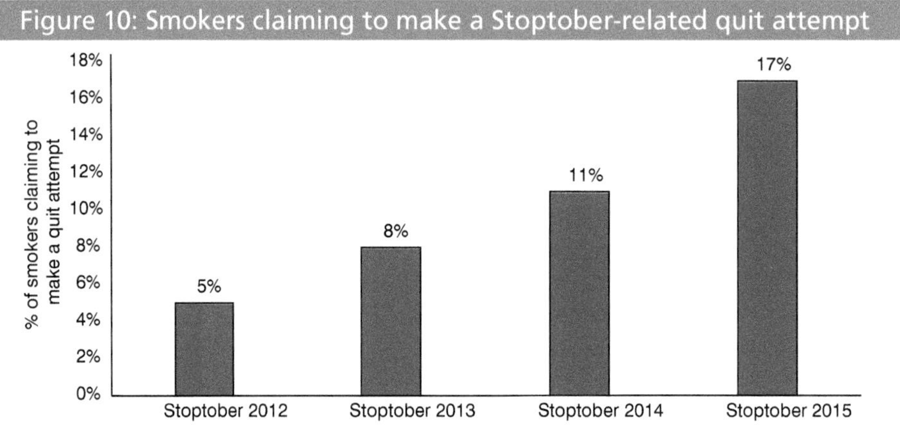

Source: TNS BMRB smoking cessation national tracker 2011–2015

2. Improving the chances of success for those that try to quit

Stoptober has seen the highest reported successful quit attempts by a smoking campaign, significantly improving on the Quit Kit 2010 campaign with 62% of all Stoptober participants reporting a quit attempt lasting four weeks or more (Figure 11).

Figure 11: Successful quit attempts – Stoptober vs. Quit Kit 2010

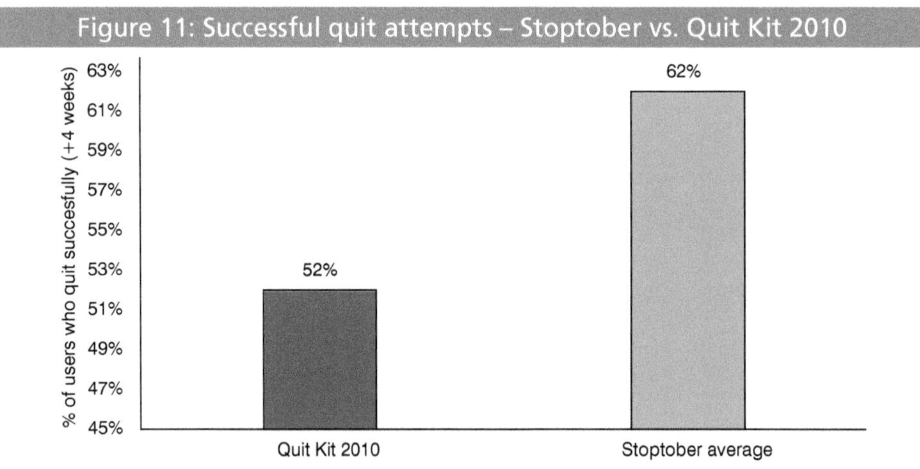

Source: COI Artemis CRM Programme Analysis/TNS Tracking

Stoptober managed to do this by delivering on the strategic pillars we set out earlier:

- Engaging less motivated smokers
- Providing smokers with a range of tools
- Recreating the 'January effect':
  - The 'herd effect'
  - SMART goals – quitting on a specific day
- Becoming an 'austerity-proof' solution.

Engaging less-motivated smokers

To meet the 18.5% prevalence target we knew we had to trigger quit attempts from smokers who did not usually respond to smoking campaigns. Figure 1 shows that Stoptober, for the first time, triggered more smokers who were only *thinking* rather than had *decided* to quit, into making a quit attempt (Figure 12).

Figure 12: Type of smoker triggered Stoptober vs. previous smoking campaigns

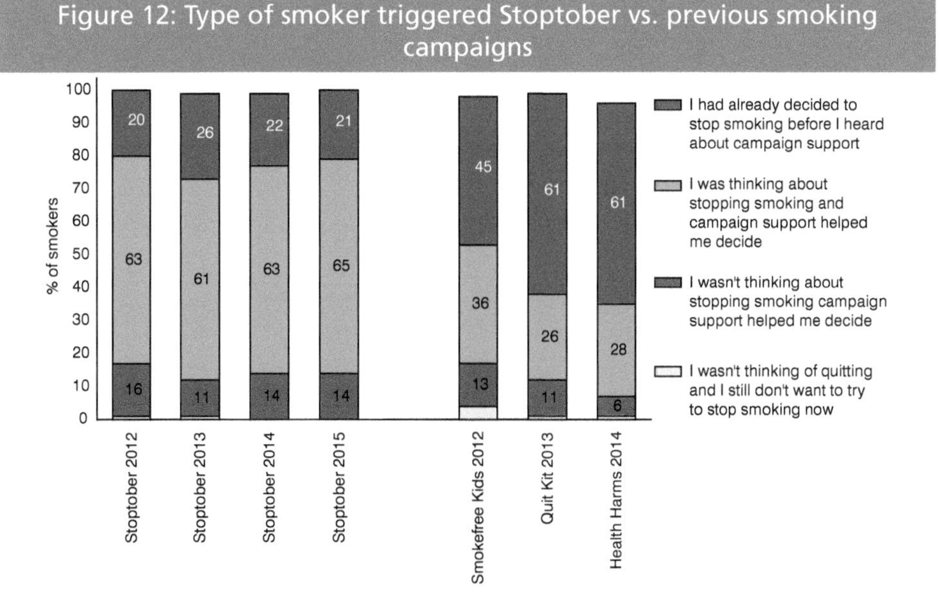

Source: TNS BMRB smoking cessation national tracker 2011–2015

Unlike previous smoking campaigns, Stoptober managed to particularly engage heavy smokers, with 79% of heavy smokers making a successful quit attempt using Stoptober, significantly higher than the average (Figure 13).

Figure 13: Successful Stoptober quit attempts (lasted 4+ weeks)

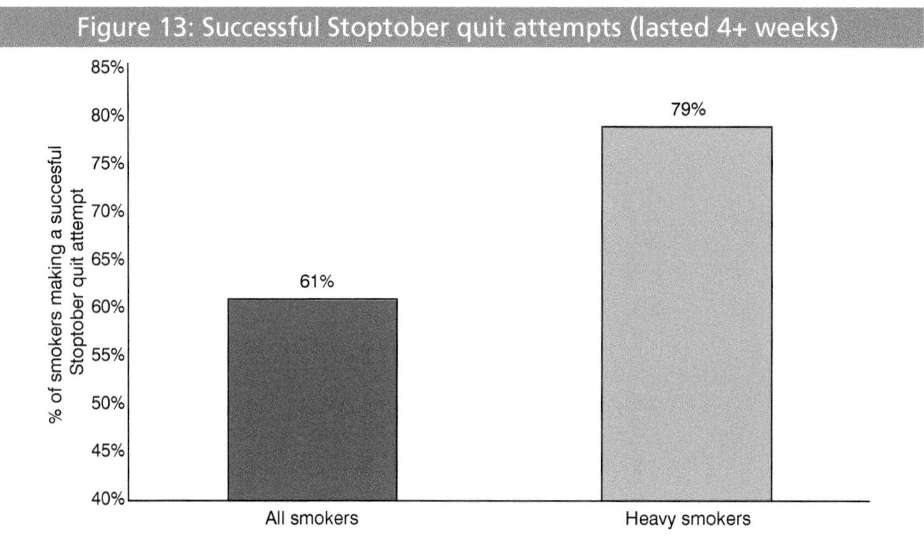

Source: TNS BMRB smoking cessation national tracker 2011–2015

Providing smokers with a range of tools that helped them quit more successfully

Over the four years, we've significantly increased the volume of support Stoptober participants use, and this has increased both the perception and the reality of Stoptober being helpful in quitting.

Each year more participants have used multiple support products (Figure 14).

Figure 14: % of Stoptober smokers using multiple support products

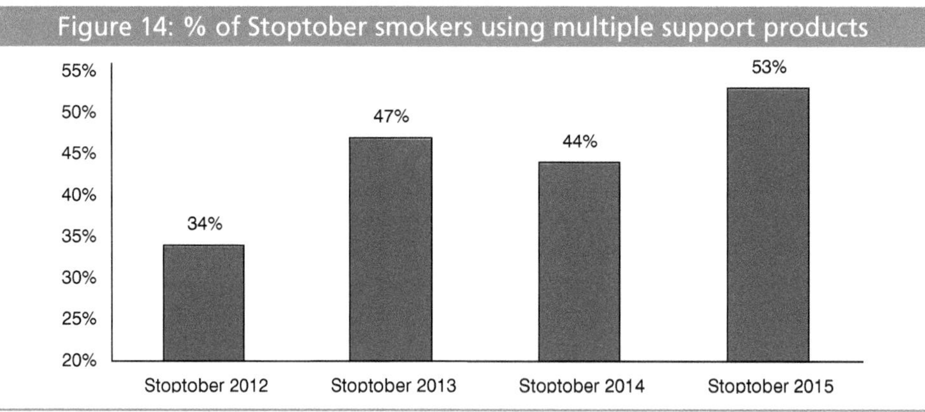

Source: TNS BMRB smoking cessation national tracker 2011–2015

And our belief that support is key has been borne out, as shown in Figure 15.

Figure 15: Support tool use impact on making a successful quit attempt with Stoptober

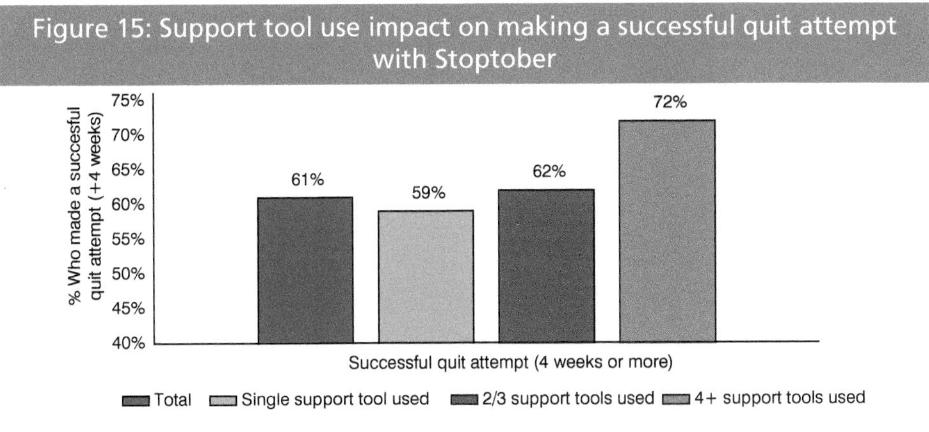

Source: TNS BMRB smoking cessation national tracker 2011–2015

Given this success it's unsurprising that smokers view Stoptober as more and more helpful as the event becomes more established (Figure 16).

Figure 16: Smokers' perception of Stoptober as a helpful quitting tool

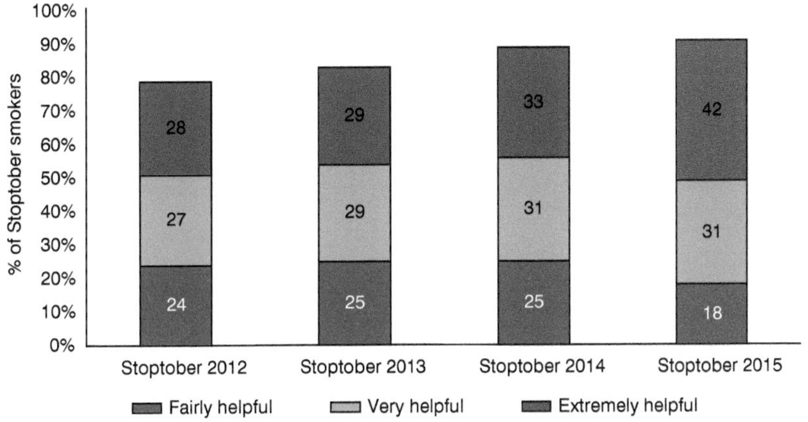

Source: TNS BMRB smoking cessation national tracker 2011–2015

Recreating the 'January effect'

Evidence that Stoptober has become an established quitting period can be found by looking at Nielsen cigarette sales data and comparing sales volumes for the year before Stoptober (2011) and those after it. 2012 onwards shows a decrease in purchase during September–October that mirrors and, in 2015, is even greater than January (Figure 17). Whilst we can't be sure if 2011 is an anomaly, the below suggests a very strong trend that October is now a time of the year when less people smoke.

Figure 17: Annual cigarette sales

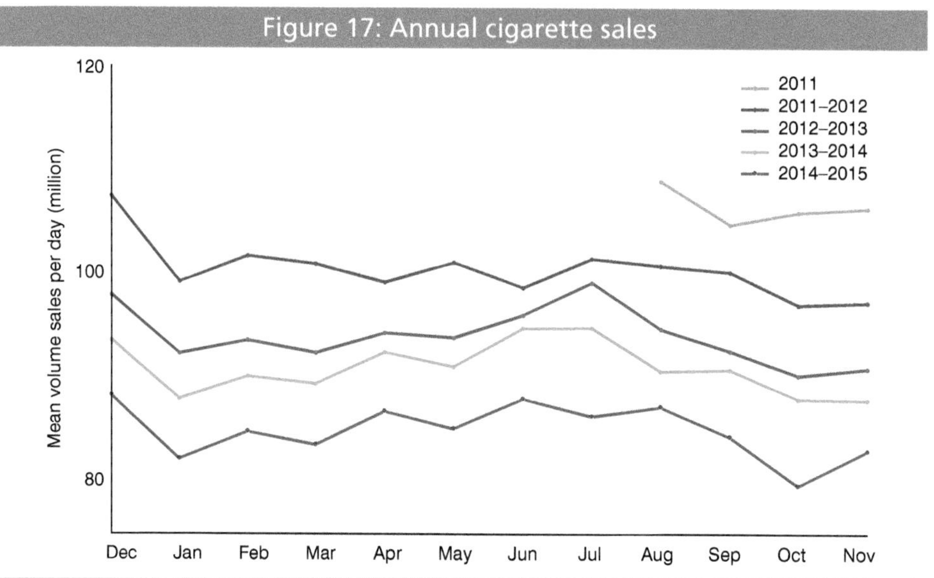

Source: Nielsen Cigarette Sales Data

Search volumes around Stoptober further support the scale created. Even from the first year, Stoptober-related search terms out-performed quit smoking-related terms in January. Stoptober also increased the generic quit-related terms in the September–October period as shown in Figure 18.

Figure 18: Stoptober vs. January quitting season search volumes

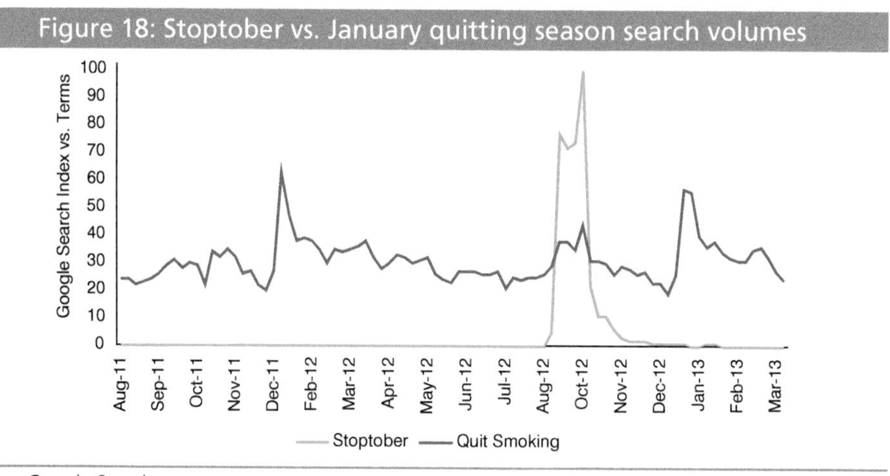

Source: Google Search

Creating the 'herd effect' – a sense that lots of other smokers were taking part

A key part of Stoptober was social norming, making it feel like everyone was quitting together, and talking about it was crucial. It did so at levels never seen before by a stop smoking campaign.

By 2015, an incredible 74% of Stoptober participants felt that lots of people were quitting together with Stoptober, whilst 72% felt Stoptober was a big event with lots of people taking part.[12]

Stoptober is highly social; in its first year, Stoptober helped increase social mentions of quitting smoking by over 150% year-on-year across September–October (Figure 19).

Figure 19: Quitting mentions year-on-year 2011 vs. 2012

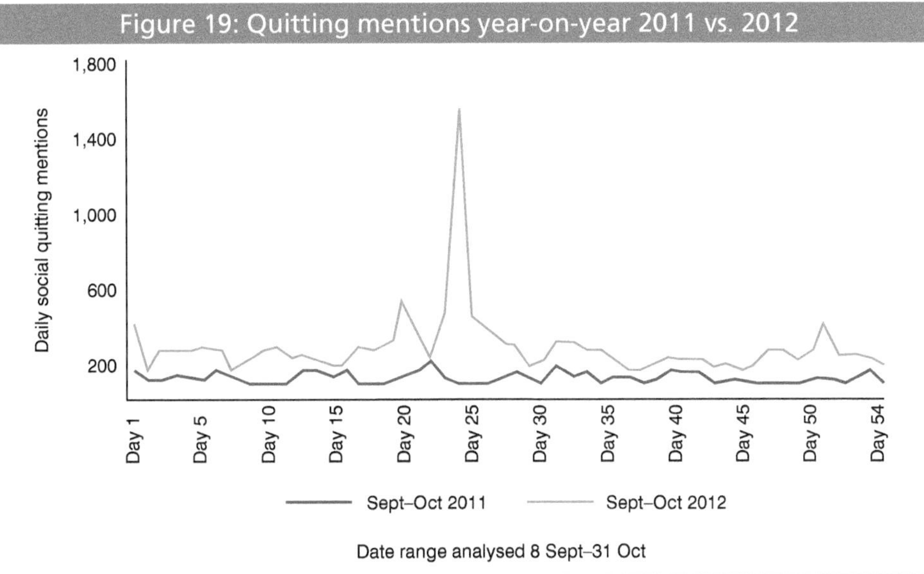

Source: Crimson Hexagon

The volume of social mentions was five times larger than any previous smoking campaign and has continuously been higher across the four years (Figure 20).

Figure 20: Average daily social mentions Stoptober 2012 vs. Quit Kit campaign 2012

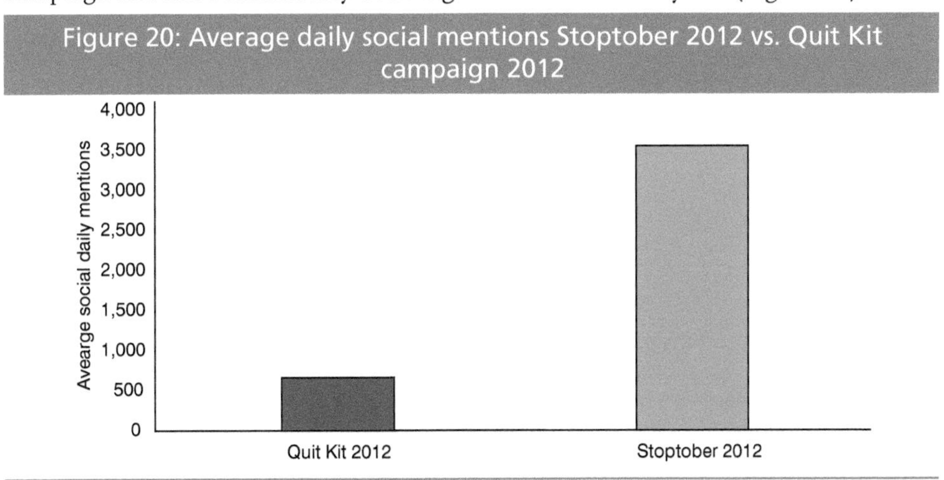

Source: Crimson Hexagon

Numerous celebrities and media organisations got involved in encouraging people too with many making a public quit attempt themselves (including Ewan McGregor) (Figure 21).

Figure 21: Selected celebrity and media coverage

PR value has exploded since Stoptober began, with more media outlets talking about quitting than ever before. PR value more than doubled in scale across the four years whilst media spend for Stoptober has slightly decreased (Figure 22).

Figure 22: PR value vs. media spend

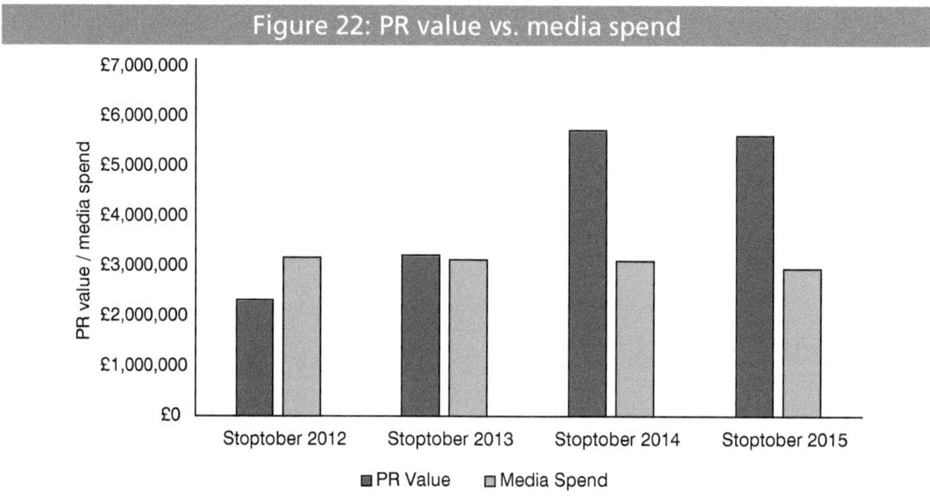

Source: Freud PR/MEC

Smokers registering to participate in Stoptober are 80%+ more likely to discuss their involvement with family / friends compared to previous smoking campaigns.

Figure 23: Discussed with family/friends Quit Kit vs. Stoptober

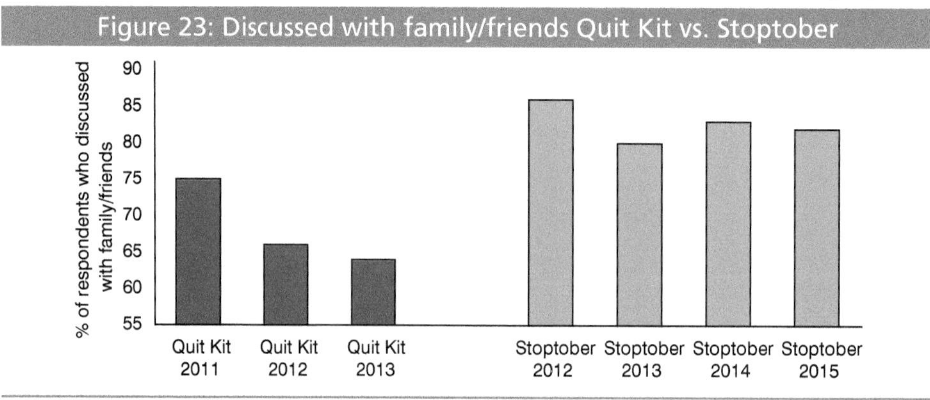

Source: TNS BMRB smoking cessation national tracker 2011–2015

And it's not just in England

Stoptober is now being copied by clinicians globally. The Netherlands and New Zealand both have now launched their own Stoptober, and more countries including France are set to follow in 2016. This is the first time that the UK has successfully exported a health prevention campaign and a huge step in positioning the UK as a world leader in this field (Figure 24).

Figure 24: Selected international 'Stoptober' campaigns

SMART goals – quitting on a specific day

Registration data also shows that even from the first year Stoptober benefited from being an event with a clear start date, with registrations peaking clearly on 1 October (Figure 25).

Figure 25: Stoptober TVRs vs. Stoptober registrations launch year

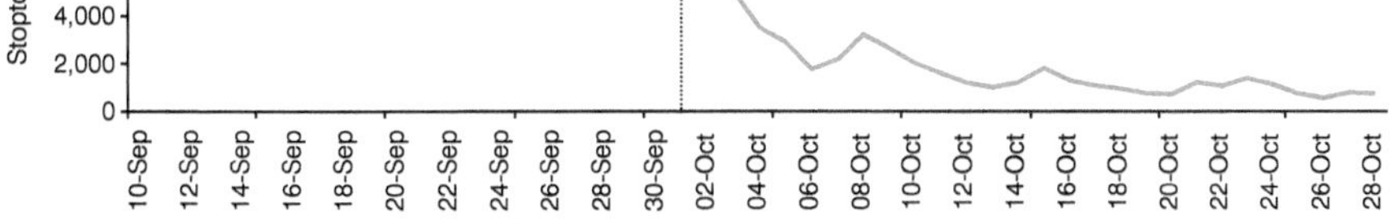

First day of Stoptober

Stoptober Registrations by day: 0, 2,000, 4,000, 6,000, 8,000, 10,000, 12,000, 14,000, 16,000, 18,000, 20,000

10-Sep, 12-Sep, 14-Sep, 16-Sep, 18-Sep, 20-Sep, 22-Sep, 24-Sep, 26-Sep, 28-Sep, 30-Sep, 02-Oct, 04-Oct, 06-Oct, 08-Oct, 10-Oct, 12-Oct, 14-Oct, 16-Oct, 18-Oct, 20-Oct, 22-Oct, 24-Oct, 26-Oct, 28-Oct

Source: Data Lateral Registration Data

Like January, Stoptober has now become an expected annual event in smokers' calendars with 80% now expecting Stoptober to happen every year (Figure 26).

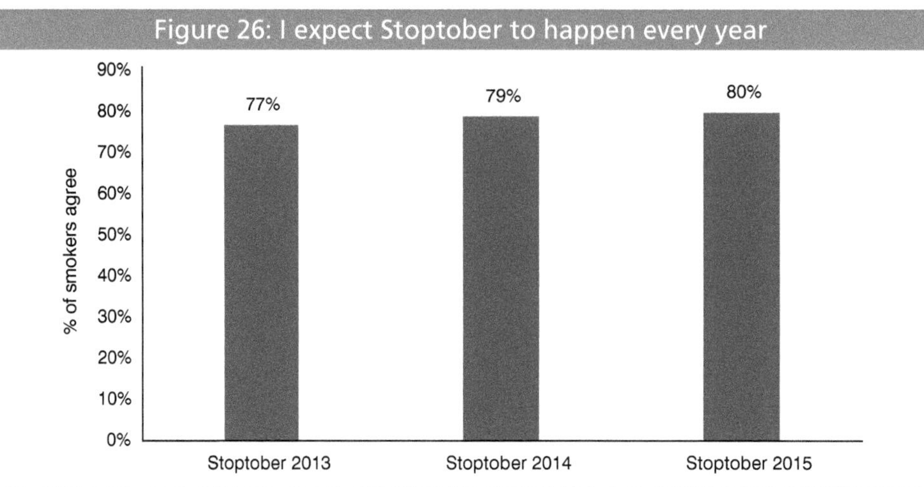

Source: TNS Tracking

Stoptober has started to establish October as a 'good time to quit' in the minds of smokers. Almost half now perceive October in this way (Figure 27).

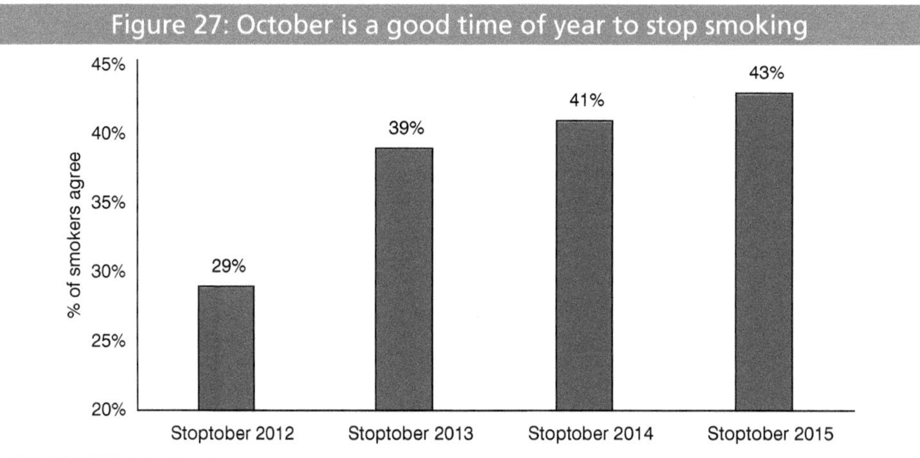

Source: TNS Tracking

Becoming an 'austerity-proof' solution

In the face of likely budget cuts, we needed a solution that would start to work independently of direct media support. Incredibly, this has been achieved.

Our agent-based model shows that since Stoptober has launched, it has directly driven 1.5m quit attempts, with over 65,000 more quit attempts generated in its last year compared with its first year – from a smaller population of smokers.

Evidence that Stoptober has, as intended, built to become a self-sustaining event can be found by looking at registrations to participate in Stoptober against the volume of smokers who claimed to take part. This shows a growing disparity, as more smokers take part in Stoptober without feeling the need to officially register (Figure 28).

Figure 28: Growing levels of smokers particpating in Stopober without registering

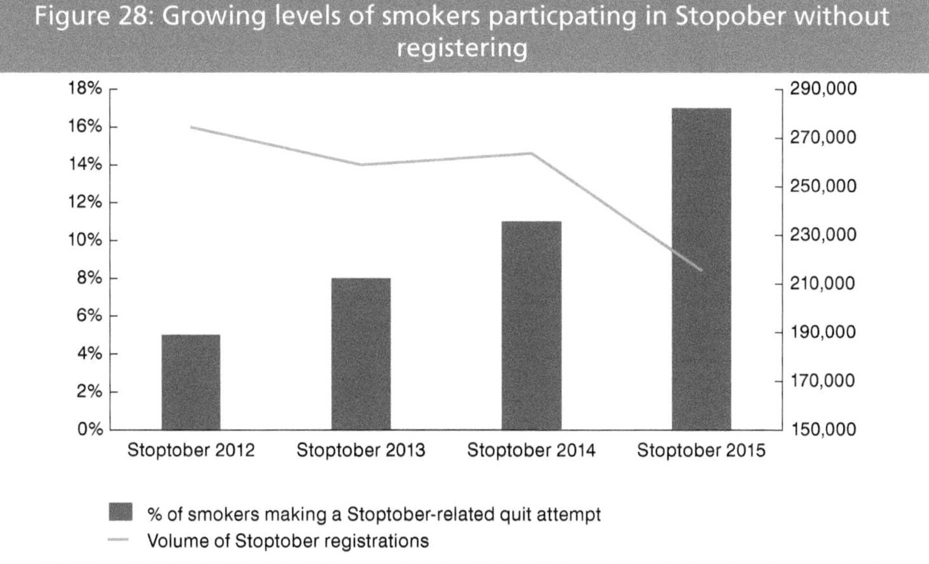

Source: TNS Tracking / Data Lateral Registration Volumes

Determining the financial payback of Stoptober

Stoptober's contribution to generating quit attempts and reducing smoking prevalence was calculated by comparing the results of the simulation with the Stoptober campaigns in place and without them, as shown in Figure 29.

Figure 29: Stoptober's contribution to generating quit attempts and reducing smoking prevalence

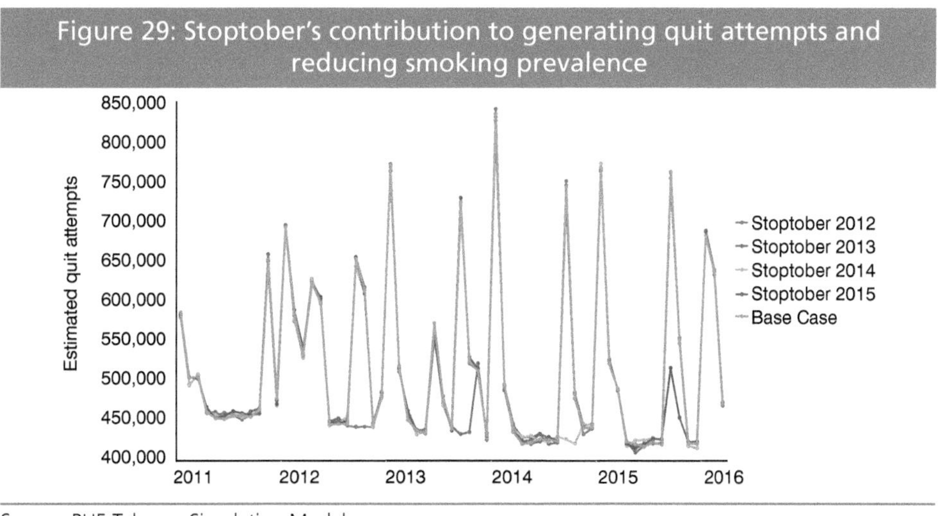

Source: PHE Tobacco Simulation Model

Our task is about lives, not return on investment. But the two are clearly linked.

In order to calculate the short term economic impact of Stoptober, we have used the official tobacco ROI tool endorsed by NICE.[13] The NICE tool allows us to determine, for a campaign with a given level of uptake and effectiveness (which we have derived from the model), the costs and benefits of a campaign, and provides us with the data we need to calculate a ROMI.

For simplicity, and due to the limitations of the tool in modelling variations in campaigns over several years, we calculated the impact of Stoptober using average values for quits generated and reductions in smoker numbers across the four years of the campaign from the Tobacco Simulation Model. (For the purposes of replicability, Stoptober was captured in the tool as a subnational tobacco control programme in an alternative package to the NICE-recommended standard package of interventions.)

In the short term (over two years), Stoptober generates over £16,000,000 in savings. With an average Stoptober campaign cost of £5,600,000 this gives us a ROMI of £2.85 for every £1 invested.

In the longer term, according to our peer-reviewed evaluation paper, the first Stoptober alone will save some 10,400 disability-adjusted life years (DALYs).[14] Scaling this number up based on quits per campaign, the four campaigns to date will save 43,409 DALYs.

Other contributors to the reduction in prevalence

In addition to the success of Stoptober and the 70,000 non-smokers it has contributed to the target, other factors proved to be successful too.

E-cigarette growth

E-cigarettes appeared in 2011 and according to analysis they contributed a reduction of over 20,000 smokers in 2014.[15] To achieve this they have spent £28 million on media since 2013 (not including digital, social or PR).[16] That's twice as much per annum as Stoptober, to convert people to a different kind of drug. In addition, when asked outright which method they believe will help them quit smoking for good, smokers have more faith in Stoptober than in e-cigarettes:

Figure 30: Percentage of smokers believing use will help quit attempt

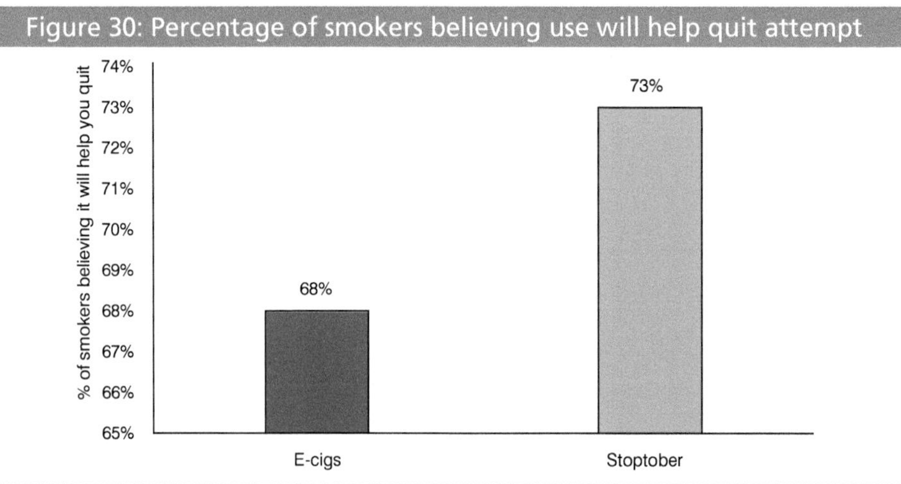

Source: TNS Tracking

The tobacco products display ban

This came into effect in 2012 (larger shops) and 2015 (smaller shops). Early analysis regarding the 2012 element shows that it has had some impact, a report in the *British Medical Journal* said that 'there was a significantly greater decrease in current smoking after the introduction of the tobacco POS display ban', but concluded that it is too soon to assess how the second wave of the ban will impact the market.[17]

However, we're still confident we can isolate the impact of Stoptober. The modelled Stoptober quit attempts show a clear seasonality focus on the period when Stoptober ran. It's highly unlikely that the display ban would drive additional quit attempts with this distinct seasonality.

In October 2015 a further ban came into place, this time for those in cars travelling with children under the age of 18. Given the timing, it is too soon for this measure to have had an impact on the results discussed in this paper.

The economy

Whilst austerity continues in the UK, it has little, if any impact on smoking. Quitters citing 'the cost of smoking' as a factor in their decision to quit have stayed fairly constant since pre-Stoptober.[18] In addition, the 2014 Feeding Britain Report[19] brings together a number of data sets that categorically evidence that poorer people are more likely to find the money for cigarettes.

Figure 31: Comments on Stopober in social media

It's tomorrow I am getting exited like it's Christmas eve 190.00 with my patches that I have bought taken off , feel like I have achieved something big

Like · Reply · 2 · October 27, 2015 at 5:19pm

I did Stoptober last year and am still smoke free. It's not easy but it can be done. Just think, this time next year you too could say, 'I'm a non-smoker'. Good luck everyone and do use and share this page, it really will help you.

Like · Reply · 8 · September 27, 2015 at 10:30am

Tomorrow I will be 365 days smoke free - all thanks to signing up with Stoptober in 2014.

Like · Reply · 20 · September 29, 2015 at 7:36pm

I have saved £120-00 so far this month, thanks to Stoptober, for all your encouragement, I will never smoke again.

Like · Reply · 3 · October 27, 2015 at 8:43pm

And I thank each and every one of you I have tried to quit smoking so many times and failed I don't think I'd have managed this time without the support of this page and all its members x

Like · Reply · 4 · October 27, 2015 at 12:58pm

In conclusion

When we launched Stoptober four years ago we knew we had to rewrite the rule book on what works in tobacco control marketing to have a chance of hitting the 18.5% prevalence target. We used this opportunity to not only help thousands of smokers quit for good, but to prove that, despite the success of previous campaigns, if we kept challenging what had gone before, we could always do more. Stoptober is about inspiring people to quit, being a positive force for good when people need it most. And to know we've done a good job, we just need to listen to some of the 70,000 people that are happier, and healthier as a result... We'll leave the last word to just a few of them (Figure 31).[20]

Notes

1. See Brown, J., Kotz, D., Michie, S., Stapleton, J., Walmsley, M., & West, R. (2014). How effective and cost-effective was the national mass media smoking cessation campaign 'Stoptober'? *Drug and Alcohol Dependence*, 135(1), 52–58. http://doi.org/10.1016/j.drugalcdep.2013.11.003
2. For the definitive study demonstrating these effects, see McVey, D., & Stapleton, J. (2000). Can anti-smoking television advertising affect smoking behaviour? Controlled trial of the Health Education Authority for England's anti-smoking TV campaign. *Tobacco Control*, 9(3), 273–282. http://doi.org/10.1136/tc.9.3.273
3. For a more detailed discussion of the benefits of agent-based modelling for understanding smoking behaviour in a public health context, see Robert Wallace, Amy Geller and V. Ayano Ogawa, *Assessing the Use of Agent-Based Models for Tobacco Regulation*, The National Academies Press, 2015.
4. In September 2015, Public Health England made their first statement about e-cigarettes which proposed that they were 90% less harmful than cigarettes.
5. West, R. – http://www.rjwest.co.uk/resources.php
6. TNS BMRB Topline Tobacco control summary
7. Kotz, D., & West, R. (2009). Explaining the social gradient in smoking cessation: it's not in the trying, but in the succeeding. *Tobacco Control*, 18(1), 43–46. http://doi.org/10.1136/tc.2008.025981
8. West, R – http://www.rjwest.co.uk/resources.php
9. Tobacco Control: a new approach to an old problem (2010); and Health Promotion Board Singapore: I QUIT – From anti-smoking to pro-quitting
10. UCL Smoking Toolkit Study
11. TNS BRMB Stoptober 2012 Campaign Evaluation
12. TNS BMRB smoking cessation national tracker 2011–2015
13. https://www.nice.org.uk/about/what-we-do/into-practice/return-on-investment-tools/tobacco-return-on-investment-tool
14. Ibid.
15. West, R. (2015) Estimating the population impact of e-cigarettes on smoking cessation and smoking prevalence in England. Retrieved from http://www.smokinginengland.info/downloadfile/?type=sts-documents&src=24
16. Nielsen Media Research
17. Kuipers, M. A. G., Beard, E., Hitchman, S. C., Brown, J., Stronks, K., Kunst, A. E., ... West, R. (2016). Impact on smoking of England's 2012 partial tobacco point of sale display ban: a repeated cross-sectional national study. *Tobacco Control*, http://doi.org/10.1136/tobaccocontrol-2015-052724
18. TNS BMRB smoking cessation national tracker 2011–2015. Concerns about health remains the number one reason for people making a quit attempt, with influence of family and friends and cost of smoking interchanging frequently as the second most common reason.
19. https://foodpovertyinquiry.files.wordpress.com/2014/12/food-poverty-feeding-britain-final.pdf
20. Taken from hundreds of such messages on the Stoptober Facebook support page

The Economist

Raising eyebrows and subscriptions

By Darren Burnett, Proximity London Ltd
Contributing authors: Nick Baker and Sarah Brown, Proximity London Ltd; Iain Noakes, *The Economist*; Neil Peace, UM London
Credited company: Promixity London Ltd; *The Economist*, UM London

Summary
The Economist's quality content is a given. But you still need crafted, provocative advertising to make people sit up and take notice. This case study demonstrates how the power of content and context can deliver long-term effects for a brand. By re-structuring teams and deploying the right data-driven infrastructure including 'newsrooms' to produce topical ad copy, *The Economist* used tailored, programmatic platforms to find more than five million previously unseen, retargetable users at a time when they were likely to be receptive to commercial messages. The activity created 64,000 paid subscriptions. Using the projected lifetime value of subscribers, this is estimated to equal a payback of £25 of revenue for every £1 invested.

Editor's Comment
This was the stand-out case of how to use digital to maximum effect – a combination of the right message to the right people in the right place, it allowed them to draw a straight line between the creative and the results.

Client Comment

Mark Cripps, EVP, Brand and Digital Marketing, The Economist

During this campaign, I've learnt to:

- **Be even braver.** We were making a radical shift away from a well-established, famous and successful campaign. This demanded confidence and collaboration across the team – and a commitment to following through.
- **Have faith.** We have always believed *The Economist*'s content was the hero, but now we were putting it front and centre. When 'progressives' read our content, they'd experience the quality of insight and analysis – and see its relevance to them.
- **Make the technology work hard.** We recognised the potential that programmatic advertising represented, but available tools blunted our ambition. So we built our own.
- **Use creative to unlock the power of the machine.** We tested machine-generated, dynamic creative – and it was consistently and significantly outperformed by crafted communications. But we needed a lot of executions. Creating the volume of work we needed wouldn't work with traditional processes.
- **Restructure**. We (and our partners) changed team structures and ways of working to accelerate turnaround at every stage, without compromising the final result.
- **Build strong relationships**. We, Proximity and UM worked as a single, virtual team. Shared objectives and trust are essential. And the same's true internally. We've built stronger relationships between marketing and editorial.

Perhaps a final learning we can all take is this: the rise of data – and of MathMen – doesn't mean the death of creativity. It can be the fuel that fires it.

It's easy to fix the damage wrought by a bad advertising campaign. But how do you handle the unintended consequences of a brilliant one?

The Economist's iconic poster work of the past two decades cemented its reputation as the house publication for the man that wants to get ahead. It was clever and flattered its readers' intelligence.

Unfortunately, it worked so well that people who saw themselves as outside this closed group felt distanced from the brand. A whole generation of people grew up thinking *The Economist* wasn't relevant to their lives. They had dismissed the title as 'a handbook for the corporate elite'.

Circulation started to plateau and digital conversion declined as the traditional prospect base became tapped.

We had to make a radical change. We had to persuade a new audience that *The Economist* was relevant to them and, specifically, get them to raise their hands and become prospects that we could target in the future. They had to see what our readers saw, experience what devoted readers term, the 'Economist Epiphany' – the story that connects and shows how *The Economist* can make you see an issue differently.

Our strategy came from an insight that underpins the publication itself – '*There is nothing more provocative than the truth*' – and we applied it to three tasks:

1. *Provoke the intellectually curious.* Surprise them with tailored, provocative headlines that showcase *The Economist*'s wit and intelligence.
2. *Demonstrate* The Economist*'s relevance.* Speak to them about the topics they've shown an interest in – when they're most interested.
3. *Give them their own 'Economist epiphany'.* Nudge them to read more, targeted content so that they experience their own 'epiphany' and subscribe.

The effect from this largely digital display campaign was incredible – and unanticipated.

We directly provoked *5.2m new people* into exploring *The Economist* content – a new addressable audience that is continuing to convert into subscribers.

We have grown the paid subscription base by *64,405* (looking only at the uplift on sales from digital channels in a period when ad spend was down, newsstand sales were down and pricing and promotions were static).

The campaign is already responsible for delivering *£51.7m in lifetime revenue* and a revenue *ROMI of over 25:1* from our year one spend of £2.03m.

This is only the beginning.

These subscribers are precisely the 'progressive' audience we were seeking – much younger than traditional subscribers. We also succeeded in addressing a historical gender imbalance, by bringing more women to *The Economist* through the campaign.

We've changed their perceptions, with more of them now seeing the newspaper as relevant and compelling.

And we've shown how even that most creatively derided channel – programmatic display – can deliver powerful, business-changing brand effects when you harness its full potential – the combined power of content, creativity and context.

The Full Story

Victims of our own success

For decades, *The Economist* promoted itself as the ticket to career success for white-collar warriors (Figure 1).

Figure 1: 'I never read The Economist'

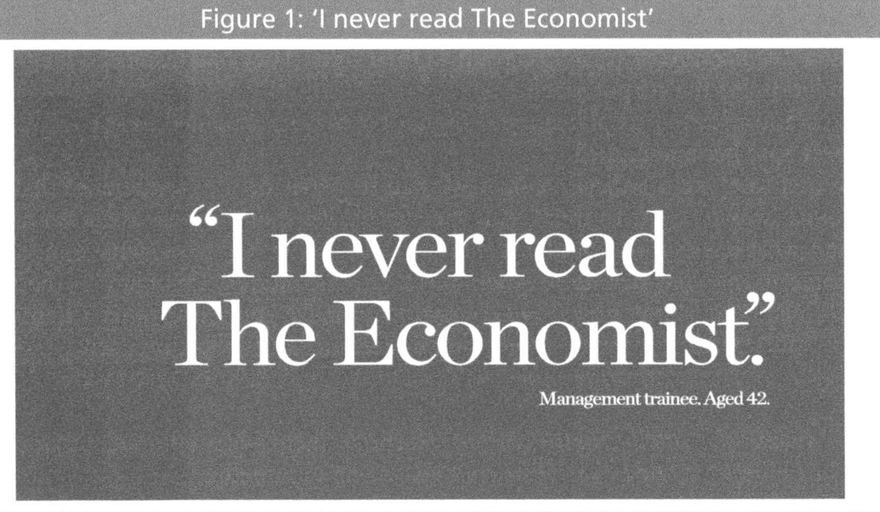

This approach fuelled successful growth and earned its status as a classic campaign. However, its very brilliance had unintended consequences. *The Economist* was often dismissed by people who weren't interested in reading a handbook for the corporate elite.

As the global prospect pool of aspiring businesspeople was exhausted, circulation started to plateau (Figure 2).

Figure 2: *The Economist* global circulation, print and digital

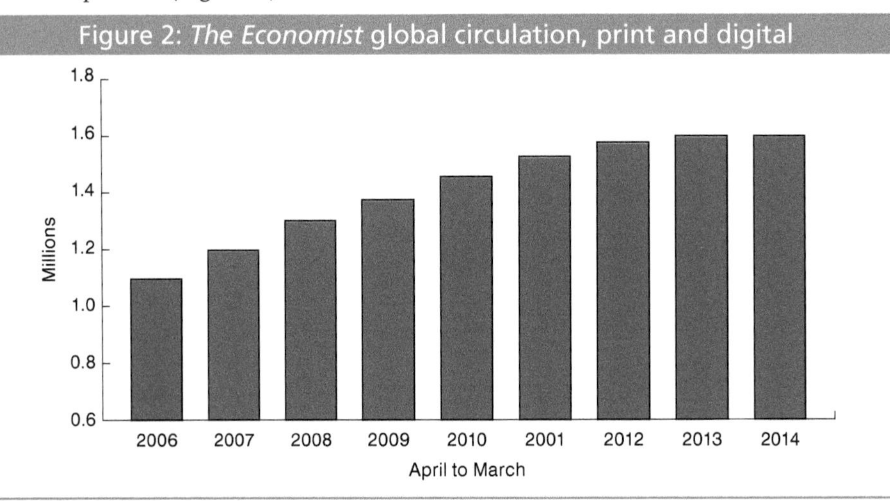

Source: Economist Group Annual Report 2015

Furthermore, research showed that, even in the UK, *The Economist* simply lacked relevance for many people (Figure 3).

Figure 3: Relevance of media outlets to people with a university degree (ranked on a 100 point scale)

Media outlet	Relevance
Facebook	93.5
YouTube	89.8
The Guardian	40.6
Twitter	32.3
Daily Telegraph	30.4
New Scientist	17.2
Sunday Times	14.3
The Independent	13.3
Financial Times	10.5
The Economist	9.5
Private Eye	5.5
The Wall Street Journal	0.2

Source: Young & Rubicam study 'Economist Brand Valuator 2014'

We needed to open up a brand-new audience by spurring a sudden re-evaluation of everything they thought they knew about us. We needed to persuade them to raise their hand and allow us to show them how *The Economist* was relevant to them so that we could turn these rejecters into readers – and ultimately, into subscribers.

But as we'd spent decades and millions of pounds unintentionally convincing them that *The Economist* wasn't for them, we'd have to do something radical to smash their preconceptions.

Our specific objectives were as follows.

Communication objectives

- *Prompt 650,000 previously unseen targets*[1] *to click, read content and join our prospect pool to re-target with future marketing activity (Primary Objective).*
- Shift perceptions of *The Economist* among a younger audience, particularly in terms of consideration, willingness to recommend and specific brand attributes (relevance, shareable content).

Marketing objectives

- Create a global pool of previously unseen prospects that we can re-target for future conversion.
- Shift subscriber profile – away from an older, very male profile – to create a platform for future growth.

Commercial objectives

- Deliver profitable subscription growth globally (target: 9,000 subscriptions).
- Help *The Economist* to return to circulation growth.

All for a global budget of £2m.
No small order.

The chasm – and the bridge

Non-readers often dismiss *The Economist* as a yawn-inducing tome of finance and business articles, as starkly revealed in non-readers' drawings of imagined subscribers (Figure 4).

Figure 4: Non-readers' drawings of imagined subscribers

Source: 2012 AMV prospect research

But once they actually read *The Economist*, non-readers realised that it is nothing like they expected.

Research showed just how far non-readers' perceptions diverged from the truth (Figure 5).

Figure 5: Readers' and non-readers' perceptions

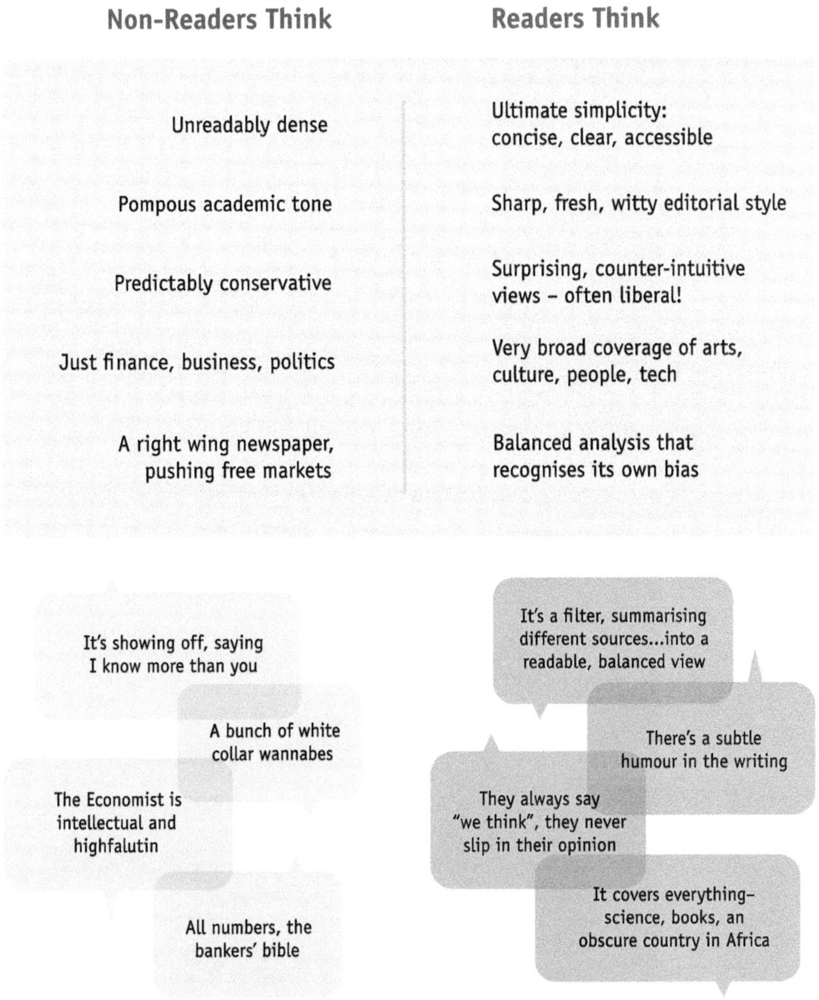

Non-Readers Think	Readers Think
Unreadably dense	Ultimate simplicity: concise, clear, accessible
Pompous academic tone	Sharp, fresh, witty editorial style
Predictably conservative	Surprising, counter-intuitive views – often liberal!
Just finance, business, politics	Very broad coverage of arts, culture, people, tech
A right wing newspaper, pushing free markets	Balanced analysis that recognises its own bias

It's showing off, saying I know more than you

A bunch of white collar wannabes

The Economist is intellectual and highfalutin

All numbers, the bankers' bible

It's a filter, summarising different sources...into a readable, balanced view

There's a subtle humour in the writing

They always say "we think", they never slip in their opinion

It covers everything– science, books, an obscure country in Africa

Research sources: 2014 focus groups by Acacia Avenue, 2013 reader research by Big Island, 2012 AMV prospect research

In fact, *Economist* readers believe there is no better source for efficiently gaining an informed, objective understanding of the issues that matter.

Converting the intellectually curious

Data from TGI shows that what unites *Economist* readers isn't just career ambition or an interest in finance; it is a broad interest in learning about global cultures and issues (Table 1).

Table 1: *The Economist* readers' interests

Statement	% *Economist* readers definitely agree	% General population definitely agree
I read the financial pages	31%	6%
I am interested in other cultures	41%	12%
I like different peoples, cultures, ideas and lifestyles around me	32%	11%
I am interested in international events	43%	14%
My work is a career, not just a job	33%	14%

Research told us there is an audience of millions who have 'a thirst to understand the important issues around the world'.[2] These people have a 'detached macro-economic view of current affairs' and seek insight 'almost entirely removed from political bias'.

We call them 'progressives', true global citizens seeking to objectively understand international issues.

And we wanted to show them that *The Economist* is their natural home.

Creating epiphanies on a mass scale

Devoted readers describe an 'Economist epiphany' when they realise that *The Economist* is peerless in reaching incisive conclusions through relentless logic. After that, everything else just feels too lightweight (Figure 6).

Figure 6: *The Economist* focus group comment

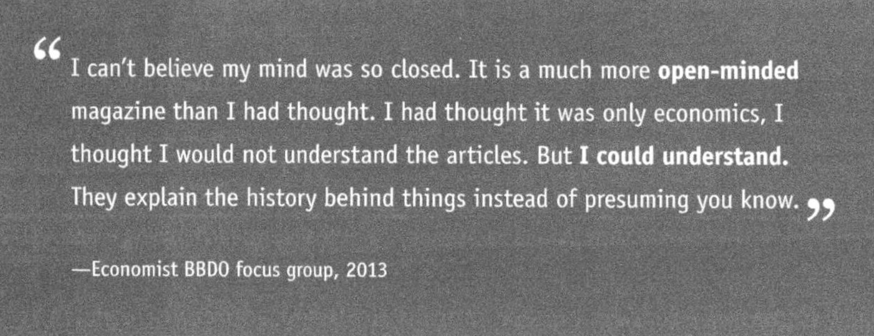

So how could we get people who were convinced we were of no interest to them to read even a single word?

Truth: the ultimate provocation

There is no better tool for arresting the attention of 'progressives' than the profound truths found in *The Economist*.

This gave us the root of our creative strategy (Figure 7).

Figure 7: *The Economist* creative strategy

There is nothing more provocative than the truth

We would provoke our audience – make them sit up and see how smart *The Economist* content was (rather than talk about how clever our readers are).

Luring our 'progressive' audience

We applied this to three tasks:

1. *Provoke the 'progressives'.* Use enticing questions and provocative insights to draw people in, uprooting misperceptions and demonstrating its accessibility, simplicity, humour, and the breadth of topics covered – stretching far beyond pure 'economics'.
2. *Demonstrate* The Economist*'s relevance.* Find 'progressives' where they're already exploring relevant topics – and directly link our incisive truths and articles to the stories they're currently reading.
3. *Give people their own 'Economist Epiphany'.* Having piqued their curiosity, let them find out more by reading the related article, then (knowing it usually takes four or five articles to consider subscription), nudge them to read more targeted content.

We used *The Economist's* own content to stop people in their tracks and make them want to find out more. We scoured recent editions for the most provocative insights, the most fresh and arresting views, which may run counter to common wisdom.

We spoke to issues of the moment and applied the powerful technique of speaking directly to the viewer. We addressed topics far outside business and finance and, of course, we showcased *The Economist*'s characteristic dry wit, tailored to this new audience.

The campaign idea

Our budgets were limited. We had a total budget of **£2.03m to spend on a global campaign** that had to provoke a resistant audience, demonstrate relevance and nudge people towards subscription.

We had to be very efficient in our media use – only digital display could provide the global reach we needed at this cost – but we would have to use it extremely effectively.

Unlocking the true power of programmatic display

We used the combined power of content, creativity and context to surprise people, change their minds and stimulate action.

We broke the campaign into two phases – an initial spike in Q4 2014 to deliver a first pool of prospects that we could re-target in the future, while translating initial learnings to inform lower level, always-on activity in phase two (see Figure 8).

Figure 8: Brand response media spend

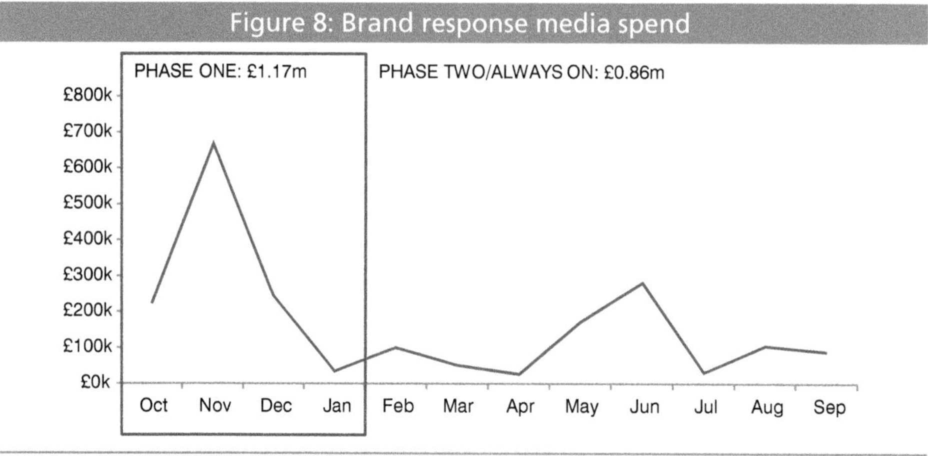

Source: Universal McCann

Delivering against our three tasks

1. Provoking our Progressive audience

Our provocative display advertising pulled readers directly through to the relevant article on our bespoke content hub. Here, we managed their journey and presented the content they would be most likely to want to read next.

Having experienced the elegance and insightfulness of *The Economist*'s content first-hand, we directed them to register for more and, ultimately, subscribe.

The classic 'why, try, buy'.

We built a live Newsroom with a direct line to editorial meetings. As soon as articles were approved for publication, we created ads on the spot to put *The Economist* at the centre of current debate.

This ad in response to *The Economist*'s coverage of the CIA's use of torture was produced and made live within hours of the Senate report's publication (Figure 10).

Figure 9: Examples of display advertising

Our contextually-placed ad linked to an article detailing an upcoming court decision that could allow employers to place pregnant workers in physically onerous jobs on unpaid leave

This ad led to an article exploring how back pain sufferers can copulate in comfort

Figure 10: Immediate display advertising

For increased cut-through, our innovative, speed-reading style '10 Second Summary' blipvert demonstrated *The Economist*'s unrivalled ability to condense complex issues into concise take-outs (Figure 11).

2. Demonstrating *The Economist*'s relevance

Tools available in the market simply couldn't offer the degree of targeting sophistication we needed, so we built our own 'dynamic contextualised content engine' (DyCCE) from the ground up – powering the dynamic adserver to target our 'progressives' in the most contextually relevant places.

We analysed web and app usage of *The Economist*'s most active subscribers, so we knew what content they preferred to consume and when. We matched cookie data to a variety of data sets to build seven robust segments reflecting the sections of *The Economist* (Free Trade Economics, Politics, Social Justice, Doing Good, Careers, Science & Tech, and Culture) and created look alikes. Finally, we repurposed contextual targeting technology to enable our adserver to scan the content of the page the user was currently reading, making the message even more on point.

Then, the really clever bit – matching the right content to the right people at the right time:

- *In-feed advertising:* Our audience is highly mobile and consume most media as a feed. We didn't want to interrupt the flow, so we placed content into feeds based on data points and context. Facebook and Twitter covered social; whilst ShareThrough and Outbrain delivered *Economist* content into a long tail of quality publications such as *Wall Street Journal* and CNN.
- *Dynamic advertising:* We mixed dynamic ads (display ads composed of *Economist* content and built in real-time) with dynamically-targeted prebuilt

Figure 11: The 10 second summary

The 10 Second Summary.

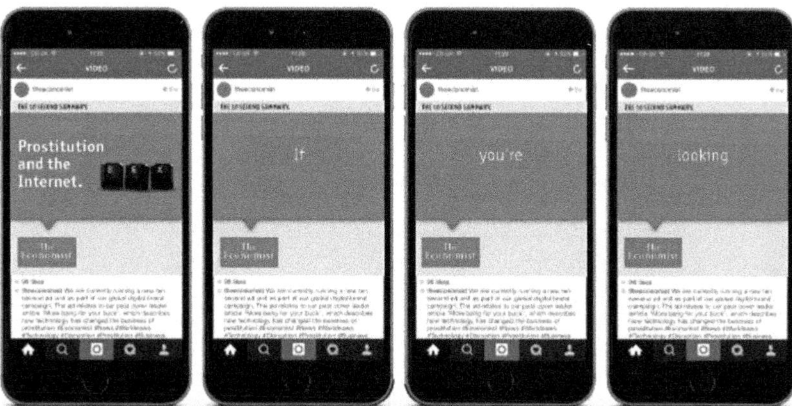

› for › commercial › sex › in › Berlin › a › new › app › called › Peppr › makes › life › easy. › Type › a › location › and › up › pops › the › nearest › prostitute › along › with › pictures › prices › and › physical › particulars. › Results › can › be › filtered › and › users › can › arrange › a › session › for › a › small › booking › fee. › The › Internet › has › disrupted › many › industries. › Sex ›

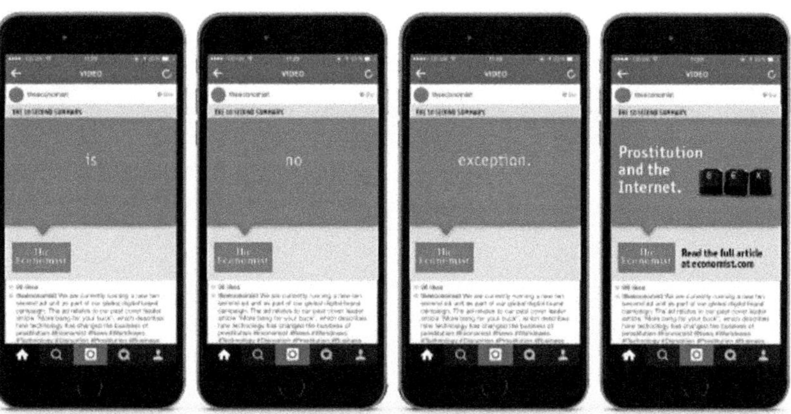

ads and matched them to page context and viewer profile. We used a feed from *The Economist* – containing thousands of articles, infographics and special reports – to build dynamic creative. And we crafted over 100 executions that could be deployed in the right context.

Figure 12: Matching content to the right people at the right time

3. Giving people their own 'Economist epiphany'

Our ads pulled readers directly through to our bespoke content hub.

Serving them the content likely to be of most interest, we nudged them to register and, ultimately, subscribe.

We developed an algorithm that delivered content in sequence, gradually learning which topics, in which order, generated the warmest prospects (Figure 12).

Figure 13: Matching content to prospects

Continually optimising

Built into our plan was continual optimisation – essential as we moved to 'always on' – through specific testing (balancing ads and content that provoked an initial read, but also created warmer prospects) and also through the learning algorithms within 'DyCCE'.

Each time we generated a quality prospect, we honed our audience definition and targeting even further, delivering ever-greater contextual relevance.

Results

Initial results – and an embarrassing mistake

Ok, hands up, that's the worst kind of humblebrag. But we did quickly realise we'd made a genuine mistake in predicting how successful this campaign would be.

The quality of *The Economist*'s writing *almost* sells itself. If you can just provoke people to read the relevant stories for themselves – not just once, but enough times for them to see the breadth of coverage, the surprising analytical insight, the complex made clearer. And that's exactly where we succeeded.

The first thing we could measure was the number of re-targetable leads generated (our primary measure of success).

There were smiles all round when we hit 50% of target – 650k new, re-targetable prospects – in just nine days.

At five weeks, when we'd hit double, we got really excited.

But corks started popping when we discovered that, from Phase One alone, we got over *2.7m* new people to take action immediately, sample *The Economist*, and become re-targetable contacts. An incredible result considering a global circulation of 1.6m.

We'd exceeded our primary target four times over – and would ultimately deliver *5.2m* new, re-targetable prospects.

Figure 14: Re-targetable unique visitors clicking on BR advertising

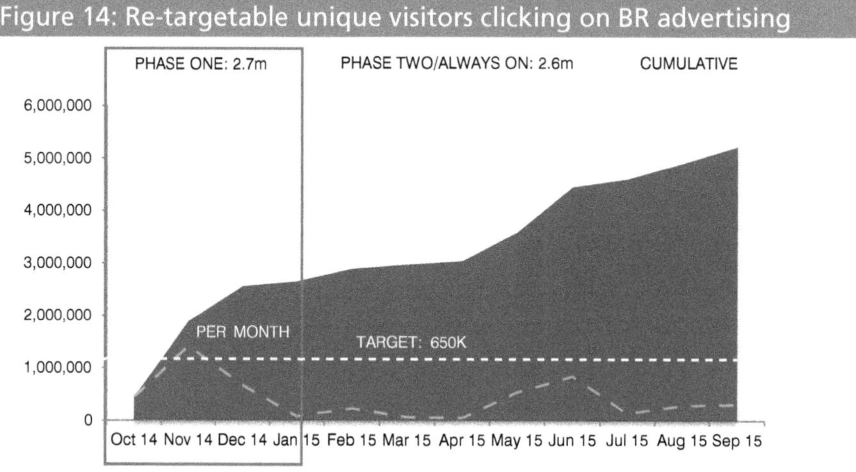

Source: *The Economist*; Adobe response tracking

But this was always about more than just immediate response...

A key comms objective was also to change how 'progressives' perceive *The Economist*. We needed to make them see it in a completely different light. And we did.

Campaign tracking run by UM,[3] comparing exposed audiences to carefully selected look-a-likes, shows that audiences exposed to our advertising have been made more likely to consider *The Economist*, to want to recommend it to others, recognise it as relevant to them and more pre-disposed to purchase.

In the UK, using 'very likely' and 'likely' as combined scores, *consideration rose by 32%* and *willingness to recommend rose by 24%* (Figure 15).

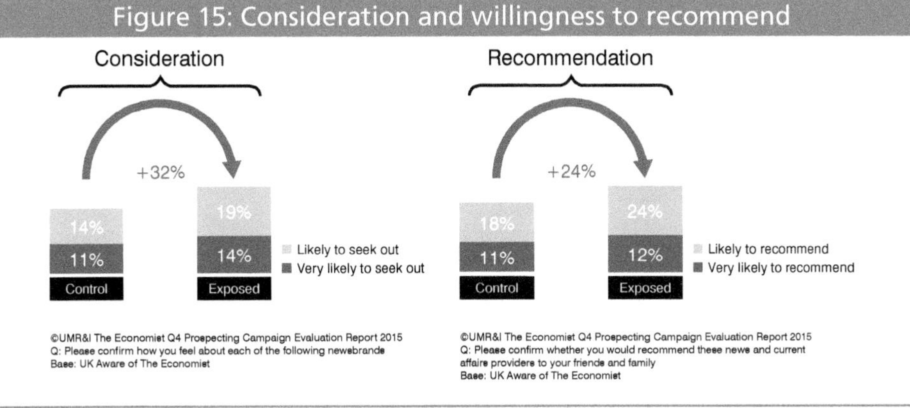

Figure 15: Consideration and willingness to recommend

We saw increases across a broad range of critical brand attributes, like 'trustworthy', 'expert', 'has content worth sharing', 'progressive' and 'relevant to you' (Figure 16). (Equally importantly, we saw declines in negative attributes, like 'academic' and 'not for you'.)

Figure 16: Which words would you associate with *The Economist*?

Expert, International, Trustworthy, Useful, Has content worth sharing, Best in class, Relevant to you, Progressive, Liberal minded, Provocative, Pioneering

0%, 5%, 10%, 15%, 20%, 25%, 30%, 35%, 40%, 45%, 50%

©UMR&I The Economist Q4 Prospecting Campaign Evaluation Report 2015
Q: Which of the words below would you associate with The Economist?
Base: Aware of The Economist

Exposed
Control

Source: *The Economist* Q4 Prospecting Campaign Evaluation Report 2015

In the US, where we faced awareness as well as perception issues, *awareness jumped 64%* (Figure 17).

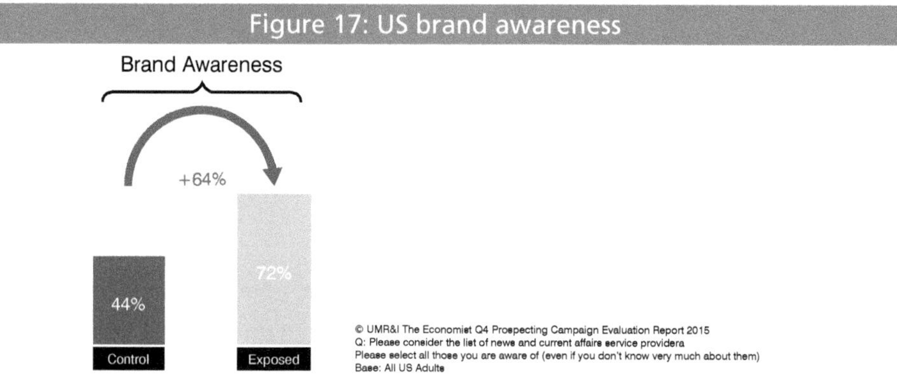

Figure 17: US brand awareness

Source: *The Economist* Q4 Prospecting Campaign Evaluation Report 2015

Consideration rose by 22% and *willingness to recommend rose 10%* – again, combining 'very likely' and 'likely' scores (Figure 18).

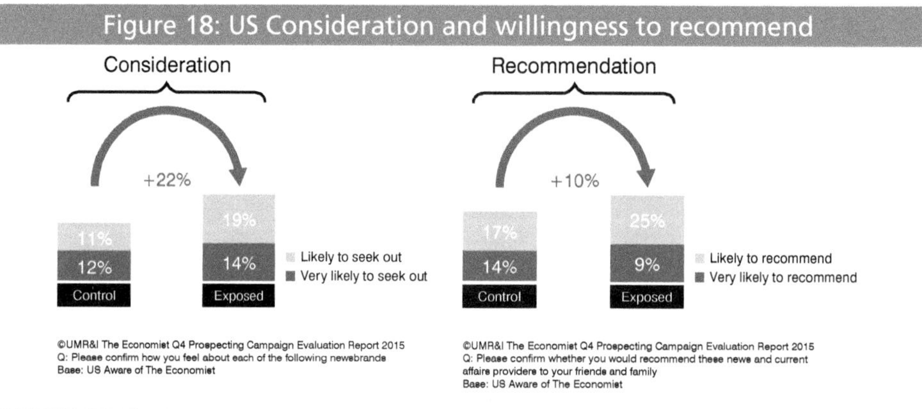

Figure 18: US Consideration and willingness to recommend

Source: *The Economist* Q4 Prospecting Campaign Evalution Report 2015

And *globally, we saw 'intention to pay' rise by 85%* amongst those that were likely to seek us out (Figure 19).

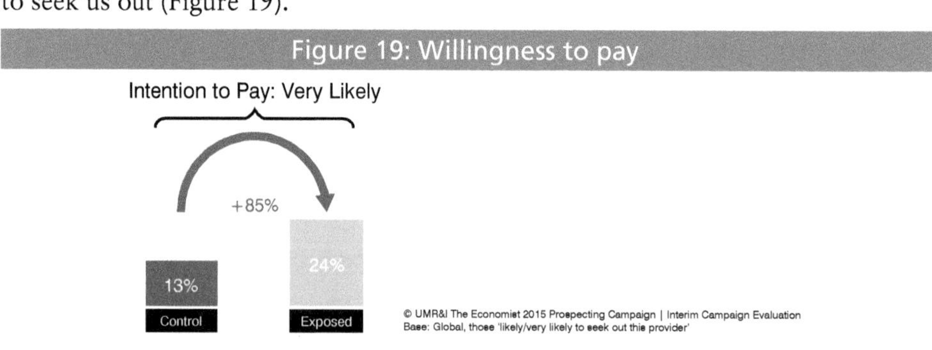

Figure 19: Willingness to pay

Source: *The Economist* Q4 Prospecting Campaign Evaluation Report 2015

After the shift in perceptions came the desire to read more... and more

Just tracking immediate clicks from an ad only tells part of the story, particularly when changing perceptions. We know that it usually takes four or five articles for people to experience their 'Economist epiphany'. That tends not to be one, intensive reading session – it takes an average of 6–8 weeks of reading before people are likely to subscribe.

In measuring the impact of our campaign, we isolated our analysis to the sources of business it directly affects – for example, digital subscriptions prompted through search or a direct visit to economist.com.

This means we excluded 88% of all paid subscriptions from our analysis – all offline acquisitions; even other, 'noisier', digital acquisition channels that could have influenced results, such as social media not explicitly linked to one of our ads.

The red layer in Figure 20 shows the 12% of subscriptions we included in our analysis.

Figure 20: Paid subscripton starts, by source of business

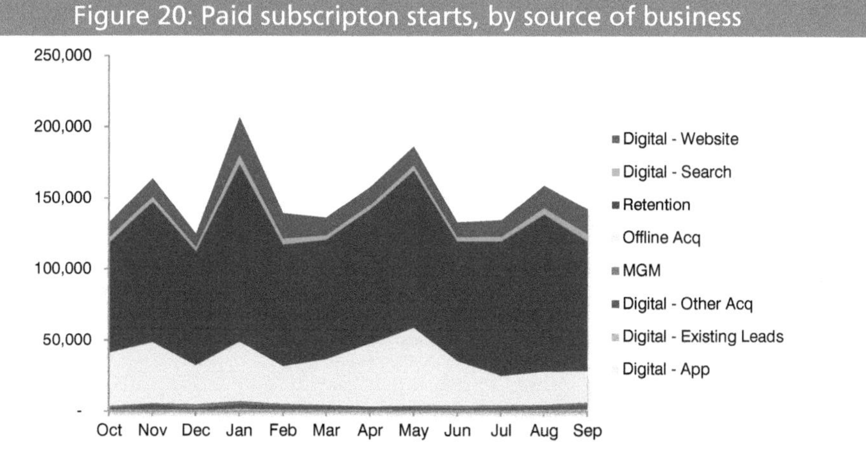

Source: *The Economist*; Adobe response tracking. 'Digital –search' include paid search only; natural search is accounted with 'Digital – website'

Our analysis shows that this campaign provoked *an extra 60,183 people* to take paid subscriptions through these channels during the campaign period (vs. original target of 9,000). That's *an uplift of 38%,* year on year (Figure 21).

Figure 21: Uplift on paid subs

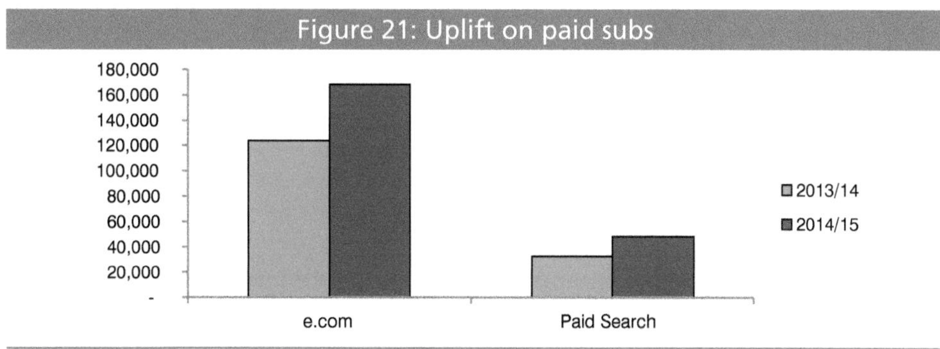

Source: *The Economist*; Adobe response tracking

We found our new audience

A key marketing objective was to change our subscriber profile – recruiting Progressives, irrespective of age and gender. Building for the future as well as delivering for today.

The Economist traditionally skews heavily male and older, so we wanted more female, younger subscribers. In profiling subscribers we acquired against the legacy base, we saw we succeeded in addressing the imbalance (Table 2).

Table 2: Subscriber profiles

Age	New Acq	01–Oct–14	Index
16–20	2.9%	0.4%	837
21–29	33.0%	7.3%	455
30–39	28.4%	18.5%	153
40–49	14.7%	21.3%	69
50–64	13.8%	28.4%	49
65 & Older	7.2%	24.2%	30
Gender	**New Acq**	**01–Oct–14**	**Index**
Male	65.3%	76.1%	86
Female	34.7%	23.9%	145

We successfully delivered younger subscribers – *64% were under 40 (vs. just 26% of existing base).*

And while we still have work to do in recruiting women to the brand, we did improve the gender balance, recruiting 35% female subscribers (vs. 24% of existing base – a 45% improvement).

A good start – and we're seeing optimisation of advertising creative and targeting improve it further.

Continually learning, continually getting better

Our focus on constant optimisation – through structured testing and the learning algorithms within DyCCE – paid (and continues to pay) dividends, as Figure 21 shows.

We almost *halved the cost of acquiring* prospects after Phase 1.

We've learned what content is most likely to recruit a quality lead, so prospects now read more (page views up over 20%) and are *more likely to subscribe immediately* (conversion up 25%).

The bottom line[4]

This campaign is responsible for delivering an estimated **£51.7m in lifetime revenue so far**, equating to a revenue *ROMI of 25:1.*

Let's break that down a bit...

Figure 22: Improvements post phase 1

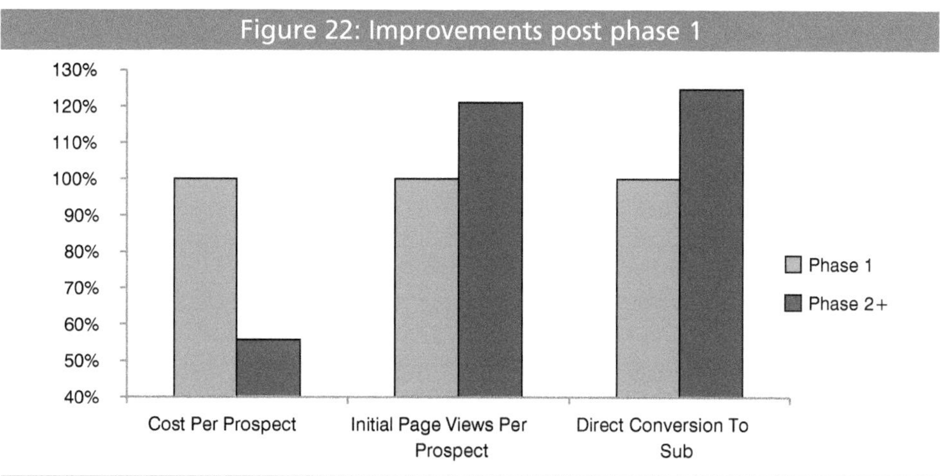

Source: UM BR Adspend; *The Economist*; Adobe response tracking

Subscriber revenue

Reflecting *The Economist* retention rates, we use a 10-year LTV for newly acquired subscribers of **£795.87.**

So the *64,405* acquired subscribers are estimated to deliver **£51,258,007** in LTV subscription revenue over 10 years (excluding price increases).

Additional revenue from advertising

Each visitor to the website also generates revenue for *The Economist* through advertising sales. The additional traffic provoked by *our campaign delivered £450,620 in incremental ad revenues.*[5]

Total revenue: £51,708,627.[6]

Costs

The campaign media cost was **£2,034,179** during the campaign period.[7]

Return on marketing investment of 25:1 (revenue)[8]

Figure 23: Campaign cost vs. revenue

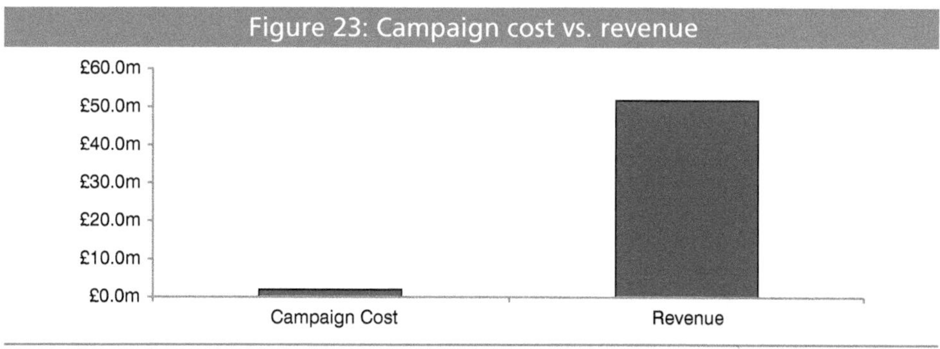

Proving it was this campaign

We have ensured that we isolated the impact of this campaign through a number of actions.

1. *We only analysed subscriptions from channels most likely to be influenced by our activity:* As explained earlier, we excluded from our analysis 88% of all paid subscriptions, e.g. all offline acquisition and even other, 'noisier', digital acquisition channels that we're likely to affect, such as social media.
2. *We can see it wasn't due to other marketing activity:* Other marketing spend only increased by 1%. This uplift came from an increased spend in local experiential marketing. Resulting subscriptions from this activity are tracked separately and are excluded from this analysis (Figure 24).
3. *We confirmed that pricing and promotions were identical in 2013/14 and 2014/15:* £184 for a full annual subscription, leading with a '12 weeks for £12' (or local equivalent) acquisition incentive.
4. *We checked it wasn't due to a surge in demand because of more newsworthy stories:* If it were, we would see some a correlation in increased news-stand sales, but these were down 7% across the year (which is consistent with trends in previous years) (Figure 25).
5. *We confirmed it wasn't due to PR stories that occurred during the campaign:* Two significant stories hit the press about *The Economist* in the period we're measuring. At the end of January 2015, Zanny Minton Beddoes became the first female editor of the newspaper, and in August 2015, *The Economist* announced it would become fully independent following its sale from the Pearson group.

Figure 24: Other marketing spend

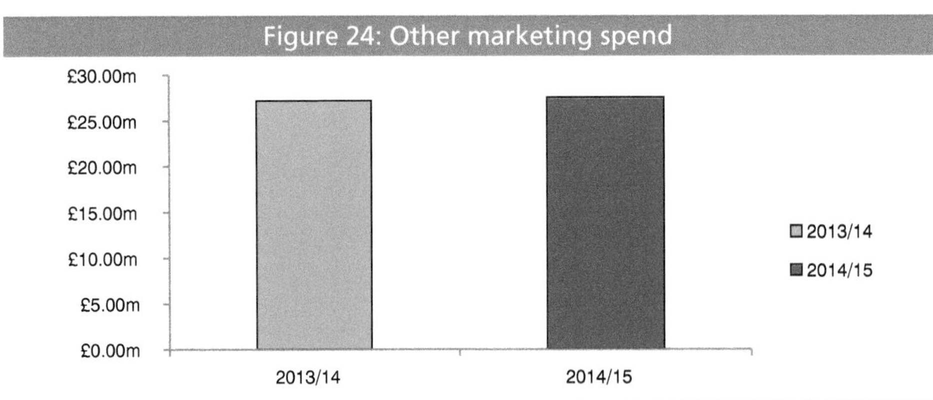

Source: *The Economist* Circulation Finance. Includes all other marketing spend excluding trade/retail

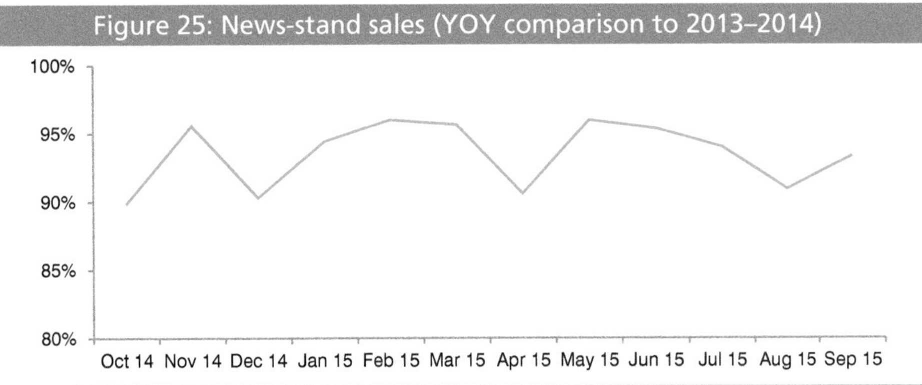

Figure 25: News-stand sales (YOY comparison to 2013–2014)

Source: *The Economist*; QlikView/QSS

These were both significant stories and will be expected to deliver business benefit over the long term. However, when we look at sales uplifts year-on-year, they do not correlate with these news stories (Figure 26).

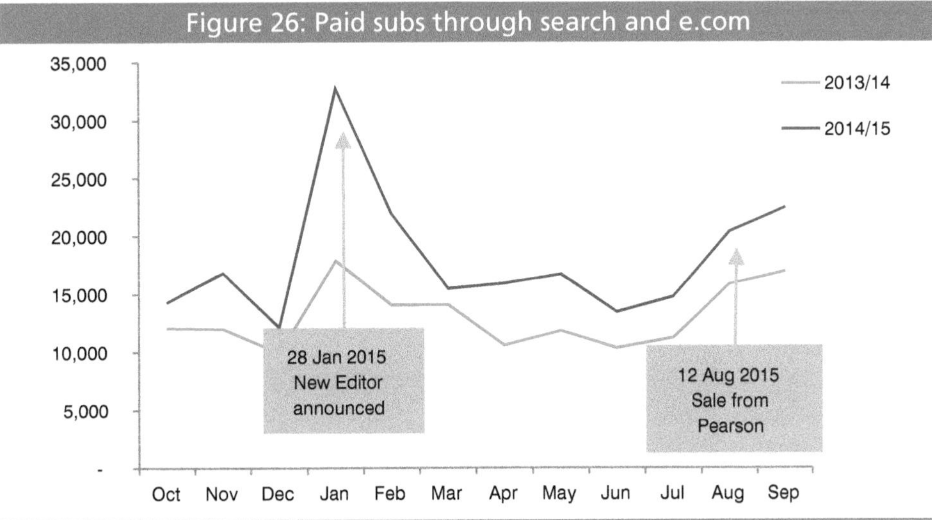

Figure 26: Paid subs through search and e.com

Source: *The Economist*; Adobe response tracking

The spike in January hits well before the editorial appointment announcement, and the uplift actually drops from 83% to 56% from January to February (when the impact would be felt). Similarly, in August, following the sale, year-on-year uplift was 29% (slightly down from July's 32%).

This is not to suggest these important moves will have no impact on digital subscriptions, but that this will be a gradual effect as benefits for readers become apparent.

The increases do, however, correlate with the average two-month window that we see between initial exposure and sign-up from prospects not immediately clicking through to subscribe.

Conclusion

The Economist is an iconic brand that had become a victim of its own success. We needed to open the minds of millions of non-readers who had come to believe that the publication had little relevance to them.

We used *The Economist*'s most powerful tool, its brilliant content, to win the attention and change the minds of intellectually curious people – 'progressives'.

Recognising in our core strategic thought that, 'There is nothing more provocative than the truth', we created a campaign that spiked the audience's intellectual curiosity to draw them in while demonstrating the wit, incisiveness, and accessibility of *The Economist* content.

We targeted people who were reading about specific topics with intriguing insight and compelling content closely related to that very topic.

We proved that *The Economist* is just as relevant to new readers as it is to our traditional audience and we opened up a whole new audience to build on *The Economist*'s past success.

We exceeded our communication objectives:

- Prompted 5.2m previously unseen people to find out more and become re-targetable (vs. our target of 650k) – our primary objective
- Dramatically shifted brand perceptions – awareness went up in low awareness markets, consideration and willingness to recommend went up and we saw significant improvements against critical brand attributes.

We exceeded our marketing objectives:

- Created a 5.2m strong global pool of previously unseen, re-targetable prospects for future conversion
- Delivered younger, more gender-balanced subscribers.

We exceeded our commercial objectives:

- Created 64,405 new, paid subscribers within the first year of the campaign (vs. 9,000)
- We delivered £51.7m revenue from £2.03m spend – a revenue ROMI of 25:1.

And we helped *The Economist*'s plateauing circulation to rise again in 2015 (Figure 27).

All through the perfect marriage of smart, programmatic targeting, provocative first-touch creative and content that keeps surprising you.

Raising eyebrows and raising subscriptions.

Figure 27: *The Economist* global circulation, print and digital

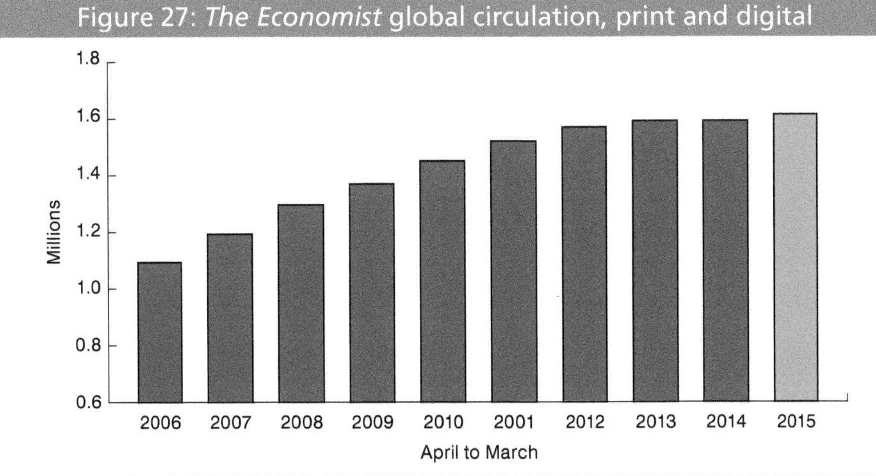

Source: Economist Group Annual Report 2015

Notes

1. i.e. Not previously visited economist.com.
2. Source: 2013 Big Island research.
3. Source: UMR&I *The Economist* Q4 Prospecting Campaign Evaluation Report 2015.
4. Note: due to the sensitive nature of margin information, profit generated and profit ROMI are not included.
5. Source: *The Economist* advertising sales team. Details of calculation withheld due to commercial sensitivity.
6. £51,258,007 subs revenue + £450,620 ad revenue.
7. Source: Universal McCann.
8. £51.7m revenue from £2.03m spend.

SECTION 3

Silver winners

The Simon Broadbent Prize for Best Dedication to Effectiveness (Unilever)
Best Commercial Effectiveness for Good (President's Prize)

Dove

Beautifully effective: how Dove turned cultural resonance into ROI

By Marie Maurer, Ogilvy & Mather
Contributing authors: Dove Team, Unilever; Jakob Kofoed, Data2Decisions; Sam Pierce, Ogilvy & Mather
Credited companies: Ogilvy; Data2Decisions; Edelman; Havas; Mavens; Millward Brown; Mindshare; Nielsen; PHD

Summary

This case study shows how the Unilever brand, Dove, articulated a strong point of view that beauty should be a source of confidence and not anxiety for women. It argues that Dove's marketing of this viewpoint and its product communications generated sales, with the combination yielding further rewards. Encompassing the ads, 'Sketches', 'Patches' and 'Choose beautiful', this paper provides evidence that having a social purpose can pay back for a brand in both the long and short term. Econometrics shows the combined ROI of 'Sketches' and 'Patches' was US $4.42 for every US $1 invested, and that a masterbrand approach has had a multiplier benefit across Dove advertising.

Client comment

Steve Miles, Global SVP, Dove

Dove's purpose is at the heart of how we market Dove. We know it works – and we know it's the right thing to do. Our experience of a new communications approach since 2013 has confirmed several other points.

First, Dove's cultural point of view communication leads directly to sales – short term, not just long term.

Second, Dove's category communications also drive sales (something we've always known).

Third, the combination of these two sells even more. This gives even more fuel and confidence to our belief in Dove, and all across Unilever – by no means a generally accepted one in the marketing and financial communities – that brands with purpose are not just socially beneficial, but are the pathway to superior growth.

To read the full case study visit www.ipa.co.uk/ease or www.warc.com

John Lewis Insurance

The power of true brand extension marketing

By Tom Sussman, adam&eveDDB
Contributing authors: Les Binet, adam&eveDDB; Ric Roberts, Manning Gottlieb OMD
Credited companies: adam&eveDDB; Manning Gottlieb OMD

Summary

This paper outlines an approach for organisations that want to extend existing brand equities into new categories. It sets out how the retailer John Lewis partnered with the insurer, RSA, to create a new, John Lewis-branded range of insurance products to cut through with consumers in a category where the existing providers were often fighting to win business mainly by offering the cheapest quotes. The strategy used advertising, including the celebrated 'Tiny dancer' TV spot, and a drip-feed media policy that focused on premium placements and regional upweighting. John Lewis Insurance earned £1.17 in insurance commissions for every £1 spent on advertising, and generated an estimated £16.7m of incremental sales for its retailer parent.

Client comment

Margaret Burke, Head of Marketing, John Lewis Financial Services

The main thing that I believe we've learnt from this journey is that there is a massive opportunity to think very differently about how to market insurance – bringing the John Lewis principles of service, quality, love and trust to life.

We deliberately chose not to follow the sector norms, i.e. to focus on a specific product feature or talk about the discounts you can get for switching, and we do not perpetuate the portrayal of fearful moments – which we know from qualitative research only lead to consumers labelling an insurance purchase as a 'necessary evil'.

Life is full of unplanned, accidental mishaps and insurance is there to help smooth the path – which is very much an extension of the John Lewis way of thinking. Far from being a 'necessary evil', it actually allows you to just get on with your life free from worrying about what might be round the corner.

That's hugely liberating and ultimately a positive thing. The fact that our latest campaign generated such a high level of engagement has meant that the change we're making is to be even braver in how we think about bringing a John Lewis-inspired positivity to a sector which is currently playing on the 'fear factor'. Insurance does not need to be a grudge purchase; it can and should be something you feel good about having.

John Lewis Insurance

To read the full case study visit www.ipa.co.uk/ease or www.warc.com

Lidl

How Lidl found itself atop the grocers' Christmas tree

By John Lowery, TBWA\London
Contributing author: Louise Cook, Holmes and Cook
Credited companies: TBWA\London; Hall & Partners; M2M Media; Starcom MediaVest

Summary

This is the story of how investment in brand advertising helped propel Lidl into the position of being Britain's fastest-growing grocer. The 'Lidl Surprises' campaign challenged the idea that the chain's keenly-priced food must be of poor quality. Using varied contexts from farmers' markets to taste tests and groups sitting down to Christmas lunch, the advertising showed Lidl products being favourably received by consumers. This case study demonstrates the contribution of advertising to increasing Lidl's penetration and share of till roll. Econometrics calculated the campaign generated a net profit return of £1.97 for every £1 invested by the end of 2015, which was estimated to rise to £5.20 over 2016.

Client comment

Ronny Gottschlich, former Managing Director, Lidl UK

We continue to set ourselves challenging targets and to meet customers' growing appetite for our best quality for the best price. We've now been Britain's fastest growing supermarket for the longest period in our history and advertising has helped to propel us there.

Claire Farrant, Marketing Director, Lidl UK

We had total faith in advertising's ability to unlock the Lidl brand's potential in the UK. An engaging, disruptive creative platform, harnessing the advocacy of real people, has delivered brand reappraisal, sales growth, and astounding levels of customer engagement. It's a campaign that is still paying back to the business and providing a platform for future brand growth.

Lidl

To read the full case study visit www.ipa.co.uk/ease or www.warc.com

SILVER

L'Oréal Paris Age Perfect

How L'Oréal Paris *Age Perfect* transformed its fortunes by showing older women that they are still 'worth it'

By Emily Ellis, McCann London; Vasileios Kourakis, L'Oréal UK
Contributing author: David Frymann, McCann London
Credited companies: McCann London; Maxus

Summary

In 2015 L'Oréal Paris Age Perfect anti-ageing moisturiser had big ambitions. However, sales of Age Perfect skincare were down 14% – worse than the market's decline. Furthermore, there were no exciting product developments on the horizon and many UK women felt little affinity with the brand. This case details how a powerful insight (women aged 55+ felt invisible) unlocked an idea to celebrate 'bold, not old' women. From Age Perfect, 'The Perfect Age' campaign with Helen Mirren was born. The communications won back value share, brought in 78,000 new buyers, and changed brand perceptions. It was estimated that the activity generated a revenue ROI of £2 per £1 invested, rising to £4.50 over the longer-term.

Client comment

Adrien Koskas, General Manager L'Oréal Paris

The 'Helen Mirren' campaign was an important milestone that helped us revaluate the way that we work

This success of a consumer insight led approach has given us an additional frame of reference going forward – changing the lens from starting with a product portfolio (e.g. skincare) to looking at our audience portfolios. So having cracked the platform for our 'Perfect Agers', next up is Gen X and Millennials.

This campaign has also helped us see the importance of working with a role model, rather than just a spokesmodel. Whilst this may seem obvious, the fact that Helen Mirren has both style and substance means we can leverage what she has to say rather than just how she looks, making her both aspirational and relatable to our UK audience.

L'Oréal Paris Age Perfect

To read the full case study visit www.ipa.co.uk/ease or www.warc.com

Pepsi Max

Unbelievable

By Tim Whirledge, AMV BBDO
Contributing author: Hannah Stockton, OMD
Credited companies: AMV BBDO; Freuds; OMD

Summary

Brands as old as Pepsi in flat or declining markets rarely experience a growth surge that outperforms their category. This is the story of how a switch to a content-led digital strategy, that focused on the no-sugar variant, Pepsi Max, re-engaged a millennial audience. Starting with a film which featured the magician, Dynamo, to position Pepsi as a brand that made 'anything possible', the approach invested in using film clips, a YouTube channel and outdoor sites to bring surprising and entertaining content to audiences, including gymnastic stunts and simulated invasions of city streets by aliens and giant insects. The approach generated an additional £54m in revenue and a marketing ROI of £2.25 for every £1 spent.

Client comment

Alex Nicholas, Senior Brand Manager, Pepsi UK

Our marketing function re-engineered itself to deliver an idea that could truly resonate with its audience. We went from a traditional marketing model using globally created assets and above the line media, to adopting a digital first marketing approach and becoming a YouTube publisher brand at scale.

Pepsi Max

To read the full case study visit www.ipa.co.uk/ease or www.warc.com

Plusnet

The pride of Yorkshire: how Plusnet's adverts transformed its fortunes against ever-increasing odds

By Emma Lodge, Maxus; Matt Sadler, Karmarama; Alex Steer, Maxus
Contributing authors: Chris Cotterill, Plusnet; Georgia Protopapa, Maxus
Credited company: Karmarama

Summary

This paper charts five years in the life of Plusnet, the Yorkshire-based broadband provider – from its first national advertising in 2010 to its most integrated and innovative campaign in 2015. As a small provider battling some of Britain's biggest advertisers, Plusnet could not compete on price or technical innovation, but succeeded by articulating its Yorkshire values, creating impactful advertising, and rigorously adjusting its communications mix.

Plusnet's customer growth was triple the market average and, according to WPP's BrandZ brand database, the contribution of Plusnet's brand equity to its annual volume share rose from 58% in 2011 to 69% in 2015. It is estimated that advertising delivered £193m of incremental revenue, equivalent to £4.05 of revenue for every £1 spent.

Client comment

Chris Cotterill, Senior Acquisition & Brand Marketing Manager, Plusnet

Plusnet's advertising history is a topic that's really close to my heart, as I've been part of the Plusnet marketing team for eight years now, in two stints. First, for three years before this campaign broke (2006–2009) and then for five years afterwards (2011–now).

And, as someone who's been there across the journey, I can truly say that this campaign has had a transformational effect on Plusnet's brand and business.

When I first joined Plusnet, our marketing was limited to local activity. Creative was purely tactical, media was bought on an instinctive vs strategic basis and we had no way of measuring the effectiveness of our spend. Since we started working with Karmarama and Maxus, all this has changed.

Together, we've launched Plusnet on a national stage and developed a powerful communications vehicle, a highly optimised media approach and a rigorous degree of evaluation across everything we do. We are as committed as ever to short-term sales, but now also focus on building the brand for the long term.

And, whilst consistency has helped us punch above our weight, we have also developed the confidence to keep innovating, with new media and new messages, knowing that we have the systems in place to test, learn and demonstrate effectiveness.

Over the last five years, we've forged all this together, through building client-agency teams that are as straight talking, warmhearted and ambitious as our advertising. As such, I'm proud of the way we've transformed Plusnet together, proud of the way we've faced our challenges together and proud to share this story with you.

Plusnet

To read the full case study visit www.ipa.co.uk/ease or www.warc.com

Sainsbury's

Christmas is for sharing

By Craig Mawdsley, Lisa Stoney and Cat Wiles, AMV BBDO

Contributing authors: Alice Beauchamp, HPI Research; Laura Boothby, Sainsbury's; Sophie Caron, AMV BBDO; Ruth Cranston, Sainsbury's; Liam Doyle, PHD Media; Michael Florence, PHD Media; Simon French, Sainsbury's; Mark Given, Sainsbury's; Anna Hancock, PHD Media; Chris Magniac, PHD Media; Sarah Mamou, Analog Folk; Jack Miles, HPI Research

Credited companies: AMV BBDO; Annalect; Harper Collins; Golin; The Royal British Legion

Summary

This case study focuses on the fame-generating 'Christmas is for sharing' campaigns run by Sainsbury's in 2014 and 2015 during tough market conditions. These include the emotive 'Christmas truce' film which marked a World War I anniversary in partnership with the Royal British Legion, and the follow-up, 'Mog's Christmas calamity', which promoted child literacy with Save the Children. It provides evidence that both iterations achieved high, positive brand scores, prompting consumers to share content and buy specific products, which raised money for charity partners. In successive years, Sainsbury's outperformed its big four rivals in value and volume share. The 2014 campaign was estimated to have generated a profit ROI of £24.34 for every £1 invested, and the 2015 activity to have paid back at least as much again.

Client comment

Mark Given, Director of Marketing Communications, Sainsbury's

The journey we've been on has revolutionised the way we, as a business, approach Christmas communications.

These results have proven that taking a longer-term view yields not only a significantly stronger ROI but has also given us a point of view at the most important time of year in the retail calendar.

It would have been relatively easy to keep everything ticking over, doing the same as we always had and, in truth, we would probably have yielded acceptable results. But none of us ever felt that 'just ok' was not good enough, and it certainly would not have set us up to weather the turbulent market conditions.

Looking back, our decision was a brave and bold one – though to us at the time (because we knew we were doing it for the right reasons) it never felt like that. Pursuing a 'fame' strategy was the only strategy that we truly believed in. Though we could never have anticipated the extent to which a 'fame' strategy would deliver greater efficiencies and year-on-year increases in ROI.

The 'Christmas is for sharing' platform has been so successful because it is anchored in a fundamental truth about the season. It is a platform that is strident, bold and welcoming – it is not an idea that is self-conscious, complicated or overly intellectual. It's the sheer simplicity of the platform that is its strength – the power of this simplicity reminds me that sometimes the best strategies can be those that are sitting right in front of you.

Sainsbury's

To read the full case study visit www.ipa.co.uk/ease or www.warc.com

SILVER

Sensodyne

Solving problems, not selling benefits

By Catherine McPherson, Grey London
Contributing authors: Brooke Elmlinger and Matt Gladstone, Grey London
Credited companies: Grey London; Ipsos; Millward Brown; PHD

Summary

This case study describes a 10-year strategy from Sensodyne toothpaste to raise 'condition awareness' of sensitive teeth by replicating the experience of learning about the problem from a dentist or trusted friend. The case details several phases of the strategy, which has spread from Ireland and the UK to other markets, and been adapted for new variants such as Sensodyne Pronamel, which treats dental erosion from acidic food and drink. This paper cites general increased consumer awareness of dental sensitivity and of Sensodyne's particular messages about the condition, resulting in a long-term rise in the brand's penetration and value share, with growth outperforming Colgate's rival sensitivity toothpaste which sold at a lower price. The long-term profit ROMI was estimated at £1.38 for every £1 invested.

Client comment

Gareth Rudduck, Global Marketing Director, Sensodyne

Anywhere in the world that Sensodyne is advertised, the 'Condition awareness' model is at the heart of our advertising.

Before the campaign launched, there were 14 different ad campaigns running around the world. The simple executions and globally replicable model have enabled us at a global level to have tight control over how our brand grows and succeeds around the world; while at the same time being very localised and relevant to consumers in each market.

Because we do not have to start from scratch with new idea development, we are free to explore fully the very best way to deliver our global message to consumers in each market. We are also able to invest more in researching how to optimise advertising, maximising our media investment by running the most effective versions of our campaign year after year.

Our biggest learning has been to stick to a model that is proven to work, but to evolve it and stretch it to accommodate the needs of local markets. We've also learned that the advertising is not just about selling products, but about using the mass reach we get to start helping consumers understand the conditions that our products help them live with.

Sensodyne

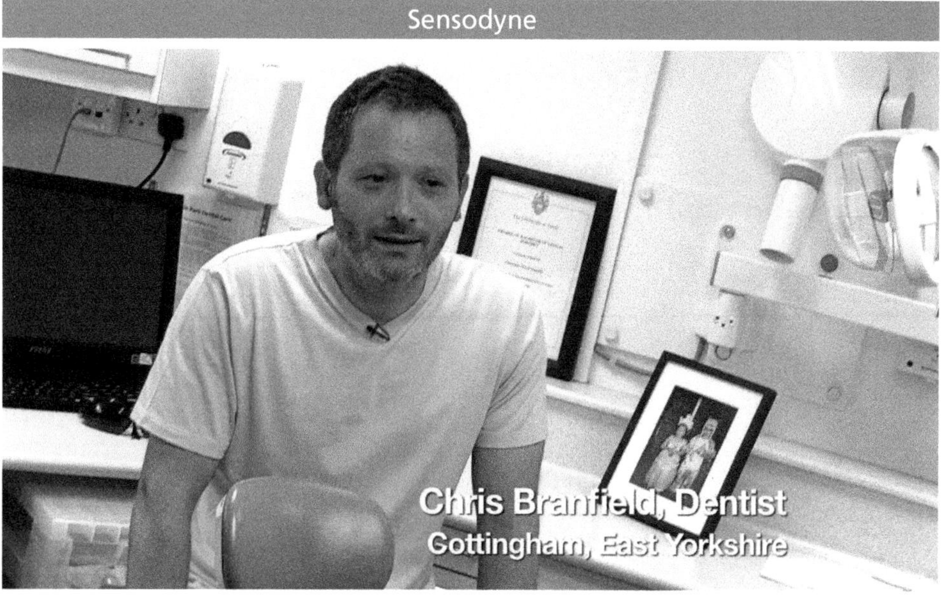

To read the full case study visit www.ipa.co.uk/ease or www.warc.com

SILVER

Sixt

How Sixt challenged car hire culture, and changed its fortunes

By Oliver Pople and Rachel Walker, Grey London
Contributing author: Matthew Gladstone, Grey London
Credited companies: Grey London; Manning Gottlieb OMD

Summary

In the car rental market where consumers mostly stick to suppliers they have used before, Sixt Rent a Car, a challenger brand, was stuck in a rut. From a low starting point and equipped with a modest £500,000 budget, Sixt needed to disrupt consumers' habitual choices, and do so fast. Based on an insight about how much people enjoyed being seen driving an expensive car they were renting for a bargain price, the 'Drive Smug' campaign aimed to challenge customer inertia. Rather than spread its efforts widely, the brand focused its media spend on dominating the branding opportunities at Canary Wharf tube station, which many of its target affluent male consumers travelled through. As a result of the campaign, key brand measures grew, local sales responded, and Sixt rented more luxury cars. The communications activity's estimated net profit return was £0.80 for every £1 invested.

Client comment

David Jackson, Head of Marketing & Channel Management UK, Sixt

This was our first advertising campaign for Sixt in the UK. Being a fairly small player in the market and having a limited budget, our concern was how to avoid our communications from getting lost in the competitive clutter. We knew there was a real need for standout to make an impact.

The key learning for us in achieving our goals, was that a strong local consumer insight makes a powerful difference. 'Drive Smug' might not necessarily be right for German consumers, in our home market, but it was right for the UK. The insight that people feel great driving a flash car at an economy price, translated into bold and motivating creative executions.

We also learned that on small budgets like ours, it helps to sacrifice reach for domination. We focused our media buy primarily at Canary Wharf tube station in

London which allowed us to create real standout, a decision that paid off. The station was perfect for our target audience but also fitted our premium brand positioning. It allowed us to use our media budget to maximum effect.

'Drive Smug', which really celebrates the great feeling of driving a premium car at economy prices, has given us a long-term platform that works across different media touch-points.

Sixt

To read the full case study visit www.ipa.co.uk/ease or www.warc.com

The Guardian and The Observer

Time for transformation

By Kate Nettleton and Achim Schauerte, BBH London
Credited companies: BBH London; Data2Decisions

Summary

This is a paper about how marketing can generate the time and money to help a business transform itself in an environment where such change is critically needed. It details how in response to declining circulation and advertising revenue, The Guardian Media Group marketed its weekend papers with the brand idea of 'Owning the weekend' expressed across channels including cinema, TV, outdoor and digital media. The strategy delivered short-term benefits, £4.8m of long-term incremental revenue, and a profit ROMI of £1.83 for every £1 invested, with the last campaign analysed delivering the highest return. The strategy provided money and time for the group as it developed a new business model.

Client comment

Tim Hunt, Marketing Director, Guardian News & Media

The 'Own the weekend' campaign has been a real success story. It was critical to *The Guardian*'s revenue performance and continues to drive revenue for the most profitable part of our business and our ongoing transformation.

As our IPA paper outlines, we iterated and tested different approaches and the latest campaign was our most effective since we started using econometric modeling. We are most proud of the fact that the campaign promoted *The Guardian*'s own content and journalism and not 'borrowed interest'. Past incentive-led campaigns were not able to deliver the same results, even in the short term.

There are a few key things we learned from 'Own the weekend'. Always value your product (even if your competitors do not) and price accordingly. We have been able to increase prices above the market average. The campaign has been a critical part of our pricing strategy.

The value of insight was critical in understanding the relationship people have with media and the role of habit in people's lives. The campaign's success was built on the role our papers play in our readers' busy lives and reminding them of their weekend ritual.

Differentiating between brand and direct response is arbitrary. With the right tone of voice everything can drive both brand measures and conversion. Finally, the campaign is a good reminder and a demonstration that paper is far from over. It is the bridge to *The Guardian*'s future.

The Guardian and The Observer

To read the full case study visit www.ipa.co.uk/ease or www.warc.com

SILVER

The Royal British Legion

Fortune favours the brave

By Alison Hoad, RKCR/Y&R
Contributing authors: Heather Griffiths and Francesca Miles, RKCR/Y&R
Credited companies: RKCR/Y&R; Maxus

Summary

The 2014 centenary of World War I was a big year for the Royal British Legion. How many organisations would have been brave enough to undergo a re-brand at such a pivotal time? Yet when people understand that RBL is as concerned with the welfare of today's armed forces as it is with 'remembrance of yesterdays', they are significantly more likely to give. This case describes how RBL's position was turned on its head, and made about life, not death, so that the organisation's 2015 Poppy appeal, 'Live on', focused on the welfare of current military as well as the fallen. Donations rose to record levels – delivering a profit ROI of £7.70 for every £1 invested which is expected to rise to £8.28 for every £1 when full 2015 data is counted.

Client comment

Gary Ryan, Marketing Director, The Royal British Legion

'Live on' has been vital to the recalibration of our brand. It has given us a way to unify both aspects of what the Royal British Legion does – both the welfare of today's armed forces, veterans and their families, and remembrance of those who have lost their lives on active service in conflicts past and present.

This is helping us to broaden understanding among people who know us just as a remembrance charity – and it's drawing younger people to the brand with messaging that feels more relevant to them today.

It's given us a way to future-proof the Royal British Legion so that we can help even more beneficiaries in the years to come. The other thing that has been particularly helpful is that 'Live on' has become a kind of North Star for us. We use it to guide everything we do – from the Poppy Appeal right through to the welfare services that the Royal British Legion provides.

The Royal British Legion

To read the full case study visit www.ipa.co.uk/ease or www.warc.com

SILVER

Three

Sorry (not sorry) for all the holiday spam

By Nick Exford, Wieden+Kennedy London
Contributing authors: Martin Beverley, adam&eveDDB; Paul Sturgeon, Mindshare; Matt Walters, Wieden+Kennedy London
Credited companies: Wieden+Kennedy London; Mindshare

Summary

To grow its business, Three Mobile, which was at the time the smallest of the UK's four main mobile networks, needed to give people a reason other than price to choose it. Three decided to differentiate itself by addressing consumer anger about the data roaming charges typically imposed on mobile customers when they used their phones abroad. The network abolished roaming charges and launched communications featuring tongue in cheek 'apologies' for the increase in 'bragging' photos sent or posted by Three users from abroad. Research showed the campaign led to Three being viewed as more appealing and customer-friendly, with its roaming policy identified as a reason for users to stay with the company. At the end of 2014, Three reached an all-time high with 10.4m UK customers and 13.3 per cent market share. According to econometric analysis, the campaign delivered a net profit return conservatively estimated at £1.46 for every £1 invested.

Client comment

Lianne Norry, Director of Brand and Communications, Three

'Feel at home' and 'Holiday spam' are great examples of when we're at our best. They show a proper, deep understanding of customers both in the proposition we created and the way we communicated it.

This goes beyond surface-level insights to tap into the motivations for why people do the things they do, and the way they really use their phones. It's a reminder that bravery pays.

There were lots of opportunities to pull our punches. We could have watered down the offer to be commercially cautious, or played it safe creatively by steering clear of the whole idea of an 'apology', but that is not 'the Three way'.

We try to do things in our own tone of voice, and when we get it right we stand out. This demonstrates the importance of being integrated. There are more and more ways to connect with our audience. 'Holiday spam' shows that when we have an idea that can bring together paid, owned and earned channels, and be executed all the way through to our stores, it really adds up to more that the sum of its parts.

Thinking about it as an integrated campaign with social at its heart (rather than a bolted-on auxiliary channel) meant we had to be really hard on creating something that people would want to engage with and talk about. It continues to set the bar for the propositions we create, the level of insight we look for and the quality of creativity we expect.

Three

To read the full case study visit www.ipa.co.uk/ease or www.warc.com

Wall's

Getting the long tail wagging again: how Wall's said 'Goodbye' to a serious business challenge

By Les Binet and Sarah Carter, adam&eveDDB
Credited companies: adam&eveDDB; Mindshare; TMW Unlimited

Summary

Faced with the twin forces of globalisation and the need to optimise the efficiency of marketing spend, large companies often opt to focus their media firepower on fewer, bigger brands. This case explains how a new campaign grew profit from a long tail of previously unsupported brands in the Wall's ice-cream portfolio owned by Unilever. On a small budget and by combining older and newer media in novel ways, the 'Talking ice creams' campaign profitably grew the sales and share of Wall's Classics for the first time in years. It generated £1.84 of incremental short-term revenue for every £1 invested. The campaign has been adapted for 120 previously unsupported ice-cream brands in 30 countries.

Client comment

Sarah Hogan, Global Marketing Director, Wall's

It is fair to say that this campaign has had a disproportionately big effect in terms of what I've learnt and how I've changed how I work as a result, despite it being a small budget campaign.

First, it was a great reminder of the value of evaluation of a new campaign. It is very unusual for a campaign developed in one country to be adopted round the world so quickly and by so many countries. Everyone intuitively loved and believed in this campaign when they saw it. But key to its fast and widespread uptake and roll-out I believe, was the work undertaken to properly evaluate all its effects in the UK. This gave immediate confidence to other countries in terms of what it could do for them too.

In the future this will lead us to prioritise the evaluation of all aspects of new campaigns as soon as feasibly possible (creative and media, brand and sales measures).

I also learnt how it is perfectly possible to do a full business effects evaluation, even for a campaign like this that includes no TV and a heavy focus on social media. In particular, the careful work done to analyse exposures by individual channels, which then meant we could compare on a like-for-like basis effectiveness and efficiency by channel was new thinking for us. We will do this more routinely in the future to help plan media more effectively.

It was also a reminder of the power of posters especially for 'impulse products' something we can forget as clients when faced with the multitude of new media opportunities available now. But this will not be an either/or choice for us; we found that posters were even more effective when turbo-charged by new media.

Wall's

To read the full case study visit www.ipa.co.uk/ease or www.warc.com

SECTION 4

Bronze winners

Coors Light

Van Damme good results: how Jean-Claude transformed the fortunes of Coors Light

By Richard Clay, ZenithOptimedia; Michael Lee and Sarah Mason, VCCP
Contributing authors: Guy Edwards, ZenithOptimedia; Andrew Perkins, VCCP; Richard Shotton, ZenithOptimedia
Credited companies: ZenithOptimedia; Ninah

Summary

Coors Light was stuck outside the UK's top 20 of beer brands, losing sales and struggling on key brand scores. Humorous advertising featuring Hollywood action star Jean-Claude Van Damme enabled Coors Light to reconnect with popular culture and create a distinct brand world that connected to the product's ability to offer a refreshing, cold-serve beer. From the first Van Damme-fronted execution onwards, Coors Light established momentum which turned Coors Light into a top 10 UK beer brand within three years. The integrated TV, outdoor, social, digital and experiential campaign delivered an estimated net profit return of £4.13 for every £1 invested.

Client comment

Alison Pickering, Brand Director Portfolio, Molson Coors

By far the most powerful learning has been an irrefutable recognition that even the most audacious of business objectives can be realised, if you and your agencies are prepared to take the bold steps needed.

Although pre-campaign research on Jean-Claude was positive, we had huge amounts of internal and external resistance to overcome to get the campaign out of the door.

Coors Light is now held up by Molson Coors as a first-class example of how communications can transform a brand, and the wide-reaching effects of the campaign are well-known and admired internally. Having such a case study within our portfolio allows us to be bolder in our thinking as a business and to believe that any objective, however ambitious, can be achieved.

To read the full case study visit www.ipa.co.uk/ease or www.warc.com

Costa

Creating a nation of coffee lovers

By Will Hodge and Matthew Waksman, Karmarama
Contributing authors: Caroline Harris, Whitbread; Sid McGrath, Karmarama
Credited companies: Karmarama; ZenithOptimedia

Summary

In 2008 Costa was the number two player suffering its lowest brand preference and facing the worst UK recession since World War II. Working with Karmarama, Costa invested in brand communications to shake up customer inertia in its category. Over the six-year period covered by this case study, the brand dramatically increased brand preference and sales. To achieve this, Costa used a mixture of strategies, from punchy rational agitation to iconic emotional relevance, becoming the leading coffee shop in revenue and the nation's favourite coffee-shop brand six years in a row.

Client comment

Caroline Harris, Marketing Director, UK & Ireland, Costa

From a retail perspective, we've learned that whilst the in-store experience and coffee quality remain the most important factors for our business, we cannot rely on these alone to differentiate and drive preference. We've learnt we have to communicate what makes us different and why customers should choose us.

We learnt that the most powerful way to do this is to base it on a powerful and unarguable brand purpose than can build the brand from the inside out. We also learnt to be open to approaching every challenge differently. Whilst we managed to drive preference and sales growth with each campaign, how we did it varied, from aggressive rational proof through to emotional brand-building symbols.

As a result, we're a client and agency team that is consistently looking for new ways to build the brand, from being the first UK coffee-shop brand on Periscope, to partnering with BuzzFeed, to continuing to build equity at Christmas time. We've become a team that is proactively on the look out for new challenges and is always open-minded in how we tackle them when they arise.

Costa

To read the full case study visit www.ipa.co.uk/ease or www.warc.com

Eurotunnel Le Shuttle

Eurotunnel Le Shuttle: engineering success

By Jack Hemens and Thibaut Pfeiffer, OMD UK
Credited companies: OMD UK; Eurotunnel Le Shuttle

Summary

This case study details how Eurotunnel sucessfuly overhauled the marketing of its Le Shuttle service. The new strategy developed a segmentation to identify the most valuable customer groups, and then communicated to those audiences separately and appropriately. Over the five years covered by this case, the integration of this segmentation across communications actvities led to a 20.8% increase in cars carried through the Tunnel. It is estimated that the advertising delivered a cumulative profit of £258.7m over five years, and the overall net profit return was estimated at £11.40 for every £1 invested.

Client comment

Allan Steatham, Head of Marketing, Eurotunnel

Prior to 2010, the marketing strategy was a one size fits all approach. In order to deliver continued business growth, the marketing strategy had to recognise the changes in consumer purchase behaviour and use channels that would take the brand to new customer audiences.

What was required was a professionalisation of the marketing strategy in order to achieve our business objectives. Our strategy was to adopt a targeted marketing approach, adapting the marketing mix according to the segment of customer we wanted to target, and using traditional media channels to drive brand awareness and consideration whilst at the same time utilising the performance media channels to harvest the interest and demand in to sales.

This approach was not without challenge, as the business value and perception of marketing channels were not clear to the organisation. An econometrics model and our customer segmentation proved the value of these channels in generating business performance, resulting in consistent year-on-year growth.

Eurotunnel Le Shuttle

To read the full case study visit www.ipa.co.uk/ease or www.warc.com

first direct

Made for millennials

By Alex Huzzey, J. Walter Thompson
Contributing authors: Andrew Miles, HSBC; Robert Webb, Mindshare
Credited companies: J. Walter Thompson; we are social

Summary

To safeguard its future profitability, first direct needed to attract younger customers. This is the second chapter of the brand's 'Unexpected bank' story, which was the subject of a bronze IPA Effectiveness Award in 2014. It shows how by going back to the brand's founding challenger spirit, and communicating it in a new way, the bank put itself back on the radar with millennials. Following the campaign, first direct grew consideration against heavier-spending banks, increased its share of new accounts, and lowered the average age of new customers. Econometric analysis estimated the campaign delivered a profit ROI of £1.50 for every £1 invested.

Client comment

Jo Thornton, Senior Manager, Advertising & Acquisition, first direct

At first direct, we are different to high-street banks, and always have been. The continued success of the 'Unexpected bank' campaign into its second and third year has taught us about the power of not being afraid of that.

In fact, being authentic and true to the genuine culture of the organisation has been crucial in connecting with this newer, younger audience. The 'Barry the platypus' character communicated that difference effectively right from the start, and with 'Hissy lizard' we have managed to refresh the campaign in a way that continued that work, connecting further with the new generation of customers we needed to draw in.

first direct

To read the full case study visit www.ipa.co.uk/ease or www.warc.com

First4Adoption

Start your adoption story

By Jared Shurin, Kindred
Contributing authors: Sharon Bange, Kindred; Katie Florence, Department for Education; Gemma Gordon-Johnson and Paul Sutton, First4Adoption
Credited companies: Kindred; M4C

Summary

This case study shows how adoption can be reframed as a means of helping adults and children achieve the family they deserve. Facebook, adoption agency partners and local media were used to recruit potential adopters. The First4Adoption Agency Finder tracked the number of people that were prompted by communications to contact their local adoption agency. By using the estimated saving to the public purse from children being adopted and therefore kept out of the care system, it is calculated that the activity generated a return of over £10 for every £1 invested. The initiative also created a new process that unified local agencies into a single voice and, most importantly, it brought children and families together.

Client comment

Katie Florence, Strategic Communications Manager, Department for Education

The legacy of the campaign will encourage local agencies to be bolder in their efforts. They can utilise tried and tested national resources that save them time and money to achieve life-changing results for children, young people and families. It was really encouraging to see organisations such as PACT, one of the UK's leading voluntary adoption agencies, re-brand its Facebook page using our resources and messaging. We're seeing pockets of excellent examples like these: agency brands aligning into one national brand for adoption.

Many in the sector were fearful of using social media, but it's now become a self-moderating, safe place for potential adopters to engage and it's growing organically. We can now offer advice, resources and shared learning to any agency looking to improve its social media output.

This is especially important considering the return on investment this campaign demonstrated in recruiting via low- and no-cost channels. It's important to note that before this campaign, the sector had no national benchmark as to what was effective in adoption recruitment marketing. By identifying some of the tactical costs, this campaign for the first time set a national benchmark. This is invaluable for future local campaign success, and represents significant progress for the sector and our mission to ensure all children have the stable and loving families they deserve.

First4Adoption

To read the full case study visit www.ipa.co.uk/ease or www.warc.com

Kenco

Coffee vs gangs: how a strong brand purpose changed lives in Honduras and changed fortunes for Kenco

By Alex Huzzey and Eleanor Metcalf, J. Walter Thompson
Contributing author: Grace Kite, The Effectiveness Partnership
Credited companies: J. Walter Thompson; Proximity; PHD Media

Summary

This paper demonstrates how brand purpose can contribute to a societal good as well as a substantial commercial return. An ethical stance has long been a distinctive part of Kenco's brand and a reason for people to buy its product. However, similar messages from competitors eroded its status as the ethically leading brand, and sales suffered.

The 'Coffee vs gangs' campaign revitalised the brand's ethical positioning among consumers and helped defend its profitable, premium-priced position in the market.

With an estimated revenue ROI for its television advertising which is three times the FMCG average, the campaign delivered a strong return on investment as well as making a beneficial societal impact. This case also evinces the multi-faceted value of social media in purpose-led campaigns.

Client comment

Martin Andreasen, Category Lead Hot Beverages, Mondelēz International

Two things have really landed with us as a result of doing this campaign.

First, we've learned about the power of the authentic in communications, the considerable impact of actually doing something genuine to change people's lives. We've learned that given the chance, most people will cheer on brands and companies who are championing for a better world and genuinely aren't afraid to do the right thing. We were gratified to see this also translate into uplifts in advertising reach and efficiency as we cut through with our purposeful message.

Second, we've learned just how powerful social media can be when you have an interesting and authentic story. 'Coffee vs gangs' engaged consumers beyond any normal benchmarks and showed us how important relevant content with a customised execution for social media is to unlocking people's involvement.

Kenco

To read the full case study visit www.ipa.co.uk/ease or www.warc.com

Mattessons

The Mattesson-aissance

By Raquel Chicourel and William Poskett, Saatchi & Saatchi
Contributing authors: Richard Bradley, Vizeum; Michael Cross and Spencer Lucas, Brightblue
Credited companies: Saatchi & Saatchi; Brightblue; Vizeum

Summary

This is a story of how a video gaming-centric strategy at Mattessons Fridge Raiders created a new commercial and creative era for the small meat-snacking brand. The resulting campaigns turned the struggling Fridge Raiders, owned by conservative Kerry Foods, into a category leader. Fridge Raiders went from speaking to a safe and retailer-friendly heartland of mums to addressing the notoriously fickle world of teens. It took money out of TV and into digital, and transformed itself from a conventional above-the-line advertiser to one that created content including an artificially intelligent robot and a helmet that equipped gamers for hands-free snacking. The Mattessons gaming era achieved a long-term revenue ROI of £3.97 for every £1 invested and a long-term net profit return of £2.34 for every £1 spent (totalling £3.1m profit).

Client comment

Sue McVie, Strategic Marketing Director, Meats, Kerry Foods

Targeting teens and infiltrating their world through our innovative gaming content was a commercial turning point and game-changer for Mattessons.

From a brand in decline, Mattessons Fridge Raiders overtook Peperami, becoming the leader of the meat-snacking category. This commercial and creative victory is something Kerry Foods feels proud of and takes as model and inspiration to all other brands we have in our portfolio.

Mattessons

To read the full case study visit www.ipa.co.uk/ease or www.warc.com

BRONZE

McVitie's

Waking the sleeping giant

By Daniel Sherrard, Grey London
Contributing authors: Matthew Gladstone and Rachel Walker, Grey London
Credited companies: Grey London; 3 Monkeys Zeno; Grey Possible; Grey Shopper; MEC

Summary

McVitie's was a sleeping giant in the UK sweet biscuit category. Despite its size and history, the brand did not enjoy fame or customer love, and was not perceived as dominant by the industry. Since retailers were looking to reduce the number of category products they stocked, McVitie's needed to assert its authority and increase consumers' love for the brand. The resulting campaign supported the McVitie's masterbrand, rather than specific product brands. Its central idea celebrated the warm emotions that biscuits arouse by featuring cute animals that prompted similar feelings. The campaign increased penetration and frequency of purchase, and helped McVitie's resist distribution cuts better than its competitors. The long-term profit ROMI was estimated to be at least £0.49, and as high as £1.06 for every £1 invested.

Client comment

Sarah Heynen, Marketing Director, United Biscuits

The campaign demonstrated the importance of evoking an emotional response rather than leaning on rational persuasion. It taught us the benefit of being a brand that people talk about – a big, famous, popular brand that is embedded in culture and front-of-mind when people step instore.

Acting as a masterbrand helped us to be seen as the category leader we really are: internally, by consumers and by the trade. Our fame-driving, masterbrand approach galvanised the business, focused our approach, and awoke the sleeping giant of McVitie's.

We have a host of great individual brands within McVitie's, which we used to treat in splendid isolation of each other. But we've seen that really utilising the scale of the united McVitie's masterbrand is a massive driver of success. With this approach we've had greater halo sales across the portfolio and greater effectiveness – and it's an approach we intend to continue.

We're confident that it's this approach that will help us to achieve our goal of becoming a true megabrand and take ourselves from a top 10 to a top 5 grocery brand.

McVitie's

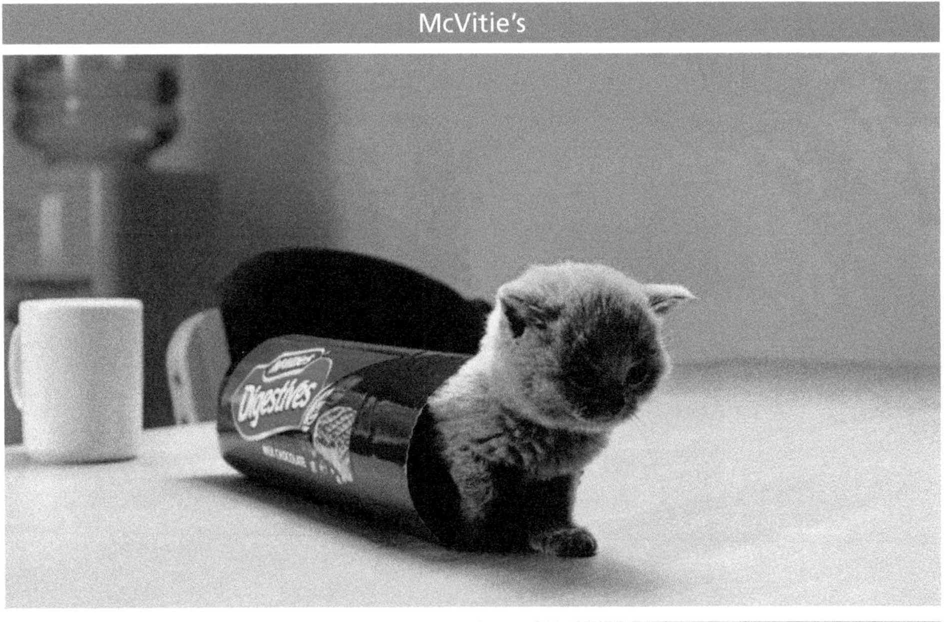

To read the full case study visit www.ipa.co.uk/ease or www.warc.com

Officeworks

How Officeworks realised its own big idea

By Pieter-Paul von Weiler, AJF Partnership
Contributing authors: Bruno Chami, AJF Partnership; Lyndelle O'Keefe, Initiative
Credited companies: AJF Partnership; Anomaly; Columbus; DT; Haystac; Track

Summary
This paper illustrates how a new positioning shifted the fortunes of Officeworks, Australia's largest retailer in office products. By focusing communications on how office products enable people to realise their ideas and goals, the company achieved record growth in sales and enviable brand health in a market dominated by product and price advertising. The case argues that taking a combined approach to sales activation and brand building can have a greater impact on the bottom line than separating the two. It is estimated the positioning helped deliver a total gross profit of AUD 206m over 40 months, representing a net profit ROI of AUD 0.46 for every AUD 1 invested.

Client comment

Karl Winther, National Marketing Manager, Officeworks

As an integrated team, we've learnt a great deal from repositioning Officeworks. Shifting the company's focus from selling stuff to helping people realise their ambitions has helped Officeworks become more meaningful.

Taking a customer-centric approach to everything we do has allowed us to connect on a deeper and more emotional level with customers. And putting customers' motivations – instead of lowest prices – at the heart of communications has increased people's loyalty and preference for our brand.

Making sure that every piece of our communications builds a perception of the brand, instead of separating brand communications from sales communications, has delivered very strong efficiency and effectiveness results.

The repositioning has not only changed how Officeworks communicates externally but also internally. It has shaped Officeworks' purpose and made 6,500 team members realise we don't just sell pens and paper, computers and office furniture, but we help make bigger things happen for our customers.

This has been translated right throughout the organisation. Recruitment ads now open with the line 'We want your big ideas' and our market results to the investors now talk about how we are a business that helps customers achieve their big ideas. Confidence in the strategy continues to grow, driven by strong sales and brand results.

Officeworks

To read the full case study visit www.ipa.co.uk/ease or www.warc.com

Santander

From 'who?' to hero: how Santander became king of the switchers

By Rachel Baynes, Santander and John Crowther, The Engine Group
Contributing authors: Beatriz Balaguer, Carat; Louise Cook, Holmes & Cook; Grace Kite, Gracious Economics; Victoria Nicholson, Santander; Stuart Williams, The Engine Group
Credited companies: The Engine Group; Havas Worldwide

Summary

At the end of 2009, Santander didn't exist as a UK high-street brand. Within six years, the bank had emerged as 'king of the switchers', taking share from competitors that had dominated the market for decades. This is the story of advertising's contribution to Santander's growth. By disrupting the usual retail banking communications model, deploying a media strategy that exploited a short window of opportunity, and developing a convention-challenging approach that featured ambassadors from sport such as Jessica Ennis-Hill, communications drove 27 per cent of the bank's account openings. The estimated net profit return from the activity was £2.22 for every £1 invested between March 2012 and March 2016.

Client comment

Rachel Baynes, Head of Marketing Strategy and Planning, Santander

We've learned that when a company has a genuine, customer-focused purpose, with products and services fully aligned behind it, and a communications strategy that delivers to these, amazing things can happen. Our strong brand purpose, single-minded communications focus, and creative strategy that broke category rules have seen us gain more net current account switchers than any other bank. And this was despite spending less on advertising than competitors, and in a market where it's said you're more likely to change your spouse than your bank.

We've also learned never to be complacent. If it's not working, change it, but conversely if it isn't broken, don't try to fix it. We learned to set clear objectives and key performance indicators, rigorously test delivery against those and take action accordingly.

We tried a couple of different creative approaches before hitting the jackpot with our use of ambassadors, and since then the creative strategy has only needed evolution not revolution. Overall, Santander's success has been as a result of a crystal clear purpose, supported and delivered throughout the organisation, with the communications strategy playing a very significant part in helping our customers and our business to prosper.

Santander

To read the full case study visit www.ipa.co.uk/ease or www.warc.com

Spies Travel

Do it for Denmark and do it for Mom

By Søren Christensen, Robert/Boisen & Likeminded and Eva Lundgren, Spies Travel
Contributing authors: Janey Bullivant and Warwick Cairns, The Effectiveness Partnership
Credited companies: Robert/Boisen & Likeminded; Annalect; Be On; Radius Kommunikation

Summary

With Danes increasingly taking advantage of budget airlines and travel websites to organise their leisure trips, this case study explains how provocative advertising helped re-establish the relevance of the 60-year-old Spies travel operator which was synonymous in Denmark with family package holidays to the Mediterranean. By suggesting Danish couples should travel to have more sex and boost the country's flagging birth rate, the tongue in cheek 'Do it for Denmark' and 'Do it for Mom' campaigns generated huge attention. They gave the brand a role in a national conversation about population trends and grew sales of Spies city breaks and activity holidays. On a modest budget of €670,000, the combined campaigns generated an estimated return for every €1 invested of €15.8 of revenue and €1 of net profit.

Client comment

Jan Vendelbo, Managing Director, Spies Travel

Both 'Do it for Denmark' and 'Do it for Mom' have had a very impressive effect on Spies as a business and as a leading Danish travel brand. We did not expect the reach this campaign managed to achieve, globally as well as within Denmark.

Commercially, the campaign has more than paid for itself. Crucially for Spies, it has changed an entrenched perception about what Spies offered to Danish consumers within a very competitive, price-driven sector. This campaign has genuinely made Spies stand out amongst its competitors and driven unprecedented fame for our brand.

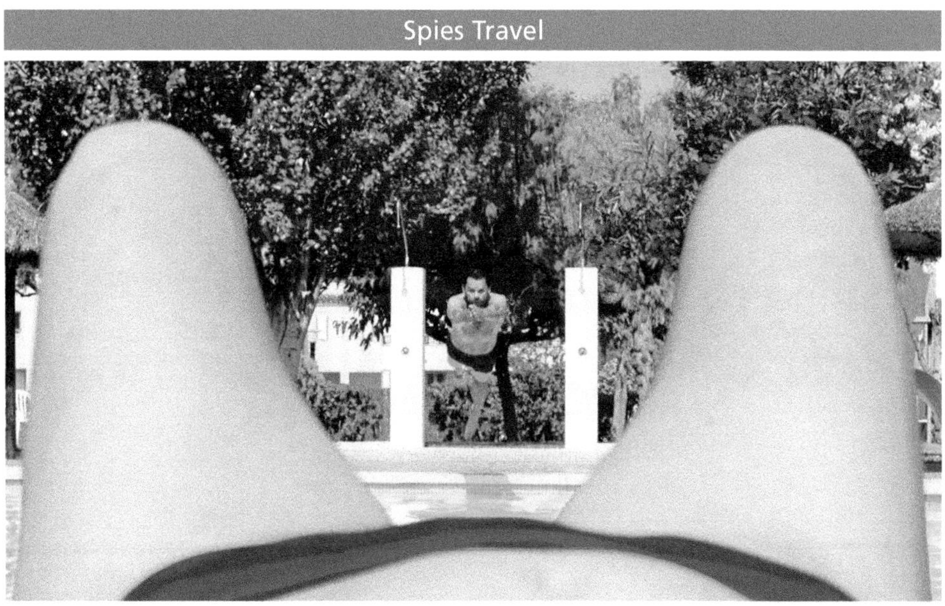
Spies Travel

To read the full case study visit www.ipa.co.uk/ease or www.warc.com

The Conservative Party

Winning the benefit of the doubt

By Richard Storey, M&C Saatchi
Contributing author: Steve Parker, M&C Saatchi
Credited companies: M&C Saatchi; Crosby Textor; The Conservative Party

Summary

In 2015, The Conservatives secured an unexpected election victory. This paper outlines how communications earned the benefit of the doubt to help achieve this. Specifically it demonstrates paid-for advertising's marginal contribution in target seats, over and above the omni-channel onslaught of election campaigns. Rather than 'swing' Labour supporters, the strategy 'swayed' UKIP, Lib Dem voters and 'don't knows', by evoking the prospect of a minority Labour government 'in SNP's pocket'. Seat-by-seat analysis shows this swayed sufficient target voters to secure the outright Conservative majority, an outcome representing reasonable use of marketing assets (RUMA).

Client comment

Andrew Feldman, Chairman, The Conservative Party

I am very proud of everyone who pulled together to secure the first Conservative-majority government for over twenty years. Our team worked hard at focusing on the battles we most needed to win and the strongest themes to communicate to do so.

As a result, our advertising was notable for its ability to reach target voters with the right messages. Winning over a new generation of supporters will be key to future elections and I am committed to extending our approach to embrace more of those who didn't vote for us, or didn't vote at all.

To read the full case study visit www.ipa.co.uk/ease or www.warc.com

UK Government

The missing millions: giving ex-pats their voice

By Nicola Strange, Ogilvy & Mather London
Contributing author: Tricia Quiller-Croasdell, The Prime Minister's Office
Credited companies: Ogilvy; Data2Decisions

Summary

Before the 2015 General Election, the UK Government set an ambitious target of increasing the number of British ex-patriates on the electoral register from about 23,000 to more than 100,000. The target group was among the most diverse and geographically dispersed imaginable, the media budget was a modest £330,000, and the timescale was exceptionally tight. The resulting campaign emphasised that ex-pats had a personal stake in the election result because they had UK-based relatives or were themselves planning to return to the UK, and used messaging across digital, print and radio in key overseas markets. It proved more effective than communications simultaneously issued by the Electoral Commission. The voter registration target was exceeded at a lower cost per registration than in the previous election, with the campaign directly responsible for an estimated 21,151 registrations. Without the campaign, the goverment would have missed its target.

Client comment

Tricia Quiller-Croasdell, Head of Campaigns, The Prime Minister's Office

The overseas voter campaign was designed to strike a different tone amongst our UK ex-pat communities. Other domestic voter registration campaigns were taking place simultaneously, but none with such a self-selecting excluded audience. There were three key lessons from this campaign which have now shaped the UK Government's engagement with and legislation for overseas voters.

- *Emotional over rational.* The language used during this campaign, versus the more straightforward information given by the Electoral Commission campaign, demonstrated the need to emotionally connect and increase the relevance to UK citizens overseas. This emotive language was the basis of the Electoral Commission's campaign in the run-up to the EU Referendum.

- *The 15 year rule.* We were aware that this issue – by which British citizens who lived abroad for more than 15 years lost their vote – would come up during the campaign. A significant number of vociferous comments were made on our promoted posts. Our campaign, unintentionally, served to highlight this issue prompting articles, blog posts and letters. Whilst it couldn't be addressed in the run-up to the election, the law was later the subject of a government bill.
- *Social over display.* The difference in our engagement rate for social over display was notable. Reaching our audience, as HM Government, seemed to resonate when our audiences were reminded and connected to those from 'home' via social. Social was 4.4 times more effective in generating action amongst our audiences, than display.

UK Government

To read the full case study visit www.ipa.co.uk/ease or www.warc.com

Volkswagen Commercial Vehicles UK

From manufacturer to service partner: how Volkswagen Commercial Vehicles did more with less

By David Mortimer, adam&eveDDB
Contributing author: Emma Whitehouse, MediaCom Business Science
Credited companies: adam&eveDDB; MediaCom; MediaCom Business Science; Proximity; Tribal Worldwide

Summary

In 2013, Volkswagen Commercial Vehicles (VWCV) UK faced competition from market leaders and economy brands with much newer vehicles. Fighting with an ageing fleet and a halved marketing budget seemed an impossible challenge. Instead, VWCV reshaped its entire business around the customers' needs, shifting perceptions of the brand from being just a van manufacturer to a service partner for small businesses. This case study demonstrates the transformation increased brand awareness, orders and market share, delivering the best results in 60 years. The approach grew the brand's profit ROMI of £7.41 for every £1 in 2013 to a ROMI of just over £11 for every £1 in 2014.

Client comment

Karen Hilton, National Communications, Retailer and Digital Marketing Manager, Volkswagen Commercial Vehicles UK

'Working with you' has been an important step in moving the Volkswagen Commercial Vehicles brand forward. It has given us a clear and competitive point of differentiation against the competition and allowed us to communicate more aspects of our business offering, such as local service, which were being largely ignored in the category.

Since it launched, 'Working with you' has become an important consideration in every brief – from brand communications to events – as we look to provide an empathetic, supportive and insightful partnership for UK businesses.

Volkswagen Commercial Vehicles UK

To read the full case study visit www.ipa.co.uk/ease or www.warc.com

BRONZE

Volvo Cars

'Or by': how two little words made Volvo's safety promise matter again

By Matthew Gladstone and Wiktor Skoog, Grey London
Credited companies: Grey London; Albedo100

Summary

Volvo LifePaint is an innovative spray paint which protects cyclists by making them more visible. Positioning Volvo on the less expected side of the safety dialogue between motorists and cyclists, this new product earned huge amounts of editorial and social coverage. Among those interested in the LifePaint product, intent to purchase Volvo cars rose, and it is calculated that customers who bought LifePaint also went on to buy an estimated 298 Volvo cars in the UK and 1,013 worldwide. Volvo treats LifePaint as a safety initiative, not a profit centre, but the revenues from more than 75,000 sales of LifePaint have covered the vehicle-maker's investment in the project. This case offers several ways of calculating the value created by the launch, including by assessing the paid media equivalent of the editorial coverage generated, and the product's role in driving quality leads to Volvo's website.

Client comment

Georgina Williams, Head of Marketing, Volvo Cars UK

Grey think differently. The agency's response to a brief to showcase different innovations within our cars wasn't a TV script, or some out-of-home. It was a product, inspired by Volvo's Intellisafe system, which on a small budget reached millions of people around the world.

LifePaint was not a big idea that made a splash and then disappeared. It's now rolling out around the world while continuing to highlight one of our key differentiators, safety. This is what modern advertising should look like.

Volvo Cars

To read the full case study visit www.ipa.co.uk/ease or www.warc.com

How to access the IPA Effectiveness Awards Databank

The IPA Databank represents the most rigorous and comprehensive examination of marketing communications working in the marketplace, and in the world. Over more than 30 years of the IPA's Effectiveness Awards competition, we have collected over 1,400 examples of best practice in advertising development and results across a wide spectrum of marketing sources and expenditures. Each example contains up to 4,000 words of text and is illustrated in full by market, research, sales and profit data.

IPA Effectiveness Awards Search Engine (EASE)

You can use the EASE search engine at www.ipa.co.uk/ease to interrogate over 1,400 detailed case studies from the IPA Databank. You can search the case studies by keywords and/or filter by any parameter from questions asked in the Effectiveness Awards Entry Questionnaire. EASE is free to use and is the first search engine on the web which allows you to do this. IPA members can also contact the Information Centre directly where more complex searches can be commissioned and the results supplied by e-mail.

Purchasing IPA case studies

Member agencies can download case studies from www.ipa.co.uk/cases at a discounted rate of £25 per case study. Alternatively members can sign up to warc.com (see overleaf) at a beneficial IPA rate and can then download case studies as part of that subscription. Non IPA members can purchase case studies from the IPA website (www.ipa.co.uk/cases) at £40 per copy.

Further information

For further information, please contact the Information Centre at the IPA,
44 Belgrave Square, London SW1X 8QS
Telephone: +44 (0)20 7235 7020
Fax: +44 (0)20 7245 9904
Website: www.ipa.co.uk
Email: info@ipa.co.uk

warc.com

Warc is the official publisher of the IPA Effectiveness Awards' case histories. All IPA case studies are available at warc.com, alongside thousands of other case studies, articles and best practice guides, market intelligence and industry news and alerts, with material drawn from over 50 sources across the world.

Warc.com is relied upon by major creative and media agency networks, market research companies, media owners, multinational advertisers and business schools, to help tackle any marketing challenge.

IPA members can subscribe at a 10% discount. To find out more, request a trial at www.warc.com/trial.

www.ipaeffectivenessawards.co.uk

On our dedicated Awards website you can find out everything you need to know about the annual IPA Effectiveness Awards competition, including how to enter, and who's won what since 1980.

As well as viewing case study summaries and creative work, you'll also find a series of over 30 brand films from over three decades of the Awards including:

- HSBC
- John Lewis
- Marmite
- Yorkshire Tea
- Cadbury Dairy Milk
- Walkers
- PG Tips

IPA Databank case availability

* Denotes winning entries
** Denotes cases published in *Area Works* volumes 1–5
S Denotes cases published in *Scottish Advertising Works* volumes 1–4

NEW ENTRIES 2016
2016 5 Gum
2016 Age UK
2016 Allianz
2016 Art Fund*
2016 AYGO
2016 Barclays
2016 Bolia.com
2016 Butlins
2016 Cancer Research UK
2016 Coors Light*
2016 Costa*
2016 Direct Line*
2016 Dixons
2016 Domino's
2016 Dove*
2016 Eurotunnel Le Shuttle*
2016 Extra Gum
2016 first direct*
2016 First4Adoption*
2016 Foxtel
2016 Guinness*
2016 Help to Buy
2016 Honda Odyssey
2016 John Lewis*
2016 John Lewis Insurance*
2016 Kenco*
2016 Lidl UK*
2016 L'Oréal Paris Age Perfect*
2016 M&S Food
2016 Macmillan Cancer Support*
2016 Mastercard
2016 Mattessons*
2016 McVitie's*
2016 Narellan Pools*
2016 National Lottery
2016 NICEIC & ELECSA
2016 Octasa
2016 Officeworks*
2016 OVO
2016 P&O Cruises
2016 Pepsi Max*
2016 Plusnet*
2016 Rugby World Cup 2015
2016 Sainsbury's*
2016 Santander*
2016 Save the Children*
2016 Sensodyne*
2016 Sixt*
2016 Slurpee Flavour Fest
2016 Slurpee Xpandinator
2016 Snickers*
2016 SPC #MyFamilyCan
2016 SPC #SPCSunday
2016 Speeding (New Zealand Transport Agency)*
2016 Spies Travel*
2016 Stoptober*
2016 Tennent's Lager
2016 The Conservative Party*
2016 *The Economist**
2016 *The Guardian* and *The Observer**
2016 The Philippines
2016 The Royal British Legion*
2016 THINK!
2016 Three*
2016 Travel & Surf
2016 TSB
2016 UK Government*
2016 Vodafone
2016 Volkswagen Commercial Vehicles UK*
2016 Volvo Cars*
2016 Vype
2016 Wall's*

NUMERICAL
2016 5 Gum
2003 55 Degrees North**
2006 100.4 smooth fm
2000 1001 Mousse*
2012 2011 Census

A
2004 AA Loans*
1982 Abbey Crunch
1990 Abbey National Building Society
1980 Abbey National Building Society Open Bondshares
1990 Aberlour Malt Whisky*
2004 Ackermans (SA)

2008 Acquisition Crime*
2006 Actimel*
2012 Admiral
1996 Adult Literacy*
2002 Aerogard Mosquito Repellent (Australia)
2016 Age UK
1999 Agri Plan Finance**
1986 AGS Home Improvements*
1988 AIDS
1994 AIDS*
1986 Air Call
2010 Albert Bartlett Rooster Potatoes
2012 Aldi*
2014 Aldi UK & Ireland*
1990 Alex Lawrie Factors
1980 All Clear Shampoo*
1988 Alliance & Leicester Building Society*
1990 Alliance & Leicester Building Society*
1992 Alliance & Leicester Building Society*
1984 Alliance Building Society
2016 Allianz
1990 Allied Dunbar
1984 Allinson's Bread
1984 Alpen
1990 Alton Towers
2003 Alton Towers 'Air'**
1999 Alton Towers 'Oblivion'**
2010 Always
2012 American Golf
1990 Amnesty International*
1992 Amnesty International
2009 Ancestry.co.uk
1990 Anchor Aerosol Cream
1988 Anchor Butter
1994 Anchor Butter
2011 Anchor Squirty Cream
1986 Andrex*
1992 Andrex
1994 Andrex Ultra
1986 Anglia Building Society
1996 Anglian Water
2002 Anti-Drink Driving*
1997 Anti-Drink Driving (DoE Northern Ireland)**
2006 Anti-Drugs (Scottish Executive)
2007 Anti-Drugs (Scottish Executive)*
1990 Anti-NHS Reform Campaign (BMA)
1994 Anti-Smoking
2011 Aquafresh Kids*
2007 Aqua Optima*
2000 Archers*
2006 Ariel
2007 Army Cadet Force
1998 Army Recruitment*
2004 Army Recruitment*
2005 Arriva Buses*
1996 Arrol's 80
2012 Art Fund*
2016 Art Fund*
1994 Arthur's (cat food)
2005 ATS Euromaster*
1988 Audi
1990 Audi*
1998 Audi*
2006 Audi
2008 Audi*
2010 Audi*
2012 Audi*
1982 Austin Metro*
1980 Austin Mini*
1990 *Auto Express*
1996 Automobile Association*
2012 Aviva
2014 Aviva*
2006 Axe
2012 Axe
2016 AYGO

B

2002 B&Q
2004 B&Q
2012 B&Q
1988 Babycham
1988 Baby Fresh
1996 Bacardi Breezer
1998 Bacardi Breezer
1992 Bailey's
2002 Bakers Complete*
2005 Bakers Complete*
2006 Bakers Complete*
2005 Bank of Ireland
1988 Barbican
1990 Barbican Health & Fitness Centre
1992 Barclaycard
1996 Barclaycard*
2010 Barclaycard*
2010 Barclays*
2012 Barclays
2016 Barclays
1998 Barclays Bank Current Account
2006 Barclays Global Investors (iShares)
2010 Barclays Wealth*
2002 Barnardo's*
2012 Barnardo's
1994 Batchelors
1998 Batchelors Supernoodles*
2005 Baxters Soup[S]
2008 BBC iplayer
2004 Beck's Bier (Australia)
2005 Belfast City
2001 Belfast Giants**
1998 Bell's Whisky
2002 Benadryl*
2006 Bendicks
2009 Benecol
1986 Benylin*
2010 Berocca*
2006 Bertolli

2007 Big Plus, The (Improving Scotland's adult literacy and numeracy)
1990 Billy Graham's Mission 89
1986 Birds Eye Alphabites*
1992 Birds Eye Country Club Cuisine
1994 Birds Eye Crispy Chicken
1982 Birds Eye Oven Crispy Cod Steaks in Batter*
1999 Birmingham, City of**
1988 Birmingham Executive Airways
2010 Bisto*
1990 Black Tower
1996 Blockbuster Video
2005 Blood Donation*
2014 Blue Dragon
1982 Blue Riband
2000 Bluewater*
2005 bmi baby
1994 BMW*
2004 BMW Films – The Hire*
1994 Boddington's*
2016 Bolia.com
2012 Bombay Sapphire
2008 Bonfire Night
2003 Bonjela**
1994 Book Club Associates
2012 Boots*
1998 Boots Advantage Card
1988 Boots Brand Medicines
2004 Bounty (paper towels)*
1994 Boursin
1998 Boursin
1986 Bovril
2000 Bowmore
2008 Bradesco
1986 Bradford & Bingley Building Society*
1990 Bradford & Bingley Building Society
2006 Branston Baked Beans*
1980 Braun Shavers
1982 Bread Advisory Council*
1982 Breville Toasted Sandwichmaker
2002 Britannia Building Society*
1994 British Airways*
1996 British Airways
2004 British Airways*
1984 British Airways Shuttle Service
1994 British Diabetic Association*
1980 British Film Institute*
2012 British Gas*
1994 British Gas Central Heating
1988 British Gas Flotation*
2006 British Heart Foundation* (Anti Smoking)
2009 British Heart Foundation – Watch Your Own Heart Attack*
2009 British Heart Foundation – Yoobot*
2014 British Heart Foundation – Stayin' Alive*
1988 British Nuclear Fuels
1988 British Rail Young Person's Railcard
1982 British Sugar Corporation
1980 British Turkey Federation
2005 Broadband for Scotland*S
2006 Brother
2007 Brother*
1992 BT
2008 BT
2009 BT
2010 BT
2012 BT*
2014 BT
2004 BT Broadband*
2005 BT Broadband (Consumer)
1994 BT Business
1996 BT Business*
2000 BT Business
1992 BT Call Waiting*
2002 BT Cellnet*
1986 BT Consumer*
2001 BT Internet (Northern Ireland)**
1999 BT Northern Ireland**
1986 BT Privatisation*
2002 BT Retail*
2007 BT Total Broadband
2010 BT Total Broadband*
1998 Bud Ice
1988 Budweiser
2002 Budweiser*
2006 Bulldog 2004
1980 BUPA
2000 BUPA
2002 BUPA
2004 BUPA
2016 Butlins
1996 Butter Council

C
1996 Cable Television
2008 CABWISE (Transport for London)*
2008 Cadbury Dairy Milk
2010 Cadbury Dairy Milk*
2010 Cadbury Dairy Milk (India)
2012 Cadbury Dairy Milk (India)*
2008 Cadbury's Biscuits*
1994 Cadbury's Boost*
1992 Cadbury's Caramel
1984 Cadbury's Creme Eggs
1988 Cadbury's Creme Eggs
1998 Cadbury's Creme Eggs
1992 Cadbury's Crunchie
1984 Cadbury's Curly Wurly*
1980 Cadbury's Dairy Box
2004 Cadbury's Dream (SA)
1982 Cadbury's Flake
1984 Cadbury's Fudge*
1994 Cadbury's Highlights
1999 Cadbury's Jestives**
1990 Cadbury's Mini Eggs
1994 Cadbury's Roses*
1986 Cadbury's Wispa

1988 Café Hag
1996 Californian Raisins
2009 California Travel & Tourism Commission
2011 California Travel & Tourism Commission
1980 Campari*
1992 Campbell's Condensed Soup
1988 Campbell's Meatballs*
1994 Campbell's Soup
1996 Cancer Relief Macmillan Fund
2014 Cancer Research UK
2016 Cancer Research UK
1984 Canderel
2008 Capital One
1992 Caramac
1994 Car Crime Prevention
1997 Carex**
1998 Carex
2003 Carex**
2007 Carex*
2008 Carex
2010 Carling
1994 Carling Black Label
1996 Carling Black Label
1984 Carousel
1998 Carrick Jewellery
1986 Castlemaine XXXX*
2006 Cathedral City*
1992 Cellnet Callback
1988 CenterParcs
2004 Central London Congestion Charge*
1992 Central Television Licence Renewal
2010 Change4Life
2000 Channel 5
1990 Charlton Athletic Supporters Club*
1980 Cheese Information Service
1996 Cheltenham & Gloucester Building Society
1988 Chessington World of Adventures
1998 Chicago Town Pizza
2002 Chicago Town Pizza
2003 Chicago Town Pizza**
1994 Chicken Tonight
2000 Chicken Tonight Sizzle and Stir*
1992 Childhood Diseases Immunisation
2007 Child Protection on the Internet (Home Office)
1994 Child Road Safety
2004 Children's Hearings (Scottish Executive)*
2005 Children's Hearings System*
1990 Children's World
2001 Chiltern Railways (Clubman Service)**
1984 Chip Pan Fires Prevention*
1990 Choosy Catfood*
1992 Christian Aid
1998 Christian Aid*
2007 Churchill Square (Shopping Centre)
1994 CICA (Trainers)*
1992 Citroen Diesel Range
2010 Civic
1988 Clairol Nice 'n Easy
1988 Clarks Desert Boots*
1996 Classic Combination Catalogue
1994 Clerical Medical
1992 Clorets
1984 Clover
1988 Clover
2007 Coca-Cola Zero*
1980 Cointreau
1998 Colgate Toothpaste*
1990 Colman's Wholegrain Mustard
2014 Colombian Ministry of Defence's Group of Humanitarian Attention to the Demobilised*
2010 Comfort Fabric Conditioner*
2010 Commonwealth Bank
2000 Confetti.co.uk*
2005 Consensia/Police Service of Northern Ireland
2000 Co-op*
1994 Cooperative Bank*
1996 Cooperative Bank
2004 Co-op Food Retail
2016 Coors Light*
1990 Copperhead Cider
2007 Cornwall Enterprise
2010 Corsodyl*
2016 Costa*
1982 Country Manor (Alcoholic Drink)
1986 Country Manor (Cakes)
1984 Cow & Gate Babymeals*
1982 Cracottes*
2004 Cravendale (Milk)*
2000 Crime Prevention
2003 Crimestoppers Northern Ireland**
1980 Croft Original
1982 Croft Original
1990 Croft Original*
2011 CrossCountry Trains
1999 Crown Paint**
2002 Crown Paint
2003 Crown Paint**
2000 Crown Paints*
2004 Crown Paints
1990 Crown Solo*
1999 Crown Trade**
1999 Crown Wallcoverings**
1984 Cuprinol*
2014 Cuprinol*
2007 Curanail
1999 Cussons 1001 Mousse**
1986 Cyclamon*
2009 Cycling Safety*

D

2014 Dacia*
1996 Daewoo*
1982 *Daily Mail**

2002 Dairy Council (Milk)*
2000 Dairylea*
1992 Danish Bacon & Meat Council
2008 Danone Activia*
2012 Danone Activia*
1980 Danum Taps
2003 Data Protection Act
1990 Data Protection Registrar
2008 Dave*
1980 Day Nurse
1994 Daz
2006 Daz*
2008 De Beers*
1996 De Beers Diamonds*
2002 Debenhams
1980 Deep Clean*
2005 Deep River Rock – Win Big
2000 Degree
2003 Demand Broadband**
2011 Department for Transport
2012 Department for Transport*
2011 Depaul UK*
2006 Dero*
2008 Dero
1980 Dettol*
2014 Deutsche Telekom AG*
2009 Dextro Energy
2002 DfES Higher Education
2010 DH Hep (C)
1984 DHL Worldwide Carrier
2012 Digital UK*
1998 Direct Debit
2004 Direct Line*
2016 Direct Line*
1992 Direct Line Insurance*
2008 Direct Payment*
2007 Direct Payment (Department of Work and Pensions)*
2006 Disability Rights Commission
2003 District Policing Partnerships (Northern Ireland)
2016 Dixons
1990 Dog Registration
2006 Dogs Trust
2000 Domestic Abuse*
2016 Domino's
2002 Domino's Pizza*
2009 'Don't be a Cancer Chancer'*
2014 Doritos
2011 Doro Mobile Phones
2008 Dove*
2012 Dove*
2016 Dove*
2010 Dove Deodorant*
2012 Dove Hair*
2002 Dr Beckmann Rescue*
2001 Dr Beckmann Rescue Oven Cleaner**
1980 Dream Topping
1988 Drinking & Driving
1998 Drugs Education*
1994 Dunfermline Building Society
1980 Dunlop Floor Tiles
1990 Duracell Batteries
1980 Dynatron Music Suite

E

1988 E & P Loans*
2007 E4 Skins (Channel 4)*
2011 East Midlands Trains*
2004 East of England Development Agency (Broadband)*
2000 easyJet*
2014 easyJet*
2009 Eden and Blighty*
2014 EDF Energy*
1994 Edinburgh Club*
1990 Edinburgh Zoo
1980 Eggs Authority
2004 Electoral Commission (Northern Ireland)
2003 Electoral Commission/COI (DoE Northern Ireland)
1992 Electricity Privatisation
2009 Elephant Chakki Gold (ECG)
2009 Ella's Kitchen
1980 Ellerman Travel & Leisure
1996 Emergency Contraception
1986 EMI Virgin (records)*
1980 English Butter Marketing Company
1986 English Country Cottages
1992 Enterprise Initiative
2014 Enterprise Rent-A-Car
2003 Equality Commission of Northern Ireland
1992 Equity & Law
2007 Erskine*
2010 essential Waitrose*
1990 Eurax (Anti-Itch Cream)
2012 Europcar
1999 EuroSites (continental camping holidays)**
2004 Eurostar*
2006 Eurostar
2008 Eurostar
2016 Eurotunnel Le Shuttle*
1994 *Evening Standard* Classified Recruitment
2010 Everest*
2014 Everest*
2004 Evergood Coffee (Norway)
1984 Exbury Gardens
2014 Expedia*
2016 Extra Gum

F

2008 Fairy Liquid
2014 Fairy Liquid*
2008 Fairy Non Bio
1990 Family Credit
1998 Famous Grouse, The

2006 Famous Grouse, The*
1982 Farmer's Table Chicken
1996 Felix*
2000 Felix*
2006 Felix*
1980 Ferranti CETEC
1990 Fertilizer Manufacturers' Association
2011 Fiat*
1982 Fiat Auto UK
1980 Findus Crispy Pancakes
1988 Findus French Bread Pizza & Crispy Pancakes
1992 Findus Lasagne
1982 Fine Fare*
1984 Fine Fare
2005 Fire Authority for Northern Ireland*
2014 Fire Safety*
2016 First4Adoption*
2005 First Choice*
1996 First Choice Holidays
1998 first direct*
1992 first direct
2004 first direct
2011 first direct*
2014 first direct*
2016 first direct*
2005 First Great Western and First Great Western Link
2007 First Scotrail
2003 Fisherman's Friend**
1992 Flowers & Plants Association
2002 Flowers & Plants Association
2003 Flymo Turbo Compact**
1994 Fona Dansk Elektrik
2014 Ford
2012 Ford C-Max
1980 Ford Fiesta
1998 Ford Galaxy*
1986 Ford Granada*
1982 Ford Model Range
2010 Forevermark*
1984 Foster's
2014 Foster's*
1995 Fox's Biscuits**
2005 Fox's Rocky*
2016 Foxtel
1998 French Connection
2000 Freschetta*
1999 Freschetta Pizzas**
2009 FRijj*
1982 Frish*
1996 Frizzell Insurance*
2002 Fruitopia
1994 Fruit-tella
2000 ft.com*
2005 Fybogel

G
1997 Gala Bingo Clubs**
1999 Gala Bingo Clubs**
2004 Garnier
2014 Garnier Ultralift*
1986 General Accident
2003 George Foreman Grills
2009 ghd*
2014 Gillette
1992 Gini (Schweppes)*
2010 Ginsters
2007 Glasgow City
1986 Glasgow's Lord Provost
1986 GLC's Anti 'Paving Bill' Campaign*
2000 Glenmorangie*S
1995 Glow-worm Boilers (Hepworth Heating)**
1996 Glow-worm Central Heating
2001 GoByCoach.com (National Express)**
1996 Gold Blend*
1984 Golden Wonder Instant Pot Snacks*
1988 Gold Spot
1980 Goodyear Grandprix
2012 Gordon's*
1984 Grant's Whisky
1988 Greene King IPA Bitter
1992 Green Giant
1990 Greenpeace
1988 Green Science
2014 Groupe Média TFO
2012 Gü*
2016 Guinness*
1990 Guinness (Draught) in Cans
1996 *Guinness Book of Records*

H
1992 Haagen-Dazs*
2009 Halifax*
2006 Halifax Bank of Scotland
1982 Halifax Building Society
1992 Halifax Building Society
1994 Halifax Building Society
2002 Halifax Building Society*
1980 Halifax Building Society Convertible Term Shares
1994 Halls Soothers*
1982 Hansa Lager
1999 Hartley's Jam**
2007 Hastings Hotels
2002 Hastings Hotels (Golfing Breaks)*
2001 Hastings Hotels (Golfing Breaks in Northern Ireland)**
2000 Health Education Board for Scotland
2012 Health Promotion Board Singapore*
2014 Health Promotion Board of Singapore
2014 Heart and Stroke Foundation of Canada*
1994 Heineken Export
2010 Heinz*
2008 Heinz Beanz Snap Pots
1980 Heinz Coleslaw
1984 Hellman's Mayonnaise*
2016 Help to Buy

1982 Henri Winterman's Special Mild
1996 Hep30 (Building Products)
1990 Herta Frankfurters
1992 Herta Frankfurters
2008 Hewlett Packard Personal Systems Group (PSG)
2005 Hidden Treasures of Cumbria*
2005 Highlands and Islands Broadband Registration Campaign
2011 Hiscox
2007 Historic Scotland*
2006 HM Revenue & Customs (Self Assessment)*
1980 Hoechst
1992 Hofels Garlic Pearles
1984 Hofmeister*
1982 Home Protection (Products)
1984 Home Protection (Products)
2006 Homebase
2012 Homebase
1990 Honda
2004 Honda*
2016 Honda Odyssey
1986 Horlicks
1994 Horlicks
2006 Horlicks
1986 Hoverspeed
1992 Hovis
1996 Hovis
2002 Hovis*
2010 Hovis*
1990 H. Samuel
2010 HSBC*
1984 Hudson Payne & Iddiols
1996 Huggies Nappies
1994 Hush Puppies

I
2012 IBM*
1996 I Can't Believe It's Not Butter!*
2008 Iceland
1992 Iceland Frozen Foods
1980 ICI Chemicals
1984 ICI Dulux Natural Whites*
1992 IFAW*
2014 IKEA
1998 Imodium
2001 Imperial Leather**
2002 Imperial Leather
2003 Imperial Leather**
2004 Imperial Leather*
1990 Imperial War Museum
1998 Impulse
1988 *Independent, the*
2006 ING Direct*
1998 Inland Revenue Self Assessment
2005 Inland Revenue Self Assessment*
1988 Insignia
1982 International Business Show 1981
1990 International Wool Secretariat
1992 IPA Society
2005 *Irish News, The*
2007 *Irish News, The* (Recruitment)
1992 Irn-Bru
2009 Irn-Bru
2007 Irn-Bru 32
2003 Ironbridge Gorge Museums**
1994 Israel Tourist Board
2010 It Doesn't Have to Happen
2014 ITV

J
2006 Jamie's School Dinners*
1998 Jammie Dodgers
1994 Jeep Cherokee
2001 Jeyes Bloo**
2002 Jeyes Bloo
1992 Jif
1999 JJB Super League**
1988 Job Clubs
2012 John Lewis*
2016 John Lewis*
2016 John Lewis Insurance*
2002 John Smith's Ale
1982 John Smith's Bitter*
1994 John Smith's Bitter*
2006 Johnnie Walker
2008 Johnnie Walker*
2011 Johnnie Walker
1998 Johnson's Clean & Clear*
2011 Jungle Formula*
2010 Juvederm Ultra

K
1992 K Shoes*
1995 K Shoes (Springers)**
1992 Kaliber
1996 Kaliber
2010 Kärcher Pressure Washers*
2014 Kärcher Window Vac*
1990 Karvol
1980 Kays Catalogue
1992 Kellogg's All Bran*
1984 Kellogg's Bran Flakes*
1984 Kellogg's Coco Pops*
1994 Kellogg's Coco Pops
2000 Kellogg's Coco Pops*
1982 Kellogg's Cornflakes
1980 Kellogg's Frozen Waffles
2000 Kellogg's Nutri-Grain*
2002 Kellogg's Real Fruit Winders*
1980 Kellogg's Rice Krispies*
1982 Kellogg's Super Noodles*
2005 Kelso Racecourse
1998 Kenco
2010 Kenco
2016 Kenco*
1986 Kensington Palace*
2009 Key 103
1984 KFC
1998 KFC

2008 KFC*
2010 KFC*
2000 KFC USA
1988 Kia Ora*
2014 KitKat
2004 Kiwi (SA)
1984 Kleenex Velvet
2007 Knife Crime (Police Service of Northern Ireland)
2009 Knorr*
1990 Knorr Stock Cubes*
2010 Kodak*
1988 Kodak Colour Print Film
1984 Kraft Dairylea*
1994 Kraft Dairylea
1980 Krona Margarine*
1986 Kronenbourg 1664
2006 Kwik-Fit*

L

1990 Lada
2012 Ladbrokes
2004 Lamb (Meat & Livestock Australia)*
2010 Lamb (Meat & Livestock Australia)
2005 Lancashire Short Breaks*
1990 Lanson Champagne*
2012 LateRooms.com
2005 Lay Magistrates
2014 Lay's Global
2014 Lay's US
1980 Lea & Perrin's Worcestershire Sauce
1990 Lea & Perrin's Worcestershire Sauce*
2008 Learndirect*
1992 Le Creuset
1982 Le Crunch
1988 Leeds Permanent Building Society
1988 Lego
2004 Lego Bionicle
2014 The LEGO Movie
1984 Leicester Building Society
1996 Lenor
1986 Le Piat D'or
1990 Le Piat D'or
1996 Le Shuttle
1988 Levi's 501s*
2002 Levi Strauss Engineered Jeans (Japan)
1980 Levi Strauss UK
1992 Levi Strauss UK*
2014 Lidl
2016 Lidl UK*
2014 Lifebuoy
2005 Lift Off
2012 Lights by TENA
1990 Lil-lets*
1996 Lil-lets
1996 Lilt
1992 Limelite*
1980 Limmits
1999 Lincoln Financial Group**
2000 Lincoln Insurance
2000 Lincoln USA
1980 Lion Bar
1988 Liquorice Allsorts
1992 Liquorice Allsorts
1980 Listerine
1988 Listerine*
2004 Listerine
1998 Littlewoods Pools
2011 Liverpool ONE
1984 Lloyds Bank*
1992 Lloyds Bank
2010 Lloyds TSB*
1999 Local Enterprise Development Unit (NI)**
1990 London Buses Driver Recruitment
2009 London Business School*
1982 London Docklands
1984 London Docklands*
1990 London Philharmonic
1992 London Transport Fare Evasion
1986 London Weekend Television
2016 L'Oréal Paris Age Perfect*
1980 Lucas Aerospace*
1996 Lucky Lottery
1980 Lucozade*
1992 Lucozade
2008 Lucozade Sport*
1988 Lurpak
2000 Lurpak*
2008 Lurpak
2014 Lux*
2012 LV=*
2002 Lynx*
2011 Lynx*
2004 Lynx Pulse*
1994 Lyon's Maid Fab
1988 Lyon's Maid Favourite Centres

M

2014 Maaza
2004 M&G
1988 Maclaren Prams
2016 Macmillan Cancer Support*
2003 Magna Science Adventure Centre**
2007 Magners Irish Cider*
1999 Magnet Kitchens**
2004 Magnum
2012 Magnum Gold?!*
2009 Make Poverty History
2006 Make Poverty History (Comic Relief)
1990 Malibu
2006 Manchester City*
1999 Manchester City Centre**
2001 Manchester City Centre**
2002 *Manchester Evening News* (Job Section)*
2003 *Manchester Evening News* (Job Section)**
2003 ManchesterIMAX**
1982 Manger's Sugar Soap*

1988 Manpower Services Commission
2011 Marie Curie Cancer Care*
2016 M&S Food
1994 Marks & Spencer
2006 Marks & Spencer*
2004 Marks & Spencer Lingerie*
1998 Marmite*
2002 Marmite*
2008 Marmite*
2011 Marmite XO
1998 Marmoleum
1988 Marshall Cavendish Discovery
1994 Marston Pedigree*
2001 Maryland Cookies**
2006 Mastercard
2008 Mastercard
2016 Mastercard
2016 Mattessons*
2014 Mattessons Fridge Raiders*
2009 Maximuscle*
1986 Mazda*
1986 Mazola*
2008 McCain
2012 McCain
2014 McCain Ready Baked Jackets*
2011 McCain Wedges*
1996 McDonald's
1998 McDonald's
2010 McDonald's
2012 McDonald's*
2008 McDonald's Eurosaver
2014 McDonald's Sponsorship London 2012
2014 McDonald's Virtual Coins*
1980 McDougall's Saucy Sponge
1988 Mcpherson's Paints
1990 Mcpherson's Paints
2016 McVitie's*
2000 McVitie's Jaffa Cakes
2004 McVitie's Jaffa Cakes
2010 Medicine Waste
2012 Mercedes-Benz
2014 Mercedes-Benz*
2012 Mercedes-Benz (Germany)
1992 Mercury Communications
2005 Metrication
1988 Metropolitan Police Recruitment*
2012 Metropolitan Police Service*
2003 Microbake
1988 Midland Bank
1990 Midland Bank
1992 Miele
1988 Miller Lite*
2014 MILO*
2014 MINI UK
2014 Missing People
2000 Moneyextra*
2010 Monopoly
2006 Monopoly Here & Now*
2006 More4*
1999 Morrisons**
2008 Morrisons*
2009 Morrisons*
2010 Morrisons
1988 Mortgage Corporation*
2008 Motorola*
2012 Motorola
2002 Mr Kipling*
1984 Mr Muscle
2010 MTR*
1995 Müller Fruit Corner**
1994 Multiple Sclerosis Society
2010 Munch Bunch
1996 Murphy's Irish Stout*
2000 Myk Menthol Norway*

N

2005 Nambarrie Tea[S]
2016 Narellan Pools*
2000 National Code and Number Change
1980 National Dairy Council – Milk
1992 National Dairy Council – Milk
1996 National Dairy Council – Milk*
1992 National Dairy Council – Milkman*
2014 National Depression Initiative (NDI)*
1996 National Lottery (Camelot)
2012 National Lottery
2014 National Lottery
2016 National Lottery
1999 National Railway Museum**
1996 National Savings
1984 National Savings: Income Bonds
1982 National Savings: Save by Post*
2007 National Trust (Northern Ireland)
1986 National Westminster Bank Loans
1982 Nationwide Building Society
1988 Nationwide Flex Account
1990 Nationwide Flex Account
2006 Naturella*
1990 Navy Recruitment
1988 Nefax
1982 Negas Cookers
1982 Nescafé
2000 Network Q
1992 Neutrogena
2003 Newcastle Gateshead Initiative
1982 New Man Clothes
2014 New York Bagel Company
1994 New Zealand Lamb
1980 New Zealand Meat Producers Board
2001 NHS Missed Appointments**
2016 NICEIC & ELECSA
2006 Nicorette*
1994 Nike
1996 Nike
2012 Nikon*
2012 Nissan*
1994 Nissan Micra*
1986 No.7
2005 Noise Awareness*
2000 No More Nails*

2010 Plenty
1980 Plessey Communications & DataSystems
2016 Plusnet*
1998 Polaroid*
2007 Police Community Support Officers
1994 Police Federation of England and Wales
2004 Police Officer Recruitment (Hertfordshire Constabulary)*
2002 Police Recruitment*
2002 Police Recruitment (Could You?)
2002 Police Recruitment Northern Ireland
2001 Police Service of Northern Ireland**
2007 Police Service of Northern Ireland (Recruitment)
1996 Polo Mints
1984 Polyfoam
2007 Pomegreat
1986 *Portsmouth News*
2004 Postbank (Post Office SA)
2002 Post Office*
2012 Post Office
1980 Post Office Mis-sorts
1986 Post Office Special Issue Stamps
1996 Potato Marketing Board
1998 Pot Noodle
2008 Power of One
2014 PowerPacq
2014 Premier Inn*
1984 Presto
1980 Pretty Polly*
2010 Pringles
2012 Pringles
2006 Privilege Insurance
2011 Program of Humanitarian Attention to the Demobilised*
2005 Progressive Building Society – Financial Services
2011 Promote Iceland*
1992 Prudential
2008 Public Awareness Campaign for Helmet Wearing*
2014 Public Health England*

Q

1984 QE2
2003 Qjump.co.uk
1988 Quaker Harvest Chewy Bars*
1982 Qualcast Concorde Lawn Mower*
2014 QualitySolicitors
1986 Quatro
1986 Quickstart
1996 Quorn Burgers

R

1982 Racal Redec Cadet
1990 Radion Automatic*
1990 Radio Rentals
1994 Radio Rentals
2008 Radley*
1980 RAF Recruitment*
1996 RAF Recruitment
2004 Rainbow (evaporated milk)*
1994 Range Rover
2014 Range Rover Sport
2000 Reading and Literacy*
1992 Real McCoys
2000 Rear Seatbelts*
1984 Red Meat Consumption
1998 Red Meat Market*
1988 Red Mountain*
1996 Reebok*
1990 Reliant Metrocabs
1994 Remegel
2010 Remember a Charity*
2012 Remember a Charity
1998 Renault
1986 Renault 5
1990 Renault 19*
1992 Renault Clio*
1996 Renault Clio*
1984 Renault Trafic & Master
2009 Resolva 24H*
2005 ResponsibleTravel.Com
2010 Retail OTP
1982 Ribena*
1996 Ribena
2001 rightmove.co.uk**
2001 right to read (literacy charity)**
2002 Rimmel*
1986 Rimmel Cosmetics
2008 Road Safety*
2009 Road Safety
2006 Road Safety – Anti-Drink Driving (DoE Northern Ireland)
1999 Road Safety (DoE Northern Ireland)**
2003 Road Safety (DoE Northern Ireland)
2004 Road Safety (DoE Northern Ireland)*
2007 Road Safety (Republic of Ireland Road Safety Authority/DoE Northern Ireland)
2006 Road Safety – THINK! (Department of Transport)
2010 Robinsons Fruit Shoot*
1996 Rocky (Fox's Biscuits)
1988 Rolls-Royce Privatisation*
2004 Roundup
2005 Roundup Weedkiller*
1988 Rover 200
1982 Rowenta
1990 Rowntree's Fruit Gums
1992 Royal Bank of Scotland
1986 Royal College of Nursing
2002 Royal Mail
1986 Royal Mail Business Economy
1997 Royal Mint**
1990 Royal National Institute for the Deaf
1996 RSPCA
2011 Rubicon
2016 Rugby World Cup 2015
1988 Rumbelows

1984 St Ivel Gold*
2016 Stoptober*
2002 Strathclyde Police
1994 Strepsils*
2010 Stroke Awareness*
1990 Strongbow
2009 Strongbow
2007 Subway*
1982 Summers the Plumbers
1980 Sunblest Sunbran
1990 Supasnaps
2014 Supermalt
2000 Surf*
2010 Surf*
1980 Swan Vestas*
1984 SWEB Security Systems
1992 Swinton Insurance
2009 Swinton Taxi Division*
1996 Switch
1998 Switch
2003 Syndol (painkillers)**

T
2012 Ta Chong Bank*
2012 Talk Talk
1992 Tandon Computers
1990 Tango
2010 Tango
1986 TCP*
2010 TDA Teacher Recruitment*
2006 Teacher Recruitment*
2001 Teacher Training Agency**
2003 Teacher Training Agency**
1986 Teletext
2016 Tennent's Lager
1986 Territorial Army Recruitment
2000 Terry's Chocolate Orange*
1980 Tesco
2000 Tesco*
2002 Tesco*
2007 Tesco (Green Clubcard)
1990 Tetley Tea Bags
2010 The Army
2016 The Conservative Party*
2010 The Co-operative Food*
1992 *The Economist**
2002 *The Economist**
2011 *The Economist**
2016 *The Economist**
1982 *The Guardian*
2004 *The Guardian**
2016 *The Guardian* and *The Observer**
2010 The Happy Egg Co.
2012 The National Lottery*
2004 The Number 118 118*
2016 The Philippines
2016 The Royal British Legion*
2010 thetrainline.com*
2010 THINK!*
2016 THINK!

1984 Thomas Cook
2008 Thomas Cook
2016 Three*
1990 Tia Maria
1992 Tia Maria
2014 Tide Naturals
1990 *Times, The*
1994 Tizer
2005 Tizer*
1980 Tjaereborg Rejser*
2010 T-Mobile*
2010 Tobacco Control*
2004 Tobacco Control (DH)*
1980 Tolly's Original
2002 Tommy's: The Baby Charity*
1984 Torbay Tourist Board*
1986 Toshiba*
2012 TOTAL 0% Greek Yoghurt
1986 Touche Remnant Unit Trusts
1992 Tower of London
2004 Toyota Corolla
2014 Toyota Daihatsu
1996 Toyota RAV4
2008 Toyota Yaris
2003 Translink CityBus
2007 Translink Metro
2003 Translink Smartlink
1982 Trans World Airlines
2016 Travel & Surf
2005 Travelocity.co.uk*
2006 Travelocity.co.uk*
1984 Tri-ac (Skincare)
2009 Tribute Ale
2008 Trident*
2007 Trident (Metropolitan Police)*
2004 Tritace
1980 Triumph Dolomite
2006 Tropicana Pure Premium*
1986 TSB*
1988 TSB*
1994 TSB
2016 TSB
2004 TUI (Germany)
1982 Turkish Delight*
1986 TV Licence Evasion*
2006 TV Licensing*
2012 TV Licensing
2014 Twix
2000 Twix Denmark

U
1984 UK Canned Salmon
2016 UK Government*
1986 Umbongo Tropical Juice Drink
2003 UniBond
1999 UniBond No More Nails**
2005 UniBond Sealant Range*
2005 University of Dundee*S
1998 UPS
2003 UTV Internet

Index

Introductory note: when the text is within a table, the number span is in *italic*; when the text is within a figure, the number span is in **bold**.